Palgrave Studies in Victims and Victimology

Series Editors
Pamela Davies, Department of Social Sciences,
Northumbria University, Newcastle upon Tyne, UK
Tyrone Kirchengast, Law School, University of Sydney,
Sydney, Australia

In recent decades, a growing emphasis on meeting the needs and rights of victims of crime in criminal justice policy and practice has fuelled the development of research, theory, policy and practice outcomes stretching across the globe. This growth of interest in the victim of crime has seen victimology move from being a distinct subset of criminology in academia to a specialist area of study and research in its own right. *Palgrave Studies in Victims and Victimology* showcases the work of contemporary scholars of victimological research and publishes some of the highest-quality research in the field. The series reflects the range and depth of research and scholarship in this burgeoning area, combining contributions from both established scholars who have helped to shape the field and more recent entrants. It also reflects both the global nature of many of the issues surrounding justice for victims of crime and social harm and the international span of scholarship researching and writing about them.

Editorial Board
Antony Pemberton, Tilburg University, Netherlands
Jo-Anne Wemmers, Montreal University, Canada
Joanna Shapland, Sheffield University, UK
Jonathan Doak, Durham University, UK

Rachel Locke · Kelsey Paul Shantz ·
Andrei Serbin Pont · Jai-Ayla Sutherland
Editors

Identity-Based Mass Violence in Urban Contexts

Uncovered

palgrave
macmillan

Editors
Rachel Locke
Kroc Institute for Peace and Justice
University of San Diego
San Diego, CA, USA

Kelsey Paul Shantz
Mass Violence and Atrocities
Stanley Center for Peace and Security
Muscatine, IA, USA

Andrei Serbin Pont
Economicas y Sociales
Coordinadora Regional Investigaciones
Económicas y Sociales (CRIES)
Buenos Aires, Argentina

Jai-Ayla Sutherland
Mass Violence and Atrocities
Stanley Center for Peace and Security
Muscatine, IA, USA

ISSN 2947-9355   ISSN 2947-9363 (electronic)
Palgrave Studies in Victims and Victimology
ISBN 978-3-031-98067-1   ISBN 978-3-031-98068-8 (eBook)
https://doi.org/10.1007/978-3-031-98068-8

This work was supported by the Stanley Center for Peace and Security.

© The Editor(s) (if applicable) and The Author(s) 2026. This book is an open access publication.

Open Access This book is licensed under the terms of the Creative Commons Attribution-NonCommercial-NoDerivatives 4.0 International License (http://creativecommons.org/licenses/by-nc-nd/4.0/), which permits any noncommercial use, sharing, distribution and reproduction in any medium or format, as long as you give appropriate credit to the original author(s) and the source, provide a link to the Creative Commons license and indicate if you modified the licensed material. You do not have permission under this license to share adapted material derived from this book or parts of it.

The images or other third party material in this book are included in the book's Creative Commons license, unless indicated otherwise in a credit line to the material. If material is not included in the book's Creative Commons license and your intended use is not permitted by statutory regulation or exceeds the permitted use, you will need to obtain permission directly from the copyright holder.

This work is subject to copyright. All commercial rights are reserved by the author(s), whether the whole or part of the material is concerned, specifically the rights of translation, reprinting, reuse of illustrations, recitation, broadcasting, reproduction on microfilms or in any other physical way, and transmission or information storage and retrieval, electronic adaptation, computer software, or by similar or dissimilar methodology now known or hereafter developed. Regarding these commercial rights a non-exclusive license has been granted to the publisher. The use of general descriptive names, registered names, trademarks, service marks, etc. in this publication does not imply, even in the absence of a specific statement, that such names are exempt from the relevant protective laws and regulations and therefore free for general use.

The publisher, the authors and the editors are safe to assume that the advice and information in this book are believed to be true and accurate at the date of publication. Neither the publisher nor the authors or the editors give a warranty, expressed or implied, with respect to the material contained herein or for any errors or omissions that may have been made. The publisher remains neutral with regard to jurisdictional claims in published maps and institutional affiliations.

Cover photo: A rooftop lambe-lambe installation by Alberto Pereira in Rio de Janeiro, Brazil, in a neighborhood with one of the highest rates of violence in the city. Photo by Thiago Maurílio.

This Palgrave Macmillan imprint is published by the registered company Springer Nature Switzerland AG
The registered company address is: Gewerbestrasse 11, 6330 Cham, Switzerland

If disposing of this product, please recycle the paper.

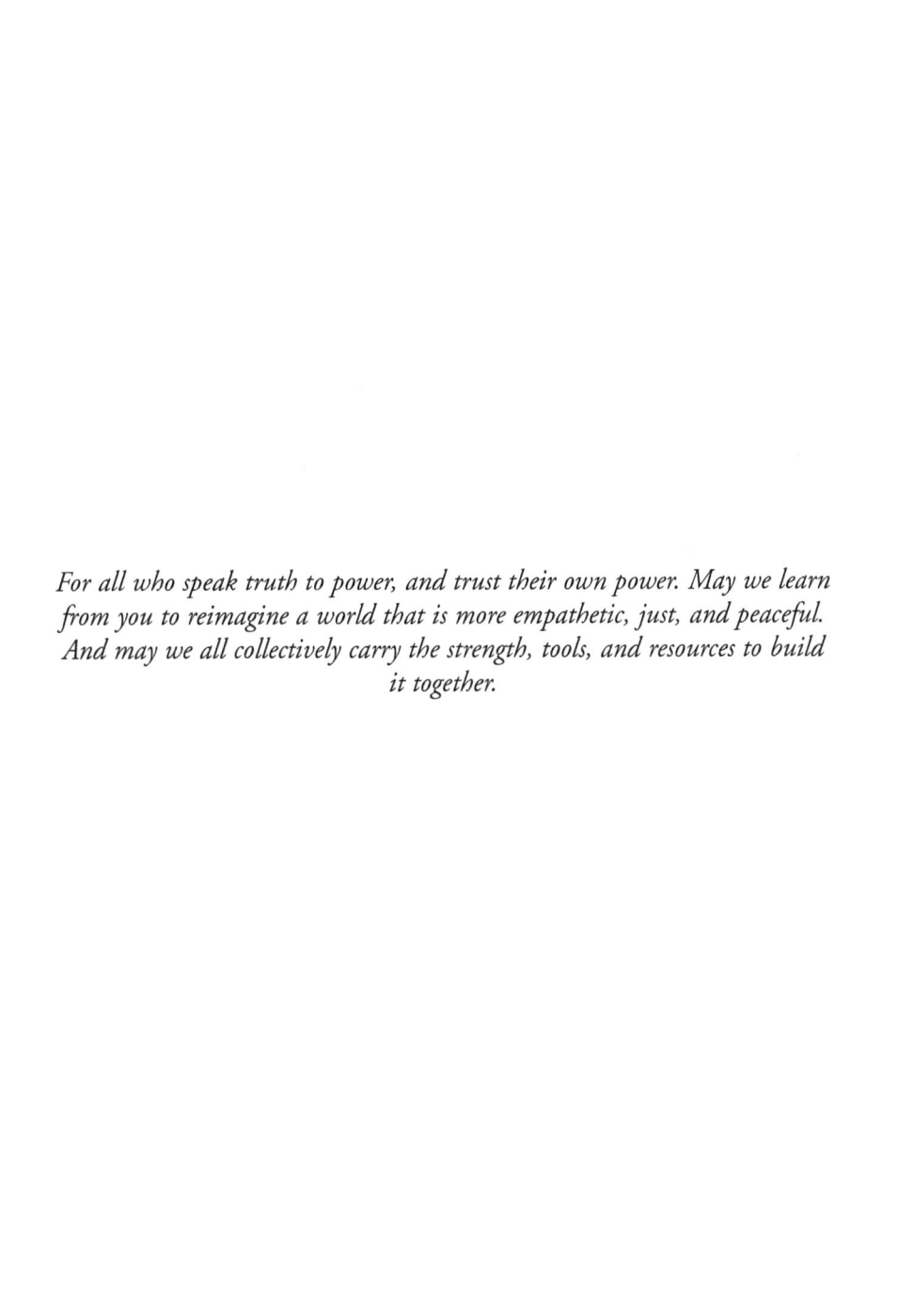

For all who speak truth to power, and trust their own power. May we learn from you to reimagine a world that is more empathetic, just, and peaceful. And may we all collectively carry the strength, tools, and resources to build it together.

Foreword

Dear Reader,

I write this to you as a father, who worries about the safety of the community our children are raised in and stands in solidarity with other parents who feel the same. As a man, who as a boy received an award that changed the trajectory of my future and understands the power of a helping hand. As a citizen, who sees my home suffering from cycles of violence that are preventable. And as a human, with a voice that will be used to do something about it.

Since 2017, the United Kingdom has experienced alarming increases in knife crime. This violence tragically takes the lives of its victims and leaves devastating ripples in its wake, impacting the lives and communities of their loved ones who must live on and repair from the pain and trauma. Too often they do so alone, without the support of their local and national leaders to offer resources that can help. There is nothing more crushing than sitting with the loved one of a young person who has been killed, left to navigate the abrupt change in the future they had never planned. We have to listen to their stories.

We know the root causes of this violence. Knife crime in the United Kingdom has far less to do with the color of one's skin than the structural and socioeconomic conditions in which these kids grow up. Of course, this is true anywhere because violence is cyclical, not racial; it feeds especially in any community where young people faced with limited access, support, and opportunity find themselves entangled with gangs or crime that use violence as a main tool of control and influence.

Tackling knife crime by punishment alone doesn't work. Yet we live in systems so accustomed to fast and sharp reactions that our tools for proactivity to address those underlying, root causes have been blunted. This is true for both individuals seeking revenge and community and city leaders who need to prevent the next attack. In all cases, there is evidence that these cycles can be broken, through community engagement, trauma healing, and meaningful support.

As my friend Serena Wiebe, who you will read about later in this volume, often tells me, "People just need to do something." By something, she really means anything. She says, "Just come and talk to us. Start there. Listen." Because these kids do have dreams. They want a brighter future, and we should not assume otherwise. But without strong governmental support and community engagement to protect them and offer better alternatives, we will continue to see them caught up in these cycles of violence.

Knowing Serena and other young people I have learned from about this violence, I remain hopeful. I hope their voices will be heard. I hope we can see their potential and show up to support them. I hope our communities and political leaders will step up to acknowledge all that needs to be done before violence takes place, to shine light on their futures and offer a helping hand—the same way I received one in my youth. We can do more, and we can save lives. This volume will help us see how. What an honor to introduce you to it.

London, UK   Idris Elba

Preface

In your hands, you hold a community. A community that crosses borders, ages, languages, nationalities, genders, experiences, and disciplines. We—the contributors, editors, and reference group members who created this volume—have learned from, critiqued, cried and laughed with, and supported one another over the past several years. Together, we have seen wars start and others end. We have held closely people forced to flee their homes, and poured hope into those with the opportunity to return. We have held one another's trauma and celebrated one another's joy.

We met in person three times—in San Diego, Barcelona, and Mexico—and virtually countless others. Building this work together has been instrumental in its unique outcome. Each chapter was developed independently from the others; but as the reader you will find the contents speak to one another in ways that could not occur by design only. The words reflect the disturbing reality of identity-based mass violence. They also emanate the respect and honor that can be cultivated within a diverse community. It has been an incredible privilege to work with each contributor.

We imagined this volume to respond to several challenges across urban violence reduction, peacebuilding, and atrocity prevention.

First, these different fields of study, policy, and practice are generally isolated, lacking collaboration and shared learning from one another. As a result, there are missed opportunities to generate valuable insights for prevention. Where urban violence focuses hyperlocally, atrocity prevention tends to focus nationally and internationally. Yet in practice, they both seek to unearth and address root, structural causes for violence, navigating sources of power that impede or enhance prevention, while simultaneously developing and deploying practices to address escalating or continued cycles of violence.

Second, despite the reality that most people live in, or are moving to, cities, there is insufficient investment in preventing large-scale harm that takes place in urban areas against specific groups of people. As such, there is also a failure to acknowledge how these harms set the stage for acute or spectacular escalations of violence.

And third, systemic or large-scale identity-based violence is used as a tool of power, often so subterraneous that it is accepted or ignored within the frameworks of certain communities and their direct experiences with violence.

Despite these challenges, cities are important because they bring together unique capacities and connections to local dynamics. City leaders in governmental and civil spaces understand their communities best, and with the right power brokers and community leaders in place, they present important opportunities for prevention.

We needed to challenge the mold. The systems have not been serving the most vulnerable, preventing the worst violence, or adequately acknowledging local knowledge and expertise. We needed new energy, new approaches, new leaders, and a platform to present it all together. Thus, this book.

We have designed this volume to reach your mind *and* your heart. You will read impactful stories supported by rigorous research. You will be welcomed into fields of practice adjacent to your own, asked to consider how, as a community dedicated to strengthening peace and reducing violence, we can assist and honor the resilience and strength of communities and push back against the forces that aim to tear them apart. This book does not skip over the work that is always and already being done; rather, it highlights examples and opportunities for actors outside of and within cities to catch up to, support, and generate additional space for work that resists acute and structural identity-based mass violence. We recommend that you read the contributions to this volume with pause, and hold space to consider the humans behind each piece. The content is quite heavy. Engage deeply, take breaks, and be in community. Share and discuss the ideas that stay with you with trusted friends and colleagues.

This volume combines academic rigor and humanity, offering individual stories alongside research to expand our collective understanding and evidence. The book includes art, photos, and poetry to accompany much of the text. And online at ibmv.org, you will discover additional media, including videos that capture and place some of the stories and lessons, and more photos and resources. Although much of the content is haunting, we believe this book will offer you hope. Hope that there are answers, there is work being done, and there always has been. It is on us to challenge the status quo, and we are glad to welcome you to this community.

San Diego, USA
Muscatine, USA
Buenos Aires, Argentina
Casper, USA

Rachel Locke
Kelsey Paul Shantz
Andrei Serbin Pont
Jai-Ayla Sutherland

Acknowledgments First and foremost, this edited volume would not have come together without our tremendous contributors. We as co-editors owe you more than what our gratitude can convey. You gave us grit, heart, authenticity, and thoughtfulness through numerous drafts and several gatherings. Writing can often happen in quiet moments, in between the busyness and heaviness of daily life: jobs that came—and went; loved ones sadly lost; new life arrived. Through it all, you stuck with this project and embodied our collective, ambitious hope. You held one another through tears, cheered one another in successes; and you demonstrated your own personal commitments to creating peace in your communities and spheres of influence. Thank you; we are forever changed by the gifts you have given to this project, and we continue to learn so much from you.

We are tremendously grateful for our esteemed reference group. From your earliest support in identifying and validating core conceptual components to this volume, to your ongoing buoying through intellectual curiosities and challenges, you've been with us through so many eras of this volume as our brain trust. Your fingerprints are evident throughout. We are so very grateful.

To our anonymous peer reviewers: thank you so ardently for your careful consideration of so many of these chapters. Your expertise coupled with your ability to see the intention of the work made for a revision process that was always supported with rigor, enlightenment, and empathy. Thank you for committing yourselves to this project; we are all better because of your support.

This work can at times be deeply personal. Long nights, busy days. Quick phone calls just to check on one detail. Long Zoom meetings to really work through core planning—this effort saw it all. Without a doubt, this book would not exist without the commitments and efforts of those working directly with the editors as part of our editorial team. Tori, Ioli, Jessica, and Julia: in many ways, you are contributors of your own to this volume. Thank you for bringing your hearts, energies, and minds to this work. We are your biggest champions.

To our agent, communications mentor, and friend Mark: you somehow simultaneously kept us on track with our deadlines while also reminding us to laugh. Thank you for not only seeing the potential of this work but also imagining ways to bring that potential to larger audiences. Alex, thank you for working with us to create space for this work to live and continue online; we are forever grateful for all that you do. And to Amy, who worked meticulously into the final hours to design and compile our manuscript.

Andy and Jen: thank you for believing in us. Thank you for seeing the value of this work and for always being our thought partners.

Our gatherings of contributors along with reference group members really established and maintained a community among us all—one that showed deep empathy and care not just for the subjects studied and discussed but for one another. Gathering a diverse group in locations scattered across the world is a challenging, time-consuming feat; one that Sydney and Eleanore carried out with such professionalism and care. Thank you for all that you brought to this effort and to creating community; you each have been core to this journey.

With over twenty contributors to this volume, it takes a ton of effort to keep a ship like this sailing. Anne, thank you for all of your work to organize and process key components of this work. Nicole and Patty, thank you for your steadfast support of this community.

To our friends at Tectonic—Andrew, Greg, Doug, and Danny—thank you for being our story keepers and so beautifully capturing the essence of this work through the accompanying story videos. In an era when content floods our screens, you choose to share stories of impact and community building. Thank you for being our partners.

To our interpreters, both for our in-person meetings and our writing, you helped us communicate across boundaries and connect deeply through this work. Thank you for your time, your commitment, and your patience with us while we tried, and failed, to learn to talk slowly.

...

The genesis of this compendium goes back several years ago to a small, glass-walled meeting room with a whiteboard full of ideas in San Diego, where several of the co-editors gathered to strategize addressing and preventing violence and power inequities in cities. Looking back to that time, we likely had no idea of the community that would form over the course of the following five years (and counting). It has been a tremendous privilege to be co-editors together. To our readers, we welcome you in this community and hope you will join us.

...

In memoriam to Mireya Pont and all those no longer with us but who still inspire and compel us along this journey.

Competing Interests Authors received a commissioning fee from the Stanley Center for Peace and Security. There are no other conflicts of interest to declare that are relevant to the content of this edited volume. This collective work represents the points of view of the authors and not necessarily of any affiliated institutions.

Praise for *Identity-Based Mass Violence in Urban Contexts*

"In a troubled world, *Identity-Based Mass Violence in Urban Contexts* offers a compelling analysis of violence along identity lines in cities and provides a critical understanding of where these come together with power and place to sustain violence. As I grapple with identity and leadership questions by studying Professor Heifetz's work at Harvard and reflect on my experience with the PAZOS strategy in Palmira, Colombia, to address the social roots of violence, I have found this book's multifaceted approach and focus on bridging across different disciplines and linking insights for practitioners and city leaders to be immensely valuable. This book is an essential resource for anyone who is committed to seeing past stereotypes and understanding that efforts beyond black and white are urgently needed for building safety, belonging, and resilience in cities worldwide."

—Oscar Escobar, *Former Mayor, Palmira, Colombia*

"A curious divide exists in the Peacebuilding field between how we consider violence that occurs within cities (often written off simplistically as 'gun violence' or 'gang violence,'), and how we think about mass atrocities and violence in civil war or cross-border contexts. Of course, this is a false divide, as this vibrant and compelling volume makes clear.

The authors of this book highlight the links between structural, acute and mass violence in clear and elegant terms, describing how cities hold the potential for violence in both particular and also universal forms. Even more important, the volume makes a strong case for how to center the work of community led peacebuilders, and how to build urban-based structures for peace, healing, and restoration. This is a deeply important contribution to the peacebuilding literature, during a turbulent time for cities—and the world."

—Melanie Greenberg, *Managing Director, Programs, Humanity United*

"*Identity-Based Mass Violence in Urban Contexts* delivers a powerful wake-up call for everyone committed to violence reduction. The epicenter of today's most devastating violence is not the battlefield, but the city block. Drawing from a rare combination of empirical research, front-line testimony, and policy experience, Rachel Locke, Kelsey Paul Shantz, Andrei Serbin Pont, and Jai-Ayla Sutherland reframe identity-based mass violence as a global urban crisis hiding in plain sight. Its contributors don't just diagnose the problem—they offer blueprints for urban resilience and violence prevention rooted in inclusion and equity. If we're serious about building peace in the 21st century, decision-makers, practitioners, and citizens must start by confronting the quiet brutality embedded in our cities. For anyone working at the intersection of urban safety, human rights, and development, this volume is not just relevant—it's indispensable."

—Dr. Robert Muggah, *Co-Founder, Igarape Institute; Commissioner, Lancet Commission on Global Gun Violence and Health*

"*Identity-Based Mass Violence in Urban Contexts*: Uncovered is a timely and essential contribution to the fields of violence prevention and peacebuilding. By centering the voices of both scholars and those directly impacted by identity-based violence, this volume offers a rare and powerful lens on how urban environments become flashpoints—and sites of potential healing. Its focus on the intersections of identity, power, and place challenges conventional frameworks and points toward deeply contextual, community-driven strategies for prevention. In a world where most violence unfolds outside formal war zones, this book is an urgent call to reimagine peacebuilding where it is needed most: in our cities."

—Vasu Gounden, *Founder and Executive Director, ACCORD*

"This important volume comes at exactly the right time; practitioners, policymakers, and the general public are all looking for hope, answers, and a semblance of sense in an increasingly chaotic world. Marrying theory with practice, personal with policy, domestic with global, *Identity-Based Mass Violence in Urban Contexts* offers innovative ideas and solutions through the lenses of identity, cities, and mass violence. Centering identity and lived experience makes this work relatable to all of us, as does the weaving in of art and storytelling. What a breath of fresh air!"

—Alexandra Toma, *Executive Director, Peace and Security Funders Group*

"*Identity-Based Mass Violence in Urban Contexts* is a powerful and timely contribution that challenges the boundaries between fields too often siloed—urban violence prevention, atrocity prevention, and peacebuilding. Drawing from rich analysis and grounded in the lived experiences of people most affected by violence, the authors shine a light on how identity, marginalization, and exclusion fuel conflict in cities worldwide. It offers an important call to action for practitioners, policymakers, and funders to rethink how we engage at the local level, where meaningful violence prevention must begin. As someone who has spent decades working on violence reduction and community-led development, I find *Identity-Based Mass Violence in Urban Contexts* to be a vital guide for those seeking to address violence not just as isolated incidents, but as symptoms of deeper structural issues. The volume's emphasis on inclusive, grassroots solutions and city-based leadership makes it both practical and visionary. It's an essential resource for anyone committed to building just and peaceful societies."

—Enrique Roig, *Former Deputy Assistant Secretary in the Bureau of Democracy, Human Rights, and Labor at the US State Department*

Contents

Identity-Based Mass Violence and Cities: An Introduction   1
Rachel Locke, Kelsey Paul Shantz, Andrei Serbin Pont, and Jai-Ayla Sutherland

"My Homeland Is Not for Sale": On the Destruction of Cities   13
Ammar Azzouz

Paper City and Papers, Cities, Lambe-Lambe, and Young People   29
Alberto Pereira

Using Evidence and Data to Monitor Identity-Based Mass Violence   41
Gary Milante

What Dwells in Casa de Luz   65
Areli Palomo Contreras

Understanding Structural, Acute, and Identity-Based Mass Violence in Cities as Process   81
Kate Ferguson and Andy Fearn

Urban Patterns of Segregation and Violence in Jerusalem 109
Michal Braier and Efrat Cohen Bar

The Next Big Thing: A Preamble to Urban Atrocities
in Four Acts 127
Ariana Markowitz

"Empire Saved My Life" 161
Serena Wiebe and Alexander Turner

Urban Mechanisms of Armed Violence: Exclusionary
Boundaries and Acute Forms of Spatial Division 177
Antônio Jacinto Sampaio

Tearing the Seams: Cycles of Structural and Acute
Violence in Aleppo 203
Alhakam Shaar

Nourish You 233
Juan Martínez d'Aubuisson and Sarah Meléndez

Reimagine, Reclaim, and Repurpose Urban Space
for Justice and Healing 255
Kerry Whigham

From the Jungle to the City Asha's Journey 273
*Mariana Medina Barragán, Luz Adriana López Medina,
and Alejandra Medina Barragán*

Toward Urban Violence Prevention: Committing
to a Multisite Ethics of Care 297
Friederike Bubenzer

We Want to Learn! Restorative Justice to Protect Black
Girls in Education 321
Barbara Sherrod

Identifying, Amplifying, and Learning from Local
Peacebuilders: A Transformative Journey 341
Prince Charles Dickson

Mending the Fabric: Healing Communities Through Trauma Resilience and Awareness *Rose Mbone*	369
Urban Planning with Identity: Exploring Alternative Methods and Possibilities for Preventing Identity-Based Mass Violence *Natalia Garcia Cervantes*	381
Harnessing Art and Crowdsourcing to Prevent Gender-Based Violence *ElsaMarie D'Silva*	411
Urban Violence: Common Elements of Good and Promising City-Led Prevention and Protection Practices *Flávia Carbonari*	429
To Get Revenge or Not, That Is the Question *José Luis Pardo Veiras and Felipe Luna Espinosa*	469
Hafiz *Shukria Dellawar*	493
Policy Recommendations and Ways Forward *Rachel Locke and Jocelyn Getgen Kestenbaum*	509
Identity-Based Mass Violence and Cities: Concluding Thoughts *Rachel Locke, Kelsey Paul Shantz, Andrei Serbin Pont, and Jai-Ayla Sutherland*	531
Index	535

About the Editors

Rachel Locke is co-founder and Acting Executive Director of Peace in Our Cities, a network of cities around the world working to prevent and reduce serious violence through evidence-informed and rights-based strategies. She previously directed the Violence, Inequality and Power Lab (VIP Lab) at the Kroc Institute for Peace and Justice, University of San Diego. She has also been Head of Research for violence prevention at New York University's Center on International Cooperation and Senior Policy Adviser with the US Agency for International Development (USAID), where she developed agency-wide policies on issues concerning conflict, violence, and fragility. She holds an MA in international affairs from Columbia University and has published widely on violence prevention, humanitarian aid, conflict, and transnational organized crime.

Kelsey Paul Shantz is Program Officer for Mass Violence and Atrocities at the Stanley Center for Peace and Security and a co-facilitating partner of the Peace in Our Cities Network. At the Stanley Center, she works to prevent identity-based violence by developing evidence and global networks of policymakers, researchers, and practitioners. She primarily focuses on city-level approaches to address structural violence, including investigating how identity is weaponized through power and systems. Her work—both personal and professional—has informed city-level strategies for violence reduction and community resilience. Her prior research has spanned topics of defense and security, global economic governance, and microfinance for think tanks and research institutions in Canada, the United States, and the Netherlands. Paul Shantz has an MA in International Relations from the Maxwell School of Citizenship and Public Affairs at Syracuse University and an MPP from the Hertie School of Governance in Berlin, Germany. She also has a BA in International Studies from the University of Evansville.

Andrei Serbin Pont is the President of the Coordinadora Regional de Investigaciones Económicas y Sociales (Regional Coordinator for Social and Economic Research) known as CRIES. He is also CEO of InnovAcción Hub by Pensamiento Propio, Regional Representative for the Global Partnership for the Prevention of Armed Conflict (GPPAC), Adjunct Director of Pensamiento Propio, a Consulting Member of the Argentine Council for International Relations, and Senior Fellow at the Jack D. Gordon Institute for Public Policy. He holds a Ph.D. in International Relations from Universidad Complutense de Madrid, a master's degree in International Relations from the San Tiago Dantas Program in Sao Paulo, Brazil, and a BA in Liberal Arts with a Specialization in Public Policy from Universidad Nacional de San Martín—Buenos Aires.

Jai-Ayla Sutherland is Program Officer for Mass Violence and Atrocities at the Stanley Center for Peace and Security, where she supports efforts to prevent structural and acute violence by working with representatives from government and civil society. Her work focuses predominantly on the role of cities, locally and internationally, in implementing evidence-based prevention strategies. Her team is part of the secretariat of the Peace in Our Cities Network, a global network of cities and organizations working together to reduce violence at the municipal level. She has worked in North and South America, Europe, Africa, and Asia and has experience conducting research on the roots of violent conflict in

Africa and the Middle East and analyzing the structural needs and policy approaches to preventing mass atrocities worldwide. She has an MA in International Security from the Josef Korbel School of International Studies at the University of Denver and a BA in International Relations from the University of Southern California.

# List of Figures

"My Homeland Is Not for Sale": On the Destruction of Cities

Fig. 1   The state of destruction in Homs, Syria in 2025. Photo by the author   16
Fig. 2   Kaaba in Mecca, Saudi Arabia circa 1910. *Source* Matson photograph collection, Library of Congress. https://www.loc.gov/resource/matpc.04659   19
Fig. 3   A view from near the Kaaba, dominated by the Abraj al-Bayt Towers, in 2024. Photo by the author   20
Fig. 4   The state of destruction in Homs, Syria in 2025. Photo by the author   23

xxx List of Figures

Paper City and Papers, Cities, Lambe-Lambe, and Young People

Fig. 1 Sento e Onze (Project 111), by the author, presents an image of André Avelino (left), João Cândido (center), and Manoel Gregório (right) in Praça Marechal Âncora, facing Guanabara Bay, Rio de Janeiro, Brazil. This was a transit area during the Revolta da Chibata (Chibata Revolt)—a mutiny by sailors led by João Cândido that occurred between November 22 and 27, 1910, and was mainly motivated by the dissatisfaction of Black and Brown sailors with the physical punishments to which they were subjected: whips. The area around the square became his refuge and home, where he carried baskets of fish to survive after the social and economic sanctions imposed by the Brazilian Navy throughout his life. Today it is a place of remembrance, where his statue stands at the site of the urban intervention. Photo by Cochi Guimarães 31

Fig. 2 Application of 100 square meters of paper on the grounds of the Praça Marechal Âncora public square, in the historic center of Rio de Janeiro, Brazil, with assistance from the BXD Lambe collective. Photo by Gabriela Azevedo 35

Using Evidence and Data to Monitor Identity-Based Mass Violence

Fig. 1 What might be included in identity-based mass violence? *Source*: the author 44

Urban Patterns of Segregation and Violence in Jerusalem

Fig. 1 Israel and the region (*Source* Bimkom) 111
Fig. 2 Map of Jerusalem (*Source* Bimkom) 112
Fig. 3 Map showing Jerusalem segregation (*Source* Bimkom) 114
Fig. 4 Comparison between the Israeli Talpiyot Mizrach and Palestinian Jabel al Mukaber neighborhoods (*Source* Bimkom) 118

Fig. 5	Map showing the area of Wadi Abdalla. The Ash-Shayyah demolition orders are marked in red (*Source* Bimkom)	120

"Empire Saved My Life"

Fig. 1	Serena sits with her nephew in front of the St. Paul's Advice Center, a charity that provides advice and resources to fight poverty and inequality in Bristol	162
Fig. 2	Across the suburb of St. Paul's in Bristol, seven large murals depict Black role models who organized the first carnival to celebrate the bus boycott of 1968, which led to the United Kingdom's first equality laws	164
Fig. 3	Martin Bisp (left) and Jamie Sanigar (right) started Empire Fighting Chance in 2006 in St. Paul's	165
Fig. 4	Serena sits at a desk where she attended primary school, Sefton Park. The school offered her a place to feel secure at a time when her home life was very difficult	166
Fig. 5	Ground remains cracked where a statue of Edward Colston, a famous slave trader, was torn down in Bristol amidst global antiracism demonstrations that followed the murder of George Floyd in the United States in 2020	168
Fig. 6	Marvin Rees, former Mayor of Bristol, was the first directly elected Black Mayor of a European city and was created a life peer in February 2025	169
Fig. 7	At Serena's secondary school, Fairfield High School, the flags of more than 80 countries hang in the atrium, representing the diverse backgrounds of staff and students	170
Fig. 8	Serena has been working since she was 14; her job at a local Indian restaurant helped her avoid some of the economic reasons why her peers got involved in criminal activities	171
Fig. 9	Clifton Suspension Bridge is often viewed as a symbol for Bristol, but for many in the city, Serena says, it represents a division of class and opportunity	172
Fig. 10	Empire Fighting Chance gym and coaches offered Serena an alternative to therapy and counseling that was not working for her	173

Fig. 11 Serena hugs her mother, Rackzon Hudson, at Empire Fighting Chance. She credits the organization with saving her life   174

We Want to Learn! Restorative Justice to Protect Black Girls in Education

Fig. 1 Illustration by Octavia Ink, Pretty in Ink Press (1)   335
Fig. 2 Illustration by Octavia Ink, Pretty in Ink Press (2)   336

Mending the Fabric: Healing Communities Through Trauma Resilience and Awareness

Fig. 1 The author, Rose Mbone, during an event with young women and men who have been directly affected by extrajudicial killings. Photo by Francis Namaba   370
Fig. 2 A site in Mathare, an informal settlement in Nairobi, that has been reclaimed by youth and transformed into a people's park, providing a safe space for young people to gather. Photo by Francis Namaba   372
Fig. 3 A circle process during a trauma-healing session led by the author and her organization, The Legend Kenya. Photo by Francis Namaba   373
Fig. 4 The author and her team from The Legend Kenya, briefing before a session with young women and men directly impacted by extrajudicial killings. Photo by Francis Namaba   375
Fig. 5 Tree planting along the creek embankment. This location was the site of an effort by the government to remove housing. Community healing includes healing the land as well. Photo by Francis Namaba   378

Urban Planning with Identity: Exploring Alternative Methods and Possibilities for Preventing Identity-Based Mass Violence

Fig. 1 Graffiti-covered "Peace Wall" in Belfast, Northern Ireland, marking physical and symbolic segregation between Protestant and Catholic communities. Photo by Kirk Fisher—http://stock.adobe.com   383

List of Figures   xxxiii

Fig. 2 The location of Campana-Altamira in the Metropolitan Area of Monterrey, Mexico (*Source* Gaceta Municipal of the Government of Monterrey, Volume 27, "Proyecto del Programa Parcial de Desarrollo Urbano 'Distrito Campana-Altamira 2020–2040'", 2021. https://www.monterrey.gob.mx/pdf/gacetas/2021/GacetaEnero2021EspecialDistritoCampanaAltamira.pdf)   396

Fig. 3 Green dots mark the locations of familiar/locally-representative places and red dots of insecure places in Campana-Altamira, from participants' perspective. Photos by authophotography exercise participants, collage by the author. Map data from OpenStreetMap openstreetmap.org/copyright   397

Harnessing Art and Crowdsourcing to Prevent Gender-Based Violence

Fig. 1 The poem "I Am Meera" was generated at a workshop in November 2021 organized by Red Dot Foundation in partnership with professors Verena Thomas and Jackie Kauli from the Queensland University of Technology, Australia (*Source* Red Dot Foundation)   417

Fig. 2 Screenshot of the Safecity map. The red dots indicate the number of reports per location. Map data: ©2025 Google, INEGI, Safecity https://webapp.safecity.in   418

Fig. 3 This wall mural in Lalkuan, India, translates in English to "Look with your hearts and not with your eyes." It was created during an art workshop where survivors shared their feelings and co-created the design along with the artist, painting it with her (*Source* Red Dot Foundation)   419

Fig. 4 A poster calling out sexism in Bollywood (*Source* Red Dot Foundation)   420

Fig. 5 Safecity engages young men to be agents of change to end gender-based violence. This young man, Manoj, is holding a placard saying "badlav" which means "change." Photo by the author   422

Fig. 6 A poster promoting the Safecity app used in Brazil during Carnival (*Source* Red Dot Foundation)   424

| Fig. 7 | Satya heroically participating in the "Meet to Sleep" action (*Source* Blank Noise Meet to Sleep) | 425 |

To Get Revenge or Not, That Is the Question

Fig. 1	Lomas de Plateros's proximity to major roads makes it a key passageway between different areas of Mexico City, adding to its strategic significance. In the background, the financial district and upscale neighborhood of Santa Fe. Photo by Felipe Espinosa	470
Fig. 2	Carlos (19). Photo by Felipe Espinosa	472
Fig. 3	Some of the small altars dedicated to the Virgen de Guadalupe mark boundaries or places where drugs are sold. Photo by Felipe Espinosa	473
Fig. 4	Rafael (21). Photo by Felipe Espinosa	475
Fig. 5	Located on a perilous gorge, Lomas de Plateros is well known for its complex alleyways, twisted staircases, and impossible slopes, making police persecution and monitoring a constant challenge. Photo by Felipe Espinosa	478
Fig. 6	Elements from Alto al Fuego conduct routine inspections and visits to individuals participating in the program. The neighborhood continues to be one of the major points of concentration of violence in Mexico City. Photo by Felipe Espinosa	479
Fig. 7	Aarón Pérez, a 16-year veteran, is head of the policing element of Alto al Fuego, based in the Department of Public Security. Photo by Felipe Espinosa	480
Fig. 8	Daniel. Photo by Felipe Espinosa	483
Fig. 9	Percival. Photo by Felipe Espinosa	486
Fig. 10	Karla. Photo by Felipe Espinosa	487
Fig. 11	María (50). Since 2017, her husband and two of her three sons are in prison, convicted of murder. Photo by Felipe Espinosa	488
Fig. 12	Since Alto al Fuego was initiated, the number of homicides in Lomas de Plateros has gone down by 60 percent. Photo by Felipe Espinosa	491

Identity-Based Mass Violence and Cities: An Introduction

Rachel Locke, Kelsey Paul Shantz, Andrei Serbin Pont, and Jai-Ayla Sutherland

Identity-Based Mass Violence in Urban Contexts: Uncovered begins with a core problem: violence is increasing globally, and existing models of understanding and preventing violence are falling short. The international system that prevailed after the end of World War II is being hollowed out, conflict is increasing worldwide, and individuals continue to experience exceptionally high levels of violence in places considered at peace, but where peace is experienced in widely different ways depending on one's identity. Those who are on the losing end of systems of oppression and those who dedicate their lives to help overcome these systems

R. Locke (✉)
Peace in Our Cities, San Diego, CA, US
e-mail: rachel@peaceinourcities.org

K. Paul Shantz · J.-A. Sutherland
Stanley Center for Peace and Security, Muscatine, IA, US

A. Serbin Pont
Economicas y Sociales, Coordinadora Regional Investigaciones Económicas y Sociales (CRIES), Buenos Aires, Argentina

are constantly battling not only the violence that manifests in political, economic, and social interactions but also failures of imagination within and outside their own communities. Failures to value unconventional pathways. Failures to acknowledge and respect too-long-silenced voices. Failures to understand evidence beyond one's own definitions. And failures to vest value in collaboration. This volume squares off directly against these failures, both through its chapters serving as written record and through the process of development serving as inspiration for creating community and reconfiguring structures of power. It accompanies those leaning into the idea of a more peaceful world with new tools of engagement, new frames of reference and assumptions on evidence, and new pathways of collaboration for policy and action.[1]

This volume represents the culmination of an intensive exploration into a new concept of identity-based mass violence (IBMV) within urban contexts. It is the most recent part of a comprehensive journey that began over four years ago, spearheaded by the joint collaboration of the Violence Inequality and Power Lab (VIP Lab), the Stanley Center for Peace and Security, and CRIES (Regional Coordinator for Social and Economic Research). Our work has traversed various dimensions of IBMV, unveiling its multifaceted nature in urban environments and attempting to uncover the converging pathways of solutions from the fields of urban violence prevention, peacebuilding, and atrocity prevention. This effort to intentionally draw such connections is an invitation to consider the phenomenon of identity-based violence and how often it stems from or informs the bedrock of societies experiencing violence and power inequality. An initial case study, completed in December 2020, laid the groundwork for many of the conceptualizations. This was further enriched by insightful roundtable discussions and the collective wisdom of a global reference group. This process has not only illuminated the complex landscape of IBMV but has also significantly advanced our understanding of the concept, its relevance, and practical response strategies.

The core of our mission—"our" being the editors, the team that pulled this volume together, and most importantly the contributors themselves—has been to consider how we might specifically bring the fields of atrocity prevention and urban violence prevention, as well as peacebuilding, together by exploring the alignments and overlaps between these disciplines. Why? Because the structures and root causes of mass violence exist in the spaces where people engage one another and where power brokers have influence over the degree to which those interactions are based on trust and peace, or not. Because mass violence does not just look like time-bound incidents of horror, but it is also slow, chronic violence that exists without end and terrorizes generations within certain groups in society. Because the solutions enacted and sought by urban violence and atrocity prevention practitioners are mutually beneficial, aiming at the structural conditions that make violence more or less likely, whether in an instant or over time.

We wondered how we might strengthen and learn from each field by focusing on the role of identity in targeted and mass violence—including identity in relationship to power and politics—and the potential for reducing violence by bringing expertise from these fields together at the urban level.[2] Our strategy was rooted in identifying common cause, connecting structural dimensions of violence with acute violence and its immediate responses, and prioritizing the voices of those directly impacted.

The volume you hold is a testament to this journey. Taken together, the chapters that follow present a comprehensive examination of identity-based violence in urban settings. We delve into how different types of violence are informed, categorized, and intersect with urban identity, power, and political dynamics. This volume raises critical questions about the interplay between these dynamics, offering insights and solutions for a path forward. The pages weave together conceptual arguments, practical guidance, and, necessarily, the lived experience of those who endure and resist IBMV.

Targeting a specialized audience, we speak directly to reform-minded partners and allies. *This is not just an academic exercise; it is a call to action for those poised to make real change in the face of daunting challenges.* In essence, this volume is an invitation: a beacon of hope and a blueprint for change. It is a bridge between theory and practice, guiding policymakers, practitioners, and communities toward a more peaceful and just world.

Defining and Building the IBMV Framework

Uncovered is a deep exploration of the intricate relationship between urban environments and mass violence. It is intentionally multidimensional, encompassing a wide array of violence, including sexual and gender-based violence, racial and ethnic violence, gang or group-based violence, political violence, violence against migrants, and structural violence. Throughout, the volume engages with several dualities that expose challenges and opportunities in using the framework of IBMV to understand violence in cities: visible and invisible violence, state-sanctioned and criminal violence, official and unofficial processes, and the often-blurred line between perpetrators and victims. We root our definition in Protection Approaches' work to clarify identity-based violence: "any act of violence motivated by the perpetrator's conceptualisation of their victim's identity, for example their race, gender, sexuality, religion, or political affiliation."[3] We build on this definition by calling attention to "mass" violence, by which we mean widespread or large-scale, and later discuss nuances related to the concept of mass violence.

A central focus of the volume is the relationship between structural violence and acute violence. For the purposes of this volume, we use the terms "acute violence" and "proximate violence" interchangeably. Acute violence is characterized by direct, overt acts of aggression that are intended to harm others—mostly in physical forms—and that occur in an immediate timespan as a single incident or part of a larger group of incidents of similar characteristics. We define structural violence as that which occurs over time and where acute, physical violence is not the primary intent, although control or the maintenance of fear or deprivation can be. Structural violence is the consequence of decisions that value certain identity groups over others and is embedded within social, political, and economic systems and institutions.

Structural violence is identified as a significant risk factor for acute violence that becomes chronic or massive in scale; both are forms of IBMV. This is not a new observation, but the insight is crucial for understanding and addressing the complex dynamics of violence in urban environments. Rather than seeing violence as a landscape of individual incidents, this volume demonstrates how patterns of structural and acute violence interact with one another in ways that create conditions for mass violence.

The editors of this volume made a deliberate decision to not set a quantifiable threshold for what we mean by "mass." Rather, we have trusted the authors and their understanding of communities to hear and interpret what mass violence means across contexts, placing emphasis on the *experience* of violence as more aligned with our purpose rather than imposing a strict, externally constructed definition. Throughout, we encouraged the consideration of certain characteristics of violence in determining whether it could be described as mass. Is it systemic or widespread? Are acute incidents part of a broader trend of violence toward specified groups? Is it chronic? And, fundamental to understanding *identity-based* mass violence, is it directed toward or affecting certain groups more than others—even groups conceptualized by the perpetrator(s)? We took guidance from the field of atrocity prevention, where the number of victims is captured alongside investigations of the motivations and circumstances driving those with power to impose harm. The editorial team acknowledges that not quantifying "mass" and instead adopting a more intuitive approach could be a point of frustration for some, particularly those grounded in stricter interpretations of analysis. Throughout this process, we have leaned into that discomfort rather than ignoring it, including embracing discussion and critiques from contributors themselves. Our decision to avoid a quantifiable threshold remains for two primary reasons. First, qualitative evidence is just as important as quantitative. Very often, a drive for numerical clarity feeds the very silos that our work is aiming to push back against. Second, it is only by seeing the whole picture that the roots of harm are made evident. If we look only at the trees, we will miss the very nature of the forest.

Centering cities as the main geographical focus within a broader global orientation provides a concrete and specific lens to examine institutional responses, fault lines, and the political battlegrounds that shape narratives around perceived or real threats. While these aspects are often more diffuse in rural settings, this volume recognizes that many, if not most, of the phenomena under discussion take place anywhere there is human life, whether in cities, in towns and rural areas, or in the spaces in between.

By focusing on the urban environment, we aspire in part to acknowledge the great innovation space that cities bring. This includes the power to move beyond the bounds of oppression that are often reflected in our systems—whether local, national, or international—and offer leadership and dedication to building environments where all people are able to live free from fear.

Thus, *Uncovered* represents more than a mere compendium of scholarly articles; it embodies a comprehensive, evidence-based narrative that navigates the intricacies of violence within urban landscapes. This work, through its in-depth exploration and critical analysis, confronts and questions long-standing paradigms, shedding light on the often-overlooked subtleties of violence that pervade city life. Its chapters collectively offer a diverse range of perspectives, each contributing to a richer, more nuanced understanding of IBMV.

What occurs locally is often, if not always, influenced by external factors. For instance, global weapons industries—particularly gun manufacturers—and the flow of small arms and light weapons share immense responsibility for local violence conditions worldwide. Likewise, dedicated campaigns, rapidly spreading disinformation through the global media landscape—alongside simultaneous widespread assaults on the free press itself—undercut truth and peace in enormous ways. Trade, tariffs, environmental degradation, and illicit trafficking networks all have an impact on people in their local communities. While the effect of global systems on local conditions is not the sole focus of this book, we recognize that these forces affect individuals and systems everywhere.

Volume Structure

This volume unfolds over a thoughtfully structured compilation of chapters, each delving into different facets of IBMV with a keen focus on cities as epicenters of chronic and systemic mass violence as well as, importantly, a focus on effective interventions. Interwoven throughout are creative and academic works, fostering an important dialogue between the conceptual framing of IBMV and the grounded implications from lived experience. In this way, the volume is a collection of innovative approaches, using creative storytelling and graphic design to illuminate the lived experiences and human impact of IBMV. The sum total is a poignant exploration of chronic and large-scale acute violence, the embedded biases in responses to violence, and the polarizing effects of such violence on individuals and their cities.

The authors of this volume and the themes of their chapters have been deliberately and carefully curated. Each chapter intentionally asks the reader to expand their perspective on what is meant by IBMV, identifying how insidious it can be in the daily lives of individuals, and the long-standing impact of trauma—not just on directly affected groups but on whole societies.

From here, the second chapter offers a grounding—both literal and metaphorical—of cities as the scope of our exploration. It delves deep into the relationships between urban spaces, their inhabitants, and the systems governing them. It lays the groundwork for understanding how urban processes and systems relate to violence. The chapter discusses the interactions of spaces, identities, and systems that foster cohesion or generate competition over resources, power, and influence.

Chapter 4 further establishes the underpinnings of evidence and IBMV, exploring what information is taken to be evidence, by whom, and toward what ends. It contends with issues such as inherent assumptions in data, the potential for data to reinforce biases, and essential questions about whose data is prioritized and why. This analysis of how violence is studied and understood identifies unsolved challenges, setting the groundwork for a deeper understanding of IBMV.

The rest of the first half of the volume integrates power and politics into the discourse of IBMV, featuring chapters that dissect and draw together structural and acute forms of violence. These chapters illuminate how these forms of violence interact and can escalate to mass violence, emphasizing the roles of identity, power, and space.

As the narrative progresses, the volume enters the second half, focused on the solutions to identity-based mass violence. Here, each chapter is dedicated to different ways of addressing and preventing further IBMV, from reimagining urban spaces for justice to learning from local peacebuilders. This section is rich with case studies and practical examples, providing tangible solutions and highlighting successful models of urban violence prevention, and includes a focus on the impact of these solutions through personal, illustrative stories. Throughout, the transformative power of restorative practices, youth leadership, and innovative urban planning are highlighted in addressing IBMV.

Next, a collection of recommendations gathered from across the volume is presented in a penultimate chapter. We offer those recommendations to varied influencers in policy and practice, including academics, practitioners, governmental representatives, and funders.

The volume closes by highlighting opportunities, insights, and areas for further study and work.

What We Imagine

One of the key aspirations of this volume is to lay the foundational stones for the ongoing development of IBMV as a distinct yet interconnected field of study, one that seeks to break away from the traditional siloed approach that characterizes academic research, policy, funding, and practice. Instead, the framing of IBMV advocates for a more integrated and inclusive perspective, one that is continually enriched by a diversity of inputs. This approach recognizes that the complexities of IBMV can only be fully understood and sustainably addressed through a multifaceted lens, drawing on insights and knowledge from a wide array of disciplines. It intentionally avoids oversimplifying realities; the lure of simplicity undermines the potential of appropriately complex and informed awareness and action.

Through this work, we aim for the volume to achieve the following key objectives in creating the environments of peace in cities globally:

1. Clarification of IBMV's Multidimensionality: We have developed and dissected the intricate nature of IBMV, offering a nuanced understanding that goes beyond traditional narratives.

2. Articulation of Politics and Power: We have held prominently throughout our exploration the role of politics and power in shaping violence and influencing prevention outcomes.
3. Urban Governance and Prevention: We have established strong support for prevention-focused work and policymaking at the urban governance level.
4. Practical Foundations for Action: Our volume lays out concrete steps for collaborative, prevention-focused action and policymaking in urban settings.
5. Elevating IBMV on Policy Agendas: We have successfully brought the issue of city-based IBMV to the forefront of national and international policy discussions.

The volume thus serves as an invitation to scholars, practitioners, and policymakers from diverse fields to engage with the concept of IBMV. It is designed to stimulate cross-disciplinary dialogue, encouraging contributions from sociology, urban studies, political science, public health, anthropology, and beyond. By doing so, it aims to foster an environment where learning is shared and collaborative, and where the richness of different perspectives is not just acknowledged but actively sought out and valued.

Moreover, this volume is underpinned by a bold, hopeful vision that through such collaborative and inclusive approaches, new pathways can be forged in the study and prevention of mass violence. It anticipates that the insights and strategies presented within its pages will not only inform current practices and policies but will also inspire new research, leading to deeper understanding and more effective interventions. This forward-looking perspective is critical, especially in a world where urban environments continue to evolve rapidly and where the dynamics of violence are ever changing.

In this way, *Uncovered* emerges as a pivotal resource. It is essential reading not just for those already immersed in the study of subjects that come together under IBMV but also for anyone keen on contributing to the evolution of this important field in its own right. The volume's commitment to an expansive, inclusive approach to understanding and addressing IBMV makes it a significant contribution to both academic discourse and practical efforts aimed at reducing violence and promoting peace in urban settings worldwide. This volume promises to change the way you think about identity, violence, and space. It will touch your mind and heart, as it has done ours, through its thoughtful research and storytelling. Thank you for joining us.

A Note from the Editors on Reading This Volume

This book is designed to reach you in dynamic ways, through both head and heart. The information and stories will leave you with deep sorrow and with immense hope. You will see yourselves and your loved ones in these pages, recognizing that we all face risk and also that there is much opportunity to embrace one another and work to retain and improve our collective, lived experience. Those who created these pages haven't given up, and we cannot either. But please take care, take breaks, and take breaths as you navigate the material. And know that we are with you in solidarity through the end and, most importantly, in the work that lies ahead.

Notes

1. Rustad, Siri Aas. "Conflict Trends: A Global Overview, 1946–2023." Conflict Trends: A Global Overview, 1946–2023, 2024. https://www.prio.org/publications/14006.
   Boo, Gianluca, and Gergely Hideg. "Broken Ambitions: The Global Struggle to Halve Violent Deaths by 2030." Broken Ambitions: The Global Struggle to Halve Violent Deaths by 2030, November 2024. https://www.smallarmssurvey.org/resource/broken-ambitions-global-struggle-halve-violent-deaths-2030.
2. This aligns with the ambitious goal of Sustainable Development Goal 16 to significantly reduce all forms of violence by 2030 as well as a range of other international commitments and ambitions.

3. On Protection Approaches' current definition, see https://protec tionapproaches.org/identity-based-violence; for more information on their work to develop the concept and definition see "Understanding identity-based violence", Protection Approaches, 2014, which builds on Kate Ferguson, "Masking genocide in Bosnia" in The Routledge History of Genocide, eds Cathie Carmicheal and Richard C. Maguire, (London, Routledge, 2015), p. 310.

Open Access This chapter is licensed under the terms of the Creative Commons Attribution-NonCommercial-NoDerivatives 4.0 International License (http://creativecommons.org/licenses/by-nc-nd/4.0/), which permits any noncommercial use, sharing, distribution and reproduction in any medium or format, as long as you give appropriate credit to the original author(s) and the source, provide a link to the Creative Commons license and indicate if you modified the licensed material. You do not have permission under this license to share adapted material derived from this chapter or parts of it.

The images or other third party material in this chapter are included in the chapter's Creative Commons license, unless indicated otherwise in a credit line to the material. If material is not included in the chapter's Creative Commons license and your intended use is not permitted by statutory regulation or exceeds the permitted use, you will need to obtain permission directly from the copyright holder.

"My Homeland Is Not for Sale": On the Destruction of Cities

Ammar Azzouz

While we often hear about the destruction of cities in situations of war as in Palestine, Ukraine, Syria, Yemen, and Libya, we hear less about the destruction of cities at times of "peace." In my book, *Domicide: Architecture, War and the Destruction of Home in Syria*, I argued how domicide in peace and war should be understood together, as they are linked and might lead to one another.[1] For instance, everyday violence that discriminates against communities and razes their culture in a slow-violence mode that stretches across years or decades might eventually accumulate and explode to reach an extreme domicide. In their book, *Domicide: The Global Destruction of Home*, Douglas Porteous and Sandra E. Smith have given two categories for domicide: "everyday domicide," which is frequent, smaller scale, and "normal," and "extreme domicide," which is

---

This chapter was completed before the fall of the Assad regime in the last weeks of 2024. On December 8, Bashar al-Assad fled Damascus, signaling the end of 54 years of the Assads' rule and 61 years of rule by the Baath Party.

A. Azzouz (✉)
University of Oxford, Oxford, UK
e-mail: ammar.azzouz@ouce.ox.ac.uk

generally infrequent, massive, and abnormal.[2] In the following, I provide more details on domicide in "peace" and war.

Destruction of Cities

There are times when even having the daily bread becomes a struggle—waiting for hours in the breadlines to feed a starving family. But even in the waiting, life is at risk: A bomb drops on innocent civilians. The daily bread is mixed with blood. The bakery shop is the target. Civilians are the target.

This was the case in Aleppo, a city that turned into a battlefield between Syrian government forces and their Russian allies against opposition groups and civilians. On August 21, 2012, a bomb from a helicopter hit a breadline in Bab al-Hadid. Twenty-three people were killed and more than 30 were wounded. It was not an accident. A report by Human Rights Watch, which investigated a period of three weeks in 2012, noted that the Syrian government forces dropped bombs and fired artillery at or near at least 10 bakeries in Aleppo Province.[3] This continued throughout the years, with 174 attacks on bakeries and breadlines between 2011 and 2021.[4] But why does a bakery shop get targeted?

Around the world, cities have turned into sites of violence, destruction, and collective punishment. Based on ethnicity, political opinion, sexual orientation, faith, religion, or other categories of identity, some communities have been seen as undesired, unwanted, illegal, or terrorists, labeled in terms describing them as animals or abnormal. Violence takes different forms against them as they are seen as disposable—not worthy of the land they live on. In the process of being harmed and punished, these communities are not only killed, imprisoned, or forcibly evicted, but their material culture is also wiped out to make their cities—for them—uninhabitable, to remove the evidence that these people have lived there. Those who remain struggle to live in extreme conditions after the destruction of their homes, the killing or displacement of their family members. The bakery shop is targeted to force people to leave their cities, to make them kneel or die.

However, it is much more than just their bakeries. In extreme instances, their schools, universities, homes, libraries, archival institutes, theaters, museums, religious buildings, monuments, and hospitals are razed. The world insists on marking these destructions part of our everyday consciousness with a sea of images and videos of destroyed cities. In other instances, slower waves of violence include underinvestment in the neighborhoods of certain marginalized communities. They might be living in cities with a degree of safety—their homes or heritages have not been destroyed—but they are nonetheless pushed away from decision-making, from access to adequate housing, or the right to shape the present and future of their cities. We must never make this "normal."

The deliberate destruction of peoples' social and built environments has come to be known as domicide, from *domus* (home in Latin) and *cide* (killing), similar to genocide or suicide. Hence, domicide is the planned and systematic killing of home. This violence ranges in its scale from destroying peoples' most intimate and private spaces such as bedrooms, kitchens, and living rooms (their physical homes) to bulldozing their entire neighborhoods, razing their gardens, parks, and public spaces— the mass destruction of the city. Increasingly, researchers around the world have been utilizing the concept of domicide as a way to center the suffering of its victims. The alternative is often to turn peoples' pain into statistics, such as when an international organization reports the numbers of displaced people or percentage of damage in cities without focusing on the human suffering. Centering the suffering of domicide's victims "not only contributes to raise awareness and generate empathy so that political intervention can be formulated, but also helps to reflect and confront the more disturbing question as to the ignorance or denial of human suffering in the first place."[5]

The impact of domicide moves beyond the physical. It destroys family networks, damages their sense of place and belonging. It could create a sense of disorientation in the world, even when victims live in the comfort of new homes or in their exile in cities such as Istanbul, Cairo, Berlin, New York, or Dubai. After domicide, they yearn for and mourn the place they used to know and grieve their forced eviction and the memory they accumulated in their lost home. It also breaks their livelihoods, as their life savings are destroyed. Balakrishnan Rajagopal, the

United Nations' special rapporteur on the right to adequate housing, has been calling for recognizing domicide as an international crime while explaining the multilayered loss people experience when they lose their home:

> I have witnessed how in just a few seconds a home—the culmination of a life-long effort and the pride of entire families—can be wiped out and turned to rubble. Destroyed is not only a home. Destroyed are the savings of entire families. Destroyed are memories and the comfort of belonging. Along with this comes a social and psychological trauma that is difficult to describe or imagine.[6] (Fig. 1)

Fig. 1 The state of destruction in Homs, Syria in 2025. Photo by the author

Domicide in "Peace"

In many cities around the world, peoples' homes have been bulldozed at times of "peace." Governments often legitimize forced eviction and mass destructions as being for the "public good." They come with architectural and urban visions to "modernize" and "develop" cities but often at the expense of the poor and marginalized targeted communities. In these processes of "modernization," layers of memory are erased, and people are uprooted from their homes. Sometimes an individual building or an infrastructure project is proposed: a bridge, a highway, or a stadium. Other times, new neighborhoods or even cities are envisioned. Entire neighborhoods are therefore razed, leaving civilians with extreme sense of loss and grief. Their homes are labeled "informal" or are in the way of these "development projects." But in almost all circumstances, these destructions are marketed as beneficial for the "public good."

Take India as an example. In a recent report published by the Housing and Land Rights Network, it was noted that in a period of two years, 2022 and 2023, over 153,820 homes were demolished in the country, evicting more than 738,438 people. In 2023, evictions increased exponentially, resulting in the highest recorded figures over the last seven years that the network has been observing. The eviction and destruction have been accompanied by media reporting that uses "strong language of criminalisation of the poor, referring to low-income communities as 'encroachers' and 'illegal.'"[7] The government justifies the destruction under the names of "development" projects, "city-beautification" and "slum clearance." A similar pattern can be found in Egypt, where cultural heritage sites and everyday architecture are threatened in the name of development.

In Saudi Arabia, many cultural heritage sites have been destroyed in Mecca, the holiest city in Islam. There, near the Kaaba, historical sites associated with Prophet Muhammad and various eras of Islam's history were replaced with shopping centers, restaurants, and hotels in the name of "both iconoclasm and modernising the infrastructure in the yearly pilgrimage"[8]. In the words of Mecca's governor, Khalid ibn Faisal Al Saud, modernization is meant to transform Mecca into a "first world" city. Mega projects in central Mecca have resulted in the displacement from their homes of thousands of residents who come from different socioeconomic backgrounds. "The former residents have received meagre compensation in return and are without legal recourse," Harvard University historian Rosie Bsheer has written. "Some have ended up in slums less than a mile away from the Grand Mosque, hidden from visitors' eyes by the Abraj al-Bayt Towers and other large-scale developments."[9]

In Jeddah, several neighborhoods have been demolished as part of a strategy to achieve Saudi Vision 2030, which was launched in 2017. Pro-state news channels released a stigmatizing narrative about the residents of these neighborhoods, claiming many of them are undocumented and the neighborhoods are rife with drugs, crime, diseases, and theft. In 2022, Amnesty International released an investigation report on the mass demolitions and forced evictions in Saudi Arabia. The organization reviewed an official public document that showed residents were given a notice period for demolition ranging from 24 hours in one neighborhood to six weeks in others. A foreign national who lived in one of these neighborhoods for three years before he was forced to leave told Amnesty International in February 2022:

> I only found out about the eviction through spray paint on our building on 22 January and a paper posted on our ground floor stating that we had to leave before the end of the month. I never saw or spoke to any municipality or government officials.[10]

What is often missing in the stories of domicide are the voices of those whose lives have been shaped by destruction and displacement. The voices of those who lose their home, "if not completely omitted, often occupies a marginal position in the rhetoric space."[11] Therefore, we hear about the major projects of "urban development" but not the stories of people who are forcibly evicted from their homes. Many people would be fearful to express their opinions, as they would be punished when resisting domicide. When NEOM city in Saudi Arabia was being proposed, Abdul Raheem al-Huwaiti, whose home is on the proposed site for the new city, rejected his eviction order. He released several videos on social media explaining how the new city is aimed at attracting foreigners and providing them safety, education, and health benefits that might not be given to the local Saudi citizen. "People here are opposing [eviction] and even if you pay them 100 million for their home, I swear by Allah, they wouldn't accept," al-Huwaiti said in his video. People had been arrested for opposing the project, he said, and his turn would come. He said he would not be surprised if the security forces would come to kill him at home.

> This is my home... I don't have the intention to sell it or take a compensation. Yes, it's correct it is my possession, it represents my ownership in this area, but if I sold it, then I have sold my entire home, my entire homeland. And my homeland is not for sale.[12]

Al-Huwaiti was killed by security forces in April 2020. Alia Hayel Aboutiyah al-Huwaiti, an outspoken activist and a member of the same tribe as al-Huwaiti, told *The Guardian* that "for the Huwaitat tribe, Neom is being built on our blood, on our bones."[13] (Figs. 2 and 3)

Fig. 2 Kaaba in Mecca, Saudi Arabia circa 1910. *Source* Matson photograph collection, Library of Congress. https://www.loc.gov/resource/matpc.04659

Fig. 3 A view from near the Kaaba, dominated by the Abraj al-Bayt Towers, in 2024. Photo by the author

Domicide in War

Domicide takes more extreme forms at times of occupation, wars, and armed conflict. Cities become the sites of battlefields and urban misery. Aleppo, Mariupol, and Mosul have become symbols of ruin and destruction in the last decade, and before them, so many cities were destroyed in the last century, including Beirut, Dresden, Coventry, Hiroshima, and Warsaw. Throughout the years, cities have been divided by conflict infrastructure (e.g., fences, walls, and checkpoints), besieged, bombed, and ruined. Civilians have found themselves at the heart of these battles, internally displaced multiple times to save lives. The changing dynamics of war keep following them as they move, and people get displaced multiple times within their city or to other cities around their countries. Millions of people eventually flee their countries, as nowhere is safe any longer for them. At times of wars, destroyers often label their destruction and killing as "ethical," "moral," and "just," fought against "terrorists" with "precision." But what we have seen in many areas is that these are wars to destroy an entire people. A war on civilians. As Lyse Doucet, the BBC's chief international correspondent, has said:

> Wars of our time, sometimes fought in our name, are not in the trenches; they're fought street-to-street, house-to-house, one home after another. Why does a hospital, a kindergarten, always seem to be hit in every outbreak of hostilities? After nearly four decades of reporting on conflict, I now often say: civilians are not close to the front lines; they are the front line.
> In Syria and Ukraine, and wars before and beyond, this kind of destruction has often been called "collateral damage," or civilians "caught in the crossfire"—the kind of language which can sanitise, even be used to excuse. Potential war crimes.[14]

In the months since Hamas's attack on Israel in October 2023 and Israel's response, the Gaza Strip has been turned into a site of ruins.[15] As of April 2024, around three quarters of the population, approximately 1.7 million people, were internally displaced in Gaza, and more of than half of the population was on the brink of famine. The destruction of Gaza includes everyday architecture, such as universities, schools, homes, shops, mosques, and hospital,[16] and also cultural heritage sites, such as the Rashad Shawa cultural center in Gaza's Rimal district, the Qasr al-Basha (the Pasha's Palace), and the Reyad El-Alami center for Palestinian heritage, a 430-year-old house in the Daraj neighborhood of the old city of Gaza. Cultural heritage is being deliberately destroyed in cities across the world in what has come to be known as cultural genocide.

While studies on cities and wars have often focused on the destruction of cultural heritage sites, fewer efforts have been directed toward understanding the wider destruction of a city, especially the destruction of peoples' homes. This was the case, for instance, in Syria, where Palmyra, with its celebrity-like statues, has led to the emergence of projects, exhibitions, initiatives, and research collaborations on the use and abuse of heritage at times of wars. But not much research or architectural projects, until today, have been done on the destruction of everyday life, on peoples' homes.

With the start of the revolution in Syria in 2011, Homs, the third-largest city after Damascus and Aleppo, was nicknamed Capital of the Revolution because of the courage and resilience people have shown in the face of the brutality of the regime. This was part of a wider wave of protests across several countries in the Arab region known as the Arab Spring. As people in Homs marched across their neighborhoods to raise their voices and express their demands for justice, freedom, and dignity, government forces started arresting and killing civilians in peaceful protests. The conflict that started peacefully took a different direction with the government's brutal response. Many members of the Syrian army started defecting, and the Free Syrian Army was formed in opposition to the regime. More armed groups started to emerge. The Capital of the Revolution has turned into ruins. In Homs—my city—more than half of the neighborhoods have been heavily destroyed, and around one quarter of the neighborhoods have been damaged. Now, even when bulldozers have left the city, even when checkpoints have been removed, and when snipers no longer remain on the city's towers, Homs remains in ruins. Syria, a forgotten war—but not for those whose lives have been shattered and broken into pieces. There are no reconstruction projects, even years and years after the end of the fighting in Homs. People wait for a reconstruction yet to come.

The Afterlife of Domicide

The afterlife of domicide remains one of the gaps in our knowledge about violence and cities in "peace" and war. The world's attention moves quickly. But what happens after the destruction of peoples' homes? Where are the people who were evicted in Egypt, Saudi Arabia, India? Where are the people who lost their homes in Ukraine, Palestine, Syria? Who will rebuild their homes and when? Ending the destruction is not by any means the end of the suffering. The aftermath of domicide leaves people in deep grief and suffering for years, and even for a lifetime. When these countries disappear from the consciousness of the world's fast news reporting, the pain continues slowly, as life in itself turns into a war for survival. When I talk to or meet with Syrians who remain in Syria, they say that the years after the war are harder than the years of the war. One has told me, "People live there, because of the lack of death." The city remains in ruins, with a collapsed economy, extreme poverty, destroyed livelihoods, and silenced grief (Fig. 4).

But my city is not an exception. As I have highlighted in this chapter, many cities around the world have turned into sites of contentions and battlefields. We need to think about the everyday violence, and respond to it, rather than neglecting it so it turns into extreme war violence. We also need to open a global conversation on the word "reconstruction." Reconstruction must be taught in architecture and urban planning schools and presented to global leaders and decision-makers. What does reconstruction look like? How can we deconstruct the word to think about its different dimensions (such as memory, heritage, economy, and

Fig. 4 The state of destruction in Homs, Syria in 2025. Photo by the author

community), and imagine a future without ruins? While the volume that follows is not narrowly focused on reconstruction but rather integrates concepts and ideas of identity-based mass violence in cities with the impact and opportunities for prevention and recovery, the work in this volume is well positioned to move such a conversation forward.

Notes

1. Ammar Azzouz, Domicide: Architecture, *War and the Destruction of Home in Syria* (London: Bloomsbury, 2023).
2. Douglas Porteous and Sandra E. Smith, *Domicide: The Global Destruction of Home* (Montreal: McGill-Queen's University Press, 2001).
3. Human Rights Watch, "Syria: Government Attacking Bread Lines: Civilian Deaths at Bakeries Are War Crimes," August 30, 2012.
4. Syrian Network for Human Rights, "At Least 174 Attacks on Bakeries Have Been Documented Since March 2011 to Date, 149 of Them at the Hands of the Syrian-Russian Alliance," Syrian Network for Human Rights, September 16, 2021.
5. Yunpeng Zhang, "Domicide, Social Suffering and Symbolic Violence in Contemporary Shanghai, China," *Urban Geography* 39, no. 2 (February 7, 2018): 191.
6. United Nations Office of the High Commissioner for Human Rights, "'Domicide' Must Be Recognised As an International Crime: UN Expert," United Nations Office of the High Commissioner for Human Rights, October 8, 2022.
7. Anagha Jaipal, Anuj Behal, and Aishwarya Ayushmaan, "Forced Evictions in India: 2022 & 2023," Housing and Land Rights Network, New Delhi, 2024, 9.
8. Rosie Bsheer, "Heritage As War," *International Journal of Middle East Studies* 49, no. 4 (November 2017): 732.
9. Rosie Bsheer, "The Property Regime: Mecca and the Politics of Redevelopment in Saudi Arabia," *Jadaliyya*, September 8, 2015.

10. Amnesty International, "Saudi Arabia: Mass Demolitions and Forced Evictions Marred by Violations and Discrimination," Amnesty International, June 22, 2022.
11. Zhang, *Domicide*, 190.
12. Abdul Raheem al-Huwaiti, "Al-Huwaiti against NEOM's Eviction," YouTube, 2020. https://www.youtube.com/watch?v=0kt4fyZxsWc.
13. Ruth Michaelson, "'It's Being Built on Our Blood': The True Cost of Saudi Arabia's $500bn Megacity," *The Guardian*, May 4, 2020, accessed March 30, 2024, https://www.theguardian.com/global-development/2020/May/04/its-being-built-on-our-blood-the-true-cost-of-saudi-arabia-5bn-mega-city-neom.
14. Azzouz, *Domicide*, xiii.
15. United Nations Office of the High Commissioner for Human Rights, "Gaza: Destroying Civilian Housing and Infrastructure Is an International Crime, Warns UN Expert," United Nations Office of the High Commissioner for Human Rights, November 8, 2023; Kaamil Ahmed and Elena Morresi, "Airstrikes on Gaza Bakeries Add to 'Catastrophic' Food Shortages," *The Guardian*, October 28, 2023, https://www.theguardian.com/global-development/2023/oct/28/airstrikes-on-gaza-bakeries-add-to-catastrophic-food-shortages.
16. Niels De Hoog, Antonio Voce, Elena Morresi, Manisha Ganguly, and Ashley Kirk, "How War Destroyed Gaza's Neighbourhoods—Visual Investigation," *The Guardian*, January 30, 2024, accessed March 30, 2024, https://www.theguardian.com/world/ng-interactive/2024/jan/30/how-war-destroyed-gazas-neighbourhoods-visual-investigation; Chandni Desai, "The War in Gaza Is Wiping Out Palestine's Education and Knowledge Systems," *Conversation*, February 8, 2024, https://theconversation.com/the-war-in-gaza-is-wiping-out-palestines-education-and-knowledge-systems-222055.

References

Ahmed, Kaamil, and Elena Morresi. "Airstrikes on Gaza Bakeries Add to 'Catastrophic' Food Shortages." *The Guardian*, October 28, 2023. https://www.theguardian.com/global-development/2023/oct/28/airstrikes-on-gaza-bakeries-add-to-catastrophic-food-shortages.

Al-Huwaiti, Abdul Raheem. "Al-Huwaiti against NEOM's Eviction." YouTube, 2020. https://www.youtube.com/watch?v=0kt4fyZxsWc.

Amnesty International. "Saudi Arabia: Mass Demolitions and Forced Evictions Marred by Violations and Discrimination." Amnesty International, June 22, 2022.

Azzouz, Ammar. *Domicide: Architecture, War and the Destruction of Home in Syria*. London: Bloomsbury, 2023.

Bsheer, Rosie. 2017. "Heritage As War." *International Journal of Middle East Studies* 49, no. 4 (November 2017): 729–734.

Bsheer, Rosie. 2015. "The Property Regime: Mecca and the Politics of Redevelopment in Saudi Arabia." *Jadaliyya*, September 8.

De Hoog, Niels, Antonio Voce, Elena Morresi, Manisha Ganguly, and Ashley Kirk. 2024. "How War Destroyed Gaza's Neighbourhoods—Visual Investigation." *The Guardian*, January 30, 2024. Accessed March 30, 2024. https://www.theguardian.com/world/ng-interactive/2024/jan/30/how-war-destroyed-gazas-neighbourhoods-visual-investigation.

Desai, Chandni. "The War in Gaza Is Wiping Out Palestine's Education and Knowledge Systems." Conversation, February 8, 2024. https://theconversation.com/the-war-in-gaza-is-wiping-out-palestines-education-and-knowledge-systems-222055.

Human Rights Watch. "Syria: Government Attacking Bread Lines: Civilian Deaths at Bakeries Are War Crimes." August 30, 2012.

Jaipal, Anagha, Anuj Behal, and Aishwarya Ayushmaan. "Forced Evictions in India: 2022 & 2023." Housing and Land Rights Network, New Delhi, 2024.

Michaelson, Ruth. "'It's Being Built on Our Blood': The True Cost of Saudi Arabia's $500bn Megacity." *The Guardian*, May 4, 2020. Accessed March 30, 2024. https://www.theguardian.com/global-development/2020/may/04/its-being-built-on-our-blood-the-true-cost-of-saudi-arabia-5bn-mega-city-neom.

Porteous, Douglas, and Sandra E. Smith. Domicide: The Global Destruction of Home. Montreal: McGill-Queen's University Press, 2001.

Syrian Network for Human Rights. "At Least 174 Attacks on Bakeries Have Been Documented Since March 2011 to Date, 149 of Them at the Hands of the Syrian-Russian Alliance." Syrian Network for Human Rights, September 16, 2021.

United Nations Office of the High Commissioner for Human Rights. "'Domicide' Must Be Recognised As an International Crime: UN Expert." United Nations Office of the High Commissioner for Human Rights, October 8, 2022.

United Nations Office of the High Commissioner for Human Rights. 2023. "Gaza: Destroying Civilian Housing and Infrastructure Is an International Crime, Warns UN Expert." United Nations Office of the High Commissioner for Human Rights, November 8, 2023.

Zhang, Yunpeng. 2018. "Domicide, Social Suffering and Symbolic Violence in Contemporary Shanghai, China." Urban Geography 39, no. 2 (February 7, 2018): 190–213.

Ammar Azzouz is a research fellow at the School of Geography and the Environment, University of Oxford. His research has appeared in the New York *Times*, *Conversation*, *New Statesman*, *New Lines Magazine*, *Middle East Eye*, and peerreviewed journals. He studied architecture in his home country of Syria, and he is the author of *Domicide: Architecture, War and the Destruction of Home in Syria* (London: Bloomsbury, 2023).

Open Access This chapter is licensed under the terms of the Creative Commons Attribution-NonCommercial-NoDerivatives 4.0 International License (http://creativecommons.org/licenses/by-nc-nd/4.0/), which permits any noncommercial use, sharing, distribution and reproduction in any medium or format, as long as you give appropriate credit to the original author(s) and the source, provide a link to the Creative Commons license and indicate if you modified the licensed material. You do not have permission under this license to share adapted material derived from this chapter or parts of it.

The images or other third party material in this chapter are included in the chapter's Creative Commons license, unless indicated otherwise in a credit line to the material. If material is not included in the chapter's Creative Commons license and your intended use is not permitted by statutory regulation or exceeds the permitted use, you will need to obtain permission directly from the copyright holder.

Paper City and Papers, Cities, Lambe-Lambe, and Young People

Alberto Pereira

Prologue: Paper City

I don't remember the last time I died. Maybe I'm dying right now in some corner of the city. This is how I live, not in any one place, but in all places at the same time, sneaking around the poles, walls, electrical boxes, telephone booths, little entrances, doorways, metal siding; in all the avenues, small streets, alleys. From Gávea to Guadalupe, I'm central, suburban. I'm in the projects, in all the shit, in the Altos, the Baixada, Niterói, São Gonçalo, but I don't stop in Rio. Nobody looks at me and thinks I'm from another city, another state, another continent.

Nobody thinks I can speak several languages, or that I've seen everything in this world, that I've been involved with the clergy and nobility, in West-to-East manufacturing or vice versa, promoting performances from the French Belle Époque or formulating ideas in the old Soviet Union. I have been present at every conceivable campaign; I've helped

A. Pereira (✉)
Artist represented by Aborda, Rio de Janeiro, Brazil
e-mail: comigo@albertopereira.com.br

elect presidents without even sharing ideas with them. Fuck it. In the situation I've been surviving in, I've never had the chance to think about morality; no. I have taken part in tons of conflicts while playing on both sides. I've *totally* done false advertising; I tell several lies and a lot of truths—it just depends on your point of view.

I keep on being born, dying, and living again. Like a Jesus from the streets, three days go by, and there I am again; I resuscitate. I don't know if I'm violating the city or if I'm the one being violated. I'm like a cloth that hugs the walls, but that people tear apart. In my eyes, I thought people liked me, because there are people who walk by and actually say they like me, but it's obvious I have my flaws, isn't it? The other day I was thinking, I've been around for many centuries, resisting, even with the world tearing at me. And notice that I don't even say anything; that's the way it is with me, straight talk, eye to eye. I'm judged, read, understood (or not) by other people's eyes, speaking directly about my thoughts, you know what I mean?

My voice can only be heard through looking. A silent scream. I think it's funny that this big world keeps evolving; some crap gets left behind, devices appear, gadgets, trinkets, and even then, I'm still sustained and sustainable. My best technology is, perhaps, simplicity and discretion. Attentive 24 hours a day, seven days a week, on constant watch. Only those who look at me are the ones who can see me, it's as simple as that. I might even seem arrogant by talking about all these things, but even without false modesty, I'm fucking awesome. In my situation, I have to value myself, since everybody abuses me, and very rarely do people give me any value.

Just imagine: You're left behind somewhere, living, but without food, without affection, without speaking to anyone, dirty, getting assaulted, getting various suspicious looks, with rarely a sincere exchange, a smile— and caught out in the sun, rain, heat, cold, and wind the whole time. Your self-esteem goes way down, damn. I even try to encourage some kind of dialog, but it's often based on disagreements, really. I'd rather sit up above where no one can reach me, but if I have to stay on the ground, it would only be to call attention to something greater. The reality is that I need to believe in myself—and for this, I need you to believe too. I can be hard, tight against the wall, as sharp as a knife, act in such a way that

I crumple, stretch, rip, stick, blow, sneak, slash, recycle. Some call me a street poster, banner, ad, sticker, maybe art, maybe advertising, maybe trash, definitely historical and history. Maybe much more than a piece of paper.

Fig. 1 Sento e Onze (Project 111), by the author, presents an image of André Avelino (left), João Cândido (center), and Manoel Gregório (right) in Praça Marechal Âncora, facing Guanabara Bay, Rio de Janeiro, Brazil. This was a transit area during the Revolta da Chibata (Chibata Revolt)—a mutiny by sailors led by João Cândido that occurred between November 22 and 27, 1910, and was mainly motivated by the dissatisfaction of Black and Brown sailors with the physical punishments to which they were subjected: whips. The area around the square became his refuge and home, where he carried baskets of fish to survive after the social and economic sanctions imposed by the Brazilian Navy throughout his life. Today it is a place of remembrance, where his statue stands at the site of the urban intervention. Photo by Cochi Guimarães

Introduction

The objective of this essay is to establish parallels among a group (perhaps a scene) of young people in street or public art, commonly identified as urban art. I will propose some considerations about social and political action, the articulation of the territory and characteristics that approximate and resignify some of the considerations presented by Rossana Reguillo and Jesus Martín-Barbero. These considerations will be based on a specific section of public art, through the technique and expression of posters and stickers in general present in cities, characterized in Brazil by the name of lambe-lambe. *Lambe-lambe* is the name given to the paper or poster that is fixed with industrial or handmade glue in public places. It varies in technique, size, and format. It can be printed by hand, by a commercial printer, or written or painted by hand. It can be in black and white or color. Its shape can be rectangular, square, or irregular, adapting to the illustration or message inscribed on it. The technique is traditional and can be used for both advertising and artistic purposes.[1]

Production of Vandalism and Vandalism as a Product

In their publications, Rossana Reguillo and Jesus Martín-Barbero present young people as agents with an active role in their relations with the world and the context that surrounds them. They are social and political actors, broadening the notions of doing politics beyond a partisan sense. According to Reguillo, the fact that many young people do not opt for partisan or institutional practices and forms of gatherings and do not seem to participate in traditional, explicit political projects may conceal the new meaning of the politics that shape the communication networks from which the social world is processed and disseminated.[2] These new forms mean that doing politics is not directly related to a system of preestablished regulations, norms, and rules but to a constant overlapping, a variable network of beliefs, actions, and layers, a collage of forms and lifestyles. In this sense, *lambe-lambe* posters overlap with young people in one of their many concomitants: that of being political beyond the traditional spheres of doing politics, through other languages, methods, formats, and suggestions, which Barbero contextualizes as an experience of overflow and displacement, both of discourse and political actions among young people. He states, "Following paths beyond traditions, politics is rediscovered from culture," and part of this act is present in paper and glue across ordinary territories. The street poster is part of the daily passage of the landscape and traffic, and above all, it becomes another layer of the city and a mirror of the social environment.[3]

Always at the crossroads between politics, the city, and the poster, as Reguillo points out:

> For certain "readings," young people are disposable as political subjects, a source of "contempt" and suspicion. For other "readings," young people are seen as soap opera and movie characters, libertarian emblems, pure power. Scorn or exaltation.[4]

Urban artistic activities are part of the set of "certain 'readings'" in the fields of the art market and advertising, which focus on the city and its spaces as an institution. In the visual arts as a whole, the expressions present in the streets are not assimilated into the mold of traditional art market practices, which, above all, remain centered on the forms considered classical: paintings and sculptures in certain formats. This hidden process of exclusion from urban practices of the white cube[5] is often associated with a supposed literalness of the work, an absence of techniques, artistic identity, methods, and conceptual research that would involve these urban makers. However, labeling an artist as street or urban does not indicate where he or she comes from, what his or her background, social class, or educational level is, simply where most of his or her recognized work takes place. In the city cluster, we can consider that spaces for urban art are competing with spaces intended for advertising. Municipal bodies often raise money through decrees, laws, and taxes by determining which formats and spaces are to be occupied by commerce and advertising. However, it is precisely in many advertising images where the use of street expression, street clothes, urban dances, and music is present, symbolically occupying several campaigns and generating millions of dollars through creative power that is mostly peripheral, unpretentious, transgressive, and young. Official and legalized art is excluded, but as commercial discourse it is exalted, appropriated as virtual image and discourse, but in its origin it is devoid of value. Where is the protagonism of the productions of street artists?

A collage made in the street has an involuntary expiration date, as it suffers from weathering, interactions, and erasures. The end is part of the work; it does not conform to the practical order of fulfilling a function of announcing something, nor does it go through maintenance or restoration processes, nor does it contribute economically to the treasury of a governmental institution. Likewise for the art market, in addition to the conventions that qualitatively exclude these practices, posters and other street languages commonly do not fit into the commodification of traditional art mechanisms, based on a unique material item, high-value commerce, social distinction, and exclusivity. Although they cannot be stored, preserved, controlled, or transported, they can be accessed, photographed, shared, idealized, and sold, always on the boundary between negation and affirmation. We could substitute the term "youth" for "street art" and "subject" for "object," in Barbero's words:

> On the one hand, young people are turning into subjects of consumption, becoming protagonists in the consumption of clothes, music, soft drinks and technological gadgets. On the other hand, this is produced through a gigantic and sophisticated advertising strategy that transforms new sensibilities into raw material for narrative and audiovisual experimentation.[6]

Finally, Reguillo brings us the disenchantment of young people in relation to the social landscape, which ranges from the institutional dynamics of the State, from traditional political relations to the economic and social contexts. Based on the elaborations and stigmas of urban art and the artist who produces it on the streets, one hypothesis to be considered is that for contexts in which the official department of the municipality does not participate by collecting through fees, deciding through permits and profiting through the sale of public spaces, such expressions can be classified as production of vandalism, depredation, and environmental crime (according to the municipal law of Rio de

Fig. 2 Application of 100 square meters of paper on the grounds of the Praça Marechal Âncora public square, in the historic center of Rio de Janeiro, Brazil, with assistance from the BXD Lambe collective. Photo by Gabriela Azevedo

Janeiro) based on subjective criteria that classify what, when, and where an expression is considered artistic or not.[7] However, in a scenario in which this department receives through fees, the production that was previously the result of vandalism transmutes into vandalism as a product.

City and Youth

Another point to think about is the relationship between the city, youth, and art present in these spaces. Lia Osório Machado, quoted by Milton Santos, reminds us that cities are open and complex systems, rich in instability and contingency.[8] Santos affirms that the city is the place where the world and human beings move the most. Copresence teaches people the difference between the two. That is why the city is the place of education and reeducation. The bigger the city, the more numerous and significant the movement, the wider and denser the copresence, and the greater the lessons and learnings.[9]

We can think of the presence of visual arts in public environments as an experience of copresence, movement, and reeducation of urban visualities. A reeducation because this practice still has to compete for space without full institutional and social acceptance. At the same time, it generates movement among artists and sympathizers in urban areas of different social classes, where young people of different social strata live, a concept expanded by Mario Margulis and Marcelo Urresti, which suggests that certain groups have the possibility of postponing social stages such as the formation of a family for an increasingly longer period and have the opportunity to study and advance in their education and professionalization.[10] In this sense, it is also an exercise in copresence, bringing together divergent trajectories, social groups, and territories through a common sense: making and observing art in the streets.

Occupying the streets with art goes beyond knowing the city; it implies recognizing it in its multiplicity: inequalities, diversities, mobilities, temporalities, and cultures. Artists sometimes start in their hometown but move to other territories between the luminous and opaque spaces of the cities, as conceptualized by Milton Santos, either by the search for new places to occupy, by the exchange with other artists, or by the need to travel, which may involve leisure, study, and/or work practices. In addition to artists, we can include admirers, professionals of tourism, architecture, communication, geography, researchers, and other groups.

From a technical point of view, in the specific case of *lambe-lambe* and stickers, the work is often sent to other cities, states, and countries. This double process of territorialization and deterritorialization has three directions and meanings to reflect on: the first direction is to think that although the practice and production of stickers are the result of a specific territory and location, as part of a local collective and perspective, it also finds meaning when it occupies other locations, expanding the idea of frontier to a new globalized and hybrid dimension. As much as they differ in their trajectory, they meet in their origins: poster culture, hip-hop movement, and punk scene are examples that encompass any collage action in the streets.

As a second point, we can also think about the virtualization of these territories and, consequently, their spatial deterritorialization, since many times the only possibility of approaching the work is through social networks and records published on websites, either because of their distant location or because of their nonexistence due to the consequences of ephemerality.

The third point is a counterpoint to the identity palimpsest conceptualized by Jesus Martín-Barbero as a double movement of dehistoricization and deterritorialization that fuses cultures.[11] Many Brazilian urban art productions include history and territory as a dual element in their conceptual constitution. This is due to a characteristic of the work of some artists who combine creation and territory in their conceptualization.

They start from very particular perspectives, historical, territorial, and local, involving above all class, gender, and race, triggering memories through the image—memories that the very regime of the city, the obsolescence of everyday life, and the time of modernity try to erase. These occupations go against the ephemerality of street practices and, ultimately, the fate of any materiality at this level. They are either erased or they fade away, are torn and disappear in the gray of urban palimpsests. And what remains beyond the erasure is the record of the erasure: the *lambe* goes away, the archive remains (Figures 1 and 2).

Notes

1. Luiz Navarro, Pele de Propaganda: Lambes e Stickers em Belo Horizonte [2000-2010] (2016), 62.
2. Rossana Reguillo, "Las culturas juveniles: un campo de estudio; breve agenda para la discusión," Revista Brasileira de Educação (2003): 114.
3. Jesús Martín-Barbero, "Jóvenes: des-orden cultural y palimpsestos de identidad," in Viviendo a toda: jóvenes, territorios culturales e

novas sensibilidades, ed. Humberto Cubides and Mario Margulis (Bogotá: Siglo del Hombre Editores, 1998).
4. Reguillo, "Las culturas juveniles," 115.
5. "'White cube,' in the definition of artist Brian O'Doherty, refers to a spatial configuration that seeks to remove from the artwork all indications that interfere with the fact that it is 'art.'" This implies isolating the artwork "from anything that might hinder its self-appreciation" through a rigorous neutralization of the gallery environment: the outside world must not enter, so windows are usually sealed. The walls are painted white. The ceiling becomes a source of light. The wooden floor is polished so that you produce austere creaks when walking or carpeted so that you walk in silence. The art is free, as it was said, "to take on a life of its own." G. Menotti, "Obras à mostra: articulações do trabalho de arte pelo desenho de exposição," ARS 11, no. 22 (2013). https://doi.org/10.11606/issn.2178-0447.ars.2013.80656.
6. Martín-Barbero, "Jóvenes: des-orden cultural".
7. Presidency of the Republic of Brazil, Lei Nº 9.605, De 12 De Fevereiro De 1998, accessed October 27, 2023, https://www.planalto.gov.br/ccivil_03/leis/l9605.htm.
8. Milton Santos, Técnica, Espaço, Tempo: Globalização e Meio Técnico-Científico Informacional (São Paulo: Hucitec, 1994), 40.
9. Ibid.
10. Mario Margulis and Marcelo Urresti, "La construcción social de la condición de juventud," in Viviendo a toda: jóvenes, territorios culturales e novas sensibilidades, ed. Humberto Cubides and Mario Margulis (Bogotá: Siglo del Hombre Editores, 1998).
11. Jesús Martín-Barbero, "Jóvenes: des-orden cultural y palimpsestos de identidad," in Viviendo a toda: jóvenes, territorios culturales e novas sensibilidades, ed. Humberto Cubides and Mario Margulis (Bogotá: Siglo del Hombre Editores, 1998).

Reference

Campos, Ricard, and Alix Sarrouy. "Juventude, criatividade e agência política." *Revista Tomo* 37 (July 2020): 17–46. https://doi.org/10.21669/tomo.vi37.13371.

Enciclopédia Itaú Cultural de Arte e Cultura Brasileira. "Fatura." São Paulo: Itaú Cultural, 2023. Accessed October 24, 2023. http://enciclopedia.itaucultural.org.br/termo50/fatura.

Margulis, Mario, and Marcelo Urresti. "La construcción social de la condición de juventud." In *Viviendo a toda: jóvenes, territorios culturales e nuevas sensibilidades*, edited by Humberto Cubides and Mario Margulis. Bogotá: Siglo del Hombre Editores, 1998.

Martin-Barbero, Jesús. "Jóvenes: des-orden cultural y palimpsestos de identidad." In *Viviendo a toda: jóvenes, territorios culturales e novas sensibilidades*, edited by Humberto Cubides and Mario Margulis. Bogotá: Siglo del Hombre Editores, 1998.

Menotti, G. "Obras à mostra: articulações do trabalho de arte pelo desenho de exposição." *ARS* 11, no. 22 (2013): 53-69. https://doi.org/10.11606/issn.2178-0447.ars.2013.80656.

Navarro, Luiz. *Pele de Propaganda: Lambes e Stickers em Belo Horizonte [2000-2010]*. 2016.

O Globo. "Alberto Pereira inaugura obra gigante no Rio em homenagem a João Cândido." Accessed October 27, 2023. https://oglobo.globo.com/ela/alberto-pereira-inaugura-obra-gigante-no-rio-em-homenagem-joao-candido-1-25312488.

O Globo. "Projeto Negro Muro retrata personalidades negras em paredes do Rio." Accessed October 26, 2023. https://oglobo.globo.com/fotogalerias/projeto-negro-muro-retrata-personalidades-negras-em-paredes-do-rio-25047544.

Presidency of the Republic of Brazil. *Lei Nº 9.605, De 12 De Fevereiro De 1998*. Accessed October 27, 2023. https://www.planalto.gov.br/ccivil_03/leis/l9605.htm.

Reguillo, Rossana. "Las culturas juveniles: un campo de estudio; breve agenda para la discusión." *Revista Brasileira de Educação* (2003): 103-118.

Santos, Milton. *Técnica, Espaço, Tempo: Globalização e Meio Técnico-Científico Informacional*. São Paulo: Hucitec, 1994. Accessed October 26, 2023. https://reverbe.net/cidades/wp-content/uploads/2011/livros/tecnica-espaco-tempo-milton-santos.pdf.

The Art of Punk—Dead Kennedys—The Art of Winston Smith. *Art + Music—MOCAtv.* Accessed October 24, 2023. https://www.youtube.com/watch?v=CiMLQqNFTyI.

Alberto Pereira is a Brazilian communicator and visual artist. His works have been presented in solo and collective exhibitions, digital and urban art festivals, and contemporary art salons in Argentina, Brazil, Egypt, France, Italy, and Lebanon. In 2016, he created the Lambes Brasil network, focused on publicizing, valuing, and producing events and opportunities for street artists who create posters across the country.

Open Access This chapter is licensed under the terms of the Creative Commons Attribution-NonCommercial-NoDerivatives 4.0 International License (http://creativecommons.org/licenses/by-nc-nd/4.0/), which permits any noncommercial use, sharing, distribution and reproduction in any medium or format, as long as you give appropriate credit to the original author(s) and the source, provide a link to the Creative Commons license and indicate if you modified the licensed material. You do not have permission under this license to share adapted material derived from this chapter or parts of it.

The images or other third party material in this chapter are included in the chapter's Creative Commons license, unless indicated otherwise in a credit line to the material. If material is not included in the chapter's Creative Commons license and your intended use is not permitted by statutory regulation or exceeds the permitted use, you will need to obtain permission directly from the copyright holder.

Using Evidence and Data to Monitor Identity-Based Mass Violence

Gary Milante

Introduction

Atrocities are atrocious. We don't need statistics or charts to know when violence is wrong. Some acts are so atrocious that data fails to capture their impact. Would a genocide that killed 1 million people be more atrocious if it was 1.1 million? Probably. Would it be less atrocious if it was "only" 900,000? Doubtful. In such cases, a word like "immeasurable" captures how statistics are insufficient, not because the phenomenon cannot be measured. Yet we measure acts of violence every day. These measurements are both communication tools to inform policy and part of the ritual of remembrance. We stack these statistics up to build collective memory and, we hope, to change behaviors in the future.

This chapter is about the evidence we use to identify and understand identity-based mass violence (IBMV). Throughout the remainder of the volume, the reader will encounter a number of chapters in which authors

---

G. Milante (✉)
The World Bank, Washington, D.C., USA
e-mail: gmilante@worldbank.org

© The Author(s) 2026
R. Locke et al. (eds.), *Identity-Based Mass Violence in Urban Contexts*, Palgrave Studies in Victims and Victimology, https://doi.org/10.1007/978-3-031-98068-8_4

will "make a case" of identity violence. The terms "case" and "evidence" are intentional; in many ways, the chapters that follow are similar to what a prosecutor might argue: the authors will present evidence that what they are reporting is identity-based mass violence. Extending the analogy makes you, the reader, a judge or jury, and this chapter is guidance for the judge or instructions for the jury.

It will be shown that the evidence of IBMV need not be only quantitative (e.g., incidence data, statistics) or qualitative (e.g., interviews, accounts, testimonials). Indeed, neither solely quantitative nor qualitative evidence is sufficient to make a case of identity-based violence. Rather, it is the artful blending of qualitative approaches that yield insights on intent, impact, and suffering with quantitative approaches, informing scale and frequency. Qualitative and quantitative evidence can be connected geospatially or temporally to inform timelines. They can also come from formal and informal sources. This chapter will start by situating the concept of identity-based mass violence amid the wider spectrum of violence. It will continue with some important concepts on the measurement and identification of violence and conclude with challenges that the nascent field faces in building the evidence base.

What Do We Mean by Identity-Based Mass Violence?

This volume starts from the premise that IBMV is a nascent field. There are no gold standards for data or evidence on this topic. Nor is all evidence of equal quality or the same type. Some situations may call for highly localized survey data. Others may be served best by qualitative assessments of those most affected. Indeed, expanding our understanding of what counts as evidence by including various forms of information allows us to understand how societal systems contribute to violence and the range of solutions to reduce it.

When I was invited to contribute this chapter, I was not convinced that we needed a new term called "identity-based mass violence." There are already quite a few terms for different types of violence, some of which are still contested in the field. However, as the tragedy in Gaza unfolded in 2023–2024 and professional and academic debate raged about whether the violence by Israel against the Palestinians constituted genocide, it became clear that our modern language was insufficient. Genocide or not is a false choice, and we cannot ignore the structural components of the conflict. Michal Briar and Efrat Cohen Bar in Chapter 7 lay out the systemic violence for Palestinians in Israel. Those structural conditions are clearly related to the outbreak of acute and atrocious violence we are currently witnessing.

We have other terms: "crimes against humanity," "crimes of aggression," "one-sided violence," and "political violence" (described below). But as we will see, these terms have been carefully ring-fenced to identify what they include. As a result, I've come around on the idea of a larger term to cover the breadth of possible violence that is and can be driven by identity. Identity-based mass violence is just such a larger concept that holds a number of these other terms usefully within it.

"Identity-based mass violence" is defined in Chapter 1. It is a useful category of violence that includes diverse forms of violence across a spectrum. This is illustrated in Fig. 1 with two dimensions: (1) horizontally by "identity"—violence motivated by identity is to the right in the figure, crimes less driven by identity, with other motivations, are toward the left; and (2) vertically by severity—more severe violence is higher in the figure than less-grave violence. A notional cut-off for "mass violence" is included as well. These are all generalizations; violence of any type can have multiple motivations and vary by both the number of people impacted and severity.

To provide further context, some indications of institutional mandates are included. The purview of the International Criminal Court (ICC) is at the top of the figure. Some types of violence are only enforced informally through norms and culture or locally. Between these would fall crimes and violence regulated by the state at whatever level. Obviously, what crimes are investigated and prosecuted in different jurisdictions varies greatly.

At the top of Fig. 1, the ICC has jurisdiction over four crimes: genocide, crimes against humanity, war crimes, and crimes of aggression.[1] The latter two are crimes that states or their armed groups perpetrate in violation of the Geneva Convention and against the sovereignty, integrity, or independence of another state, respectively. Genocide is

```
                War Crimes                    Genocide         ICC
                        Crimes Against Humanity
                    Crimes of
                    Aggression              Hate-Crimes (Violent)
                            Gender-Based Violence
    Community
    Violence         PoliticalViolence       Systemic Violence
                        One-Sided Violence   Structural Violence
    Interpersonal
    Violence            Terrorism
                        State Violence
    Entrepreneurial
    Violence        Hate Crimes (Non-Violent)    IBMV

                                                    LOCAL
                        Mass
                        Violence
                        Cut-Off
```

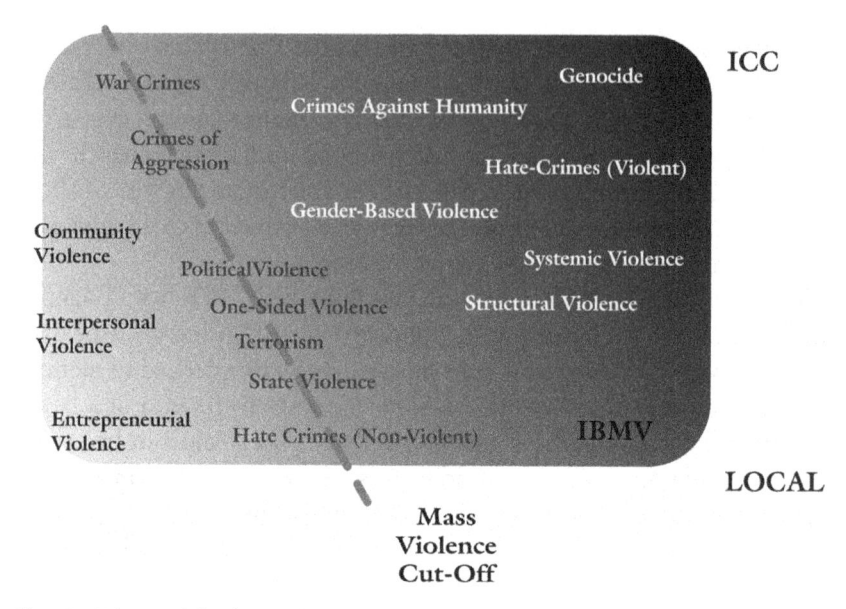

Fig. 1 What might be included in identity-based mass violence? *Source*: the author

defined by the intent to destroy a national, ethnic, racial, or religious group—the intent to destroy a group of people through any means based on their identity. Genocide is indisputably identity based and mass violence. Crimes against humanity include the use of various forms of violence against civilians (not necessarily by identity), which can include crimes like imprisonment, disappearances, enslavement, apartheid, and deportation. These actions often manifest with an identity component. Thus, among the crimes over which the ICC has jurisdiction, genocide, at the upper right, is included firmly in the diagram in Fig. 1 as identity-based mass violence (IBMV) and as mass violence.[2] Crimes against humanity, midway on the spectrum, may not have an identity component or be mass violence (but they often do and are).[3] Even in the cases with the highest quality documentation of evidence, records, data, and interpretation may be political.[4] Of the crimes over which the ICC has jurisdiction, war crimes and crimes of aggression are perhaps least likely to have an identity component and be considered IBMV, and are shown near the border.

Farther down the figure, classification becomes more difficult. Crimes typically enforced by state authorities include political violence, criminal violence, and gender-based violence. Political violence around elections or other political processes that suppress the vote, intimidate voters, secure outcomes by force (including coups and civil wars), or otherwise use violence to affect the outcome are often aligned by identity. Criminal violence is a broad category and can include community violence (often targeted against people of a certain identity), interpersonal violence, and entrepreneurial violence. Criminal violence that is not identity based is also, typically, not mass violence. Crimes intended to terrorize an identity group may be hate crimes, violent or nonviolent, and whether or how they are enforced is often a matter of local law and custom. Gender-based violence is, by definition, identity-based violence and is often mass violence.

Two special cases of political violence are one-sided violence[5] and terrorism. One-sided violence is violence against civilians, including violence by nonstate armed groups. Police violence or violence against civilians by armed forces is also one-sided violence, whether or not it is investigated or enforced by state authorities. Violence by the state against citizens/civilians may be condoned or ordered, as in the well-documented examples of extrajudicial killings under the Rodrigo Duterte regime in the Philippines and death squads under Augusto Pinochet in Chile. These may be identity based, particularly when killings are used to maintain political control in ethnically divided states. Identity groups that come into power may also use state violence against political enemies and other groups, often in retaliation, creating unbroken cycles of violence as perpetrators change. Terrorism is a special case of political violence targeting civilians with intent to achieve political goals. Terrorism can be isolated incidents or include a campaign of terrorism, and either could constitute mass violence.

As the spectrum figure shows, violence may or may not fall into the category of IBMV. IBMV is, therefore, a blanket term that can hold a range of concepts from hate crimes to genocide. As a result, there are border cases. Political violence can certainly escalate to crimes of aggression or crimes against humanity. It will be up to the authors of the volume and the readers to determine what is and is not IBMV. This is not a shortcoming of IBMV but rather a strength.

One important takeaway is the centrality of intent in determining whether violence qualifies as hate crime, genocide, crimes against humanity, pogroms, ethnic cleansing, etc.[6] In these cases, the motivations of the perpetrators evidenced by the targeting of a specific group (by identity) differentiate them from other mass atrocities, acts of aggression, and mass violence. Data or statistics on incidence can rarely inform on intent. Intent may need to be resolved in court.

Because of the centrality of intentions, one of the most pernicious and subtle forms of IBMV may be the most difficult to identify: systemic violence (also called structural violence). This indirect violence against groups of people cannot always be specifically attributed to an individual or perpetrator group with specific intent but rather to the product of societal systems perpetuated by actors who may not be consciously aware of—or aren't motivated to change—the impacts of those systems. Because this form of violence may not be explicitly planned or premeditated by a group (though often it is), it may be difficult to attribute intent or motivation and, therefore, difficult to clearly define whether it is identity based or has similar features of other forms of IBMV, thus the gray areas of the figure. Despite this, systemic violence is very clearly mass violence, as it occurs at scale. When that scale seems to largely correlate with ethnicity, gender, race, or other aspects of identity, it is likely IBMV. How systemic violence manifests (and can be measured) is discussed further below.

Most of the types of violence in Fig. 1 are well understood and defined in academic and professional literature, including most types of political, criminal, and gender-based violence that are thoroughly investigated by peace researchers and criminologists, among others. Some are less well understood or defined, such as systemic and structural violence, and have relatively recent origins in academic studies.[7] Figure 1 and the discussion above demonstrate that "identity-based mass violence" as an emergent, enveloping classification term can accommodate many forms of large-scale violence motivated by identity. It is also clear that the edges of what may or may not be IBMV remain debatable.

Why Do We Need Evidence of Identity-Based Mass Violence?

Evidence has many uses. Most directly for justice, but also to support reconciliation processes, create a historical record, understand baselines and changes within a system, and measure effectiveness. Often, we draw on data (typically statistics) that have been collected by trusted actors and are objective and replicable. But statistics alone do not constitute evidence; equally rigorous is the collection of qualitative evidence, which follows established academic and professional protocols. Further, "official statistics" or the "establishment" versions of facts may be insufficient to construct a historical record, contested as it may be. The historical record can become an institution itself, particularly useful in highly emotionally charged and political contexts surrounding IBMV. Eventually, consensus can be built on what has transpired. In the most profound cases, conscientious and meticulous studies of remembrance, like the *Bosnian Book of the Dead* and work by Yad Vashem on the Holocaust, become sources considered objective and unassailable.

This epistemological tension between knowing an atrocity when we see it and the rigor of documenting identity-based violence through high-quality evidence runs throughout this volume. Most advocates and experts don't need statistics to know when atrocities are happening. Yet their cases are stronger when they use quantitative and qualitative evidence from formal and informal sources. This is easier said than done. In some cases, those most affected cannot or will not report crimes against them. In other cases, actors (state or nonstate) either don't have the capacity to produce quality statistics or don't have the political will to provide trustworthy evidence. When data is contested, actors may speak past each other with competing evidence as they construct their own narratives. Finally, measurement is uniquely challenging. Measuring crimes and other intentionally hidden acts is already difficult, and concepts like structural violence, which implies violence at the systemic level against a specific identity group, may be incredibly hard to measure (more on this below).

Measuring IBMV

How will we know IBMV when we see it? As discussed, data may be necessary but insufficient as evidence. Evidence can be quantitative (e.g., numeric measurements and statistics) and qualitative (e.g., information gathered through other forms, such as stories, interviews, focus groups, and images). Quantitative evidence and qualitative evidence are not mutually exclusive. Qualitative data can be counted and turned into quantitative data, for example, when the results of interviews are grouped in a phrase like "Five out of six respondents agreed…" Likewise, quantitative data is often used to inform qualitative data, for example, when police commissioners and city planners are given data on crime rates before a focus group discussion.

Quantitative data is often given artificial primacy because it is perceived as more objective and/or "official" (e.g., crime statistics). Yet depending on the collection methods used and their interpretation, it can also be inaccurate, misused, or abused.[8] Data can be manipulated by those creating it to serve their own narrative purpose. And biases can enter into the most objective statistics, particularly if humans interpret or provide expert assessment at any stage of the data-production process. Relatedly, quantitative data approaches have been critiqued in developing countries for being extractive, built to serve Western donor aid models instead of created by and for national actors who would use them for policy and planning.[9] Furthermore, good quality quantitative data takes time to produce, but atrocities and violence happen very quickly—waiting for verified statistics is not always an option (see Kate Ferguson and Andy Fearn's piece in Chapter 6 of this volume).

Data is worthless if it cannot be trusted and used by policymakers, particularly if the underlying processes are not trustworthy. Cautions should be attached to all indicators introduced and discussed unless the source, methodology, and process of data collection are well known, proven, accepted, and used by the parties to which it pertains. Quantitative data at face value is no more reliable than qualitative data—trust but verify.

Evidence Involving Violent Deaths

Prominent among the violence statistics is mortality. The reasons for this are simple: it is an important, discrete, objectively verifiable event. With modern forensics and surveillance, it is possible for death data points in a mass killing event to be time-stamped to the second or minute and geolocated to within meters.[10] It also can't happen twice. With nearly every other violence statistic, an event can happen to one individual five times or five individuals once. Not so with mortality. Furthermore, it is simple (captured by the short dictum "habeas corpus"), universally understood, and has significance to us all, which is why it is nearly universally monitored (though with surprising variance in quality[11]).

The preeminence of violent death statistics led them to be adopted as the flagship indicators by the United Nations for Sustainable Development Goal (SDG) 16: Peace, Justice and Strong Institutions. The first target, SDG 16.1, is "Significantly reduce all forms of violence and related death rates everywhere." The first indicators for that goal are:

16.1.1 Number of victims of intentional homicide per 100,000 population, by sex and age.
16.1.2 Conflict-related deaths per 100,000 population, by sex, age, and cause.

The SDGs were adopted in 2015 and cover the period until 2030, though few countries are on track to meet the ambition of significantly reducing violence. Note that although goal 16.1 is reducing all forms of violence, the first indicator selected is deaths. Perceptions indicators are included for other targets and, ultimately, many aspects of violence were not included in SDG 16.[12] Also, most legal definitions of homicide include intentionality—violent deaths without intentionality are not included as indicators for SDG 16.[13] This reinforces the importance of motivation and intent when building evidence around violence, though the bar of intentionality may be higher for legal qualification of homicide than for the intent to harm or intimidate in identity violence.

Intentional homicide data is collected by national and international actors, with varying degrees of quality and coverage.[14] Conflict-related death data is highly contested, as it occurs in countries affected by conflict, and national-level statistics ought to be treated with skepticism. International sources for conflict death event data, including geocoded and time-stamped data, are available from the Armed Conflict Location and Event Database and the Uppsala Conflict Data Program, and specific country observatories.[15] Finally, mortality is not unique to violence monitoring; of the 231 unique indicators used for the SDGs, 13 are types of mortality. As we will discuss below, other forms of mortality are often used for monitoring structural and systemic violence.

In this volume, a number of authors use violent deaths as indicators. In Chapter 21, Flávia Carbonari reports on the use of city homicide rates as a means of measuring impact for the Palmira violence reduction strategy. However, as discussed, statistics alone are often insufficient for us to comprehend the impact of IBMV and its solutions. In a simple reporting of dry statistics, the qualitative aspects of loss of life are conspicuous.

In Chapter 13, Kerry Whigham notes the use of a specific number of dead (8,372) in discussing the *ŠTO TE NEMA* art project of remembrance for the Srebrenica massacre. The power of the art installation comes from 8,372 empty tea cups representing the conversations over tea that will never be. Similarly, the four volume *Bosnian Book of the Dead* does more than count the 95,940 people killed in the Balkans in the 1990s. It documents age, gender, ethnicity, profession, combat statues, and information about the death of each person named. This provides the contextual understanding of identity-based mass violence achieved only by a massive, decades-long review of more than 200,000 pieces of information.[16]

One-sided violence, by a state against citizens, is worth special attention in this volume.[17] In Chapter 10, Antônio Sampaio demonstrates how deaths attributed to state security actors in Brazil measure the use (and abuse) of violence. A locally relevant threshold of "eight or more people killed during a police operation" was introduced by the nonstate observatory reporting on violence as a marker of mass violence. When the state is the perpetrator, its own statistics may not be trustworthy. Consider two examples:

- During the Syrian conflict (2011–2024), the government reported casualty figures that faced international scrutiny. Effective monitoring required cross-referencing these official reports with data from independent sources, including humanitarian organizations and investigative journalism. This meticulous approach ensured a more accurate picture of state-perpetrated violence.[18]
- In the United States, police violence has ignited debates around official statistics versus independent accounts. Monitoring state violence entails considering official reports and evidence from civil rights groups, eyewitness testimonies, and bystander videos. In some jurisdictions, federal agencies (including the US Department of Justice) have been tasked with monitoring and validating local reporting. Despite some oversight, there remains no single standard for reporting police shootings,[19] and definitions of hate crimes vary by jurisdiction.[20]

Dual approaches to building the evidence base can overcome mistrust of official statistics, which may be necessary for future peacebuilding and policymaking.

On Other Forms of Violence

Not all violence results in death. Statistics on other forms of violence can also be used to measure and monitor IBMV. Indeed, where only mortality is used, ill-intentioned actors will simply use nonlethal violence to avoid detection. Furthermore, as global norms against killing and medical technology have improved, mortality associated with violence has decreased. As a result, violence can increase even when deaths decline. Additional statistical measures of violence include assaults, sexual violence, extortion, property crime, and simply the threat of violence. Shootings are another example, as reported in Chapter 21 by Flávia Carbonari: "In New York City and Chicago, Cure Violence has been credited with a decrease in shootings of 63 percent and 48 percent, respectively."

Qualitative evidence enhances such statistical information and includes survivor testimonies, eyewitness accounts, perceptions surveys, and focus groups. This evidence informs us on the quality of peace and the experience of violence. The harrowing experiences of LGBTQI + migrants recounted by Areli Palomo Contreras in Chapter 6 are far more powerful as evidence than likely dubious assault statistics from state actors in Tijuana. A qualitative approach also supplements data on incidence of gender-based violence. In India, ElsaMarie D'Silva Chapter 20 demonstrates how participatory processes involving poetry can address and reduce sexual and gender-based violence. Sometimes, quantitative data isn't necessary at all. We don't have to know the exact scale and scope of identity-based violence in the Baltimore grade school described by Barbara Sherrod in Chapter 16. The qualitative evidence of the experience, the survivor testimony, and the restorative process are sufficient evidence of how IBMV is being experienced and addressed.

Furthermore, when violence is difficult to observe or measure, particularly when perpetrators don't want to be observed, novel forms of evidence may be necessary. The chapters in this volume by Ammar Azzouz (Chapter 2) and AlHakam Shaar (Chapter 11) make a compelling case for an emergent form of IBMV called domicide, a strategy of urban planning and a form of structural violence that hides beneath the veneer of building codes, policies, and the market, much like redlining has done in the United States. This phenomenon is also seen in Chapter 7 by Michal Braier and Efrat Cohen Bar.

In other cases, the nature of the violence is unobservable, and the main challenge is exposing it. Consider the evidence presented in Chapter 14 by Luz Adriana López Medina, Mariana Medina Barragán, and Maria Alejandra Medina Barragán, which involves the painstaking documentation of the experiences of individuals who have been disappeared into state systems in Colombia.

Hate crimes and hate speech are both incidents of identity-based violence and risk indicators for further, potentially mass, violence. The US Federal Bureau of Investigation defines hate crimes as "a committed criminal offense which is motivated, in whole or in part, by the offender's bias(es) against a: race, religion, disability, sexual orientation, ethnicity, gender." Crucially, "even if the offenders are mistaken in their perception the victim was a member of a certain group, the offense is still a bias crime because the offender was motivated by bias."[21] Once again, as with the genocide, this definition highlights the importance of intent.

Within the United States, participation in data collection around hate crimes is not mandatory for state, local, or tribal law enforcement but is required for federal law enforcement. Other countries have similar guidance for monitoring hate crimes (e.g., Organization for Security and Cooperation in Europe's guide *Hate Crime Data-Collection and Monitoring Mechanisms*[22]), but a lack of accurate data means that academics, activists, and other civil society members are often left to track risks using media reports and other anecdotal sources to better understand hate-based crimes.

Box 1: Who Collects the Data? One of the essential roles of the state is exercising the effective and legitimate monopoly on violence. With that monopoly comes a responsibility to monitor violence by the state and its citizens, particularly if the violence is to be considered effective and legitimate. As a result, state organizations, including federal departments, provincial authorities, and municipalities often, are responsible for proper reporting of violence and crime statistics, including homicides, assaults, sexual assaults, and other common crime rates. In some cases, judicial, federal, or oversight bodies monitor and report these statistics (or are responsible for validating statistics from various sources).

Hospitals and healthcare professionals may also be a source of evidence. These actors are often required by law to report to other administrative bodies any evidence of treated gunshot wounds, assaults, sexual assaults, and possible self-harm. Legal, law-enforcement, judicial, and health-system data are collectively considered administrative sources. Yet when political will and/or capacity are weak, (nonadministrative) civil society actors may set up observatories to monitor incidences of violence, disappearances, and displacement. A unique and often underappreciated source of data is churches, which often maintain life registries for congregants, including birth, death, and other significant milestones.

On Risk of Violence and Early Warning

The international atrocity prevention community has laid the foundation for identifying the risks of many aspects of IBMV. The United Nations relies on the *Framework of Analysis for Atrocity Crimes*[23] to identify 14 risk factors and associated indicators of the risks of genocide, war crimes, and crimes against humanity.[24] While we cannot review all 14 factors here, specific factors linked to IBMV include "intergroup tensions," "intent to destroy…a protected group," "systematic attacks against a civilian population," and "plans or policies to attack any civilian population." This evidence may be quantitative in the case of event records or qualitative if accounts are collected. This is not easy; early warning and forecasting of political violence in a highly contested environment can be contentious. Following established protocols based on experience can be a start.

For example, violence along ethnic lines has accompanied past elections in Kenya, culminating in high levels of political violence during the 2007 elections. To prevent recurrence, early warning systems analyze historical conflict data, political tensions, social media, activities of gangs/other entities, and regional dynamics, much of which is qualitative. When indicators such as rising tensions or provocative rhetoric emerge, authorities, community leaders, the private sector, and civil society actors can intervene proactively. Regulations and voting rules have been adapted to reduce the incentives for violence, accompanying constitutional reforms and economic progress that reduced structural violence. As a result, though violence and "hooliganism" often accompany election cycles, the 2007 experience has not repeated.[25]

On Systemic and Structural Violence

It may be difficult to measure or collect evidence of systemic or structural violence, but it is not impossible. A negative peace is one in which systems perpetuate inequalities in protection or support, limiting access among some groups to rights and/or access to assistance, including health care. Where a group within a society (often defined by identity) suffers under systems perpetuated by the state or broader society, it is experiencing structural or systemic violence. In these cases, indicators on education and health outcomes may be more useful than measuring direct, acute violence.

One of the most extreme historical cases of structural violence is apartheid South Africa (see Chapter 15 by Friederike Bubenzer), in which state segregation led to a legacy of inequality in education, health care, and economic opportunities depending on one's identity. Much of the legacy of that inequality remains today, despite 30 years of multiparty democracy, illustrating the persistence of structural violence even in the presence of reform efforts.[26] Obviously in these situations, the system producing the structural violence may be untrustworthy to produce evidence of violence. This may be intentional or unintentional. In either case, the evidence base may need to be built by civil society or other actors with watchdog responsibilities.

Compelling evidence of systemic violence in this volume is presented in Chapter 8 by Ariana Markowitz]. In the case of Flint, Michigan, while technical, quantitative approaches to measuring water quality were used, the most compelling evidence was a qualitative assessment by the Michigan Civil Rights Commission following public hearings. The cases of Phoenix and New York in the same chapter warn of the dangers of setting targets that risk undermining the objective trying to be achieved, a tendency exacerbated by quantitative approaches. Building a case of structural violence often requires evidence that supersedes the state or system that is producing the violence. The absence of explicit violence or violent deaths may belie underlying systems of oppression.

Additional Challenges of Building the Evidence Base on Violence

The sections above demonstrate the challenges of measuring violence generally and the specific challenges that may be associated with measuring IBMV. In some instances, the count of violent deaths may be necessary to make the case of IBMV, and in others, such as oppression or structural violence, this data may be insufficient. At times, warning signs of impending IBMV may be difficult to identify. Furthermore, the official statistics may be untrustworthy, as they are created by the state or system that perpetuates the violence. This chapter concludes with two additional challenges—those of measuring the absence of violence and the political contestation of evidence through narratives.

Measuring Prevention and Peacebuilding

While violence itself is measurable, it can be difficult to measure the absence of violence and the resultant peace.[27] Additionally, in the presence of prevention and peacebuilding, the counterfactual may be unobservable. While headlines regularly report on violence, they rarely report on atrocities avoided. Attribution and causation may be difficult to assess in complex environments where randomized control trials and identifiable treatment effects are near impossible. These are more reasons why qualitative and quantitative evidence is jointly useful to triangulate peace and violence, outcomes, and impacts.

The resultant evidence base may need to be broad and drawn from a variety of sources to monitor performance. In Chapter 21, Flávia Carbonari notes the qualitative nature of programming associated with prevention and violence reduction, drawing on multilevel risk factors used for primary, secondary, and tertiary prevention in Pelotas, Brazil, which "designed a multisectoral violence prevention program comprising a series of evidence-based interventions." The evidence net may need to be cast wide.

Narratives and Evidence

In complex cases with active conflicts, evidence can be weaponized to serve a narrative by different actors (e.g., government officials, civil society groups, or international organizations). Evidence may be falsified or may be technically accurate but open to varying interpretations (or irrelevant). For example, labeling an act as terrorism in the Global Terrorism Database may undermine or discredit legitimate claims for self-determination. In these situations, competing narratives aim to shape public perception and influence international responses, often undermining peace.[28]

Media outlets play a pivotal role in the evidence ecosystem. An event reported inconsistently by various news sources muddies the waters. Quantitative databases that measure violence, such as the Armed Conflict Location and Event Database and the Uppsala Conflict Data Program, do so through monitoring media reporting, which impacts measurement. For instance, protests can be framed as legitimate expressions of discontent or as acts of rebellion and lawlessness, and coding rules will determine how these events appear as evidence.[29] Digital sources, such as social media and online reporting platforms, offer real-time data for monitoring violence and may be aggregated. Text and sentiment analysis techniques can help identify emerging trends, hate speech, and potential threats. This technology is double edged. Disinformation campaigns, cyberattacks, and other abuses of new technologies can be used by nefarious actors to accomplish IBMV by other means. Where media is censored or attacked, it can be a warning sign that IBMV is occurring.

Narratives are important because people are motivated by storytelling. A sense of agency is an important aspect of peacebuilding. Though evidence may not always be objective, one of its strengths may, indeed, be its subjectivity. For example, the Everyday Peace Indicators methodology helps communities identify what peace means and what metrics matter to them. In these cases, powerful stories are constructed by citizens themselves, which is often the source of systemic change.[30]

Conclusions

Evidence helps us to collectively understand the world and how it changes, and observable change is what we need to be able to demonstrate impact, change policies, and undertake reconciliation, among other social processes. As you read this volume, remember that evidence transcends formal data-collection processes.[31] Building evidence of IBMV involves constructing a comprehensive picture of violence. This triangulation of quant and qual, formal and informal, may be useful to find consensus in a charged political atmosphere. Keep in mind there is no numerical threshold for "mass." Authors were asked to present characteristics that make violence chronic, widespread, and systemic. As a result, it varies by context.

The evidence in the chapters that follow will include testimonials of violence, expert assessments and qualitative accounts, accounts of violent deaths, and incidents and perceptions of violence. Because IBMV is an emergent concept, there is no established right way to make this case. Further, because IBMV is a comprehensive concept that can include everything from hate crimes to police violence to structural violence to genocide, evidence will and should vary. And because IBMV may be a contested concept, the strongest cases will be made with evidence from a variety of actors, perspectives, and levels; in many cases, the actors producing evidence will have their own position on IBMV. This evidence will be used to document and remember IBMV, which is the initial step necessary for avoiding it in the future.

This is not an abstract, academic discussion; we see evidence of violence in day-to-day life. In many countries, headlines about crime report on homicides and other metrics collected by police. Headlines about war report casualties and fatalities, including deaths of civilians, numbers of refugees and displaced people, and destruction due to war. Violence measurement abounds. Understanding where this violence has an identity component and when it qualifies as mass violence is the present challenge.

Notes

1. The Rome Statute, adopted in 1998, was the International Criminal Court's founding treaty and describes this mandate. See International Criminal Court, "Rome Statute of the International Criminal Court," https://www.icc-cpi.int/sites/default/files/2024-05/Rome-Statute-eng.pdf.
2. There is no numerical cutoff for genocide; it is based on intent to destroy a group of any size. However, a group implies multiple, so certainly many groups qualify as "mass" whatever definition is used.

3. The targeted mass killings data set provides useful coding and definitional information for these categories. See Charles Butcher et al., "Introducing the Targeted Mass Killing Data Set for the Study and Forecasting of Mass Atrocities," *Journal of Conflict Resolution* 64, no. 7-8 (2020): 1524-1547.
4. See M. P. Broache and Agnes Yu, "The Politics of Descriptive Inference: Contested Concepts in Conflict Data," *International Politics* (2024): 1-23.
5. For a description and definition of armed conflict deaths, see Pettersson, Therese (2024) UCDP One-sided Violence Codebook v 24.1, https://ucdp.uu.se/downloads/.
6. Broache and Yu, "Politics of Descriptive Inference."
7. The presence of structural violence is often linked to the concept of negative peace advanced by Johan Galtung, "Violence, Peace, and Peace Research," *Journal of Peace Research* 6, no. 3 (1969): 167-191.
8. Broache and Yu, "Politics of Descriptive Inference."
9. Renee Lynch et al., "'The Tears Don't Give You Funding': Data Neocolonialism in Development in the Global South," *Third World Quarterly* 44, no. 5 (2023): 911-929.
10. Gulzhan Asylbek kyzy et al., *Gaps Report: Challenges of Counting All Violent Deaths Worldwide*, Global Registry of Violent Deaths, 2020.
11. See "Homicide Monitor," Igarapé Institute, homicide.igarape.org.br, for the most comprehensive global database on homicides by country (and excellent visualization tools). On global reporting and a complete review of methodologies and quality of data, see UN Office on Drugs and Crime (UNODC), *Global Study on Homicide*, 2019.
12. In addition to violent deaths, SDG 16.1 has two other official indicators: 16.1.3, "Proportion of population subjected to (a) physical violence, (b) psychological violence and (c) sexual violence in the previous 12 months," and 16.1.4, "Proportion of population that feel safe walking alone around the area they live after dark." These indicators are perceptions-based, requiring surveys or other experience-based data gathering to collect this

information. The first is decidedly about violence and the experience of it, whereas the second indicator lies farther along the spectrum on the experience of peace and security (discussed further below). That is to say that perceptions of "feeling safe" may not be directly related to the presence of violence, or the incidence of IBMV. Experiential surveys may be the only way to identify the prevalence of certain forms of violence, including gender-based violence. Using anonymization and aggregation, as well as statistical techniques, researchers can estimate the prevalence of violence in a population, uncover underlying risk factors, and assess the effectiveness of prevention programs. Despite the commitment to monitor these indicators through the SDG process, few countries are collecting and reporting on this data. However, they are effective methods for monitoring violence and have proven methodologies that can be replicated at any level. For example, indicator 16.1.4, "Proportion of population that feel safe walking alone…" is a standard question used in the Global Barometers Surveys, including multiyear panel studies collected through the Afro Barometer, Asia Barometer, and Arab Barometer, Eurasia Barometer, and Latinobarametro. This question could be easily incorporated into local/municipal surveys and focus group discussions to monitor local perceptions of security and safety. For a taxonomy and exhaustive list of indicators by type, source, use, etc., see UNDP, *Indicators We Want*, May 26, 2016, https://www.undp.org/publications/indicators-we-want.

13. On official international definitions of homicide, see UNODC, *Global Study on Homicide*, 2019.
14. The UN Office on Drugs and Crime (UNODC) is the UN agency tasked with collecting and monitoring homicides, through annual reporting by UN member states.
15. Ostensibly, the UN Office of the High Commissioner for Human Rights is the custodian UN agency for collecting data on conflict-related deaths; however, reporting varies by conflict because of the challenges of agreeing with member states on these statistics. See the office's *Technical Guidance Note* on measurement of SDG

16.1.2, https://www.ohchr.org/sites/default/files/Documents/Issues/HRIndicators/SDG_Indicator_16_1_2_Guidance_Note.pdf.
16. "The Bosnian Book of the Dead," Research and Documentation Center, http://www.mnemos.ba/en/home/Download.
17. On extra-judicial killings, see "Special Rapporteur on extrajudicial, summary or arbitrary executions," United Nations Human Rights Special Procedures, https://www.ohchr.org/en/special-procedures/sr-executions.
18. See the Ukraine live map adaptation for Syria at https://syria.liveuamap.com.
19. Emilee Green and Orleana Peneff, "An Overview of Police Use of Force Policies and Research," Illinois Criminal Justice Information Authority (August 15, 2022), https://icjia.illinois.gov/researchhub/articles/an-overview-of-police-use-of-force-policies-and-research.
20. See Jennifer Schweppe, "What Is a Hate Crime?," *Cogent Social Sciences* 7, no. 1 (2021): 1902643, for a full discussion of hate crimes across jurisdictions. Note that the author concludes, "It might be that a new umbrella term needs to be developed which wraps around hate incidents, hate speech, expression offences and hate crime, to cover the broad spectrum of these acts and their impacts, though I will leave it to someone else to coin this term." "Identity-based mass violence" may be a useful candidate for that umbrella term.
21. "Hate Crime Statistics," FBI, https://www.fbi.gov/how-we-can-help-you/more-fbi-services-and-information/ucr/hate-crime.
22. "Collecting data to address hate crime," OSCE Office for Democratic Institutions and Human Rights, https://hatecrime.osce.org/.
23. "Framework of Analysis for Atrocity Crimes," United Nations, 2014, https://www.un.org/en/genocideprevention/documents/about-us/Doc.3_Framework%20of%20Analysis%20for%20Atrocity%20Crimes_EN.pdf.
24. Although not legally defined under international law, ethnic cleansing is also commonly referred to as an atrocity crime and can include "murder, torture, arbitrary arrest and detention, extrajudicial executions, rape and sexual assaults, severe physical injury

to civilians, confinement of civilian population in ghetto areas, forcible removal, displacement and deportation of civilian population, deliberate military attacks or threats of attacks on civilians and civilian areas, use of civilians as human shields, destruction of property, robbery of personal property, attacks on hospitals, medical personnel, and locations with the Red Cross/Red Crescent emblem, among others." See UN Commission of Experts Interim Report S/25274, "Interim Report of the Commission of Experts Established Pursuant to Security Council Resolution 780 (1992)," United Nations Security Council, 10 February 1993, https://docs.un.org/en/S/25274.

25. Ken Opala, "Mafia-style crimes/Muted violence in Kenya's 2022 elections masked seething dissent," Enact Africa, April 24, 2023, https://enactafrica.org/enact-observer/muted-violence-in-kenyas-2022-elections-masked-seething-dissent.
26. Brian Levy et al., *South Africa: When Strong Institutions and Massive Inequalities Collide*, Carnegie Endowment for International Peace, March 18, 2021.
27. Emery Brusset et al., *Measuring Peace Impact: Challenges and Solutions*, Stockholm International Peace Research Institute, November 2022, https://www.sipri.org/sites/default/files/2022-11/measuring_peace_0.pdf.
28. Isak Svensson and Mimmi Söderbergh-Kovacs, "The Return of Victories?: The Growing Trend of Militancy in Ending Armed Conflicts," paper prepared for the seventh General Conference of the European Consortium for Political Research at Science Po Bordeaux, Domaine Universitaire, September 4–7, 2013.
29. Broache and Yu, "Politics of Descriptive Inference."
30. On the Everyday Peace Indicators see: https://www.everydaypeaceindicators.org/.
31. The United States Institute of Peace describes evidence as "both formal and informal assessments (including evaluative), analyses, and experiences." See, for example, Ruth Rhoads Allen et al., *What Constitutes Effective Use of Evidence to Inform Peacebuilding Project Design?*, US Institute of Peace, March 2023.

Gary Milante is the lead specialist on risk monitoring in the World Bank's Fragility, Conflict and Violence Group. Before that he founded N.Path and was Director of Studies for Peace and Development at the Stockholm International Peace Research Institute. He has a PhD in economics from the University of California at Irvine and has advised the Organization for Economic Cooperation and Development, the International Monetary Fund, UN agencies, and other organizations, as well as the governments of developing and developed countries.

Open Access This chapter is licensed under the terms of the Creative Commons Attribution-NonCommercial-NoDerivatives 4.0 International License (http://creativecommons.org/licenses/by-nc-nd/4.0/), which permits any noncommercial use, sharing, distribution and reproduction in any medium or format, as long as you give appropriate credit to the original author(s) and the source, provide a link to the Creative Commons license and indicate if you modified the licensed material. You do not have permission under this license to share adapted material derived from this chapter or parts of it.

The images or other third party material in this chapter are included in the chapter's Creative Commons license, unless indicated otherwise in a credit line to the material. If material is not included in the chapter's Creative Commons license and your intended use is not permitted by statutory regulation or exceeds the permitted use, you will need to obtain permission directly from the copyright holder.

What Dwells in Casa de Luz

Areli Palomo Contreras

The Other Dimension

There is a light in the gloom. It is a dim, diffuse light in a space where there is only mist. This place usually escapes the gaze of the human eye—but there are times when it comes into view. It is a different place than the one we live in every day. It is a parallel dimension that we are aware of, a part of our reality even though we usually cannot see it. What lives here and is constantly being transformed is the complex web of relationships that make up the social fabric. This dimension exists between us; it is here that the bonds we forge become tangible and visible, like vines that intertwine us in innumerable ways. It is here where our dynamics of violence, from the most trivial to the most terrible, emerge and extend their invisible tentacles into everyday life in our dimension.[1]

A. P. Contreras (✉)
Línea 84 Ethnographic Journalism and Community Action, Tijuana, Mexico
e-mail: 84linea@gmail.com

Casa de Luz in the Physical Dimension

Casa de Luz (House of Light) is a collective house in Mexico that takes in people living in situations of forced and undocumented migration. From all over the world and other parts of Mexico, these individuals are traveling through Mexico to reach the border with the United States. The house was born spontaneously out of the unprecedented mass movement of the migrant caravans in 2018 and 2019. At its core, it is a union between LGBTIQ + people and many others who forged bonds during their migration journeys.

The collective house has had three locations, all in the coastal border borough of Playas de Tijuana, at the edge of Tijuana proper in Baja California, Mexico. Casa de Luz is run by and for the LGBTIQ + community, and its doors will always be open to anyone who is enduring difficult circumstances during their migration.

Casa de Luz in the Social Dimension

In the invisible social dimension, in the space that sometimes appears in the mist, Casa de Luz is a web of relationships between people that have been gradually woven over time. In this hidden place, our relationships grow and intertwine like vines; we come together and we are transformed. The walls, the foundations, the rooms, the windows, and the doors of Casa de Luz are built from this fabric. The house inhabits this dimension of our shared humanity.

Position on Human Rights Defense

Casa de Luz was not created under the auspices of any religious institution or humanitarian organization. Although it has the legal standing of a nonprofit organization, its members do not consider themselves to be human rights defenders. They are just living expressions of what solidarity looks like. There are no saviors here, nor is anyone being saved. What is offered is the best possible support in times of migratory adversity.

The formation of the collective house as a space for refuge and protection meant embedding itself in the social spaces and the daily life of Tijuana. This included confronting the city's particular dynamics, already-existing social fabric, and narratives about "others": foreigners, migrants, and those with diverse gender identities.

Welcome to Tijuana

Playas de Tijuana, white sand beaches. Here the sea salt eats away at the monstrous metal fence that marks the border between Mexico and the United States. They call it the wall.

For a long time, this place has been rocked by waves of violence attributed to organized crime. Cartels control the flow of all kinds of illegal merchandise between the neighboring countries, as well as human trafficking and smuggling networks. They have infiltrated public security institutions throughout the border region, including Mexico's immigration enforcement agency, the National Institute of Migration (INM, per its Spanish abbreviation).

A source from Tijuana, we'll call her Marta, is dedicated to legal defense on several fronts. She tells me about Tijuana and Playas: "Two decades ago, foreign tourism—mainly Americans—was booming." Crossing to the United States was quick; there was an intense dynamic of trade, work, and recreational activities in the area. Everything changed following the attacks of September 11, 2001, and the arrival of Jorge Hank Rhon to the presidency of Tijuana in 2004. Rhon is the founder and head of the Caliente Group—one of the largest group of gambling and sports betting companies in Mexico—which has been linked to drug trafficking, money laundering, and other illicit activities. Violence exploded, and the border control as we now know it came to be.

> That was when a hanging or mutilated body, a head, dumped bodies, began to appear, and from that moment on, all of that became normal," says Marta. She adds that organized crime has always been present in

Playas de Tijuana: "There have always been safe houses in Playas, they come to dump bodies here because it's so remote.

In this context, some of those from the LGBTIQ + collective from the 2018 caravan arrived at a house that was rented by the California Roots Foundation (la fundación Raíces de California), located in a wealthy area of Playas. The members of the collective that arrived at the house at this point didn't encounter any resistance from the local community, although they recognized that there had previously been tensions with other collectives that had been present in that area. Part of the collective arrived in 2019 to the house at the far end of Playas; later, some of them would form Casa de Luz.

The Origins of Casa de Luz

The Mobile Collective Kitchen

The origin of Casa de Luz was in the caravans of 2018 and 2019, and the bonds of collaboration and camaraderie were created there. The 2019 caravan started in the center of Tecún-Uman, the most important town on the Guatemala side of the border with Mexico, which is divided by the Suchiate River. The caravan had come from Honduras and stopped there for about a week because Mexico would not let it enter the country.

A member of the caravan's kitchen staff and the LGBTIQ + community told me that the first time they served food in the early morning, they heard two men say, "You see that? It's the faggots who are cooking." Their comment was more out of amazement than contempt; giving food to everyone earned the LGBTIQ + community the recognition of the rest of the caravan. In contrast to what happened with the 2018 caravan, this time, until they arrived in Mexico City, no one openly mocked them.

The situation in Tecún-Uman was very difficult. Despite a large disturbance on the international bridge and lots of people being detained by the INM, the caravan advanced and the kitchen moved with it. Many people from a range of nationalities joined the caravan, as well as Mexicans displaced by the generalized violence in Mexico. The LGBTIQ +

community, women and families, and the pots and pans advanced, and some of them made it to Tijuana. But there was a concern: where would they rest once they got there? Following the traumatic experience of being stuck and detained at Guatemala's border with Mexico and the death of a beloved member of the collective, the LGBTIQ + group recognized the pressing need to find somewhere they could stay and not be discriminated against.

The death I'm referring to is that of Ximena. Her presence, along with the sense of closeness generated by the collective kitchen, began to form the fabric of Casa de Luz. This is her story.

Laura y Ximena

> We didn't want to migrate, we didn't want to leave. —Laura.

Ximena is a luminous root of Casa de Luz. Her everyday agony during the course of her forced displacement toward the United States and her death are a symbol of the crushing, commonplace, and violent social control imposed on undocumented migrants and aggravated by their expressions of diverse gender identities.

The paths of Ximena, from Honduras, and her friend Laura, from El Salvador, became intertwined in Tapachula, Mexico, where they met after joining the 2018 caravan. Laura is the one who opened up about the personal side of her and Ximena's journey together.

Laura escaped the violence in her country seven years ago. She arrived first in Guatemala, where the homophobia is just as severe as in El Salvador. Then she left for Mexico, but she did not find peace or protection there either.

> It's the same in Mexico—even though it's a country that takes in trans and LGBT people, it doesn't offer us the safety that we need. —Laura.

She was a sex worker on the streets of Tapachula and recounted that despite having a document that gave her permission to stay in the country, Mexican authorities did not respect her rights, much less her identity.

In 2018, the rumor began to circulate among Laura's sex worker colleagues that a large caravan was going to pass through the city. Trans and lesbian women, gay men, and other queer people started to walk together. Ximena was detached and did not socialize much with the others, "but she was very close to me," Laura tells me.

It was in Huixtla, still very close to Tapachula, that Ximena told Laura for the first time that she felt very ill and was starting to suffer from dizziness. The more they advanced, the worse she felt. Ximena was sweating profusely; she suffered from diarrhea, and her lungs were killing her. Years later, under the spell of the memory, Laura finds it hard to say that Ximena was HIV positive. As she told me, "I never, out of respect..." She never asked her about it.

They slept in parks and in shelters, walked, took the freight train and buses, and walked again. With the conditions of the caravan journey, the changes in temperature, and the lack of medication, Ximena's health deteriorated. Laura told her she had to get medical attention, but Ximena slumped into a deep fear. She was terrified of the idea that her caravan companions would find out that she was HIV positive, that they would make fun of her and leave her to die in a hospital in Mexico—a country just as violent as her own.

The angst over not getting to the United States, along with the humiliation and contempt caused by the disease—even nowadays—pushed Ximena to swallow her own existence in a terrifying silence.

It was Laura who always respected the silenced voice of her friend.

The caravan's LGBTIQ + collective that Ximena and Laura were traveling with reached Tijuana. They were constantly moving from one shelter to the next, trying to settle somewhere while they worked out how to cross into the United States. Nevertheless, except for the support they received from some nonprofit organizations, there was no refuge for their tired and overwhelmed bodies in the spaces that received them. When the LGBTIQ + collective reached the Caritas shelter in the El Soler district of Tijuana, they were received by people throwing stones at them. The mafia—Laura does not even know which one—had four unaccompanied minors who were part of the group in their sights and attempted to recruit them. Another one of the trans girls, Gema, found a piece of paper that said, "We don't want homos here, we don't want fags. We're going to burn all of you, we're going to kill you." They fled. Another shelter, El Jardín de las Mariposas, refused to take in the four minors, and the group split up. The community of El Soler ended up burning down the Caritas shelter, thinking the queer group was still inside. "A hate crime," says Laura.

Ximena and Laura stayed at El Jardín de las Mariposas along with some of the other women, but the mistreatment and abuse continued. There, Ximena's illness progressed unimpeded. In the rush to leave, they split into two groups and ended up camping in El Chaparral—on the border between Mexico and the United States—while they waited in line to turn themselves over to US authorities. Laura left with the first group; Ximena stayed behind. Her life was fading, but she managed to get to her feet and leave with the second contingent.

Laura crossed with her group into the United States, and they spent seven days in detention—the "icebox." They were then moved to Otay Detention Center in California, and it was there, seven days later, that Ximena's group arrived. She also spent seven days in the "icebox" and could not withstand the cold. Ximena demanded to be seen by a doctor but received no response. She paid dearly for the hope that her life would be respected in the United States.

Ximena was dying. By now she was unable to eat and growing thinner, with large bags under her eyes and her hair falling out in clumps, says Laura. They demanded a doctor and medication for the emergency situation, but they got nothing. The officers from Otay Detention Center put them on a plane to Cibola Correctional Center in New Mexico. Then they put them on a US Immigration and Customs Enforcement bus, where they also begged and pleaded for them to attend to Ximena, for them to call an ambulance because she could not stop vomiting. Ximena was dying, and the authorities treated her with contempt. When they arrived at Cibola, a doctor finally took her away.

It was too late.

What followed was silence. The terrifying quiet of a voice drowned in the seas of everyday violence of those whose lives are deemed worthless. Ximena died the next day.

Ximena's death helped Laura understand, for a few seconds, what exists in that place filled with fog. As the memory came back to her, her words were filled with a terrifying question: "Why? She was already in the United States, she had the right [to health care], but they didn't give her that right, they ignored that right, they trod on her right to the health care that she needed!" And every time Laura says "right," that word swells with suspicion. The lie shatters a little more, and she glimpses, from that other dimension, human dignity strangled and destroyed in the body of her friend.

The only thing the United States offered her was to die in the same way she had been treated her whole life—without dignity.

It was not just Ximena who died. With her died the fantasy of respect that many people expect to find there.

But in that dimension that Laura caught only a glimpse of, a light appeared in the vast gloom. It was Ximena's death seeking a place to rest; in that dimension, it sought a home.

Her death shook the lives of everyone who traveled with her and who, by her side, experienced the daily, constant, and oppressive violence entwined in her life. From one country to another, from one path to another, from one shelter to another, the need to have a place of refuge upon arrival at this border shone brightly.

The Spaces Inhabited by Casa de Luz

The Abandoned House

The idea of a home for Ximena and the other members of the 2019 caravan's kitchen collective was transformed into Casa de Luz when the LGBTIQ + group, together with mothers with children and unaccompanied minors, finally made it to Playas de Tijuana. They settled into an abandoned house and poured themselves into fixing it up. An individual from the LGBTIQ + community who traveled with both caravans tells me that thanks to several people, they obtained a six-month contract to "arrive at a space together, without being split up and with the idea of living as the family of caravan members that we were, mainly in support of the LGBTQ community." The Remain in Mexico program had already been implemented when the group arrived in Tijuana, and everyone wanted to request asylum in the United States.[2]

The space began to grow and take shape, becoming a home, until it became Casa de Luz—Collective House. And here at the end of Playas de Tijuana is where Alicia arrived and her life became intertwined with this space. The same space where Marta spoke of dumped bodies was where the caravan collective found a place to put down roots.

Alicia

Alicia is originally from Guatemala, but a family from Veracruz adopted her when she was seven months old. She had lived in fear of being herself since she was a child. She remembered that her adoptive father despised her and would say to her that he wanted her to act like "a little man." Her mother, the only person who accepted her gender identity and cared about her well-being, died when Alicia was still very young. All manner of things happened to Alicia, but what sticks the most in her mind is the systematic abuse by the police everywhere she lived in Mexico. She left Veracruz when she was still a teenager after her parents died. She never stayed in one place for long—she was always moving; something was always happening because of her trans identity. She arrived in Tijuana around 2017 and worked in a hotel as a receptionist. The owner's son mistreated her, insulted her, told her he did not want people like her there, but still she held out there for three years. In this city, she got into an abusive relationship with a man who almost killed her.

In 2019, she met an American volunteer who was in Tijuana supporting people arriving in the caravan, and she took her to Casa de Luz.

Alicia would disappear for days. They knew that the Tijuana police would often arrest her just for walking the streets and she would end up in La Veinte, the local precinct's detention center, where she had no choice but to stay locked up. She always said the police told her trans women could not walk along the pedestrian bridge that connects the city of Tijuana with the El Chaparral border post because it "looked bad." On innumerable occasions, the municipal police stopped her and stripped her of her possessions and money, but that was not enough for them. They always made sure to tell her she was a freak, "a jackal disguised as a princess," says Alicia.

She reappeared on May 10, 2019. This would turn out to be the true breaking point in her life. At 7:30 in the morning, Alicia was sitting on the steps in front of the city's general hospital in the Zona Río. She was waiting for visiting hours to start to see a friend who was seriously ill after having liposculpture done by a surgeon rumored to have a history of scamming patients.

Alicia says all she saw were stars, then everything went black. Someone had hit her so hard that it took her a moment to realize they were dragging her by her hair. They hauled her up some stairs to the corner of a room she didn't recognize. There were people around and she was screaming, but no one did anything.

They raped her, hit her in the face with bricks, tortured her by stabbing her with a pen while shouting at her, "If you feel like a woman, we're going to make sure you die like one!" She managed to make it to the waiting room of the hospital where her friend was and begged for help, but they turned her away. Bleeding, her face destroyed, they refused to see her because her condition "gave a bad impression." There was a police car outside. She approached it and told the officer what had happened to her, and the officer, without an ounce of pity, told her, "You'd better leave." She left and walked along the riverbank, raped, tortured, and alone. She managed to reach Enclave Caracol, where they helped her.[3] Alicia contracted HIV after that rape.

It was very difficult for her to get medical care. In the same general hospital, the doctors did not want to go near her, not even to take her blood pressure. "It was like they were disgusted by me, like I was going to give them something," she said. Some trans girls who were also at Casa de Luz insulted her and treated her as an "AIDS girl." It was the same treatment Ximena had feared so much, that she ran from.

Alicia had constant nightmares and would cry out in the night; the memories of that day in May continued to haunt her. With great effort and thanks to the connections that Casa de Luz started to build with other organizations, Alicia was able to obtain medicine to improve her health. She spent approximately two and a half years at the house until she managed to cross to the United States, where she finally obtained refugee status.

La Gruta

Eventually members of the collective house got into a big dispute with the owner of the abandoned house and had to leave. One of the people from the LGBTIQ + community found a former gym for rent, called *la Gruta* (The Cave) and they moved in there.

Amid tents for rooms, children's toys, books, pots, ladles, gas tanks, and improvised partitions to divide the large space inside La Gruta, the collective fabric of Casa de Luz was now settled into its new home for 2020. The group of people and their relations were gradually becoming more deeply connected to the social fabric of the city and of Playas de Tijuana. They were putting down roots.

The pandemic struck them at La Gruta. The administration of US President Donald Trump used the pretext of preventing the spread of COVID-19 to deport asylum seekers under public health order Title 42, leading to a large number of people becoming stranded at this and other Mexican border crossings.[4] Meanwhile, the still-in-effect Remain in Mexico program exacerbated the situation, keeping asylum seekers trapped in dangerous zones dominated by organized crime. These measures, and others not mentioned in this work, ended up violating the international protection system established by the Geneva Conventions and their Protocols.

Sonia

In 2021, when the pandemic ended and Joe Biden's term as US president began, a memo from the Department of Homeland Security began to circulate announcing that the United States would again allow asylum seekers to enter its territory.

On the Mexican side of the border is the Chaparral crossing; the US side is San Ysidro. There, migrants from Central America, Haitians, and a large contingent of Mexicans forcibly displaced by organized crime from Michoacan and elsewhere, as well as other groups, have coalesced, all seeking asylum in the United States. They formed the El Chaparral Camp near the international pedestrian bridge that links the center of Tijuana with the border crossing.

The surroundings of El Chaparral are desolate. Beyond the pedestrian bridge there is a shopping mall with the majority of its units closed. Walking by there gives you the chills. Surely at some point it was booming, as Marta said.

Despite its appearance of being abandoned, the shopping mall is controlled by the local mafia, and any activity there happens under its control. When the camp was formed, Casa de Luz was one of the organizations that was there providing help. The staff cooperated with members of the camp and set up a collective kitchen to prepare food. However, there were several attacks on the kitchen collaborators, it is unknown by whom, and the members of Casa de Luz were forced to leave. That was when chaos broke loose and the local criminal group moved in to take full control of the camp. It charged monthly rent for staying in a tent, and forced people to pay for their two daily meals. It was not possible to go out at night without permission, and the punishment for ignoring the new rules was a beating. The police refused to get involved. The members of Casa de Luz managed to transfer several people and families from the camp to the collective house.

This is when Sonia appeared—a trans girl who left the camp with her partner when the Casa de Luz collective offered her a place in the house. The local mafia wanted to force Sonia to sell drugs because "the police don't search trans girls," she said. Sonia refused, but knew it was only a matter of time before she'd have to give in. What the boss of that place said came back to haunt her: "Here, it doesn't matter what you want. If you don't want to today, you will tomorrow. Wait until the hunger burns and you'll see how you come looking for me!".

Fortunately, Sonia and her partner found protection at Casa de Luz. That supportive fabric was strong enough to hold her so that hunger would not crush her into submission. She did not have to give in to the violence greasing the power represented by the petty local mafia that dominates the destroyed marketplaces of a tongue-tied society.

Casa de Luz—Collective House

Over the years, relationships within the collective house grew stronger. Its roots extended and managed to reach people from other countries, which is how Jack Noreen got involved. An American from the LGBTIQ + community, Jack, decided to be part of the collective efforts to find a permanent home for the existing web of solidarity at Casa de Luz. The collective uprooted itself from La Gruta and left for its new home.
And that is where Sara arrived.

Sara

Sara was a Honduran trans woman with Garifuna ancestry, a Caribbean ethnic group descended from enslaved Africans and Indigenous people who rebelled and continue to resist oppression. She speaks loudly and clearly about the extreme abuses she has faced in her life, precisely because of her identity, and the reasons she arrived at this border seeking protection and respect in the United States. But she did not make it. She never got there. She disappeared in silence. And her voice, like the death of Ximena, reverberated out there in the distance, in the haze.

Today she speaks with condemnation in her reproach of social indifference and the powers that injured her. Her voice joins the death of Ximena, strengthening the fabric of this collective house, a place of refuge for people seeking dignity.

Sara speaks and her words are not simply a discourse demanding respect for her rights. Through her injured body, Sara speaks of the ruthlessness with which people's dignity is shattered.

She crossed from Honduras through the jungle to Guatemala at just 14. She witnessed the murder of Guatemalan trans companions, then migrated to Mexico. After crossing at Ciudad Hidalgo, Chiapas, she stayed for a while. But the authorities harassed her, and she decided to head north. She was brutally gang-raped in Huixtla while avoiding immigration checkpoints. They took everything, but somehow she made her way by freight train to Mexico City. There the only person who would give her a "job" was a pimp. Then one day he told her she had to pay him 5,000 pesos (about $250) a night and the goal was to attend to 50 customers. Sara migrated to Guadalajara, worked as a prostitute, and in a bordello, a hovel, they sold her. Then they drugged her and 17 men raped her. They tore up her papers, including her Mexican naturalization certificate and her Honduran documents. She approached the authorities in Guadalajara and was simply told that if she filed a report, whoever attacked her would kill her as soon as she left there. She traveled to Mexico City and tried to file a report; those authorities also turned their backs on her. Nobody helped her. Seventeen months after the gang rape in Guadalajara, Sara was still bleeding and needed surgery. The Tijuana LGBTIQ + community center referred her to Casa de Luz, that is how she arrived there.

On March 31, 2023, Casa de Luz took part in a vigil organized in El Chaparral in memory of the fire at the Ciudad Juarez Detention Center, which coincided with the International Transgender Day of Visibility.[5] That evening, Sara told her story. These were her last words: "I know I'm going to die one day. I want to get to the United States. I know I'm going to die one day, but I don't want to die on a sidewalk, and I don't want to die at the hands of someone else."

A week after speaking out publicly at that terrible border, Sara "went downtown," and, a member of the Casa de Luz team told me, "I never saw her again." A missing person's report was filed. The Casa de Luz team searched the city. She has not returned, and nobody has heard from her.

Sara and Ximena are the windows of Casa de Luz, but you have to look hard to see them. They only appear on the days when the mist comes in from the sea and travels in between the buildings, houses, and streets of Playas de Tijuana. In those moments, if we look carefully, we can peek into that dimension where there are no borders. There we will see not just the webs that unite us but also the violent relationships that crush us every day.

The End

From here, from this border, from this shore, when the fog rolls in, you get the sensation that the other dimension is there, where the entire social realm takes shape and can be seen and felt. But then the fog disappears, and all that is left is the impression of having sensed those vines—the origins of the brutality of everyday life.

There, at times, in the morning fog on the beaches of Tijuana, it seems possible to glimpse the rootlike things that become part of our bodies and of the great social structure that shapes the behavior, thoughts, and emotions of our everyday lives.

The mist clears, and all that is left is the wall.

Notes

1. The concept of the Other Dimension and its tentacles extending to everyday life is inspired by the work of Veena Das in *Life and Words: Violence and the Descent into the Ordinary* (Oakland: University of California Press, 2007), 7.
2. Remain in Mexico was a program through which the United States forced asylum seekers to remain in Mexico during the processing of their asylum applications in the United States. ACNUR México. "¿Qué Es MPP? - ACNUR México," July 3, 2020. https://help.unhcr.org/mexico/2020/07/03/que-es-mpp.
3. Enclave Caracol is a community space in downtown Tijuana. Workshops and community and cultural events are often held at this center. Enclavecaracol. "Enclave Caracol." Enclave Caracol, September 13, 2017. https://enclavecaracol.wordpress.com.
4. Carnegie Corporation of New York, "What Does the End of Title 42 Mean for U.S. Migration Policy? | Immigration | Carnegie Corporation of New York," Carnegie Corporation of New York, n.d., https://www.carnegie.org/our-work/article/what-does-end-title-42-mean-us-migration-policy.
5. On March 27, 2023, 40 migrants held at a detention center run by INM burned to death. El País, El País, and El País, "Una

Investigación Revela Nuevas Irregularidades Sobre La Cárcel Del INM En La Que Murieron 40 Migrantes En Ciudad Juárez," *El País México*, March 19, 2024, https://elpais.com/mexico/2024-03-19/una-investigacion-revela-nuevas-irregularidades-sobre-la-carcel-del-inm-en-la-que-murieron-40-migrantes-en-ciudad-juarez.html.

Areli Palomo Contreras is an award-winning ethnographic journalist who has produced investigative chronicles focusing on violence associated with Central American migration. Her work has appeared in Somos el Medio, Contra Corriente, Avispa,and other outlets across Latin America.

Open Access This chapter is licensed under the terms of the Creative Commons Attribution-NonCommercial-NoDerivatives 4.0 International License (http://creativecommons.org/licenses/by-nc-nd/4.0/), which permits any noncommercial use, sharing, distribution and reproduction in any medium or format, as long as you give appropriate credit to the original author(s) and the source, provide a link to the Creative Commons license and indicate if you modified the licensed material. You do not have permission under this license to share adapted material derived from this chapter or parts of it.

The images or other third party material in this chapter are included in the chapter's Creative Commons license, unless indicated otherwise in a credit line to the material. If material is not included in the chapter's Creative Commons license and your intended use is not permitted by statutory regulation or exceeds the permitted use, you will need to obtain permission directly from the copyright holder.

Understanding Structural, Acute, and Identity-Based Mass Violence in Cities as Process

Kate Ferguson and Andy Fearn

We wrote in 2014, when we founded Protection Approaches, that "[i]dentity-based mass violence is not a phenomenon particular to certain countries, regions or groups. Rather, it is something that we can all relate to as we have all seen prejudice in our own cities, towns and streets."[1] Protection Approaches was created as the first NGO to explicitly confront the distinct challenge of identity-based violence. Our view was then, and remains, that by first acknowledging the "pathology" of identity-based violence and then by better understanding its roots, trajectory, and implementation, we can help to transform how a spectrum of intersectional harm is prevented.[2] This understanding can transform contributions to prevention and protection, not only by community and charitable organizations but by structures, local governments, and states. Ultimately, our theory of change is to "stop responding to the

K. Ferguson (✉)
Protection Approaches, London, UK
e-mail: kate.ferguson@protectionapproaches.org

A. Fearn
Protection Approaches, London, UK

gravest crimes as individual catastrophes and begin a joined-up, collective movement that stands against identity-based violence wherever it occurs."[3]

In this chapter, we set out our understanding of identity-based mass violence as a concept and as a real-world challenge. We take the opportunity here to view identity-based mass violence and its prevention through the lens of the city. Drawing on our perspective as practitioners based in a Western capital, we set out the challenge that cities and city-based prevention actors face many propellants of identity-based mass violence. In the United Kingdom and around the world, these factors are moving in the wrong direction; without rapid and significant change of course, we face an era of increased violence across many fronts. However, we conclude that while "violence concentrates in urban centers,"[4] it may in fact often be easier from a structural and policy perspective to prevent this type of violence on the city level than elsewhere. We offer this suggestion as a constructive challenge to our colleagues and to ourselves at a time when global violence prevention feels beleaguered and broken but also existentially important.

In this chapter, we draw first on our practice, rather than the academic, spanning the experience of working in and alongside hundreds of local, grassroots organizations toward community-led change, as well as to support structural change from neighborhood, city, national, and international governance systems, from frontline services to grand strategy in domestic and international policy. In doing so, we will do disservice to our academic colleagues and the multidisciplinary literature base of the fields from which we inevitably consciously and unconsciously learn. In a different way, we will also fall short of properly attributing what we have learned from our community partners, whose expertise and knowledge drive so much of what Protection Approaches does but can be less easily referenced in the format of a footnote. What we set out below is a reflection of the last 10 years we have spent working together building an organization focused on the prevention of identity-based violence. Thus, none of what we have written would be possible or valid without the extraordinary efforts, generosity, and expertise of those we have met along the way. All errors are, of course, our own.

We have always believed that no community, society, or country is ever immune to identity-based violence[5]; rather, constant and consistent effort is required from local grassroots to political leaderships to defend and advance the fundamental rights and freedoms of all. In times of political, economic, or social crisis, societies become more vulnerable. Our experience is rooted in the United Kingdom, during a period of considerable national flux, marked economic decline, erosion of trust in domestic political institutions, and isolationism on the world stage.[6] When a sense of national anxiety becomes widespread, minority and marginalized groups often pay the greatest price; the United Kingdom and its capital are no different to anywhere else.[7] Protection Approaches is a nongovernmental organization based in London, and its work has inevitably been shaped by the dynamics of our large, complex capital—and by its relationship to the rest of the country. It is in London where British domestic and international policy meet and at times clash most explicitly, whether in the profits of identity-based mass violence being used by states such as the United Arab Emirates and by corrupt individuals to buy up the city's residential and cultural properties[8] or in the debates of, or protests toward, our parliament.

Over the past 10 years, we have sought out lessons of what works in peacebuilding and violence prevention around the world, developed alongside local organizations—very often but not only in London—to support, develop, and collect evidence for community-led solutions. At the same time, we have reached up to the national and local government levels to encourage structural and system change across UK domestic and international policy, and engaged internationally and in multilateral forums to learn from global best practice and advance normative understanding of the phenomenon of identity-based violence. Protection Approaches is founded on the principle that everyone shares a collective responsibility to protect people from identity-based violence. This commitment must be upheld within our own countries and through our global actions, ensuring that we support the protection of people from identity-based violence everywhere.[9] This chapter speaks primarily to the British experience of identity-based violence domestically and in the world and brings a focus to the lessons we have learned in and from London, but it situates our observations within a global context.

Our Understanding of Identity-Based Violence

The concept of identity-based violence is not a new one, nor was it when we founded Protection Approaches, but over the past decade we and our colleagues have worked to transform how we understand the phenomenon so we can help transform how we respond to and prevent it. Our definition of identity-based violence is "any act of violence—whether physical or structural—that is motivated by the perpetrator's conceptualization of their victim's identity, for example their race, gender, sexuality, religion or political affiliation."[10] Our definition is intentionally open and inclusive, in both capturing all its manifestations and ensuring no victim group is excluded. Thus, our approach to identity-based violence encapsulates structural violence, hate-based incidents and hate crime, violent extremism, and terrorism—which by its very nature is intrinsically rooted in a logic of collective punishment—and identity-based mass atrocities such as genocide, ethnic cleansing, and some crimes against humanity and war crimes. Without drawing any kind of equivalence of experience, identity-based violence is something we have nearly all experienced and also have likely perpetrated and/or contributed to. Likewise, all states—and again, without drawing equivalence—are both protector and perpetrator. From this position, all of us, individuals and states, can do better.

Our definition is an adaptation of Frank Chalk and Kurt Jonassohn's definition of genocide, which similarly considers the act from the perspective of the perpetrator.[11] This is important because in the moment of discrimination or attack, the challenge is never how the victims hold their own unique complex (and often movable) identity/ies but how the perpetrating individual, group, or structure acts on its interpretation of an identity marker that it has ascribed to its victim(s). This starting point, of conceptualizing the phenomenon of identity-based violence from the view of perpetrators, is integral to our understanding of how we can, collectively, better confront and prevent it.[12] This does nothing to discount the knowledge and expertise of those who experience identity-based violence; but, being aware of our own identities, the starting point for us both was of wanting to target the behavior of perpetrators and perpetrating structures rather than replicating or displacing community-led transformation efforts. While the victims of identity-based violence and the ways such violence manifest often look different, we address the common pathology—recognizing, understanding, and confronting its shared causes and effects.

Identity-based hate and violence can, when left unchecked, metastasize. When structural and physical—or acute—discriminatory violence persists, the risks it becomes extreme, widespread, or systematic increase. Depending on the context and enabling conditions, this might variously breech legal thresholds of terrorism, crimes against humanity, genocide, or, in situations of armed conflict, war crimes. Understanding identity-based violence in these terms brings in ethical and treaty obligations traditionally considered to be unrelated to the challenges of identity-based violence in cities, from the 1948 UN Convention on the Prevention and Punishment of the Crime of Genocide to the 2005 normative principle endorsed by every member state of a collective responsibility to protect populations from mass atrocity crimes.[13]

No matter where it takes place and no matter whom it targets, every act of identity-based violence is a manifestation of the deadly idea that some lives are more valuable than others. For that reason, we acknowledge that a spectrum of harms—including hate crime, violent extremism, and most mass atrocities—should be seen as a shared global crisis: the targeting of individuals or groups solely because of who they are, what they believe, or who they love.

Recognizing this spectrum of violence as representative of the same phenomenon or pathology, rather than as disparate challenges, should encourage greater focus on the shared root causes and drivers of identity-based violence while also opening far more cross learning, coordinated working, and strategic efforts to confront hate crime, violent extremism, and identity-based mass violence. Moreover, recognizing the pathology of violence as one that afflicts practically every society, state—indeed city—should help to break down the entrenched, colonial conceptual binary that identity-based mass violence occurs in some parts of the world but not others.

The Threat of Identity-Based Mass Violence

Identity-based mass violence is rising inside and outside of conflict, and not only in states with lower levels of development or stability. The driving forces behind this violence—"inequality, social fracture, democratic backsliding, resource scarcity, arms proliferation, climate change, and the internationalisation of malign networks—are all moving in the wrong direction."[14] As Kate Ferguson and Fred Carver wrote in 2021, "as COVID-19's societal, economic and political consequences deepen, climate change-induced events become more common and severe, and political dynamics become more polarised and exclusionary, widespread and systematic identity-based violence, including mass atrocities, will become increasingly frequent as we approach the mid-twenty-first century." Unless prevention thinking and prevention-first policy become central to contemporary local, national, and multilateral politics—not only in the United Kingdom but worldwide—the next political era will be characterized by escalating identity-based violence and mass atrocity. Therefore, "getting better at preventing mass violence is no longer simply a moral duty for responsible states but also an issue of strategic self-interest—albeit, rarely recognized as a core one."[15]

At the same time, in the United Kingdom at least, public expectations of how such responsibilities should be upheld continue to increase as travel, trade, and technology shrink moral and political geographies—and increase international and internationalist identities among younger people.[16] The complexities of threats that states, and indeed cities, now face are rightly driving interest in more integrated approaches to policy, recognizing the opportunities to be gained by joining up policy thinking across domestic and outward-facing government departments and embracing theories of change that "reach in" to the local as well as reaching outward through global diplomacy. States recognize that they have to do more, and have less to do it with, and so they must recalibrate their entire national approach if they are to have impact. Here, however, is an opportunity for city-level governance and devolved understanding of violence prevention. Meeting this rising threat requires a reorientation of society and policy around the idea of human rights (and safety) not only as a good unto itself but as a fundamental approach to ensuring that the unconscionable never occurs. As Zeid Ra'ad Al Hussein, former UN high commissioner for human rights, has said, "wars do not start because people are poor; neither do they start because people are illiterate. They start because of structural discrimination— a deliberate attempt to marginalise people. [...] Indeed, most of the conflicts today have their antecedents in human rights deficits."[17] We would argue that the same can be said for all manner of complex crises that cripple states, communities, and cities—from the chronic, such as gang violence and domestic violence, to the (apparently) singular, such as the Grenfell Tower fire or the 7/7 terrorist attack.[18]

We argue that those charged with upholding or contributing to local, national, or international responsibilities must accept two points: (1) widespread systematic violence against identity groups is a common occurrence in the modern world, not a rarity, and (2) the harmful impact of such violence is never limited to its immediate victims but instead erodes the rights and safety of all. Therefore, a rights-based approach is also a rational one; diagnosing and treating the root cause is not only more effective, but it is also cheaper. This will become increasingly apparent in a world where democracies are facing growing fiscal challenges in the face of aging populations and spiralling state costs, and as the impacts of new technologies, climate change, and globalization are sped up. Integrating the means of informing decision-making from the perspective of preventing identity-based violence and its antecedents is therefore necessary.

The responsibility to help protect people from identity-based violence is a collective one that stretches from the local to the national to the global. Translating this responsibility into the daily decisions of individuals, systems, and states, and measuring the success of these efforts, is integral to securing change outside of the grassroots. It is therefore important to first identify and then confront the drivers of identity-based violence. We can understand many of the risk factors as being both the cause of and effect of marginalization, by which we mean when an individual or group is excluded from full participation in a community. Marginalization of a group or individual increases the likelihood that individuals in that group not only become victims of identity-based harms but also perpetrators of them. Therefore, key to preventing acute, structural, and identity-based mass violence is preventing or dismantling the structural marginalization that creates the enabling conditions in which such violence is more likely.

Fundamental to our understanding of identity-based violence is that there are common factors and circumstances that make it more likely and contribute to its intensification. Likewise, there are common "actors" that contribute to enabling identity-based violence: the systems, institutions, and platforms whose behaviors, relationships, and transactions contribute deliberately or incidentally to driving vulnerability or violence. Likewise, an improved understanding of who is doing what to commit, incite, or otherwise enable identity-based violence is key to prevention. On the whole, these factors and actors are the same around the world, whether in a city, a town, or a village.

How these common risk factors and enabling actors come together, how the identity-based violence manifests, and who is made vulnerable and in what ways are, however, always distinct to the context. Therefore, while generalities of understanding and lessons can—and we argue should more frequently—be drawn to deepen our understanding of identity-based violence as a global preventable phenomenon, solutions will always need to be led by the particular circumstances and needs of the state, society, locality, and community in question.

Identity-Based Mass Violence and the City

What does it mean to understand identity-based mass violence and the city? The level of lethal violence in cities is greater than in nonurban areas.[19] Cities hold the highest concentration of people and so are places where different communities with perceptions of competing interests are more likely to come into more regular contact—and conflict—than areas that are less densely populated. Cities are places where enclaves of identity groups are more likely to be found and thus potentially provide easy targets for perpetrators.[20]

Inequalities are often more visible in urban environments, seen in the proximity between those who "have" and those who "have not" but also in the daily structural processes of the city, from gentrification to policing. While its population represents less than a tenth of the country, London brings in a quarter of the United Kingdom's gross domestic product.[21] However, wealth disparity in London is far greater than in the rest of England. According to the Trust for London, "In 2021/22 those in the 90th net income percentile in London took home 10 times more than those in the 10th net income percentile (a 90:10 net income ratio of 10.5). In the rest of England, the 90:10 net income ratio is 5.2."[22] Twenty-nine percent of Londoners live in poverty, and this number rises to 39 percent for nonwhite households and 33 percent for families that include someone with a disability. Certainly, cities are fertile breeding grounds for many of the risk factors of identity-based violence that we measure.

Cities bring a scale of violence. London, as a huge capital city, sees levels of varied violence that a smaller town or rural area in England would not, but that is not to say violence, including structural and acute identity-based violence, is not a deep-seated challenge in our more suburban and rural areas. Nor are the fundamental roots of the challenge different. Britain's characteristics of class, capitalism, etc, are structural and cultural realities that inform identity-based violence, and this plays out differently in rural or urban locations across the UK.

Around the world, structural and physically violent discrimination, hate crime, violent extremism, gang violence, crimes against humanity, and genocide occur across urban and rural lines; it is how that violence is perpetrated and felt that varies. Cities do experience identity-based violence differently. They are more frequently targets of terrorism and violent extremism, they are more likely to see political violence and clashes between the state and protest, and the methods of metropolitan policing and surveillance differ from more rural areas. When identity-based mass violence spikes elsewhere in the world, its ripples are often felt in global cities such as London. When Hamas launched violent incursions into Israeli settlements on October 7, 2023, deliberately targeting civilians, the Israeli government responded with a massive attack on Gaza (both, let us note, in themselves campaigns of identity-based mass violence that likely constitute crimes against humanity[23]). The mayor of London, Sadiq Khan, swiftly tweeted, "Tragically, we know that violence in the Middle East can lead to a rise in hate crime in London. I'm in touch with senior officers at the Met[ropolitan police] & communities across our city. Let me be clear—hate crime in London will not be tolerated."[24] Khan also surged emergency funds to community-building programs, particularly those supporting the capital's Jewish and Muslim communities.

Structural identity-based violence is more likely to become acute in a manner that is systematic and/or widespread in cities because of the nature of city infrastructure and the concentration of people. Strategies of identity-based mass violence that seek to destroy, remove, or displace communities can sometimes be more effectively carried out in rural areas (such as deliberate campaigns carried out in Bosnia, Sudan, and Myanmar) because cities are able to resist or are able to bring the attention of the world's spotlight and so help mitigate assault. In other situations, such as Gaza, Aleppo, Dresden, or Hiroshima, it has been the city's geography and concentration that has enabled perpetration of identity-based violence on massive scale. In contexts of identity-based mass atrocity violence—where crimes against humanity and genocide are committed against groups of people—strategic implementation of the objective to destroy or remove communities is often starkly different across cities and rural areas, even if the dreadful objective remains the same.

In Bosnia, for example, the capital of Sarajevo became a focus of armed conflict that served to distract the international community from the systematic ethnic cleansing of Bosnian Muslims from towns and rural areas. Sarajevo was besieged, subjected to relentless shelling and the deliberate targeting of civilians—in this case targeted in collective punishment for the inhabitants being seen to stand with the Muslim majority government and army but also targeted because of their Sarajevan identity, which was considered representative of a cosmopolitan Bosnia and former Yugoslavia and so the seat of political resistance to the genocidal partition of the country. In the rural areas, without the physical and political infrastructure of either resistance or protection— nor being able to draw the spotlight of the world's attention—people were separated, persecuted, displaced, and/or killed because of their Muslim identity in a manner that left whole towns, villages, and hamlets "cleansed" of that population.

The symbol of the city is a powerful one, especially of a capital city. Thus, it is not uncommon for cities to be deliberately and particularly targeted in campaigns of identity-based mass violence for total destruction, for example, Aleppo, Gaza, Grozny, Palmyra, or as collective punishment in armed conflict such as Dresden, Hiroshima, and Nagasaki. The symbolism of the city also brings a different kind of media spotlight. Coverage of assaults on Sarajevo, Kiev, Khartoum, when contrasted with coverage of more systematic or widespread identity-based displacement and eradication in the Bosnian, Ukrainian, and Sudanese rural regions, says something about how prevention and protection are conceived by, or projected to, the global public.

Our mission as an organization is to better understand identity-based violence and so help transform our collective efforts to prevent it. So, then, is this chapter seeking to assess the dynamics of identity-based mass violence within and of cities, not to establish any hierarchy of experience across an urban and rural divide but rather to explore whether assessing the city context holds new or untapped understanding that can transform our efforts to prevent and protect.

It is from this perspective that we see not only the logic of looking at identity-based mass violence and cities but the opportunities for prevention that doing so could create. We argue that cities in fact are the low-hanging fruit for prevention. While the very fundamentals of cities increase many of the risks of identity-based mass violence, so too do those fundamentals give us much of what we need to prevent that violence.

Preventing Acute and Structural Violence in Cities

The fields of atrocity prevention and hate crime prevention, which our work bridges, have in common the objectives of first identifying propellants of acute violence and then developing or supporting programming and sometimes policy to confront or reverse those trends. The UN's framework of analysis for the prevention of mass atrocity crimes says, "Atrocity crimes take place on a large scale, and are not spontaneous or isolated events; they are processes, with histories, precursors and triggering factors which, combined, enable their commission. [...] With the help of the Framework, we can better sound the alarm, promote action, improve monitoring or early warning by different actors, and help Member States to identify gaps in their atrocity prevention capacities and strategies."[25]

At Protection Approaches we use a list of risk factors drawn from the work of many others to understand any society's resilience to divisive and hate-based behaviors.[26] It is not an exhaustive list.

Society-Wide Conditions

- Local or national-level political, economic, public health, climate, resource, or other crisis.
- Intergroup tensions or patterns of discrimination against identity groups.
- Widespread, often competing, perception(s) of grievance, threat, or inequality.
- Sense of group, community, or national insecurity.
- Normalization of hate speech, dehumanizing language, and incitement to violence against identity groups.
- Legislative curtailment of the rights and freedoms of identity groups.
- Revival of historic grievance, myths of collective victimhood, politicization of national memory.
- Widespread disinformation, propaganda, and fake news.
- Widespread delegitimization of expertise and intellectualism.
- Widespread lack of trust in the media.
- Increased belief in or widespread normalization of conspiracy theories and/or grievance-based explanations of complex challenges.
- Widespread lack of trust in the government.
- Widespread belief that the democratic process cannot lead to positive change.

- Hardening of heteronormative and patriarchal societal and political norms, including but not limited to curtailments related to reproductive and abortion rights, sexual orientation, gender identity, and gender-based protection.
- Increases in domestic and/or gender-based violence.
- Increased hostility to "foreigners," "newcomers," "refugees," and "migrants."
- Disregard for or violations of international obligations and/or international law, disengagement from the international system.
- Removal of or failure to uphold human rights protections.
- Growth in number and legitimacy of groups who use violence or the threat of violence.
- Widespread access to weapons of violence.
- Impunity for those who commit, incite, or threaten violence.

Personal Conditions

- Not feeling valued by those around you.
- Not feeling represented by those who make decisions affecting your life.
- Not feeling in control of your life or its direction.
- Believing that certain groups are responsible for your problems or pose a threat to your security or prosperity and other grievance-based beliefs.
- Believing that certain groups are "less legitimate," "less human," or deserving of punishment, including violence.
- Personal networks or relationships with corrupting individuals.
- Ready access to weapons of violence, whether physical arms, being in a position of power, or access to online tools.
- Having a violent or criminal history.
- Having a history of psychological ill health.

Tackling Identity-Based Violence in Cities

Much has been written about—and many policies and programs designed, implemented, and evaluated to strengthen—how we can confront or reverse propellants of acute identity-based violence such as those listed above. A less developed approach to violence prevention, though perhaps a growing one, is the effort to map the systems, institutions, and platforms that, intentionally or not, create conditions in which identity-based violence becomes more likely.[27] Such approaches force us to understand how decisions and actions across national and local government departments, police and other security forces, civil society, and business contribute, or not, to increasing or decreasing the risk of violence. These approaches are designed to tackle the structural violence that enables the physical. In this sense, the city must approach identity-based mass violence in much the same way it approaches organized crime: tackling the root causes and drivers while also criminalizing the parts of the conspiracy that currently operate under the protection of the law, and using all tools at its disposal to map, disrupt, and dismantle the structures and networks that enable mass violence and atrocities, whether they are committed inside or outside of its city and/or state borders.

We therefore suggest that there are two key approaches to identity-based mass violence prevention: confronting the propellants of physical or acute violence through effective programming and integrating indicators of prevention into the decision-making processes of systems to reverse structural violence. Cities and large urban areas are well suited to implement both these approaches, having tools that nonurban areas do not, primarily because of the high concentration of people and the formal and informal infrastructures cities require.

We know, for example, that identity-based divisions in communities can be confronted, mitigated, and prevented when social cohesion is strong and when strong communities are recognized as contributing to social and national resilience.[28] Requisite too are long-term, meaningful interactions between different members of a community, often referred to as "contact hypothesis."[29] Such interactions can be far easier to initiate through targeted programming in cities where there is greater diversity and the proximity of the population makes it is easier to bring people together. Even without distinct interventions or programs, this social dynamic is common in many cities. In the United Kingdom, for example, using data from the British Social Attitudes Survey, researchers found that people living in major cities—especially London—displayed significantly more tolerant attitudes toward asylum seekers, concluding that "having opportunities for meaningful social contact with asylum seekers and other immigrants is a key factor underlying some of the unexplained rural–urban differences in attitudes."[30]

This dimension of the city experience, which is far from universal, should not overshadow the varied and challenging realities all cities face. Moreover, our view is shaped by the particular British city experience, which is—or was—fairly unique in seeking, during the postwar decades, to deliberately rebuild many urban areas differently. The 1950s and 1960s are generally seen as something of a golden era for British social housing, when 1.5 million new homes were built as the slums and bomb damage of the Second World War were cleared to make way for modern homes for working people. Many of the Britain's urban areas were badly bombed during the war, so large areas of London and many other cities needed to be rebuilt, which meant that new housing for poorer, working, and immigrant tenants was developed in close proximity to wealthier areas. But this was a political decision too, and it provided the stability of long-term tenancies at low rents to millions of ordinary people. It is also an example of how centering a vision for social impact in decision-making not only transformed British urban planning but also had tremendous lasting impact on British city social and political history. The French experience, by contrast, was quite different. Throughout the same decades, the banlieue were built on the edge of cities across the country, creating a suburban periphery of low-cost, large-scale social housing—and creating a new form of urban economic and racial segregation.[31] This too was a political decision, and one that has had profound and detrimental consequences for many French cities, particularly with regard to structural and acute identity-based violence and the recent history of French identity politics.

In Britain and France, the social housing project began to fall apart when financial and political investment stopped. Nor was the British vision for its cities ever implemented, or even begun, everywhere. Cities like Glasgow in Scotland and Liverpool in the north of England saw rapid builds of low-cost housing in already deprived areas that only drove existing inequities and urban challenges, propelling those cities' experiences of identity-based violence within the city systems. Since the 1980s, there has been near abandonment in UK urban planning of social impacts and the metrics of integration and cohesion, leading inevitably to a contemporary manifestation, in London particularly, of social cleansing, where profits of private enterprise have won out over community needs. This is not solely a decision to prize the landlord above the tenant—although that is a marked transformation—but the pursuit of short-term financial gains for very few has brought in fast investment, including from individuals and regimes that are enabling identity-based mass violence in other parts of the world, displacing London's poorer, more marginalized communities in the process. The city of London is now thought to launder over 40 percent of the world's dirty money, and while much of these funds are cleaned through the British trading markets or banking systems, London's property is a popular alternative.

Take Kensington and Chelsea, a borough of London that includes both the most expensive properties in the city and social housing estates, including Grenfell Tower. In 2017, over a third of properties sold in a major new development in the borough were purchased via anonymous companies or by buyers from states considered to be a high-corruption risk.[32] Kensington and Chelsea's public and private structures did not take into account in their decision-making regarding local housing the metrics of identity-based violence; as a result, those decisions and the culture of decision-making on housing alone contributed to structural, acute, and identity-based mass violence. They contributed to ongoing local displacement, grievances, and inequities; they were responsible for the fire that broke out in the residential Grenfell Tower block and killed 72 people—a preventable incident of identity-based violence and an acute consequence of deep structural violence over years by public and private decision-makers. Finally, those decisions provided safe haven for the profits of identity-based mass violence elsewhere.

Whether we call it contact hypothesis, integration, or social cohesion, strengthening shared community identities, reducing grievance, and building collective vision can only succeed "under the right conditions."[33] Such conditions are not created through any single decision or time-bound programming but require constant and consistent work. On the local level, these conditions are most often created by grassroots civil society organizations like amateur sports clubs, religious groups, and other community formations that make shared decisions around their services. While there are not necessarily more civil society groups in urban areas (indeed, in the United Kingdom there are more voluntary groups per person in rural areas than in urban),[34] cities are more densely populated and diverse. This creates greater opportunity for civil society organizations to create more meaningful interactions and should make it somewhat logistically easier for donors and local governments to help those organizations maximize their contributions to cohesion and social resilience. For example, Protection Approaches delivers a program with local and grassroots civil society organizations in cities across England that helps their staff and volunteers understand how they can better tackle marginalization and create inclusive and connected communities where the risks of identity-based mass violence can be reduced. We are able to do this in cities because we can easily and regularly bring together civil society organizations from across a city to share best practices on how to tailor their programming. To achieve the same results in nonurban areas and reach the same number of people, the significant additional resources necessary are beyond what is seen as justifiable for most funding bodies.

However, because the very nature of city infrastructure means structural identity-based violence is commonplace, the need for structural prevention—or prevention through and by structures—is critical. Inhabitants of urban centers are inevitably more likely to be in daily interaction with certain complex public infrastructure systems such as transport or policing. The daily decisions made by power holders in London's urban infrastructure—whether in the public or private sector—can have considerable impact on whether those structures and services become more or less discriminatory (or structurally violent), or make greater or lesser contributions to reducing risks of acute or physical violence. Does the property developer force social housing tenants to use a different "poor" door of a mixed tenant building—or does the developer or its contractors in fact reject pressures to do so? Do the metropolitan police prioritize implementation of a zero-tolerance policy toward police officers who have committed sex offenses or domestic violence or fail to implement its own recommendations? Does the local government officer agree to requests from tenants to remove flammable cladding from their tower blocks or leave their warnings of fire risk unreplied?

Imagine if these same daily decisions made by our urban infrastructure systems were not primarily based on what are commonly—often mistakenly—assumed to be the most immediate economic, political, or practical benefit; and that instead longer-term considerations of community knowledge, safety, cohesion, and other metrics that not only support the prevention of identity-based violence but many social, economic, and health benefits, had to be integrated into the decision-making process. The results would likely often be different.

Whether it is in the decisions that determine how, when, and where our public transport runs; how, when, and where housing is built, torn down, or redeveloped; or in our cities' policing; in how our cities interact with the climate and nature; city governance has the potential to center the safety of its populations and in so doing confront all manner of political, financial, and security challenges that cripple cities all over the world. In their day-to-day decision-making, city leaders often have far greater power than leaders in rural communities to tackle systemic and structural identity-based violence and help build more equitable communities where the risk factors that contribute to the likelihood of physical, acute, and widespread identity-based violence are substantially reduced. At the same time, they are able to draw potentially more easily on a vibrant, diverse, creative, civil society to inform their decisions and ensure that those who are most marginalized are at the table. For those outside of cities, these levers are not always so easy to pull.

Thus, we argue that in the global challenge of preventing or mitigating identity-based violence, cities are the low-hanging fruit. It is in cities that we have more of the answers and more of the resources and are able to scale solutions far more easily.

We know, as a community of practice, how to reduce identity-based violence in cities and how to foster lasting, cohesive, and trusted relationships; it is just not yet a policy priority of political leaderships to do so.

Nor have we collectively as a movement been advocating sufficiently in a joined-up manner for how this could be done. By contrast, we don't have the same answers for the countryside, where state and civil society infrastructure is far more disconnected. The fundamental tenet of community building is bringing people together in meaningful ways to build trust, relationships, and solutions. This is far less possible in the countryside or the village than in the city.

The Future of Identity-Based Mass Violence and Cities

Despite our positive proposal, the future for our cities looks bleak. Climate change will increasingly make many places more difficult to live in, and cities will be no exception. As people are displaced from their homes by floods, fires, drought, and other effects of a warming planet, cities around the world will need to deal with influxes of people looking for safety. At the same time, financial systems based on perpetual growth on a finite planet are likely to continue to be strained, while growing inequality is driving increased polarization. For financial cities such as London, it is difficult to project how these dynamics will evolve, but without radical community investment and system change, it will be those with least access to power who pay the greatest price. A warmer, less stable world will change every aspect of how we live our lives, but it will be in the arenas of identity-based violence, systemic racism, extremism, mass atrocity, and armed conflict that we will see some of the most explosive human consequences. And it is cities, for all the reasons we set out above, that will have to contend in a particular way with risk factors that will drive structural, acute, and in some instances widespread or systematic identity-based violence. Cities will have to face what is coming.

We suggest that while national governments often find themselves ensnared in the slow machinations of bureaucratic response, city leaders should emerge during this critical juncture for the prevention of identity-based violence as crucial critical actors, capable of creating the foundations for resilient urban futures. The challenge, and indeed the imperative, is to engender a shift in decision-making, rooted in the responsibility to help prevent identity-based violence and its consequences—and transferring far greater power to communities.

Transferring power within the city must go beyond what is currently granted through the majority democratic or indeed nondemocratic state systems. Today, most people feel they are unable to actively influence decisions that affect them. For example, the Pew Research Center, through a survey of populations in 19 major democracies, found the median across those 19 countries saw 65 percent believe the political system in their country does not allow people like them to have an influence on politics.[35] It is here where local leaders can play such a pivotal role in the prevention of identity-based violence. Transferring power (and so tackling marginalization) means ensuring that individuals and groups feel and are actively involved in, and able to affect, decision-making. This is something that all local leaders can pursue and help achieve. Within and across many cities, it does not require national policy changes, nor does it take vast sums of money but rather a change in ways of thinking and working—and altering priorities.

In this pursuit, city leaders must confront the exclusion of community expertise from consultation, decision-making, program delivery, and planning. It is not uncommon for national or large nonprofit and profit-making organizations or academic institutions to receive substantial funding toward the building of stronger communities or to deliver public services. This means that as services are developed and delivered, the voice, expertise, and trust of communities are lost. Without involving communities that have been marginalized or made vulnerable in developing services or policy, structural biases will be replicated, strengthening the barriers to participation, safety, and equity and further compounding marginalization.

By contrast, it is less common to find examples of patchwork, consortium, or coalition-led ways of working that see local or grassroots organizations who best understand what is needed, and are trusted by their communities being centered in strategy, policy, resource allocation, and so on. Examples of this work exist in cities and can be championed.

Not only do we know what works but we know what does not. We know that the answer cannot be a romanticization of the local or community-led, where the burden for transformation is placed wholly on local communities but without the structural support necessary to ensure deliver-system change, scaled delivery, and joined-up working.[36] Peace Direct's work on decolonizing aid, which has shown many of the flaws in current international systems of funding and delivery in global peacebuilding, holds lessons for London and elsewhere because the fundamental wrong assumptions are the same.[37] As Peace Direct writes in its report Race, Power, and Peacebuilding:

Adopting local approaches with little consideration may not shift power within the local population. Avoiding romanticising the local will enable a more honest, clearheaded appreciation of what local groups can bring, as well as their limitations. This will also help to avoid assuming homogeneity amongst locals—some local actors may disagree and hold divergent beliefs, all of which should be seen as valuable and worthy of discussion.[38]

Instead, a different approach is more effective, one of partnerships whereby there is true and meaningful local ownership of projects, programs, and decisions by local communities but in ways that don't burden those communities with the expectation that they have all the knowledge, experience, or administration systems necessary. This can be achieved in many ways, such as through consortiums where public services and other projects are owned by many local groups with the support of a larger organization that can give support on administrative burdens, coordination, and through facilitation of skills sharing and learning.

The responsibility to help protect people from the threat of identity-based mass violence is part of the modern social contract; resilient societies rely on the actions of citizens, the strength of communities, and the political support of the state. Reflecting on this responsibility at the city level only reaffirms our own conviction as practitioners that the local holds untapped opportunity for community, structural, and systems prevention. The power of people and the reality of local government meet in the city—and so offers great opportunity for new action at a time when the need for social resilience and preparedness for shocks is rising worldwide.

Notes

1. Andrew Fearn and Kate Ferguson, "Understanding Identity-Based Mass Violence," Protection Approaches, September 29 2014, https://protectionapproaches.org/news/f/understanding-identity-based-mass-violence.
2. Kate Ferguson and Fred Carver, *Being the Difference: A Primer for States Wishing to Prevent Atrocity Crimes in the Mid-Twenty-First Century*, Protection Approaches, November 2021, https://img1.wsimg.com/blobby/go/131c96cc-7e6f-4c06-ae37-6550dbd85dde/Being%20the%20difference%20Final.pdf.
3. Fearn and Ferguson, "Understanding," 2014.
4. World Bank Group, *Violence in the City: Understanding and Supporting Community Responses to Urban Violence*, April 2011, p. ix, https://documents1.worldbank.org/curated/en/524341468331181450/pdf/638880WP0Viole00BOX361532B00public0.pdf.
5. Andy Fearn and Kate Ferguson, *A Gathering Storm? Assessing Risks of Identity-Based Violence in Britain*, Protection Approaches, March 2019 https://img1.wsimg.com/blobby/go/131c96cc-7e6f-4c06-ae37-6550dbd85dde/downloads/A%20Gathering%20Storm%20Assessing%20risks%20of%20identity-.pdf?ver=1733930951875.
6. Andrew Gamble, "Britain's Eternal Decline," *New Statesmen*, September 30, 2023.
7. Fearn and Ferguson, *Gathering Storm?*.
8. Investigations have highlighted how individuals from the United Arab Emirates and other corrupt figures have been investing in London's property market, raising concerns about money laundering and the influx of illicit funds into the city's real estate

sector. Patrick Wintour, "Nearly 40% of dirty money is laundered in London and UK crown dependencies", *The Guardian*, May 14, 2024, https://www.theguardian.com/world/article/2024/may/14/nearly-40-of-dirty-money-is-laundered-in-london-and-uk-crown-dependenies.
9. The responsibility to protect principle, as articulated in the 2005 World Summit Outcome document (A/RES/60/1), see p.30. This principle was endorsed by every UN member state and represented a major moment in the history of rights in that the entire UN General Assembly acknowledged that state sovereignty is not absolute; when a state is unable or unwilling to protect populations within its borders from mass atrocity crimes (genocide, crimes against humanity, and war crimes), that fundamental responsibility to protect transfers to the rest of the world. Protection Approaches advocates a devolution of the principle, recognizing that all of us share in upholding or failing this responsibility. Ferguson and Carver, *Being the Difference*.
10. On our current definition, see https://protectionapproaches.org/identity-based-violence; for our contributions on developing the concept and definition see "Understanding identity-based violence", Protection Approaches, 2014, which builds on Kate Ferguson, "Masking genocide in Bosnia" in *The Routledge History of Genocide*, eds Cathie Carmicheal and Richard C. Maguire, (London, Routledge, 2015), 310.
11. Frank Chalk and Kurt Jonassohn, *The History and Sociology of Genocide: Analyses and Case Studies* (New Haven, CT: Yale University Press, 1990).
12. Christopher Browning's *Ordinary Men* transformed literature on and understanding of the Holocaust and was a foundational text for Protection Approaches. Christopher Browning, *Ordinary Men: Reserve Police Battalion 101 and the Final Solution in Poland* (New York, Harper Collins, 1992).
13. United Nations, Convention on the Prevention and Punishment of the Crime of Genocide, 1948; United Nations, 2005 World Summit Outcome, 2005.
14. Ferguson and Carver, *Being the Difference*.

15. Ibid.
16. Fearn and Ferguson, *Gathering Storm?*.
17. Zeid Ra'ad Al Hussein, speaking to the Foreign Affairs Committee of the House of Commons, "Oral Evidence: The FCO and the Integrated Review, HC 380," Q75, July 21, 2020, https://committees.parliament.uk/oralevidence/772/html/.
18. On June 14, 2017, a high-rise fire broke out in the 24-storey Grenfell Tower block of flats in North Kensington, West London. It burned for 60 hours, killing 74 people died. See Peter Apps, *Show Me The Bodies: How We Let Grenfell Happen* (London, Oneworld Publications, 2022). The July 7, 2005, London bombings, also referred to as 7/7, were a series of four coordinated suicide attacks carried out by Islamic terrorists that targeted commuters on London's public transport during the morning rush hour.
19. Impact:Peace and the Institute for Peace and Justice, Kroc School, University of San Diego, *Making the Case for Peace in Our Cities: Halving Urban Violence by 2030*, Evidence Brief, October 2019, https://catcher.sandiego.edu/items/usd/I_P%20Urban%20Violence%20Evidence%20Brief%203.4.20.pdf.
20. Ariana Markowitz, *Big Events on a Small Scale: Exploring Identity-Based Mass Violence in Cities*, Stanley Center for Peace and Security, November 2020, https://stanleycenter.org/publications/urban-atrocities.
21. UK Office for National Statistics, "Regional Gross Domestic Product: All ITL Regions," April 2024.
22. Trust for London, "Net Income Inequality before Housing Cost (1996/97–2022/2023)," June 2024, https://trustforlondon.org.uk/data/income-inequality-over-time/#:~:text=What%20does%20it%20tell%20us.
23. Protection Approaches, "Statement on Preventing Mass Atrocity Crimes in Israel & in Gaza," October 13, 2023, https://protectionapproaches.org/news/f/statement-on-preventing-mass-atrocity-crimes-in-israel-in-gaza.
24. Post by London Mayor Sadiq Khan, October 7, 023, https://x.com/MayorofLondon/status/1710626161292644475?s=20.

25. United Nations Office on Genocide Prevention and the Responsibility to Protect, *Framework of Analysis for Atrocity Crimes: A Tool for Prevention*, September 30, 2014, https://www.ohchr.org/sites/default/files/2021-11/Genocide-Framework-of-Analysis-English.pdf, p.iii.
26. These indicators are drawn from Protection Approaches' own risk analysis framework and global best practice, including the United Nations Office on Genocide Prevention and the Responsibility to Protect, *Framework of Analysis for Atrocity Crimes*, and *Preventing Violent Extremism through Inclusive Development and the Promotion of Tolerance and Respect for Diversity*, United Nations Development Programme, June 1, 2016.
27. Kate Ferguson, *From Network Analysis to Creative Leverage: Mapping New Horizons of Modern Atrocity Prevention*, Stimson Center, September 29, 2022, https://www.stimson.org/2022/from-network-analysis-to-creative-leverage-mapping-new-horizons-of-modern-atrocity-prevention/.
28. Derek Oakley, "Building Resilient Communities: The Case for Social Cohesion," Protection Approaches, December 2, 2024.
29. See, for example, Gordon W. Allport, *The Nature of Prejudice* (Cambridge, MA: Addison-Wesley, 1954); Thomas Pettigrew and Linda Tropp, "A Meta-Analytic Test of Intergroup Contact Theory," *Journal of Personality and Social Psychology* 90, no. 5 (2006): 751–783; and Elizabeth Paluck, Seth Green, and Donald Green, "The Contact Hypothesis Re-Evaluated," *Behavioural Public Policy* 3 (2018): 1–30.
30. Heaven Crawley, Stephen Drinkwater, and Rukhsana Kausar, "Attitudes towards Asylum Seekers: Understanding Differences between Rural and Urban Areas," *Journal of Rural Studies* 71 (October 2019): 104–113.
31. Juliet Carpenter, "The French Banlieue: Renovating the Suburbs," in *The Routledge Companion to the Suburbs*, edited by Bernadette Hanlon, Thomas Vicino, 254–265 (London, Routledge, 2018).

32. Transparency International UK, "One in Five Homes in New Kensington and Chelsea Housing Development Bought through Anonymous Companies," press release, August 9, 2017, https://www.transparency.org.uk/one-five-homes-new-kensington-and-chelsea-housing-development-bought-through-anonymous-companies.
33. Gordon W. Allport, *The Nature of Prejudice* (Cambridge, MA: Addison-Wesley, 1954). For more recent empirical support, see Thomas Pettigrew and Linda Tropp, "A Meta-Analytic Test of Intergroup Contact Theory," *Journal of Personality and Social Psychology* 90, no. 5 (2006): 751–783.
34. NCVO, UK Civil Society Almanac 2021; Data, trends, insights, September 01 2021 https://www.ncvo.org.uk/news-and-insights/news-index/uk-civil-society-almanac-2021/profile/where-are-voluntary-organisations-based/#/across-the-uk.
35. Richard Wike et al., December 6, 2022 Pew Research Center, *Satisfaction with Democracy and Political Efficacy around the World*.
36. Peace Direct, *Time to Decolonise Aid: Insights and Lessons from a Global Consultation*, 2021. https://www.peacedirect.org/time-to-decolonise-aid/.
37. Ibid.
38. Peace Direct, *Race, Power and Peacebuilding: Insights and Lessons from a Global Consultation*, 2023. https://www.peacedirect.org/wp-content/uploads/2023/09/Race-Power-and-Peacebuilding-report.v5.pdf.

Kate Ferguson is Co-Executive Director of Protection Approaches. Her education includes a master's degree from Oxford in Russian and East European studies and a PhD in the study of mass atrocities from the University of East Anglia. She is the author of Architectures of Violence: The Command Structures of *Mass Atrocities from Yugoslavia to Serbia* (Oxford: Oxford University Press, 2020). She serves on the Board of Trustees of the Holocaust Memorial Day Trust.

Andy Fearn is Co-Executive Director and head of learning and outreach for Protection Approaches. He holds an MA in human rights from Kingston University London and works to build community resilience and help individuals develop the practical skills, knowledge, and networks to confront prejudice and hate.

Open Access This chapter is licensed under the terms of the Creative Commons Attribution-NonCommercial-NoDerivatives 4.0 International License (http://creativecommons.org/licenses/by-nc-nd/4.0/), which permits any noncommercial use, sharing, distribution and reproduction in any medium or format, as long as you give appropriate credit to the original author(s) and the source, provide a link to the Creative Commons license and indicate if you modified the licensed material. You do not have permission under this license to share adapted material derived from this chapter or parts of it.

The images or other third party material in this chapter are included in the chapter's Creative Commons license, unless indicated otherwise in a credit line to the material. If material is not included in the chapter's Creative Commons license and your intended use is not permitted by statutory regulation or exceeds the permitted use, you will need to obtain permission directly from the copyright holder.

Urban Patterns of Segregation and Violence in Jerusalem

Michal Braier and Efrat Cohen Bar

We finished researching for this piece at the end of September 2023, on the Jewish new-year's eve. Though public turmoil against the ruling of an extremist right-wing government was at its height, we could not have anticipated the merciless bloodshed that would swipe through Israel and Palestine just a few weeks later. Hamas's brutal attack on Israel's southern region triggered extreme Israeli violence in Gaza, killing tens of thousands and razing its urban fabric to the ground. Yet Israeli violence against Palestinians takes many shapes and occurs at different scales and times. In this intervention, we focus on the structural, systematic, and bureaucratized violence against Palestinians as it manifests through urban planning, building, and enforcement mechanisms in the city of Jerusalem.

M. Braier (✉)
Bimkom, Jerusalem, Israel
e-mail: michal@bimkom.org

E. C. Bar
Bimkom, Jerusalem, Israel

Urban History of Segregation

For decades, Jerusalem has been at the heart of the Israeli-Palestinian conflict and a focal point of vast national, religious, and political debates. While peace negotiations over possible just and equal solutions imagined the city's future as either shared or separated, everyday realities are deeply segregated and unequal.

Jerusalem did not always feature segregation between Jews and Arabs. Separation between the two communities, albeit not a rigid one, can roughly be dated to the beginning of the British Mandate and was especially conspicuous in the modern neighborhoods built outside the Old City's walls. The 1948 war, referred to as Independence War by Israelis and the Nakba ("the catastrophe") by Palestinians, marked a significant turning point. The war divided the city by the armistice line, later known as the Green Line (marked in Fig. 1), strictly separating the two ethnonational communities. To achieve the division between the Israeli western city and the Jordanian eastern city,[1] many Palestinian communities, and some Jewish, were moved from one side to another during the war. Separate systems of government, administration, and law were set up, forming two isolated cities.

This state of affairs was profoundly altered by the 1967 war, when Israel occupied the West Bank, as well as Gaza strip, Sinai peninsula, and the Golan Heights. In Jerusalem, Israel unilaterally annexed some 70 square kilometers (43.5 square miles) only a few weeks after the end of the war, encompassing the Old City (one square kilometer/.6 square miles), the Jordanian city (six square kilometers/3.7 square miles), and 28 villages and suburbs from the city's hinterlands. Israel applied its law, jurisdiction, and administration to this newly devised municipal territory (the black line on Fig. 2). However, the Palestinian residents of the city were not afforded full citizenship but rather given a status of permanent residents, which most Palestinian Jerusalemites hold till this day. This liminal status affords them certain rights such as relative freedom of movement, employment, and some social benefits, yet they are denied the right to vote in national elections, and their residency can easily be revoked.

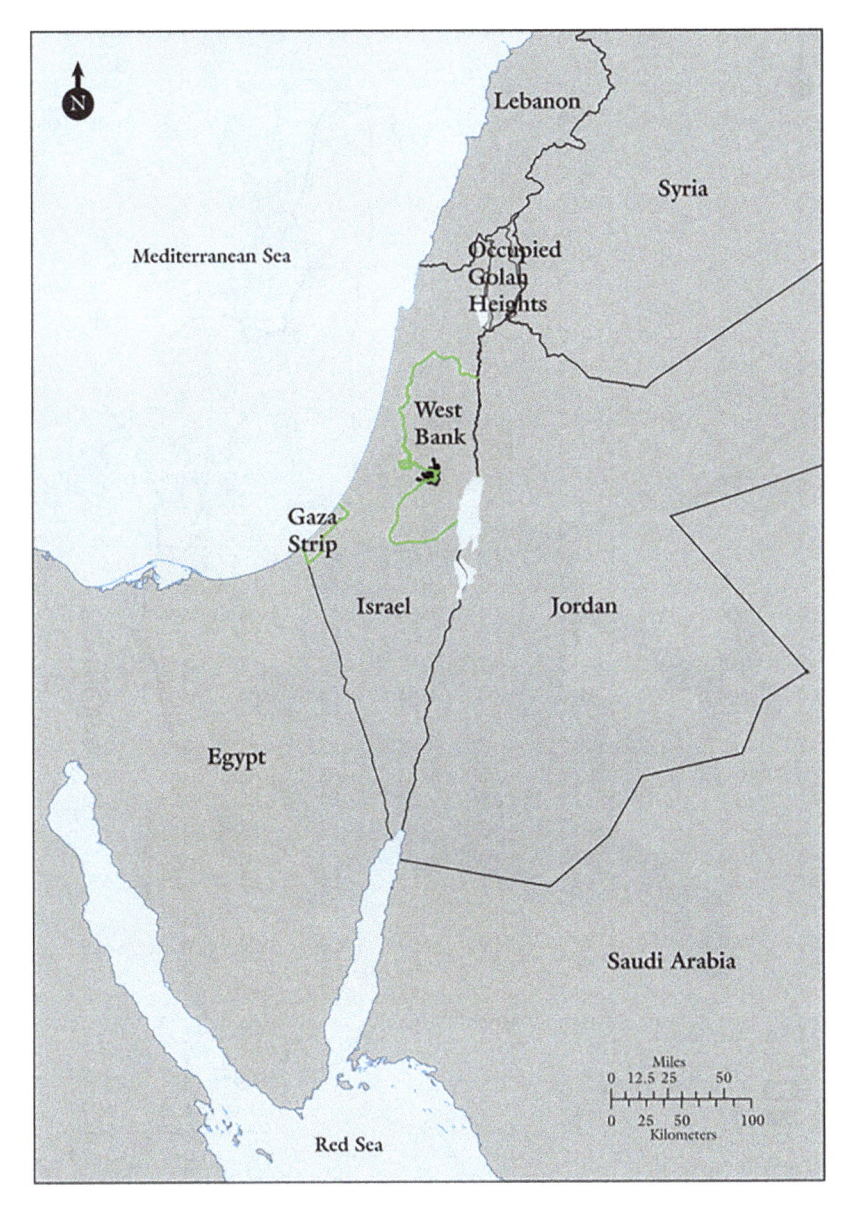

Fig. 1 Israel and the region (*Source* Bimkom)

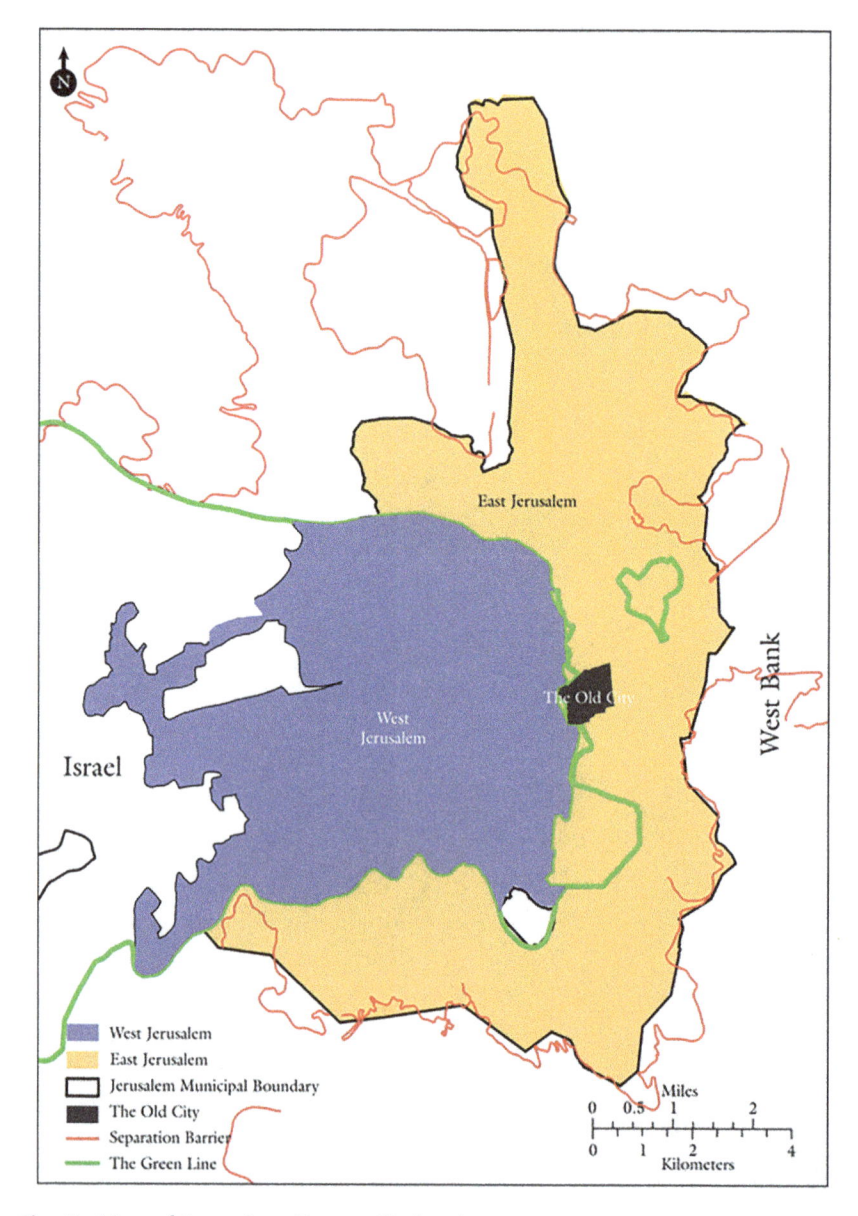

Fig. 2 Map of Jerusalem (*Source* Bimkom)

Israel immediately began to plan the so-called unified city,[2] aiming to achieve Jewish-Israeli geographic and demographic dominance over Jerusalem's vast new territory. This included expropriating large tracts of open land east of the Green Line, used for building new "satellite neighborhoods" (settlements), which functioned as purified Jewish spaces. The Israeli neighborhoods were strategically located between existing Palestinian localities, confining their development and preventing their spatial continuity. At the same time, severe building restrictions were forced on the Palestinian neighborhoods and former villages of the city. These were otherwise neglected by most municipal services and development.

Combined, the new Israeli neighborhoods that housed a large Jewish population and the grave restriction and neglect of the Palestinian population radically changed the geography of separation in Jerusalem. Both populations continued to grow, yet no real attempt to integrate Israelis and Palestinians was made. While in 1967 the city housed close to 70,000 Palestinians and 200,000 Israelis, by 2021, there were 376,000 Palestinians and 591,000 Israelis.[3] Despite constant Israeli efforts to maintain a large Jewish majority in the city, the Palestinian population grew from 26 percent in 1967 to 39 percent in 2021.

This urban growth made Palestinians a vital part of the city's economy by providing it with a cheap and unskilled labor force. Yet segregation persists in most areas of life. Neighborhoods are easily classified as either Israeli or Palestinian, as Fig. 3 shows, with few exceptions. Segregation does not only mean separate housing spaces but also high levels of separation in all services and public facilities, which are managed and operated by different agents and in different languages.

For example, education is delivered through two separate school systems, applying different curriculums and different matriculation exams. Except for one bilingual school operating in the city, most Jews and Arabs study in their own languages, posing a challenge to basic communication across groups. Overall, the public Palestinian education system is poor in resources and quality, relegating Palestinians to mostly working-class positions in the predominantly Jewish-Israeli labor market. In turn, 60 percent of Palestinians live in poverty, and almost all neighborhoods are ranked in the lowest socioeconomic decile.[4] Similarly, public transportation, health, welfare, and community services are

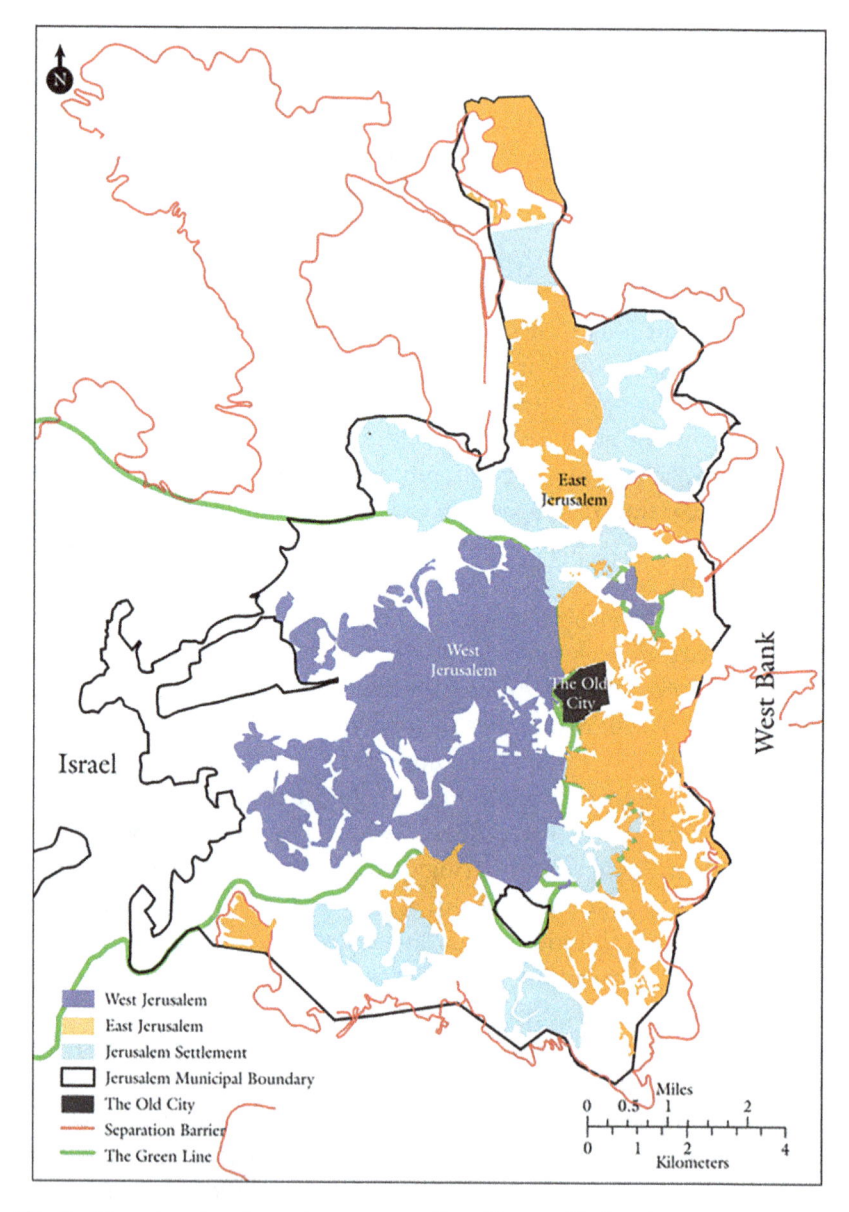

Fig. 3 Map showing Jerusalem segregation (*Source* Bimkom)

segregated, with significantly higher quality of services and facilities in Jewish-Israeli areas.

It is important to remember that for many years after occupation, everyday life in Palestinian neighborhoods and villages continued to be governed under Jordanian—and later Palestinian—auspices, including the education system, health services, public transport, and infrastructure development. Jerusalem continued to function as the Palestinian capital and economic center of the West Bank, as movement to and from the city was relatively easy.

This changed dramatically with the 1990's Oslo process, followed by the outbreak of the Second Intifada (the Palestinian uprising) and the construction of the separation wall (red line on Figs. 2 and 3) in the beginning of the 2000s. At that time, Israel began tightening the legal and physical borders between East Jerusalem and the West Bank, limiting Palestinian freedom of movement and political activity in the city. The wall divides the urban fabric of the Palestinian city, cutting it off from the West Bank. Simultaneously, Israel has made efforts to demonstrate stringent governmental control over East Jerusalem, including trying to provide more civil services in the Palestinian neighborhoods of the city. These efforts, however, are far from meeting all the acute needs or closing the existing gaps caused by years of neglect. The efforts are also met with great suspicion among Palestinian Jerusalemites, not least of all because they are often understood as measures of normalizing occupation.

1. Urban Planning as Identity-Based Violence

Urban planning and development policies have been a linchpin in shaping the segregated and unequal urban fabric of Jerusalem. Housing development is a prominent example: while in predominantly Jewish-Israeli neighborhoods (west and east of the Green Line) development and densification policies are aggressively endorsed, the Palestinian neighborhoods experience acute shortages in housing-development possibilities. By design, land available for new development is extremely limited, and development is highly restricted in terms of building heights, densities, and volumes. Infrastructure development lags far behind and is only slowly and sporadically upgraded. Public amenities and services are all but lacking. The current Palestinian housing crisis in the city is a direct outcome of Israel's long-standing discriminatory planning and development policies and practices. These have hindered the development of Palestinian neighborhoods, restricting and confining Palestinian presence in the city and condemning their residents to poverty and deprivation.

Regardless, the city's Palestinian community continues to grow. Facing systematic attacks on their livelihoods, Palestinians have countered Israeli planning policy with widespread informal urban development. Whether understood as a tactic of survival or political resistance, such development can give only a limited answer to growing housing needs. Furthermore, most development lacks access to proper public amenities and infrastructure and fails to meet safety regulations and security standards. Today, it is estimated that 50 percent of all Palestinian housing units in the city are considered illegal by Israeli authorities, criminalizing many of the city's residents. This informal construction is met with harsh institutional violence, consisting of legal procedures that culminate in dozens of home demolitions every year. As a result, many residents live under permanent conditions of fear and insecurity, and whole families are left deprived of basic, secure shelter. Thus, urban planning and identity-based mass urban violence become two sides of the same coin.

According to the Israeli Planning and Building Law (1965), a house built without a permit can only be immediately demolished during the building process or in the first 30 days of inhabitation. After that, a court order must be obtained, turning the threat of demolition into an ongoing event that affects every aspect of life. Living under the threat of home demolition, the Palestinian working class must constantly invest its scarce time and limited resources in efforts to prevent demolitions and save homes. This includes enduring and costly legal proceedings, repeated attempts to rezone the area, and incessant efforts to follow frequently changing urban policy. Planning bureaucracy and the legal system's procedures thus play a dual role of threatening Palestinian existence, both figuratively and literally, as well as allegedly offering what are tortuous paths for saving one's home. In most cases, however, the planners, lawyers, surveyors, and engineers working on behalf of individual homeowners fail to achieve any significant change.

Tracking demolition orders and actual demolitions over the decade between 2012 and 2022[5] shows that during this period, the Jerusalem Municipality issued more than 5,000 demolition orders. However, these are unevenly distributed across the city, with about 60 percent located in the Palestinian neighborhoods of the city, where 40 percent of the city's residents live. During the same period, close to 1200 demolitions were executed, 65 percent of which were in Palestinian neighborhoods.

Importantly, the type of demolitions implemented in the Palestinian neighborhoods differ from those in Jewish-Israeli neighborhoods. In Israeli neighborhoods, small building additions or modifications are generally demolished, but not entire housing units. In Palestinian neighborhoods, entire buildings, often housing multiple families, are demolished. As these figures demonstrate, home demolition is not a singular episode of violence but rather a structural, violent force that shapes both urban space and a relationship dominated by the Israeli government. Such violence is grounded in the ethnic-national conflict over the city and is part of a state mechanism that casts the Palestinian residents of the city as ever more displaceable.

Box 1: Neighborhood Comparison

Figure 4 shows an aerial view of two adjacent neighborhoods: the Israeli Talpiyot Mizrach (ITM) and Palestinian Jabel al Mukaber (PJM). ITM was built on lands expropriated from PJM. Yet the building possibilities in the two neighborhoods are completely different. In PJM, about 65 percent of the area was zoned as open landscape, forbidding any construction. In the remaining areas, only 16 percent is zoned residential, with low building densities (ratios set to 25 to 37.5 percent) that allow one-to-two-story buildings. In ITM, by contrast, about 45 percent of the land is zoned residential, allowing four-to-five-story buildings with building densities set 4 times higher (a ratio of 120 percent). Dwelling densities in the two neighborhoods provide insight into the impact of these differences. While in ITM the housing density stands at 1.0 person per room, in PJM it is 1.6 people per room. Currently, densification policy allows for building up to 30 stories in ITM, yet in PJM, six stories are the most that can be approved.

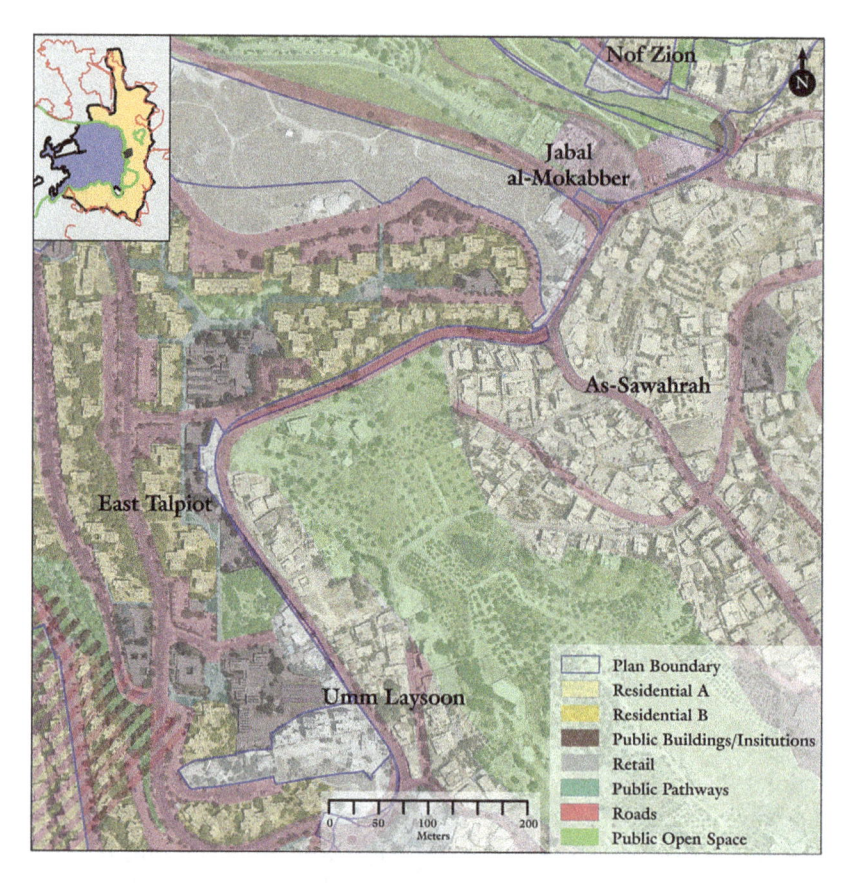

Fig. 4 Comparison between the Israeli Talpiyot Mizrach and Palestinian Jabel al Mukaber neighborhoods (*Source* Bimkom)

2. Urban Planning and Violence: The Case of the Wadi Abdalla Neighborhood

Wadi Abdalla is a small neighborhood, lying on the slopes of a steep valley, adjacent to the historic Jewish cemetery of Mount of Olives. As in most Palestinian neighborhoods in East Jerusalem, the area lacks public amenities and infrastructure such as paved roads, schools, playgrounds, street lighting, garbage disposal facilities, and much more. About 3,000 people live in Wadi Abdalla, most of them in informal houses built in the 1980s and 1990s without obtaining building permits.

The area was included in the Holy-Basin Plan (also known as Ein Mem/9), the first major Israeli statutory plan made for East Jerusalem, in 1976. The plan sought to preserve the ancient landscape surrounding the Old City as a sacred tribute to the three monotheistic religions. In practice, that plan strictly limited any development in the area, especially for housing. Wadi Abdalla was zoned as an extension of the historic Jewish cemetery, ignoring the fact that the land was owned by Palestinian residents of the nearby village of Silwan, as well as the few houses already there at the time. In 1993, a detailed plan for the area was made, allowing limited housing development on only 30 percent of the area, leaving more than 40 percent zoned as a cemetery. However, the planned public infrastructure and facilities were never implemented. Hence, the landowners remained unaware of the plan's existence (see Fig. 5).

At the beginning of the 1990s, as housing shortages for Palestinians became acute, especially in the Muslim Quarter of the Old City, small pieces of land in Wadi Abdalla were sold, and residents seeking better housing opportunities began building their homes. This informal urban environment was developed mainly according to land ownership patterns rather than the formal (statutory) land uses. For about 15 years, the Jerusalem's Israeli municipality overlooked this informal development, making no attempt to stop it. At the beginning of the 2000s, however, the municipal policy became more stringent, and building enforcement began to roll out. Many of the houses escaped the clutches of the law, but others did not, receiving demolition orders.

About a decade ago, the Israeli planning authorities accepted Wadi Abdalla's residents' long-standing demand to rezone the area from a cemetery to housing, in light of the existing reality of a rapidly urbanizing area. The Jerusalem Municipality initiated a new master plan for the area, providing some hope, but requiring additional planning procedures to be carried out by the residents themselves. The long-awaited building permits, which provide the only real protection against demolitions, are still far from being issued, requiring homeowners to continue to spend money, time, and effort dealing with painstaking bureaucracy.

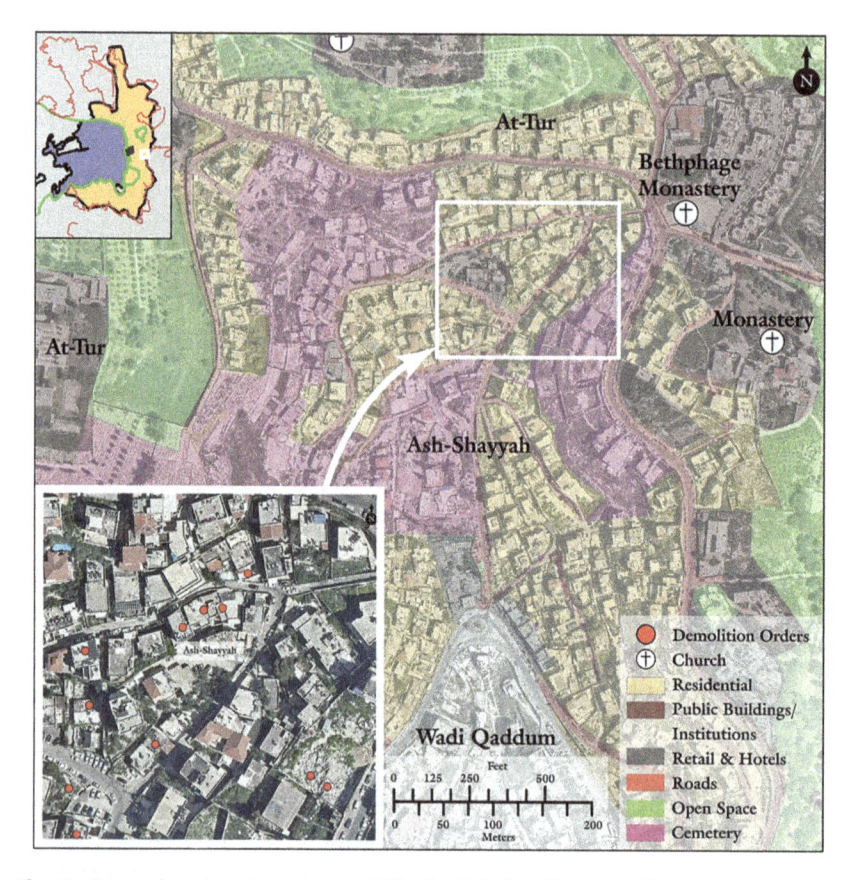

Fig. 5 Map showing the area of Wadi Abdalla. The Ash-Shayyah demolition orders are marked in red (*Source* Bimkom)

3. Testimonies: The Crusade to Save One's Home

Abed

Abed is 78 years old.[6] He is married, the father of two daughters and one son, and the grandfather of four. He lives in Wadi Abdalla, Ash-Shayyah. The interview took place on July 12, 2023, in Abed's home.

Abed was born in 1946, in the Palestinian village of Lifta, located west of the city of Jerusalem. When he was only two years old, the 1948 war broke out, bringing about the Nakba (Arabic for catastrophe) for the Palestinian people. His family was displaced, and his mother died. As Lifta was seized by the Israeli army, later becoming part of West Jerusalem, its residents were forced to flee east. Abed's family settled on agricultural land in the West Bank, then under Jordanian rule.

When Abed turned 21 in 1967, Israel conquered the West Bank, which it still occupies. East Jerusalem was unilaterally annexed to Israel, but Israeli authorities never allowed Palestinian refugees to return to their homes or lands, using various legal mechanisms.

In the beginning of the 1990s, Abed married a woman from Silwan, a Palestinian village on the outskirts of the Old City of Jerusalem. Although customarily women move into the husband's family home, Abed's family had no home or land to accommodate the newlyweds. His wife's family, however, had land close to their village, in Wadi Abdalla. Although zoning plans strictly limited any development of the area, Israeli authorities had turned a blind eye on development there, and many unauthorized homes were being built in Wadi Abdalla. In the beginning of the 2000s, when Abed and his family moved there, no demolition orders were issued, and none of the houses had been demolished.

The lax policy, however, quickly changed. As Abed was building the family's house, law enforcement deputies showed up and ordered him to stop the work. Nonetheless, as the day dawned, he poured the roof and the family moved in. The demolition order was fast to arrive. "When they come to demolish," he used to say to his children, "you will pack your most important belongings and go. No looking back. A house is only a house."

Twenty-three years later, the house still stands, having evaded demolition at least for the time being. But this has not left a sense of peace. Rather, it has been 23 years of endless attempts to lift the threat of demolition, 23 years of ceaseless worries and fright. During this time, the family has grown, the children have matured and married, and grandchildren have been born. A new floor was added for their son, somehow escaping the gaze of the building-enforcement officers. As Abed testifies, living under the constant threat of demolition is "worse than terror. In a terror attack you die at once. Here, it is a slow death. It is like a knife that keeps cutting through your flesh."

To legalize the home, Abed must first submit a detailed plan, requesting to rezone the land from cemetery designation to residential use. Only after the rezoning plan has been approved, a process that usually takes a few years, can an application for a building permit be filed, also a long and arduous process. The criteria for rezoning are burdensome and oftentimes change. The municipality regularly demands a large area to be rezoned all at once, beyond an individual house, requiring cooperation among different landowners, which is difficult to accomplish. Abed has tried several times to organize his neighbors to submit such a plan, but achieving such cooperation was hard, especially from those who do not have a demolition order, as they fear drawing any attention to their homes. Abed has spent all his family's savings paying various professionals who promised to alleviate his situation, but solutions are yet to be found.

Ibrahim

Ibrahim is 56 years old. He is married, the father of 5, and the grandfather of 12. He lives in the neighborhood of Ras al-Aamud. The interview took place on July 12, 2023, in Ibrahim's home.

Ibrahim was born in 1968, in the Ras al-Aamud neighborhood of Jerusalem to a Palestinian refugee family. He is the youngest of 12 siblings. His family is originally from the village of Kolonia, west of Jerusalem, where they lived until 1948. During the 1948 Nakba, the family fled east, first living in Jerrico and later settling in Jordanian Jerusalem. The small house in Ras al-Aamud belongs to a Silwan family and is only about 50 square meters. In 1967, the neighborhood came under Israeli rule like the rest of East Jerusalem.

In 2000, before Israel began building the separation barrier, Ibrahim moved to the neighborhood of al-Azariye, a Palestinian suburb of Jerusalem, outside the municipal boundary. But when Israeli authorities began revoking residency status for Jerusalemites living outside the municipal area, Ibrahim and his family began moving back and forth between his parents' home within the city and their own house in al-Azariye. In 2006, he finally managed to buy a house within the city boundaries, in the neighborhood of Wadi Abdalla, in Ash-Shayyah. The house was small, only two rooms on a 400-square-meter-plot, yet it allowed the family to stay in their own home, eliminating the need to constantly move into and out of the city. The house was built in the

1990s without a building permit but had not received a demolition order by the time he bought it.

To make a living, Ibrahim built a small car-repair workshop, which he ran for the next 17 years. When his sons began marrying, he added two rooms and a shower to the small house. These additions drew the attention of the building-enforcement unit, and legal proceedings were quick to hit. Inspection deputies began visiting the house, one time just hours before his daughter's wedding while the guests were in the living room. The memory of that moment still hurts so bad that it brings tears to Ibrahim's eyes: "It burns you from the inside."

For years, Ibrahim tried to save the house in every possible way. He went through 16 legal proceedings, spending time and money, but to no avail. In 2019, it became clear there was no way to save the house. Ibrahim decided to demolish the home and workshop himself in order to avoid the extra fine authorities charge when they carry out a demolition. When the enforcement officer overseeing the demolition demanded that he demolish the original house too, despite not being included in the demolition order, Ibrahim refused to obey.

"Troubles make you old and sick," Ibrahim told us. After this traumatic experience, Ibrahim sold the lot with the half-destroyed house on it and left Wadi Abdalla. He returned to his parents' home in Ras al-Aamud, where he still lives. The well-kept house has three bedrooms, a small kitchen, and a lavatory. An enclosed balcony serves as a living room. Five people live in the home: Ibrahim, his wife, their son, Ibrahim's disabled brother, and their elderly mother. The rest of the children and grandchildren have moved out after starting their own families.

The years in Wadi Abdalla were filled with struggle and fear; they were the worst in Ibrahim's life. He lost his home, his livelihood, and his joy, as he testifies: "I bought two rooms and I was happy. I built two more rooms and I was happy. Then the demolition came and brought it back down to zero—to begin everything from scratch. It is to wreck a dream, not just a house."

Ibrahim has not given up, however. He got a new job as a bus driver. And he is still searching for a home to buy.

Conclusion

Abed and Ibrahim represent only two of those who face the daily uncertainty and pressure of a bureaucratized system of identity-based mass violence. Many other residents of East Jerusalem have constructed their homes without building permits and have received demolition orders. Some have witnessed their homes being destroyed, and with it their worlds collapsing. Others, like Ibrahim, are pushed to self-demolish their most cherished asset. Still others are struggling to alleviate the burden of a demolition order, but few have succeeded. In the process, all have exhausted their scarce resources—emotional and material.

Years of segregation, discrimination, and coercion have produced prolonged violence, which penetrates every aspect of daily life. In the given political environment, planning policies and building enforcement do not serve the needs and aspirations of Jerusalem's Palestinian residents; rather, they have become tools for making Palestinian life in the city unbearable, weighing heavily on individuals and society as a whole.

Yet insisting to continue life in the city subverts the authorities' aspiration for a purified space, avowing its shared reality. Rather than denying the reality of a shared city, it can and should be embraced, redirecting the trajectories of urban development. In more concrete terms, the Jerusalem Municipality, which devised the planning and development restrictions in the first place, can invest in new plans that allow for sensitive and adequate development that meets the needs of all its residents. Such planning will not only be more suitable, practical, and implementable but will also work toward a more just and equal reality. As planners working to advance human rights and justice, we ourselves are not the targets of this type of urban violence, but we continue to work with and support the communities under attack in an effort to make Jerusalem a better city for all of us.

Notes

1. From 1948 to 1967, the Palestinian part of the city was under Jordanian rule.

2. This is the English translation of the commonly used Israeli phrase that expresses the Israeli view that Jerusalem was reunified in 1967.
3. Jerusalem Institute for Policy Research, *The Statistical Yearbook of Jerusalem* (2024), table C3. https://jerusaleminstitute.org.il/wp-content/uploads/2024/05/shnaton_C0124.pdf.
4. Assaf-Shapira, Yair, ed. *The Statistical Yearbook of Jerusalem*. Jerusalem: Jerusalem Institute for Policy Research. https://jerusaleminstitute.org.il/en/yearbook/#/4235.
5. Data obtained by Bimkom from the Jerusalem Municipality under a Freedom of Information Request; requested as "Information on Building Permits and Home Demolitions" January 2023; received June 2023.
6. All names have been changed to ensure the safety of our interviewees.

Michal Braier is an architect and urban planner specializing in urban political geography. She holds a PhD from Ben Gurion University of the Negev. Braier is head of research and publications at Bimkom—Planning and Human Rights. She is also a teaching fellow at the Urban and Regional Planning Institute at Hebrew University of Jerusalem.

Efrat Cohen Bar is an architect and urban designer. She is co-executive director of the Israeli nongovernmental organization Bimkom—Planning and Human Rights, where she manages the East Jerusalem and the Urban Renewal Departments and has served as Deputy Director of Planning.

Open Access This chapter is licensed under the terms of the Creative Commons Attribution-NonCommercial-NoDerivatives 4.0 International License (http://creativecommons.org/licenses/by-nc-nd/4.0/), which permits any noncommercial use, sharing, distribution and reproduction in any medium or format, as long as you give appropriate credit to the original author(s) and the source, provide a link to the Creative Commons license and indicate if you modified the licensed material. You do not have permission under this license to share adapted material derived from this chapter or parts of it.

The images or other third party material in this chapter are included in the chapter's Creative Commons license, unless indicated otherwise in a credit line to the material. If material is not included in the chapter's Creative Commons license and your intended use is not permitted by statutory regulation or exceeds the permitted use, you will need to obtain permission directly from the copyright holder.

The Next Big Thing: A Preamble to Urban Atrocities in Four Acts

Ariana Markowitz

> Slow violence does not persist due to a lack of arresting stories…but because those stories do not *count*, thus rendering certain populations and landscapes vulnerable to sacrifice.
> —Thom Davies, "Slow Violence and Toxic Geographies: 'Out of Sight' to Whom?".

Act One: Flint

"Hard to Spot"

In 2011, the state of Michigan was still reeling from the global financial crisis of 2008–2009. With multiple municipalities in economic distress, the state tabled a law to enable the appointment of an "emergency

A. Markowitz (✉)
University College London, London, UK
e-mail: ariana.markowitz@gmail.com

© The Author(s) 2026
R. Locke et al. (eds.), *Identity-Based Mass Violence in Urban Contexts*, Palgrave Studies in Victims and Victimology, https://doi.org/10.1007/978-3-031-98068-8_8

manager" who would sit atop local elected representatives in any municipality at risk of "financial emergency." Flint, a small city near Detroit, went into emergency management in November, the same day residents re-elected Mayor Dayne Walling.[1] Residents collected signatures to demand that the emergency management law be put to a vote, and they rejected it a year later when it was.[2] The state responded by passing a similar law with a different name.[3]

Under emergency management, Flint's water supply became inconsistent, with community organizations intervening to ensure access.[4] Then, in 2014, to cut costs, the emergency manager opted to begin pumping the city's water from the Flint River instead of the Detroit River but without implementing anti-corrosion measures that scientists advised.[5] This marked the start of 18 months of state-sanctioned contamination of the city's water supply, killing at least 12 and perhaps up to 70 people in a low-income city with a majority Black population in the mostly white state of Michigan despite concerted resident activism. "Within Flint, it is striking how the efforts of academic and medical institutions to resolve the emergency have been nationally visible," note Jennifer E. Johnson and Kent Key in their work with the Flint Water Community Narrative Group, "but the efforts of African-American community residents, which predated the academic efforts by at least a year, have been nearly invisible in the press, academic publications, and in public discourse."[6] The Michigan Civil Rights Commission's final report on the public hearings on the water crisis in 2016 concluded, "The people of Flint have been subjected to unprecedented harm and hardship, much of it caused by structural and systemic discrimination and racism that have corroded your city, your institutions, and your water pipes, for generations."[7] Dan Levy was the commission's director of law and policy during the hearings. "In theory, because things happen over a longer period, we should be able to make change more than we would in those isolated incidents," he reflected four years later. "The doors for doing good should be wider and more available, but they're hard to spot."[8]

Echoing Levy, scholars often use metaphors to illuminate the "hidden" impact of structural violence. Maren Ulriksen de Viñar highlights urban trauma's "marks and inscriptions" that sink into residents' skin and thread through the fabrics of their places.[9] Karen E. Till describes how violence and exclusion leave "wounded cities" in their wake.[10] Structural violence "may be seen as about as natural as the air around us," cautions Johan Galtung,[11] while Ann Laura Stoler amplifies the "lower frequencies" of being on the wrong side of "interior frontiers."[12] Bruce B. Lawrence and Aisha Karem have a more assertive take: "If given time and repetition...[violence] becomes routine, part of the air, and one learns how to breathe it without being asphyxiated."[13] Slow violence, which is ossified structural violence, "occurs gradually and out of sight," explains Rob Nixon, who coined the term. It is "a violence of delayed destruction that is dispersed across time and space, an attritional violence that is typically not viewed as violence at all."[14] When the US government declared a state of emergency in Flint in January 2016, the disregard and dismissal that residents endured became visible to everyone else, "like an enormous rock in a creek, impeding the free flow, creating all kinds of eddies and turbulences."[15]

Because structural violence is a precondition for atrocity violence,[16] preventing atrocities demands moving "beyond the optical facade of immediate peril."[17] One way to do that is by forefronting the lived experience of people "weathering"[18] the symptoms of structural and slow violence who are "best placed to witness its gradual injuries."[19] But adding the role of witness to people who already experience everyday violence is a weighty burden, requiring that survivors narrate their experiences over and over so the rest of us can recognize and repair what they withstood.[20] The remaining acts in this chapter focus instead on concrete, physical things that target specific groups of people in US and UK cities: shade in Phoenix, lights in New York, and social housing in London.[21] These things enact the structural, sociospatial systems and processes of identity-based mass urban violence. If they are left unchecked, left unseen, we risk closing our eyes to the next big thing.

Act Two: Phoenix

"Abate the Nuisance"

In 2022, a group of residents and business owners in Phoenix, Arizona, sued the city for having "created, maintained, and/or failed to abate a public nuisance in a neighborhood in Phoenix informally referred to as 'The Zone.'" In its March 2023 finding in favor of the plaintiffs, the Superior Court of Arizona summarized the charges:

Plaintiffs base their action on allegations, many of which are undisputed, that there is a substantial portion of homeless individuals that have moved into the area and set up semi-permanent tent encampments on the public sidewalks, public grounds, and public rights of way. Plaintiffs allege, *inter alia,* that the City refuses to enforce criminal and quality-of-life laws prohibiting loitering, disturbing the peace, drunken and disorderly conduct, drug use, domestic violence, and obstruction of streets, sidewalks, and other public grounds inside the Zone.[22]

The Zone was the largest encampment of unhoused people in Arizona, home to some 1,000 residents at its peak and occupying close to 20 city blocks. It was near a human services campus where several organizations that provide support to unhoused people are based. Though the Zone had existed for years, it expanded in 2018 and 2019 when the city "intentionally stopped—or at least materially decreased—enforcement of criminal, health, and other quality-of-life statutes and ordinances" there.[23] The court additionally determined that violent crime, public drug use, property crime, sex work, and public indecency had all increased; that there were fire hazards, road obstructions, and a deterioration of the street environment; and that the area was a biohazard. On September 20, 2023, the court ordered Phoenix "to abate the nuisance" by November 4.[24]

The city began clearing the Zone in May 2023, at the start of the "heat season." During that summer, the temperature in Phoenix exceeded 110°F/43 °C for 31 consecutive days, shattering the previous record of 18. On 16 of those days, the nighttime temperature did not drop below 90°F/32°C. Maricopa County, where Phoenix is located, reported 645 heat deaths in 2023, representing an increase of 52 percent from 2022, which was previously the worst year on record for heat-related deaths in the county.[25] Unhoused people were disproportionately impacted: they accounted for 45 percent of the death toll, though fewer than 30,000 of the county's 4.2 million residents, or seven of every 1,000 people, are unhoused or experiencing periods of homelessness.[26]

"Heat has consequences for every aspect of urban life: it compromises critical urban infrastructure, lowers educational outcomes, increases preterm births, and reduces labor productivity," explain V. Kelly Turner and colleagues.[27] In their evaluation of municipal heat governance in the largest US cities, they found that cities plan for "extreme heat events" more than they strive to mitigate chronic heat exposure. This has parallels in other fields. In the 2016 Interpeace report *Assessing Resilience for Peace*, for example, the authors painted conflict as an "internal stressor," countering the view that conflict erupts because of external shocks.[28] Mirroring that tension between internal and external, city plans often overlook shade, which improves everyday lived experiences of heat but has little impact on saving lives in a heat wave, most cities' preferred indicator of public health in heat.[29] Adaptive capacity to heat declines with chronic exposure, so residents of neighborhoods with less shade suffer gradual and mounting consequences if they are unable to reduce that exposure.[30]

The urban heat island effect, in which asphalt and concrete absorb heat during the day and release it at night, makes cities hotter than rural areas.[31] The growth of Phoenix in the mid-twentieth century, in part enabled by the expanding availability of air conditioners, coincided with the height of US suburbia as a form of metropolitan development.[32] This form is characterized by the proliferation of residential neighborhoods composed of homes for single families where leisure, entertainment, and services are mostly reachable by car.[33] The 1950s saw a fourfold increase in Phoenix's population—and an 11-fold increase in its area.[34] As in other hot and dry cities around the world, reliance on air conditioning led to some abandonment of design principles for urban heat management,[35] and the hot air that air conditioner units emit compounds heat in the city.[36]

Urban heat islands also exist at the neighborhood scale in areas where there is less greenery and more pavement.[37] These neighborhoods are often structurally unequal: sidewalks are not shaded, cars are unaffordable for the people who live there, and public transport is inadequate.[38] Residents, who are disproportionately poor and not white, experience "thermal inequity."[39] In Phoenix, low-income residents chronicle the day-to-day grind of managing heat without shade. "The distance you would have to walk…is not far, but with the heat it's like an eternity to get there, and even though you have some shade, it's hot," reports one. "You feel the heat coming from the pavement and when the cars pass by you feel the hot air that they make. You feel that desperation when you arrive at the doctor's office, you're going in for one thing and they end up checking you for another thing." A second resident describes moving "in this weird zig-zag pattern to try and walk in the shade." According to Melissa Guardaro and colleagues, "Urban heat becomes a poverty trap the way that it is currently institutionalized."[40]

Sleeping in cars, on streets, in shop doorways, in parks, and in parking lots intensifies vulnerability to heat, but there has been limited research on the impact of heat on unhoused people. Based on work they did in Columbus Park, an unhoused encampment in San José, California, C. J. Gabbe and colleagues find that "unhoused people experience thermal inequity in that they disproportionately live in areas with relatively higher temperatures."[41] In Columbus Park, despite limited access to shade and water, residents prioritize stability and access to services even as they seek to relocate, sometimes multiple times in a day, in search of shade. At night, residents may sleep with their tent or car windows closed and may use stimulants to stay awake in case someone attempts to assault them or steal their belongings. The stress of heat may also aggravate interpersonal tensions.[42] According to a resident named Aaron, his neighbors "get a little more aggressive toward people when they're hot. They try to fight each other. I'm just like, 'don't fight, it's just gonna be more hot.'" Nonetheless, they remain in the encampment because, according to Sara, another resident, "There is nowhere else to go."[43] These decisions deepen risks to their health.

In addition, residents may be unwilling or unable to access assistance, including cooling centers or shelters. Sara notes that some residents "are using, they are drinking, and don't want to leave. They feel safe in their area." She continues: "I've seen people that are so out of it from using and drinking. Some people don't even know where they are. So finding a cooling center would be impossible for them."[44] Cooling centers and shelters may also have curfews and rules against intoxication and keeping pets, and insufficient space for personal effects, and they may require people to show identification, all potential deterrents to service use.[45] In its September 2023 ruling, the Superior Court of Arizona turned the city's findings about barriers to service against it: "The City's study further confirms the finding that a sizable percentage of the individuals in the Zone are service resistant and voluntarily choose to live on the street without rules and restrictions."[46] The narrative that unhoused people are "service-resistant," a term the city cautions against using,[47] finds purchase within the unhoused community too. In response to a question about why unhoused people might not use municipal cooling centers in San José, Steven, a Columbus Park resident, replied: "Well, because they have rules and people don't like to follow rules. That is why you have so many homeless people out there. They would rather do their own thing and not follow any rules except their own."[48] Joe, a 62-year-old living on the streets of Phoenix since at least 2022, has repeatedly declined housing assistance. "I don't want to be dependent," he explains. He aspires "to spread my wings. Sleep on Mother Earth."[49]

In September 2023, the court denounced city personnel for appearing "utterly indifferent to the plight of the City's constituent property owners, their families, and small business owners that are attempting to make a living."[50] In response, the City Council voted to temporarily rezone a nearby light industrial area as an "outdoor campground," allowing up to 300 people to live there for up to three years.[51] The site began accepting residents in November, six months after the city began moving people out of the Zone. It has restrooms, showers, shade, indoor spaces for heat and cold relief, access to water, and 24-hour security. David Hondula, the director of Phoenix's Office of Heat Response and Mitigation—the first publicly funded position of its kind in the country—concedes, "The multifaceted nature of the challenge for the unsheltered community remains at the top of mind. It's not like there's one singular answer for all the different circumstances that folks are in."[52]

Indeed, local and national organizations are working many angles to address the vulnerabilities that unhoused residents face, ranging from accountability and enforcement to support and education. In June 2024, the US Department of Justice (DOJ) released the results of its three-year investigation into the Phoenix Police Department, or PhxPD. According to the DOJ, the PhxPD failed to uphold a 2019 ruling by the US Court of Appeals for the Ninth Circuit barring police from citing people for sleeping on public property when they have nowhere else to go.[53] "A person's constitutional rights do not diminish when they lack shelter," the report warned.[54]

A few weeks after the report's release, the US Supreme Court overturned the lower court's ruling. Writing for the majority, Justice Neil Gorsuch cited a brief from Phoenix. The Ninth Circuit Court "'paralyze[d]' even commonsense and good-faith efforts at addressing homelessness," according to the city, "prevent[ing] local governments from pursuing 'effective solutions to this humanitarian crisis while simultaneously protecting the remaining community's right to safely enjoy public spaces.'"[55] Elected leaders were cautiously optimistic about the ruling, with Mayor Kate Gallego expressing appreciation that the decision "provides the necessary clarity we need" to issue citations failing all else. Elsewhere in the state, officials questioned the ruling. "Let me be clear, when criminal behavior is afoot, we have and will continue to hold people accountable," explained Shawndrea Thomas from the Pima County Attorney's Office. "But arresting people for sleeping outside is not the way. While the Supreme Court might tolerate cruelty, our community does not."[56]

Meanwhile, community organizations were ramping up in preparation for another heat season in 2024. Circle the City, which provides mobile medical care for unhoused Phoenix residents, started an IV hydration program to assist people who are severely dehydrated. The street medicine team carries bags of saline solution everywhere they go so they can assist people who are unable or unwilling to go to the emergency department.[57] In addition, the Urban Heat Leadership Academy in Maricopa County launched its fourth cohort in June 2024. Using a social justice lens, the academy provides "knowledge, resources and skills to advocate for greener, healthier and cooler communities" in English and Spanish for free to county residents. "Our goal has been to plant more trees in the neighborhood," explains Silverio Ontiveros in a promotional video for the program. "We've planted probably like 14 fruit trees."[58]

Act Three: New York

"Because These Are Projects"

"I'm very happy to be here at the Wagner Houses as we start on a major set of initiatives to help residents of public housing, to make their lives better, to make their lives safer," announced Bill de Blasio six months after he became mayor of New York City in January 2014.

One of the biggest things we're going to act on is safety lighting. So there are too many parts of developments that are not in the nighttime hours safe to residents, in part because they're not well lit. Now we're already adding a lot of resources in terms of NYPD [New York Police Department] presence. But as [NYPD] Chief Gomez will tell you, the officers depend on being able to see what's going on. They know a well-lit environment creates an atmosphere of safety, it makes it harder for those who are doing the wrong thing to go about that. It makes it easier for law-abiding citizens to have a better experience.[59]

In the first stage of the Omnipresence program, the city installed 150 light towers across 15 high-crime areas of public housing developments. Each tower emitted 600,000 lumens, equivalent to 200 car headlights.[60] The temperature of the lights exceeded guidelines from the American Medical Association, which warn that high-intensity LED lighting has detrimental impacts on human and environmental health and can cause road hazards.[61] Alberto Barberá and Berta Teixidó, lighting designers from Barcelona, agree that access to darkness and having sight of the night sky are fundamental for the well-being of urban residents.[62] Shawna M. Nadybal and her colleagues warn that "the excessive use of artificial light at night is an emergent, rapidly intensifying environmental hazard known to disturb sleep patterns, trigger mental illness, and increase risks of various cancers in humans."[63]

The first environmental justice study of excessive exposure to ambient light at night in the United States found in 2020 that neighborhoods with more Asian, Latino, and Black people, and more renters than homeowners, have less access to darkness.[64] A study in 2023 confirmed these findings, concluding that people living in the most vulnerable parts of the United States are exposed to nearly 2.5 times more artificial light than people living in the least vulnerable areas of the country.[65] Nadybal and her colleagues attribute this to, first, "a concentration of residentially undesirable land use activities, which often emit high levels of artificial light at night" in poorer and nonwhite areas. Second, they note that renters have less power to contest planning initiatives, so "privileged rather than socially disadvantaged neighborhoods are more likely to experience darkened nights."[66] They predict this will worsen as access to darkness becomes more desirable.

There is a long history of using light to exert control over stigmatized populations and aid in policing and surveillance while claiming to safeguard residents from crime.[67] In the United States, white colonial administrators in the 1700s implemented "lantern laws" that required Black, mixed-race, and Indigenous people to carry a light outside at night to prevent them from gathering to plot a rebellion. Any white person could report someone for failing to comply with the law, and the consequences for violating it included physical punishment.[68] In Khayelitsha, an apartheid-planned township outside of Cape Town, South Africa, the military installed 40-meter high-mast lighting that shines 200-meter-wide spotlights during its 1980s occupation of townships. The military hoped the lights would improve surveillance while convincing Black residents that the state was committed to their protection.[69] In 2017, Dalli Weyers from the Cape Town-based Social Justice Coalition explained that Cape Town's own guidelines recommend avoiding "high-mast lights that cast dark shadows." Yet, a map from the city's Geographic Information Systems department indicated that historical Black African townships are mostly lit this way and "'effective public lighting' is almost entirely reserved for main roads, thoroughfares and other communities."[70] The coalition organized marches in 2019 calling on the city to share its lighting plans for townships. They also demanded that the plans include street-level lighting that would not cast shadows, according to the late gender justice advocate Nontando Mhlabeni. "We get raped and robbed while the mast lights are on," she said.[71] When Mayor de Blasio announced the launch of the Omnipresence program in New York, he boasted of "150 [light] towers to light up the areas that have previously been obscure and problematic, and make it easier for the NYPD to do its job."[72] The journalist and researcher John Surico questioned the mayor's characterization. "[I]t's stop-and-frisk 2.0," Surico wrote in *Vice* in 2014. "Omnipresence just adds surveillance while cutting back on actual interactions, so as to avoid bad PR."[73]

"Particularly harsh lighting has often been used in lower-income neighborhoods in part because of a belief that both darkness and poverty breed criminality," explains Mo Speller in "A History of Urban Inequality and Street Lighting in Baltimore."[74] As a result, residents and visitors in privileged spaces can enjoy "atmosphere" while people elsewhere cannot. The urban lighting scholars Joanne Entwistle and Don Slater witness the primacy of "safety" and "security" in decisions about lighting in a social housing development in central London. There, the aim of "safe" lighting is to protect residents from physical injury. Quality lighting, in contrast, is best avoided "because it might enable junkies to locate their veins" the same way that illuminating green spaces or installing seating "might attract undesirables." In these developments, lighting is "regulatory and disciplinary," places where "functional lighting defined social spaces solely as incipient problem spaces, coded for inequality" while reproducing it.[75] Separate departments with separate budgets manage internal and external spaces bound by different lighting standards, inhibiting a coherent strategy across an area. The standards fail to account for spaces that fulfill both public and private needs. Where categories are blurred, authorities opt for technical compliance rather than "destabilis[ing] practical assumptions (widely shared by institutions like the police) that brightness secures safety."[76]

Excessive lighting in urban spaces occurs partly because light is fluid. "Light spills and bleeds outside of its intended area, flooding adjacent spaces, overlapping with neighbouring designs and schemes," observe Entwistle and Slater. "This bleeding plays a significant part in the ratcheting up of light levels in cities: an over-lit area casts adjacent spaces into comparative darkness, making them feel too dark and thus 'unsafe,' and putting pressure to increase their lighting in order to compete."[77] This "arms race" can backfire, however, as it did at another public housing development in London where residents backpedaled on lighting that their local authority had installed at their request. When they saw the lights in place, they feared that they were so bright that surrounding areas might read their development as a problem area. Only a problem area, they reasoned, would have such bright lighting.[78]

Back in New York, the city rolled out light towers in 25 other neighborhoods after an evaluation of the first six months of Omnipresence found that crime had dropped by more than a third across the pilot areas. The authors of the evaluation defined success as reductions in six of the FBI's eight "index crimes": criminal homicide, robbery, aggravated assault, burglary, larceny-theft, and motor vehicle theft.[79] They excluded rape and arson "due to data constraints."[80] The evaluation reproduced the tendency to reduce lighting to "an economic and technical equation to be solved within a functionalist and technocratic framework"[81]—meeting the required standards for the lowest possible cost.

The New Yorker filmed a mini-documentary on Omnipresence in one of the pilot developments in the Bronx. The film crew did all the filming at night without having to use any additional lighting because the light towers were so bright. "I don't think the lights are gonna go away because these are projects," a young woman muses to the camera, "and usually people think bad things when they think about projects."[82]

Act Four: London

"Nothing out of the Ordinary"

Lee Chapman moved in with his partner in May 2014 as the building's nonprofit landlord was beginning a major renovation. Their apartment was on the 22nd floor of a 24-story tower block of mostly social housing in the London borough of Kensington and Chelsea, one of the wealthiest, and most unequal, municipalities in the United Kingdom. As part of the two-year renovation, constructors installed cladding, an outer shell that can enhance a building's energy efficiency and appearance. Residents suspected that the latter superseded the former in importance. In a 2017 blog post, they charged that the cladding was installed "to pimp [the building] up so that it wouldn't spoil the image of creeping gentrification that the Council is intent on creating."[83]

Some types of cladding make buildings more flammable. Chapman joined the leaseholders' association in early 2017 to demand action on fire safety issues that the refurbishment caused or exacerbated. His concerns were "made worse by the fact that our flat was on the 22nd floor, which was so high up in the building that the consequences in a fire could be terrible." Chapman and his neighbors sent emails to the tenant management organization (TMO), the borough government, and their member of parliament to convey their misgivings. "I am seriously concerned about how I will get out of this building alive in the event of a fire," Chapman wrote in one email. In another he highlighted the risks to his neighbors, some of whom had migrated from war zones. "There are many people in this building who are immobile, very young or suffer from mental health issues. I would ask for your undivided help in getting this matter resolved for all interested parties."

The replies that Chapman and his neighbors received were generic and uninformative. "Ultimately we were people who wanted to feel safe in our homes, and this should not have been perceived by the TMO as something which was annoying or bothersome. I also believe that as residents in a so-called 'social housing block,' we were treated as sub citizens or sub class." He concluded that the TMO did not know if the works they commissioned were sound "or that they knew that there were valid concerns about the safety of this proposal and were seeking to cover it up in some way, in order to avoid the cost of trying to ensure that it was done correctly and that we were safe."[84]

Chapman was in Malaysia on June 14, 2017, when his building went up in flames. The fire began in the kitchen of a fourth floor apartment and, according to a fire safety expert, "in terms of its origin and magnitude this one was nothing out of the ordinary."[85] Though firefighters arrived in minutes and extinguished the flames, the fire had already escaped the apartment. Propelled by combustible materials in the cladding, the blaze reached the top of the building, Grenfell Tower, within 20 minutes and consumed it within hours.[86] Chapman's partner survived, but 71 of their neighbors did not, and 70 others were injured.

The UK government established the Independent Grenfell Recovery Taskforce one month later to assist the Kensington and Chelsea Council. In response to the task force's first report, the council thanked the secretary of state for "much useful advice…as we work with the North Kensington community to recover from the Grenfell Tower fire tragedy."[87] News coverage of the fire in the immediate aftermath and in the years since sometimes echoes the council's language of "tragedy." More often, it refers to the fire as a "disaster," the product of hazards interacting with exposure, vulnerability, and capacity.[88] The preferred outcome or resolution of the disaster remains vague.[89]

But the human footprint in a disaster is not foregone,[90] which is why survivors of the fire advocate for alternative language. "No longer do I want to accept this as a tragedy," declared a participant in a public meeting that same July. "A tragedy is something that, you know, happens, that can't be prevented, that can't be foreseen; an atrocity is something that was well documented, well reported on prior to the absolutely horrendous situation that happened that morning. So, therefore, I think the language has to change already before we go any further." Lawyer Peter Herbert reinforced the survivor's claim. "The atrocity, and I accept that word because it is nothing less than an atrocity in London in this day and age. I have dealt with many, whether it be in Rwanda, Lebanon, Sicily, everywhere else, but this is one of the worst."[91]

That language has yet to catch on, however, because the intentionality of the loss of life in Grenfell Tower does not reside in the "cinematic violence"[92] of the conflagration. Instead, it lives in the structural violence that preceded it, an instance of "large-scale, systematic violence against civilian populations."[93] The script for *Grenfell: In the Words of Survivors*, which played at London's National Theatre during summer 2023, is taken verbatim from the public inquiry into the fire. In the *Guardian*'s review, journalist Mark Lawson accepts that the "local authority housing policy resulted in a sort of social cleansing with tenants—often diverse or disadvantaged—isolated and ignored in a corner of a super-rich postcode. Residents who raised concerns were told to be grateful for having a potential inferno over their heads."[94] Grenfell Tower was the worst residential fire in the United Kingdom since World War II.

Author's Postscript: Vienna

"Making an Exception"

On June 5, 2022, my partner, Julio, who is a citizen of El Salvador, was denied boarding on our flight from Vienna to London, where we live. The previous month, the UK government changed its migration policy for Salvadoran citizens such that UK residents, like Julio, needed a physical residence permit to travel, and Salvadoran tourists, who used to be able to enter the United Kingdom without a visa, needed to obtain one before arrival. A national government memorandum justifying the policy changes notes that the number of Salvadorans seeking asylum increased by 1,750 percent between 2017 and 2021, from 38 to 703 people.[95] For perspective, close to 90,000 people applied for asylum in the United Kingdom in 2022.[96]

When the government announced the new policy, it also announced a four-week grace period, ending June 9, for any travel booked before the law changed.[97] Though we reserved our flight in February, the airline demanded that Julio obtain a letter from the UK embassy in Vienna attesting to his compliance with the new policy. Airline staff forced us to leave the airport without providing assistance for transport, food, or lodging. It was late on Sunday night, and the next day was a bank holiday. As a US citizen, I was permitted to board, even though Julio and I share a visa. The airline rebooked us two days later, claiming they were "making an exception" for us. Thanking them for their assistance was demeaning, but we did it anyway.

As we fought to return home, we witnessed the inner workings of an opaque and unaccountable system. The UK government had moved the national border we were supposed to cross in London to the capital city of another country without any involvement by either city's government or its people. Bypassing the public sector entirely, the Austrian migration authority delegated enforcement of the UK border to an airline, a private company. That company's willful misapplication of UK policy put Julio at risk of violating the law for having followed it.

Since then, the UK government has repeatedly made decisions about migration for local governments and communities without them, quickening the decay of incendiary rhetoric into discriminatory policy. Parliament sought to deport asylum seekers to Rwanda, and when court challenges slowed the policy's implementation, the Home Office housed migrants on a barge that was contaminated with legionella. Police arrested 45 activists in South London in May 2024 for blocking a bus transporting asylum seekers to the Dorset port where the barge was moored.[98] Earlier the same year, despite censure from universities, the United Kingdom revoked the right of most international students to migrate with their partners or children, as Julio and I did in 2015 when I went back to school.[99] Cities and the communities that animate them can ease—or inflame—identity-based mass violence, but only if they have, or seize, the power to do so.

Being attentive to "things" enables us to see the structural underpinnings of identity-based mass violence in cities, like meteorologists tracking the waves that wash off tropical coasts to predict whether prevailing atmospheric conditions will enable the waves to swell into devastation. The disturbances are in our infrastructure, our homes, our interactions with public services and private companies, and our systems, processes, and documents. They mean to wear away specific types of people by discounting their knowledge, diminishing their voices, weakening their bodies, and limiting what their bodies can do.

In 2020 when I interviewed Alhakam Shaar, who has also contributed a chapter to this volume, about the siege of his hometown of Aleppo, he told me that at the beginning, "People refused to believe that you couldn't just cross" between east and west Aleppo. When the final crossing closed in late 2013, people had to drive seven hours outside the city and return from a different province. He described Aleppo's destruction as "gradual, of course,"[100] because, of course, being in the thick of it means you feel each page of the book being torn out before everyone else notices that the words binding the start to the end are gone.

Notes

1. Kristin Longley, "Dayne Walling Re-Elected Mayor as State Declares Financial Emergency in Flint," mlive, November 9, 2011, https://www.mlive.com/news/flint/2011/11/dayne_walling_re-elected_as_st.html.
2. Jennifer E. Johnson, Kent Key, and the Flint Water Community Narrative Group, "Credit Where Credit Is Due: Race, Privilege, and Injustice in Flint Water Responses," Supporting Testimony: Flint Water Crisis (Lansing: Michigan Civil Rights Commission, 2016), https://www.michigan.gov/mdcr/-/media/Project/Websites/mdcr/racial-equity/johnson-equity-in-flint.pdf?rev=ad63ec1b3b0047bf97e8d669aed2c88f&hash=FC667CA4458F1FB07A6F5584ACCD5216.
3. Michigan Legislature, Local Financial Stability and Choice Act, Pub. L. No. 436 (2013), https://www.legislature.mi.gov/Laws/MCL?objectName=MCL-ACT-436-OF-2012.
4. Johnson, Key, and Flint Water Community Narrative Group, "Credit Where Credit Is Due."
5. Matthew M. Davis et al., *Flint Water Advisory Task Force Final Report* (Lansing, MI: Flint Water Advisory Task Force, March 2016), https://www.michigan.gov/documents/snyder/FWATF_FINAL_REPORT_21March2016_517805_7.pdf.
6. Johnson, Key, and Flint Water Community Narrative Group, "Credit Where Credit Is Due," 3.
7. Dan Levy, *The Flint Water Crisis: Systemic Racism through the Lens of Flint* (Lansing, MI: Michigan Civil Rights Commission, February 17, 2017), v, https://www.michigan.gov/documents/mdcr/VFlintCrisisRep-F-Edited3-13-17_554317_7.pdf.
8. Dan Levy, online interview by Ariana Markowitz, September 16, 2020.
9. Maren Ulriksen de Viñar, "Political Violence: Transgenerational Inscription and Trauma," *International Journal of Applied Psychoanalytic Studies* 9, no. 2 (2012): 95–108, https://doi.org/10.1002/aps.1310.

10. Karen E. Till, "Wounded Cities: Memory-Work and a Place-Based Ethics of Care," *Political Geography* 31, no. 1 (January 2012): 3–14, https://doi.org/10.1016/j.polgeo.2011.10.008.
11. Johan Galtung, "Violence, Peace, and Peace Research," *Journal of Peace Research* 6, no. 3 (1969): 173.
12. Ann Laura Stoler, *Interior Frontiers: Essays on the Entrails of Inequality*, Heretical Thought (Oxford and New York: Oxford University Press, 2022).
13. Bruce B. Lawrence and Aisha Karem, eds., *On Violence: A Reader* (Durham, NC: Duke University Press, 2007), 5.
14. Rob Nixon, *Slow Violence and the Environmentalism of the Poor* (Harvard University Press, 2011), 2; see also Graeme Simpson, *The Missing Peace: Independent Progress Study on Youth and Peace and Security*, Secretary-General of the United Nations, February 23, 2018, https://www.youth4peace.info/ProgressStudy.
15. Galtung, "Violence, Peace, and Peace Research," 173.
16. Ariana Markowitz, "Big Events on a Small Scale: Exploring Identity-Based Mass Violence in Cities," Analysis and New Insights, Stanley Center for Peace and Security, December 21, 2020, https://stanleycenter.org/publications/urban-atrocities.
17. Nixon, *Slow Violence*, 62.
18. Arline T. Geronimus, *Weathering: The Extraordinary Stress of Ordinary Life in an Unjust Society* (New York: Little, Brown Spark, 2023).
19. Davies, "Slow Violence," 412.
20. Didier Fassin and Richard Rechtman, *The Empire of Trauma: An Inquiry into the Condition of Victimhood*, trans. Rachel Gomme (Princeton, NJ: Princeton University Press, 2009).
21. According to Shelter England, a housing justice organization, social housing homes are rented at rates that are genuinely affordable, secure, and stable.
22. Freddy Brown, et al. v. City of Phoenix, No. CV 2022-010439 (Superior Court of Arizona Maricopa County March 27, 2023).
23. Ibid., 3.

24. Freddy Brown, et al. v. City of Phoenix, No. CV 2022-010439 (Superior Court of Arizona Maricopa County September 20, 2023).
25. Meaghan Batchelor, 2023 *Heat Related Deaths Report*, Maricopa County Department of Public Health, April 2024, https://www.maricopa.gov/ArchiveCenter/ViewFile/Item/5820.
26. *Homelessness Trends Report: April-June 2023*, Maricopa Regional Continuum of Care, June 2023, https://azmag.gov/Portals/0/Homelessness/Reports/2023-Q2-Homelessness-Trends-Report.pdf.
27. V. Kelly Turner et al., "How Are Cities Planning for Heat? Analysis of United States Municipal Plans," *Environmental Research Letters* 17, no. 6 (June 2022): 1–21, https://doi.org/10.1088/1748-9326/ac73a9.
28. Graeme Simpson et al., "Assessing Resilience for Peace, Guidance Note," Interpeace, June 2, 2016, https://www.interpeace.org/resource/assessing-resilience-for-peace-guidance-note.
29. Turner et al., "How Are Cities Planning for Heat?".
30. V. Kelly Turner, Ariane Middel, and Jennifer K. Vanos, "Shade Is an Essential Solution for Hotter Cities," *Nature* 619, no. 7971 (July 2023): 694–97, https://doi.org/10.1038/d41586-023-02311-3.
31. Gordon M. Heisler and Anthony J. Brazel, "The Urban Physical Environment: Temperature and Urban Heat Islands," in *Urban Ecosystem Ecology*, ed. Jacqueline Aitkenhead-Peterson and Astrid Volder (Chichester: John Wiley & Sons, 2010), 29–56, https://doi.org/10.2134/agronmonogr55.c2.
32. Michael Konig, "Phoenix in the 1950s: Urban Growth in the 'Sunbelt,'" *Arizona and the West* 24, no. 1 (1982): 19–38.
33. Becky M. Nicolaides, "Suburbia and the Sunbelt," *OAH Magazine of History* 18, no. 1 (October 1, 2003): 21–26, https://doi.org/10.1093/maghis/18.1.21.
34. Konig, "Phoenix in the 1950s.'".
35. Tahani Ahmed Elbondira et al., "Impact of Neighborhood Spatial Characteristics on the Microclimate in a Hot Arid Climate—A Field Based Study," *Sustainable Cities and Society* 75

(December 1, 2021): 1–57, https://doi.org/10.1016/j.scs.2021.103273.
36. Francisco Salamanca et al., "Anthropogenic Heating of the Urban Environment Due to Air Conditioning," *Journal of Geophysical Research: Atmospheres* 119, no. 10 (2014): 5949–65, https://doi.org/10.1002/2013JD021225.
37. Sharon L. Harlan et al., "Neighborhood Effects on Heat Deaths: Social and Environmental Predictors of Vulnerability in Maricopa County, Arizona," *Environmental Health Perspectives* 121, no. 2 (February 2013): 197–204, https://doi.org/10.1289/ehp.1104625.
38. Melissa Guardaro et al., "Adaptive Capacity to Extreme Urban Heat: The Dynamics of Differing Narratives," *Climate Risk Management* 35 (January 1, 2022): 1–13, https://doi.org/10.1016/j.crm.2022.100415.
39. C. J. Gabbe et al., "Reducing Heat Risk for People Experiencing Unsheltered Homelessness," *International Journal of Disaster Risk Reduction* 96 (2023): 1–17, https://doi.org/10.1016/j.ijdrr.2023.103904.
40. Guardaro et al., "Adaptive Capacity," 8, 9.
41. Gabbe et al., "Reducing Heat Risk," 11.
42. See, e.g., Andreas Miles-Novelo and Craig A. Anderson, *Climate Change and Human Behavior: Impacts of a Rapidly Changing Climate on Human Aggression and Violence* (Cambridge: Cambridge University Press, 2022), https://www.cambridge.org/core/elements/climate-change-and-human-behavior/F64471FA47B8A6F5524E7DDDDE571D57; Kun Hou et al., "High Ambient Temperatures Are Associated with Urban Crime Risk in Chicago," *Science of the Total Environment* 856 (January 15, 2023): 158846, https://doi.org/10.1016/j.scitotenv.2022.158846; Rahini Mahendran et al., "Interpersonal Violence Associated with Hot Weather," *Lancet Planetary Health* 5, no. 9 (September 1, 2021): e571–72, https://doi.org/10.1016/S2542-5196(21)00210-2.
43. Gabbe et al., "Reducing Heat Risk," 10.
44. Ibid.

45. "Strategies to Address Homelessness," Phoenix Office of Homeless Solutions, 2020, https://www.phoenix.gov/solutions.
46. Freddy Brown, et al. v. City of Phoenix, Superior Court of Arizona Maricopa County September 20, 2023, 6.
47. *Strategies to Address Homelessness: Task Force Recommendations to the City Manager*, Phoenix Office of Homeless Solutions, April 6, 2022, https://www.phoenix.gov/solutions.
48. Gabbe et al., "Reducing Heat Risk," 11.
49. Kathy Ritchie, "Meet the Team That Delivers Health Care to Homeless Patients on the Streets of Phoenix," KJZZ, February 29, 2024, https://www.kjzz.org/2024-02-29/content-1872714-meet-team-delivers-health-care-homeless-patients-streets-phoenix.
50. Freddy Brown, et al. v. City of Phoenix, Superior Court of Arizona Maricopa County September 20, 2023, 16.
51. "Phoenix City Council Formal Meeting," September 20, 2023, YouTube, https://www.youtube.com/watch?v=dgbPqEXllpI.
52. Nina Lakhani, "Heat Deaths Surge in the US's Hottest City as Governor Declares Statewide 'Heat Emergency,'" *Guardian*, August 13, 2023, US News, https://www.theguardian.com/us-news/2023/aug/13/phoenix-heat-tsar-cooling-shelters-heatwaves.
53. Robert Martin v. City of Boise, No. 15-35845 (US Court of Appeals for the Ninth Circuit, April 1, 2019).
54. *Investigation of the City of Phoenix and the Phoenix Police Department*, US Department of Justice Civil Rights Division, June 13, 2024, 41, https://www.justice.gov/crt/media/1355866/dl?inline.
55. City of Grants Pass, Oregon v. Johnson et al., No. 23–175 (Supreme Court of the United States June 28, 2024).
56. Taylor Seely and Miguel Torres, "Phoenix Reacts to Supreme Court Ruling Clearing Its Homeless Camping Ban. What's Known," *Arizona Republic*, June 28, 2024, https://www.azcentral.com/story/news/local/phoenix/2024/06/28/supreme-court-ruling-clears-way-for-phoenix-to-enforce-camping-ban-homeless/74246396007.

57. Kathy Ritchie, "To Combat Heat Deaths, Phoenix Nonprofit Will Offer IV Hydration to Unsheltered People," KJZZ, May 24, 2024, https://www.kjzz.org/2024-05-24/content-1880885-combat-heat-deaths-phoenix-nonprofit-will-offer-iv-hydration-unsheltered-people.
58. "Application Open for the Fourth Cohort of Urban Heat Leadership Academy," Nature Conservancy, April 17, 2024, https://www.nature.org/en-us/newsroom/uhla-fourth-cohort.
59. "Transcript: Mayor Announces Plan to Make NYC's Neighborhoods and Housing Developments Safer," Official Website of the City of New York, July 8, 2014, http://www.nyc.gov/office-of-the-mayor/news/338-14/transcript-mayor-de-blasio-plan-make-new-york-city-s-neighborhoods-housing.
60. Nadia Hallgren and David Kortava, "The Controversial Floodlights Illuminating New York City's Public-Housing Developments," *New Yorker*, June 30, 2021, https://www.newyorker.com/culture/the-new-yorker-documentary/the-controversial-floodlights-illuminating-new-york-citys-public-housing-developments.
61. American Medical Association, "AMA Adopts Guidance to Reduce Harm from High Intensity Street Lights," American Medical Association, June 14, 2016, https://www.ama-assn.org/press-center/press-releases/ama-adopts-guidance-reduce-harm-high-intensity-street-lights.
62. Alberto Barberá and Berta Teixidó, "Urban-Centric Lighting Task Group: Tactical Lighting as an Innovation Strategy," *IOP Conference Series: Earth and Environmental Science* 1099, no. 1 (November 2022): 012043, https://doi.org/10.1088/1755-1315/1099/1/012043.
63. Shawna M. Nadybal, Timothy W. Collins, and Sara E. Grineski, "Light Pollution Inequities in the Continental United States: A Distributive Environmental Justice Analysis," *Environmental Research* 189 (October 1, 2020): 2, https://doi.org/10.1016/j.envres.2020.109959.
64. Nadybal, Collins, and Grineski, "Light Pollution Inequities."

65. Qian Xiao et al., "Artificial Light at Night and Social Vulnerability: An Environmental Justice Analysis in the U.S. 2012–2019," *Environment International* 178 (August 1, 2023): 108096, https://doi.org/10.1016/j.envint.2023.108096.
66. Nadybal, Collins, and Grineski, "Light Pollution Inequities," 8.
67. Nadybal, Collins, and Grineski, "Light Pollution Inequities."
68. Simone Browne, *Dark Matters: On the Surveillance of Blackness* (Durham, NC: Duke University Press, 2015).
69. Stephanie Briers, "The Violence of Lighting in Khayelitsha," *Architectural Review*, September 8, 2021, https://www.architectural-review.com/essays/the-violence-of-lighting-in-khayelitsha.
70. Dalli Weyers, "Lights, Toilets, Taxis - Situational Crime Prevention Failures in Khayelitsha," SaferSpaces (blog), May 15, 2017, https://www.saferspaces.org.za/blog/entry/lights-toilets-taxis-situational-crime-prevention-failures-in-khayelit.
71. Vincent Lali, "Marchers Call for Better Street Lighting," GroundUp News, February 20, 2019, https://groundup.org.za/article/marchers-call-better-street-lighting.
72. "Transcript: Mayor Announces Plan."
73. John Surico, "Omnipresence Is the Newest New York Police Tactic You've Never Heard Of," *Vice*, October 21, 2014, https://www.vice.com/da/article/vdpq7m/omnipresence-is-the-newest-nypd-tactic-youve-never-heard-of-1020.
74. Mo Speller, "A History of Urban Inequality and Street Lighting in Baltimore," in *Signal Station North Lighting Guidebook* (Baltimore: Neighborhood Design Center, 2021), 55, https://signalstationnorth.com/wp-content/uploads/2021/11/SSN_Lighting_Guidebook.pdf.
75. Joanne Entwistle and Don Slater, "Making Space for 'the Social': Connecting Sociology and Professional Practices in Urban Lighting Design," *The British Journal of Sociology* 70, no. 5 (2019): 5, 10, 13, https://doi.org/10.1111/1468-4446.12657.
76. Ibid., 11.
77. Joanne Entwistle and Don Slater, "Light as Material/Lighting as Practice: Urban Lighting and Energy," *Science Museum Group*

Journal, (Spring 2018), https://journal.sciencemuseum.ac.uk/article/urban-lighting-and-energy.
78. Lauren Dandridge, "Responsible Lighting at Night: Bridging the Inequality Gap," accessed August 18, 2023, https://www.designlights.org/news-events/events/webinar-bridging-the-inequality-gap.
79. FBI: UCR, "2019 Crime in the United States: Offense Definitions," FBI: UCR, 2019, https://ucr.fbi.gov/crime-in-the-u.s/2019/crime-in-the-u.s.-2019/topic-pages/offense-definitions. Note that since the evaluation was published in 2022, the FBI has added a ninth index crime: human trafficking.
80. Aaron Chalfin et al., "Reducing Crime through Environmental Design: Evidence from a Randomized Experiment of Street Lighting in New York City," *Journal of Quantitative Criminology* 38, no. 1 (March 1, 2022): 138, https://doi.org/10.1007/s10940-020-09490-6.
81. Entwistle and Don Slater, "Light as Material."
82. Hallgren and Kortava, "Controversial Floodlights."
83. Grenfell Action Group, "Grenfell Tower—The KCTMO Culture of Negligence," Grenfell Action Group blog, June 19, 2017, https://grenfellactiongroup.wordpress.com/2017/06/19/grenfell-tower-the-kctmo-culture-of-negligence.
84. Lee Jonathan Chapman, "Witness Statement," The Grenfell Tower Public Inquiry (London, February 2020), 5–6, 7, 8, 8–9, https://www.grenfelltowerinquiry.org.uk/evidence/lee-chapman.
85. Martin Moore-Bick, *Report of the Public Inquiry into the Fire at Grenfell Tower on 14 June 2017*, Grenfell Tower Inquiry (London, October 2019), 3, https://www.grenfelltowerinquiry.org.uk/phase-1-report.
86. Moore-Bick, *Report of the Public Inquiry*."
87. *Independent Grenfell Recovery Taskforce: Initial Report RB Kensington and Chelsea Response to Secretary of State* (London: Royal Borough of Kensington and Chelsea, November 1, 2017), https://www.rbkc.gov.uk/newsroom/initial-report-independent-grenfell-recovery-taskforce.

88. UN Office of Disaster Risk Reduction, "Sendai Framework Terminology on Disaster Risk Reduction: Disaster," 2019, https://www.undrr.org/terminology/disaster.
89. Maria Laura Frigotto, Mitchell Young, and Rómulo Pinheiro, "Resilience in Organizations and Societies: The State of the Art and Three Organizing Principles for Moving Forward," in *Towards Resilient Organizations and Societies: A Cross-Sectoral and Multi-Disciplinary Perspective*, ed. Rómulo Pinheiro, Maria Laura Frigotto, and Mitchell Young (Berlin: Springer International, 2022), 3–40, https://doi.org/10.1007/978-3-030-82072-5_1.
90. Ksenia Chmutina and Jason von Mending, "A Dilemma of Language: 'Natural Disasters' in Academic Literature," *International Journal of Disaster Risk Science* 10 (2019): 283–92, https://doi.org/10.1007/s13753-019-00232-2.
91. "Public Meeting" (London, July 20, 2017), 34–35, 49, https://assets.grenfelltowerinquiry.org.uk/inline-files/Public-meeting-20-July-2017.pdf.
92. Davies, "Slow Violence," 410.
93. Scott Strauss, *Fundamentals of Genocide and Mass Atrocity Prevention* (Washington, DC: United States Holocaust Memorial Museum, 2016), 40, https://www.ushmm.org/m/pdfs/Fundamentals-of-Genocide-and-Mass-Atrocity-Prevention.pdf.
94. "*Grenfell: In the Words of Survivors*—a Masterpiece of Forensic Fury," *Guardian*, July 21, 2023, https://www.theguardian.com/stage/2023/jul/21/grenfell-in-the-words-of-survivors-review-dorfman-theatre-london.
95. "Explanatory Memorandum to the Statement of Changes in Immigration Rules Presented to Parliament on 11 May 2022 (HC 17)" (London: Home Office, 2022), https://assets.publishing.service.gov.uk/media/627b7f84d3bf7f5c0d0462dd/Explanatory_memorandum_to_the_changes_in_immigration_rules_HC17__print-ready_PDF_.pdf.
96. Home Office, "How Many People Do We Grant Protection To?," 2023, https://www.gov.uk/government/statistics/immigration-system-statistics-year-ending-december-2022/how-many-people-do-we-grant-protection-to.

97. "Explanatory Memorandum."
98. Jess Warren and Chris Slegg, "Peckham: Arrests after Protesters Thwart Asylum Seekers' Coach Transfer," BBC News, May 2, 2024, London, https://www.bbc.com/news/uk-england-london-68943919.
99. Suella Braverman, "Immigration Update: Statement Made on 23 May 2023," Statements, Questions, and Answers, UK Parliament, May 23, 2023, https://questions-statements.parliament.uk/written-statements/detail/2023-05-23/HCWS800.
100. Alhakam Shaar, online interview by Ariana Markowitz, August 28, 2020.

References

American Medical Association. "AMA Adopts Guidance to Reduce Harm from High Intensity Street Lights." American Medical Association, June 14, 2016. https://www.ama-assn.org/press-center/press-releases/ama-adopts-guidance-reduce-harm-high-intensity-street-lights.

Barberá, Alberto, and Berta Teixidó. "Urban-Centric Lighting Task Group: Tactical Lighting as an Innovation Strategy." *IOP Conference Series: Earth and Environmental Science* 1099, no. 1 (November 2022): 012043. https://doi.org/10.1088/1755-1315/1099/1/012043.

Batchelor, Meaghan. *2023 Heat Related Deaths Report*. Maricopa County Department of Public Health, April 2024. https://www.maricopa.gov/ArchiveCenter/ViewFile/Item/5820.

Braverman, Suella. "Immigration Update: Statement Made on 23 May 2023." Statements, Questions, and Answers. UK Parliament, May 23, 2023. https://questions-statements.parliament.uk/written-statements/detail/2023-05-23/HCWS800.

Briers, Stephanie. "The Violence of Lighting in Khayelitsha." *Architectural Review*, September 8, 2021. https://www.architectural-review.com/essays/the-violence-of-lighting-in-khayelitsha.

Brown, Freddy et al. v. City of Phoenix, No. CV 2022-010439 (Superior Court of Arizona Maricopa County March 27, 2023).

Brown, Freddy et al. v. City of Phoenix, No. CV 2022-010439 (Superior Court of Arizona Maricopa County September 20, 2023).

Browne, Simone. *Dark Matters: On the Surveillance of Blackness*. Durham, NC: Duke University Press, 2015.

Chalfin, Aaron, Benjamin Hansen, Jason Lerner, and Lucie Parker. "Reducing Crime through Environmental Design: Evidence from a Randomized Experiment of Street Lighting in New York City." *Journal of Quantitative Criminology* 38, no. 1 (March 1, 2022): 127–57. https://doi.org/10.1007/s10940-020-09490-6.

Chapman, Lee Jonathan. "Witness Statement." The Grenfell Tower Public Inquiry. London, February 2020. https://www.grenfelltowerinquiry.org.uk/evidence/lee-chapman.

Chmutina, Ksenia, and Jason von Mending. "A Dilemma of Language: 'Natural Disasters' in Academic Literature." *International Journal of Disaster Risk Science* 10 (2019): 283–92. https://doi.org/10.1007/s13753-019-00232-2.

City of Grants Pass, Oregon v. Johnson et al., No. 23-175 (Supreme Court of the United States June 28, 2024).

Dandridge, Lauren. "Responsible Lighting at Night: Bridging the Inequality Gap." Accessed August 18, 2023. https://www.designlights.org/news-events/events/webinar-bridging-the-inequality-gap/.

Davies, Thom. "Slow Violence and Toxic Geographies: 'Out of Sight' to Whom?" *Environment and Planning C: Politics and Space* 40, no. 2 (April 10, 2019): 409-427. https://doi.org/10.1177/2399654419841063.

Davis, Matthew M., Chris Kolb, Lawrence Reynolds, Eric Rothstein, and Ken Sikkema. *Flint Water Advisory Task Force Final Report*. Lansing, MI: Flint Water Advisory Task Force, March 2016. https://www.michigan.gov/documents/snyder/FWATF_FINAL_REPORT_21March2016_517805_7.pdf.

Elbondira, Tahani Ahmed, Koji Tokimatsu, Takashi Asawa, and Mona G. Ibrahim. "Impact of Neighborhood Spatial Characteristics on the Microclimate in a Hot Arid Climate—A Field Based Study." *Sustainable Cities and Society* 75 (December 1, 2021): 1–57. https://doi.org/10.1016/j.scs.2021.103273.

Entwistle, Joanne, and Don Slater. "Light as Material/Lighting as Practice: Urban Lighting and Energy." *Science Museum Group Journal* (Spring 2018). https://journal.sciencemuseum.ac.uk/article/urban-lighting-and-energy.

Entwistle, Joanne, and Don Slater. "Making Space for 'the Social': Connecting Sociology and Professional Practices in Urban Lighting Design." *British Journal of Sociology* 70, no. 5 (2019): 2020–41. https://doi.org/10.1111/1468-4446.12657.

"Explanatory Memorandum to the Statement of Changes in Immigration Rules Presented to Parliament on 11 May 2022 (HC 17)." London: Home Office, 2022. https://assets.publishing.service.gov.uk/media/627b7f84d3bf7f5c0d0462dd/Explanatory_memorandum_to_the_changes_in_immigration_rules_HC17__print-ready_PDF_.pdf.

Fassin, Didier, and Richard Rechtman. *The Empire of Trauma: An Inquiry into the Condition of Victimhood*. Translated by Rachel Gomme. Princeton, NJ: Princeton University Press, 2009.

FBI: UCR. "2019 Crime in the United States: Offense Definitions," 2019. https://ucr.fbi.gov/crime-in-the-u.s/2019/crime-in-the-u.s.-2019/topic-pages/offense-definitions.

Frigotto, Maria Laura, Mitchell Young, and Rómulo Pinheiro. "Resilience in Organizations and Societies: The State of the Art and Three Organizing Principles for Moving Forward." In *Towards Resilient Organizations and Societies: A Cross-Sectoral and Multi-Disciplinary Perspective*. Edited by Rómulo Pinheiro, Maria Laura Frigotto, and Mitchell Young, 3–40. Berlin: Springer International, 2022. https://doi.org/10.1007/978-3-030-82072-5_1.

Gabbe, C. J., Jamie Suki Chang, Morayo Kamson, and Euichan Seo. "Reducing Heat Risk for People Experiencing Unsheltered Homelessness." International Journal of Disaster Risk Reduction 96 (2023): 1–17. https://doi.org/10.1016/j.ijdrr.2023.103904.

Galtung, Johan. "Violence, Peace, and Peace Research." *Journal of Peace Research* 6, no. 3 (1969): 167–91.

Geronimus, Arline T. Weathering: *The Extraordinary Stress of Ordinary Life in an Unjust Society*. New York: Little, Brown Spark, 2023.

Grenfell Action Group. "Grenfell Tower—The KCTMO Culture of Negligence." Grenfell Action Group blog, June 19, 2017. https://grenfellactiongroup.wordpress.com/2017/06/19/grenfell-tower-the-kctmo-culture-of-negligence.

Guardaro, Melissa, David M. Hondula, Jessica Ortiz, and Charles L. Redman. "Adaptive Capacity to Extreme Urban Heat: The Dynamics of Differing Narratives." *Climate Risk Management* 35 (January 1, 2022): 1–13. https://doi.org/10.1016/j.crm.2022.100415.

Hallgren, Nadia, and David Kortava. "The Controversial Floodlights Illuminating New York City's Public-Housing Developments." *New Yorker*, June 30, 2021. https://www.newyorker.com/culture/the-new-yorker-documentary/the-controversial-floodlights-illuminating-new-york-citys-public-housing-developments.

Harlan, Sharon L., Juan H. Declet-Barreto, William L. Stefanov, and Diana B. Petitti. "Neighborhood Effects on Heat Deaths: Social and Environmental Predictors of Vulnerability in Maricopa County, Arizona." *Environmental Health Perspectives* 121, no. 2 (February 2013): 197–204. https://doi.org/10.1289/ehp.1104625.

Heisler, Gordon M., and Anthony J. Brazel. "The Urban Physical Environment: Temperature and Urban Heat Islands." In *Urban Ecosystem Ecology*. Edited by Jacqueline Aitkenhead-Peterson and Astrid Volder, 29–56. Chichester: John Wiley & Sons, 2010. https://doi.org/10.2134/agronmonogr55.c2.

Homelessness Trends Report: April–June 2023. Maricopa Regional Continuum of Care, June 2023. https://azmag.gov/Portals/0/Homelessness/Reports/2023-Q2-Homelessness-Trends-Report.pdf.

Home Office. "How Many People Do We Grant Protection To?," 2023. https://www.gov.uk/government/statistics/immigration-system-statistics-year-ending-december-2022/how-many-people-do-we-grant-protection-to.

Hou, Kun, Liqiang Zhang, Xia Xu, Feng Yang, Baozhang Chen, Wei Hu, and Rui Shu. "High Ambient Temperatures Are Associated with Urban Crime Risk in Chicago." *Science of the Total Environment* 856 (January 15, 2023): 158846. https://doi.org/10.1016/j.scitotenv.2022.158846.

Independent Grenfell Recovery Taskforce: Initial Report RB Kensington and Chelsea Response to Secretary of State. London: Royal Borough of Kensington and Chelsea, November 1, 2017. https://www.rbkc.gov.uk/newsroom/initial-report-independent-grenfell-recovery-taskforce.

Investigation of the City of Phoenix and the Phoenix Police Department. US Department of Justice Civil Rights Division, June 13, 2024. https://www.justice.gov/crt/media/1355866/dl?inline.

Johnson, Jennifer E., Kent Key, and the Flint Water Community Narrative Group. "Credit Where Credit Is Due: Race, Privilege, and Injustice in Flint Water Responses." Supporting Testimony: Flint Water Crisis. Lansing: Michigan Civil Rights Commission, 2016. https://www.michigan.gov/mdcr/-/media/Project/Websites/mdcr/racial-equity/johnson-equity-in-flint.pdf?rev=ad63ec1b3b0047bf97c8d669aed2c88f&hash=FC667CA4458F1FB07A6F5584ACCD5216.

Konig, Michael. "Phoenix in the 1950s: Urban Growth in the 'Sunbelt.'" *Arizona and the West* 24, no. 1 (1982): 19–38.

Lakhani, Nina. "Heat Deaths Surge in the US's Hottest City as Governor Declares Statewide 'Heat Emergency.'" *Guardian*, August 13,

2023, US News. https://www.theguardian.com/us-news/2023/aug/13/phoenix-heat-tsar-cooling-shelters-heatwaves.

Lali, Vincent. "Marchers Call for Better Street Lighting." GroundUp News, February 20, 2019. https://groundup.org.za/article/marchers-call-better-street-lighting.

Lawrence, Bruce B., and Aisha Karim, eds. *On Violence: A Reader*. Durham, NC: Duke University Press, 2007.

Lawson, Mark. "*Grenfell: In the Words of Survivors*—a Masterpiece of Forensic Fury." Guardian, July 21, 2023. https://www.theguardian.com/stage/2023/jul/21/grenfell-in-the-words-of-survivors-review-dorfman-theatre-london.

Levy, Dan. *The Flint Water Crisis: Systemic Racism through the Lens of Flint*. Lansing, MI: Michigan Civil Rights Commission, February 17, 2017. https://www.michigan.gov/documents/mdcr/VFlintCrisisRep-F-Edited3-13-17_554317_7.pdf.

Longley, Kristin. "Dayne Walling Re-Elected Mayor as State Declares Financial Emergency in Flint." mlive, November 9, 2011. https://www.mlive.com/news/flint/2011/11/dayne_walling_re-elected_as_st.html.

Mahendran, Rahini, Rongbin Xu, Shanshan Li, and Yuming Guo. "Interpersonal Violence Associated with Hot Weather." *Lancet Planetary Health* 5, no. 9 (September 1, 2021): e571–72. https://doi.org/10.1016/S2542-5196(21)00210-2.

Markowitz, Ariana. *Big Events on a Small Scale: Exploring Identity-Based Mass Violence in Cities*." Analysis and New Insights. Stanley Center for Peace and Security, December 21, 2020. https://stanleycenter.org/publications/urban-atrocities.

Michigan Legislature. Local Financial Stability and Choice Act, Pub. L. No. 436 (2013). http://www.legislature.mi.gov/(S(d44tpsdd1xf0htnbarsxlwwc))/mileg.aspx?page=GetObject&objectname=mcl-act-436-of-2012.

Miles-Novelo, Andreas, and Craig A. Anderson. *Climate Change and Human Behavior: Impacts of a Rapidly Changing Climate on Human Aggression and Violence*. Cambridge: Cambridge University Press, 2022. https://www.cambridge.org/core/elements/climate-change-and-human-behavior/F64471FA47B8A6F5524E7DDDDE571D57.

Moore-Bick, Martin. *Report of the Public Inquiry into the Fire at Grenfell Tower on 14 June 2017*. Grenfell Tower Inquiry. London, October 2019. https://www.grenfelltowerinquiry.org.uk/phase-1-report.

Nadybal, Shawna M., Timothy W. Collins, and Sara E. Grineski. "Light Pollution Inequities in the Continental United States: A Distributive Environmental Justice Analysis." *Environmental Research* 189 (October 1, 2020): 1–12. https://doi.org/10.1016/j.envres.2020.109959.
Nature Conservancy. "Application Open for the Fourth Cohort of Urban Heat Leadership Academy," April 17, 2024. https://www.nature.org/en-us/newsroom/uhla-fourth-cohort.
Nicolaides, Becky M. "Suburbia and the Sunbelt." *OAH Magazine of History* 18, no. 1 (October 1, 2003): 21–26. https://doi.org/10.1093/maghis/18.1.21.
Nixon, Rob. *Slow Violence and the Environmentalism of the Poor*. Cambridge: Harvard University Press, 2011.
Official Website of the City of New York. "Transcript: Mayor Announces Plan to Make NYC's Neighborhoods and Housing Developments Safer," July 8, 2014. http://www.nyc.gov/office-of-the-mayor/news/338-14/transcript-mayor-de-blasio-plan-make-new-york-city-s-neighborhoods-housing.
"Phoenix City Council Formal Meeting," September 20, 2023. YouTube. https://www.youtube.com/watch?v=dgbPqEXllpI.
"Public Meeting." London, July 20, 2017. https://assets.grenfelltowerinquiry.org.uk/inline-files/Public-meeting-20-July-2017.pdf.
Ritchie, Kathy. "Meet the Team That Delivers Health Care to Homeless Patients on the Streets of Phoenix." KJZZ, February 29, 2024. https://www.kjzz.org/2024-02-29/content-1872714-meet-team-delivers-health-care-homeless-patients-streets-phoenix.
Ritchie, Kathy. "To Combat Heat Deaths, Phoenix Nonprofit Will Offer IV Hydration to Unsheltered People." KJZZ, May 24, 2024. https://www.kjzz.org/2024-05-24/content-1880885-combat-heat-deaths-phoenix-nonprofit-will-offer-iv-hydration-unsheltered-people.
Robert Martin v. City of Boise, No. 15-35845 (US Court of Appeals for the Ninth Circuit, April 1, 2019).
Salamanca, Francisco, Matei Georgescu, Alex Mahalov, Mohamed Moustaoui, and Meng Wang. "Anthropogenic Heating of the Urban Environment Due to Air Conditioning." *Journal of Geophysical Research: Atmospheres* 119, no. 10 (2014): 5949–65. https://doi.org/10.1002/2013JD021225.
Seely, Taylor, and Miguel Torres. "Phoenix Reacts to Supreme Court Ruling Clearing Its Homeless Camping Ban. What's Known." *Arizona Republic*, June 28, 2024. https://www.azcentral.com/story/news/local/phoenix/2024/06/28/supreme-court-ruling-clears-way-for-phoenix-to-enforce-camping-ban-homeless/74246396007.

Simpson, Graeme. *The Missing Peace: Independent Progress Study on Youth and Peace and Security*. Secretary-General of the United Nations, February 23, 2018. https://www.youth4peace.info/ProgressStudy.

Simpson, Graeme, Anupah Makoond, Patrick Vinck, and Phuong N. Pham. "Assessing Resilience for Peace—Guidance Note." Interpeace, June 2, 2016. https://www.interpeace.org/resource/assessing-resilience-for-peace-guidance-note.

Speller, Mo. "A History of Urban Inequality and Street Lighting in Baltimore." In *Signal Station North Lighting Guidebook* (Baltimore: Neighborhood Design Center, 2021). https://signalstationnorth.com/wp-content/uploads/2021/11/SSN_Lighting_Guidebook.pdf.

Stoler, Ann Laura. *Interior Frontiers: Essays on the Entrails of Inequality*. Heretical Thought. Oxford and New York: Oxford University Press, 2022.

"Strategies to Address Homelessness." Phoenix Office of Homeless Solutions, 2020. https://www.phoenix.gov/solutions.

Strategies to Address Homelessness: Task Force Recommendations to the City Manager. Phoenix Office of Homeless Solutions, April 6, 2022. https://www.phoenix.gov/humanservicessite/Documents/Task%20Force%20Recommendations%20to%20the%20City%20Manager-Final.pdf.

Strauss, Scott. *Fundamentals of Genocide and Mass Atrocity Prevention*. Washington, DC: United States Holocaust Memorial Museum, 2016. https://www.ushmm.org/m/pdfs/Fundamentals-of-Genocide-and-Mass-Atrocity-Prevention.pdf.

Surico, John. "Omnipresence Is the Newest New York Police Tactic You've Never Heard Of." *Vice*, October 21, 2014. https://www.vice.com/da/article/vdpq7m/omnipresence-is-the-newest-nypd-tactic-youve-never-heard-of-1020.

Till, Karen E. "Wounded Cities: Memory-Work and a Place-Based Ethics of Care." *Political Geography* 31, no. 1 (January 2012): 3–14. https://doi.org/10.1016/j.polgeo.2011.10.008.

Turner, V. Kelly, Ariane Middel, and Jennifer K. Vanos. "Shade Is an Essential Solution for Hotter Cities." *Nature* 619, no. 7971 (July 2023): 694–97. https://doi.org/10.1038/d41586-023-02311-3.

Turner, V. Kelly, Emma M. French, John Dialesandro, Ariane Middel, David M. Hondula, George Ban Weiss, and Hana Abdellati. "How Are Cities Planning for Heat? Analysis of United States Municipal Plans." *Environmental Research Letters* 17, no. 6 (June 2022): 1–21. https://doi.org/10.1088/1748-9326/ac73a9.

Ulriksen de Viñar, Maren. "Political Violence: Transgenerational Inscription and Trauma." *International Journal of Applied Psychoanalytic Studies* 9, no. 2 (2012): 95–108. https://doi.org/10.1002/aps.1310.
UN Office of Disaster Risk Reduction. "Sendai Framework Terminology on Disaster Risk Reduction: Disaster," 2019. https://www.undrr.org/terminology/disaster.
Warren, Jess, and Chris Slegg. "Peckham: Arrests after Protesters Thwart Asylum Seekers' Coach Transfer." BBC News, May 2, 2024, London. https://www.bbc.com/news/uk-england-london-68943919.
Weyers, Dalli. "Lights, Toilets, Taxis - Situational Crime Prevention Failures in Khayelitsha." SaferSpaces (blog), May 15, 2017. https://www.saferspaces.org.za/blog/entry/lights-toilets-taxis-situational-crime-prevention-failures-in-khayelit.
Xiao, Qian, Yue Lyu, Meng Zhou, Jiachen Lu, Kehe Zhang, Jun Wang, and Cici Bauer. "Artificial Light at Night and Social Vulnerability: An Environmental Justice Analysis in the U.S. 2012–2019." *Environment International* 178 (August 1, 2023): 108096. https://doi.org/10.1016/j.envint.2023.108096.
Zahran, Sammy, Shawn P. McElmurry, Paul E. Kilgore, David Mushinski, Jack Press, Nancy G. Love, Richard C. Sadler, and Michele S. Swanson. "Assessment of the Legionnaires' Disease Outbreak in Flint, Michigan." *Proceedings of the National Academy of Sciences* 115, no. 8 (February 20, 2018): E1730–39. https://doi.org/10.1073/pnas.1718679115.

Ariana Markowitz is an urban researcher and community-centered practitioner focused on methodology development, ethics, and organizational transformation in challenging contexts. She has worked in some 15 countries across five continents in government, academia, nonprofits, and the private sector.

Open Access This chapter is licensed under the terms of the Creative Commons Attribution-NonCommercial-NoDerivatives 4.0 International License (http://creativecommons.org/licenses/by-nc-nd/4.0/), which permits any noncommercial use, sharing, distribution and reproduction in any medium or format, as long as you give appropriate credit to the original author(s) and the source, provide a link to the Creative Commons license and indicate if you modified the licensed material. You do not have permission under this license to share adapted material derived from this chapter or parts of it.

The images or other third party material in this chapter are included in the chapter's Creative Commons license, unless indicated otherwise in a credit line to the material. If material is not included in the chapter's Creative Commons license and your intended use is not permitted by statutory regulation or exceeds the permitted use, you will need to obtain permission directly from the copyright holder.

"Empire Saved My Life"

Serena Wiebe and Alexander Turner

Serena Wiebe is a 19-year-old Bristolian of Jamaican heritage. She grew up in a racially and economically fractured city—among the United Kingdom's worst for social mobility—and her story illustrates the social, criminal, and financial drivers that ensnare and expose young people to the worst of urban violence. In 2023, Serena lost a much-loved childhood friend to one of a number of gang murders that briefly registered across the noise of the whole city. She believes recent gang violence exposes Bristol as a tale of two cities: on the one hand, it is a playground for the affluent; on the other hand, it is a war zone for the poor whose substandard living conditions and limited life chances make them vulnerable to gang exploitation (Fig. 1).

From Serena: Bristol is still segregated by race; as a dual-heritage female, I find some of the areas, classed as nice, difficult to be in. No

---

S. Wiebe (✉)
Empire Fighting Chance, Bristol, UK
e-mail: serena@empirefightingchance.org

A. Turner
Bristol, UK

Fig. 1 Serena sits with her nephew in front of the St. Paul's Advice Center, a charity that provides advice and resources to fight poverty and inequality in Bristol Photo by Alexander Turner

one looks like me, talks like me, and they seem to have their own code. Houses appear bigger, brighter, healthy cafes, shops, and you don't see drug dealing. They have supermarkets. When I walk into a beauty supply store, I am often followed by security staff. Our products are locked away, products for white hair aren't. This means I feel uncomfortable.

In the inner city, I see people who look like me, have similar experiences, but I also see litter, weapons, needles, cannisters, and open drug dealing. Houses are closer together, more run-down, and there are fast food places on each corner. We have corner shops (convenience stores) where we have to pay more.

Recently there has been a large increase in serious violence, including murders. These have all taken place in areas affected by inequality and exacerbated by not having opportunity and thinking everyone else is carrying weapons.

We aren't supported by the system; teachers don't look like me and often don't understand our culture so assume we are being aggressive.

The suspension rates for Black kids are much higher than for white kids. We all say exclusion leads to exploitation and mental health problems. I saw excluded people go from attending school daily to selling drugs.

As a Black person I know not to put my hood up or have hands in my pockets when I go anywhere, especially if I see the police. If people don't look like me how can they understand me?

Serena, now a successful sports coach with pioneering and internationally recognized Empire Fighting Chance (EFC), believes her story could have turned out very differently. Growing up in the poorer part of town in a broken family and tragically losing her brother to suicide when she was just 14, Serena was born exposed to the same violent tides she has seen drown many of her peers. Based in an inner-city boxing gym, EFC provides mental health support to the United Kingdom's most vulnerable young people. With EFC's help, Serena is rewriting her own story arc and coaching the youth behind her to do the same.

Here, with the help of EFC cofounders Martin Bisp, Jamie Sanigar, and Europe's first directly elected Black mayor, Marvin Rees of Bristol, Serena tells her story (Fig. 2).

> As a Black female, I have always struggled with feeling supported. People have always called me strong but have never asked if I was actually OK. These pictures are important to me because they represent inequality but also the power of community.

Serena spent much of her youth in St Paul's, an inner suburb of Bristol, as she had family there. It is an area that is home to much of the city's British African-Caribbean population, many of whom arrived in the 1950s and 1960s. The area's walls are home to seven large-scale murals dubbed "the seven saints of St Paul's"; the brightly colored paintings depict the seven Black role models who organized the area's legendary carnival. The carnival celebrated the successful 1968 bus boycott, which challenged discriminatory employment practices and led to the first equality laws in the United Kingdom.

Following a wave of police raids, riots, and shootings during the 1980s, St Paul's became an area that, in the minds of many, was inextricably linked to drug dealing and gang violence. Today, despite the usual

Fig. 2 Across the suburb of St. Paul's in Bristol, seven large murals depict Black role models who organized the first carnival to celebrate the bus boycott of 1968, which led to the United Kingdom's first equality laws Photo by Alexander Turner

forces of gentrification, it is still an area that struggles with poverty, deprivation, and a soaring crime rate. It was here where one summer's evening Serena's friend Eddie was stabbed to death just meters from his family and the house he grew up in. The streets here are what Serena describes as "front line," where street drug dealing is an open secret, visible to any passing visitor. Growing up, she witnessed things that would horrify children in more affluent areas, but she became used to that. Knife crime, drug safe houses, and the worst effects of drug addiction were part of her everyday landscape. Wearing her Empire hoodie has kept her safe; people know she is part of something that gives back to their community and therefore is left to do her thing.

Rather than judging her peers for their involvement in these trades, she can sympathize and understand what drove them to being involved in things such as drug dealing, recruiting young children to sell drugs, retail-based fraud, and street violence. "We're not making enough money to survive," says Serena. "If you're able to get a job, [employers] take the

Fig. 3 Martin Bisp (left) and Jamie Sanigar (right) started Empire Fighting Chance in 2006 in St. Paul's Photo by Alexander Turner

piss out of you because they want to pay you £4 an hour. A lot of these young people that I know have parents who are ill or don't make money; some don't have parents at all. Some of these young people even have to provide for their parents, which puts them in a shit position. How can you be paying a young person that amount of money? They also have to provide for a family, which leads them to do what? Selling drugs." She explains that for many young people growing up in this area, generational neglect and stigmatization have limited their life chances, their access to role models, and their access to alternative pathways before they were even born. "They live in a deprived area, and they feel they haven't really got any options. They have family members involved in gangs; gangs is the only thing that they know, which continues the violence" (Fig. 3)

Empire Fighting Chance was founded in St Paul's by Martin Bisp and Jamie Sanigar in 2006 when they witnessed two youths they vaguely knew dealing drugs in a park outside the boxing gym. They invited them into the amateur boxing session Martin was coaching—they wanted to

Fig. 4 Serena sits at a desk where she attended primary school, Sefton Park. The school offered her a place to feel secure at a time when her home life was very difficult Photo by Alexander Turner

understand the challenges these young people were facing and what was happening in their lives for them to be making these risky decisions. The following week, the young men came back and brought their friends along; within six weeks, Martin and Jamie were coaching 50 of the city's most vulnerable young people. Today EFC works with over 5000 young people each year. Martin's sentiments echo those of Serena's: "I've not yet met a 10-, 12-, or 13-year-old whose real life ambition is to be selling drugs or who wants to get involved in some of the situations they have been involved in. We have not yet met young people who have any desire to be mentally unwell. What happens is that their behavior can manifest itself in certain ways. If you look at the symptom of anger or criminal behavior, there are always underlying core problems. It may be chaotic home lives, it may be substance abuse by the parents, it could be domestic abuse, it could be sexual abuse. There is a whole series of factors that can lead into a behavior that becomes symptomatic, which then gets a young person labelled" (Fig. 4).

Unlike many of her peers, Sefton Park primary school was a form of salvation for Serena—a place to shelter from a difficult home life where, she says, she experienced things "no child my age should go through." She explains that as she moved around a lot as a child, she ended up going to a primary school that was not in her immediate area, in a more affluent part of the city. It was there she met Eddie, who was one of just three other Black students in her class. Eddie and Serena began a friendship that lasted up until his tragic death in 2023. Aged 19, he died in the hospital of multiple stab wounds inflicted just meters from his home (Fig. 5).

On June 7, 2020, antiracism protestors tore down the statue of slave trader Edward Colston (1636–1721) that had stood in the center of the city for 125 years. This catapulted the city into the center of a reckoning on institutional racism that swept the globe in response to the killing of George Floyd in the United States two weeks earlier. Debate raged internationally about the legitimacy of Bristol residents forcibly removing the statue of Colston, with UK Home Secretary Pritti Patel labeling the action "sheer vandalism." Many within the city took a more supportive view, including then Mayor Marvin Rees, who described the statue as an "affront" that he felt no sense of loss for. In the months and years that followed, city residents and institutions were left to reckon with their selves in relation to race and racism in their past and futures. "Racism isn't fixed in Bristol," says Serena. "Do we have more access to jobs? Are we living in a more equal society? Just because the statue is no longer there, that doesn't mean that the attitudes or the problems have gone away for us" (Fig. 6)

Rees, an ambassador for Empire Fighting Chance, has explained: "We have major race and class fractures within Bristol that are quite historic. Inequality in Bristol is stark: we've got all this wealth, but we've also got six areas that are in the top one percent of the most deprived in England. We have a nine-year life expectancy difference between the richest and poorest. Bristol West has amongst the highest number in higher education; Bristol South has amongst the lowest. Racism is not just about individual attitudes; racism is about the everyday structural inequalities" (Fig. 7)

When Serena was 14, her brother took his own life. After years of poor mental health for which he received little support, he went missing.

Fig. 5 Ground remains cracked where a statue of Edward Colston, a famous slave trader, was torn down in Bristol amidst global antiracism demonstrations that followed the murder of George Floyd in the United States in 2020 Photo by Alexander Turner

"Empire Saved My Life" 169

Fig. 6 Marvin Rees, former Mayor of Bristol, was the first directly elected Black Mayor of a European city and was created a life peer in February 2025 Photo by Alexander Turner

When he was found, he was dead. The effects on Serena were severe. "The system failed him," she says. "He should have had more support, but because we are poor and can't pay, we can't access help. He was hearing voices, had a history of mental health issues and previous suicide

Fig. 7 At Serena's secondary school, Fairfield High School, the flags of more than 80 countries hang in the atrium, representing the diverse backgrounds of staff and students Photo by Alexander Turner

Fig. 8 Serena has been working since she was 14; her job at a local Indian restaurant helped her avoid some of the economic reasons why her peers got involved in criminal activities Photo by Alexander Turner

attempts, but a GP only saw him once. The services also aren't suitable; if we would have known about Empire, I am sure he would still be alive."

"When it all happened, I went to school, and I just started [lashing out] There was one time where I went to the bathroom, and I had a massive mental breakdown and I kicked holes into the bathroom. My mental breakdown was so bad, I made a few of my classmates cry, and I made my teachers cry because I feel like they could see what I was going through." It was at this point where she felt the most vulnerable. "I felt the same way as him. I had this complex that I was turning into my brother. Outside my school, gang members used to hang out and they were recruiting. When you're not in the right head space you are so much more vulnerable to being involved in stupid things because you're trying to find a release. Luckily, I managed to stay away." (Fig. 8)

Serena has been working since she was 14. She had seen her mother working four jobs and inherited both this work ethic and an awareness of the economic pressures of modern life. When she was 16, motivated by

Fig. 9 Clifton Suspension Bridge is often viewed as a symbol for Bristol, but for many in the city, Serena says, it represents a division of class and opportunity Photo by Alexander Turner

a desire to ease some of her mother's financial burdens and to reduce the need to ask her for support, Serena got a job at an Indian restaurant. She says doing so helped her to resist some of the financial forces that may have seen her resort to criminal acts. The restaurant is based in a more affluent part of town, and she bonded with the Indian owner, who was also subjected to casual racism from the customers. "When I'm working, a lot of people ask me where I'm from. Why is it okay to randomly ask a Black person where they're from? Particularly when I am serving them." (Fig. 9)

Near to the restaurant is the iconic Clifton Suspension Bridge. For many it's the symbol of Bristol, but for Serena and many of her family and friends it represents the class divide within the city. "The suspension bridge is based in between Clifton and Leigh Woods," says Serena. They are two of the wealthiest areas of the country, and the life chances for children born there are significantly more encouraging than for those born in the poorer areas. "People like me tend to avoid areas like this

Fig. 10 Empire Fighting Chance gym and coaches offered Serena an alternative to therapy and counseling that was not working for her Photo by Alexander Turner

because when we're there we are looked at like we're not welcome. People from Clifton avoid areas such as St. Paul's and Easton due to their crime rate. When I was younger, I would hang out with my friends at the park in St Paul's, which hasn't changed or been repaired since I was a child. When we went on a family day out, we would go to Suspension Bridge Park, but every time we went there I felt out of place. I didn't see people that looked like me. We see buildings, parks with loads of new equipment that we haven't got. It makes us feel that Bristol doesn't care about us and that we don't matter. It's the same today—when I go to places like Clifton or the Suspension Bridge, I feel like a tourist in my own city." (Fig. 10)

After many years of therapy and counseling that Serena felt were largely ineffective, her therapist directed her to EFC. Though Serena's needs were complex and wide ranging, they were a set of issues that EFC is used to encountering in the young people it works with. "Young people arrive at our doors with a range of behavioral and emotional issues,

Fig. 11 Serena hugs her mother, Rackzon Hudson, at Empire Fighting Chance. She credits the organization with saving her life Photo by Alexander Turner

including anger, anxiety, depression and low self-esteem," says Martin. Adds Jamie, "We believe we can help anyone. The level of extremity has drastically changed over recent years. This is inner city. We're in an area of deprivation that is going through a bit of a funny change at the moment. A three-bed house will cost you over £300,000, so if you are growing up in this area with nothing—no role models, no mentors—it's practically impossible now for you to get on the property ladder. Youth services have been closed. There is nothing for them, and they are becoming more isolated." (Fig. 11)

When Serena walked through the doors at Empire, she felt at home. She started volunteering her time there and quickly became a valued and respected part of the team. After a while, she was promoted to a paid member of staff and was given the opportunity to work as a coach and mentor with vulnerable young people, many of whom are experiencing traumas similar to those she had encountered. "I can relate to these young people. I can give them advice on what I did and what I wish I had done differently in certain situations. I hope that I can be a role model for them. I don't feel like I've got my life completely sorted, but I can be truthful to them. I tell them you have to work your way up, but first you have to make sure you are on the right path," Serena says.

For Marvin, the positive impacts of the work Serena does through EFC are simple and can be felt all across the city. "The benefits to the wider city are pretty straightforward: a healthier population. You have young people who are less likely to become mentally unwell, who have more structure in their lives, and who are better able to develop their own talents, abilities, and ambitions in life. They are also less likely to become youth service users or engage in activities that take away the quality of life from other people."

Speaking as a coach, Serena wants the world to know "whatever you have been through in life, whatever you are going through—we can help you. At Empire, we are trying to find new ways to help young people and make sure that their voices are heard." Serena's own story shows that the results of EFC's work can be dramatic. In 2024, her work within the community was recognized by King Charles, who met with her to discuss national strategies for reducing youth violence. As with many other cities, the residents of Bristol are born into a story too often characterized by an inescapable segregation of wealth, education, and opportunity. However, based from a modest city center boxing gym, the 5000 young people who pass through Empire's doors each year are being encouraged and empowered to knock down these generational barriers and fight themselves into a fairer future.

It's a domino effect," says Serena. "If we can help one young person, then that young person can go on and help somebody else. My story shows that. If I could go back to my 13-year-old self now and tell her what I have done—she would probably pass out. That's what Empire has done for me. They saved my life.

Serena Wiebe has, at just 19 years old, established herself as a successful sports coach for the charity Empire Fighting Chance. Of Jamaican heritage, she was raised in the racially and economically fractured city of Bristol, UK, where she confronts the many structural and social challenges of urban violence.

Alexander Turner is a freelance photographer and journalist working in Bristol, UK. His clients include the *Guardian, the New York Times,* the BBC, and many other outlets.

Open Access This chapter is licensed under the terms of the Creative Commons Attribution-NonCommercial-NoDerivatives 4.0 International License (http://creativecommons.org/licenses/by-nc-nd/4.0/), which permits any noncommercial use, sharing, distribution and reproduction in any medium or format, as long as you give appropriate credit to the original author(s) and the source, provide a link to the Creative Commons license and indicate if you modified the licensed material. You do not have permission under this license to share adapted material derived from this chapter or parts of it.

The images or other third party material in this chapter are included in the chapter's Creative Commons license, unless indicated otherwise in a credit line to the material. If material is not included in the chapter's Creative Commons license and your intended use is not permitted by statutory regulation or exceeds the permitted use, you will need to obtain permission directly from the copyright holder.

Urban Mechanisms of Armed Violence: Exclusionary Boundaries and Acute Forms of Spatial Division

Antônio Jacinto Sampaio

Introduction

One of the seemingly contradictory facts about urban spaces is that they have been historically characterized as meeting points "for people to come together across multiple factional, socioeconomic, religious and ethnic divides to coalesce," and yet they are often marred by persistent—and sometimes intense—cycles of armed violence.[1] "No-go" areas—dangerous streets and neighborhoods—coexist side by side with glittering financial centers and wealthy residential areas. In the many global cities affected by such inequalities, residents have learned to navigate the fragmentation of the urban space brought about by violence, so as to bypass and avoid troubled areas. Although so-called normal life can continue alongside violence, risks and vulnerabilities are not equally shared but tend to concentrate in space with very real risks and limits imposed on certain populations.

A. J. Sampaio (✉)
King's College London, London, UK
e-mail: sampaio.antonio@gmail.com

The dominance of the analytical focus on states and the international system in analyses of security in our world has, until recently, relegated the urban space to a marginal role. A wave of scholars in urban studies, political science, strategic studies, sociology, and criminology has more actively challenged over the past two decades or so the view that cities are "inert receptacles" of peace and conflict dynamics, pointing out instead that they are "key elements in conflict—a target in attempts to destroy the fabric of a society, but also a necessary foundation" for peace.[2] This involvement of the urban space in, rather than just passive hosting of, conflict and violence has profound implications for global efforts to prevent and reduce violence. The urban space has specific drivers and mechanisms that affect the incentives, triggers, and social impact of violence. Of particular concern for scholars and practitioners in peace and security is how this reconceptualization of the urban space provides new insights about how—and where—certain communities are more or less vulnerable to intense and targeted violence, and what to do about it.

Identifying these dynamics specific to urban forms of violence has become a policy imperative given the rapid urbanization observed globally during the late twentieth and early twenty-first centuries, as opposed to broader violence dynamics from rural, national, or international perspectives. Alongside demographic trends, another major driver of policy and academic interest in urban dynamics of violence has been a broad perception of shifting characteristics in armed conflict that place cities as "crucial sites of political engagement," such as the insurgency against US-led forces in Iraq and (to add a more recent example) the conflict in Ukraine following the Russian invasion.[3]

One key recurring feature highlighted in numerous studies is the tendency of urban violence to fragment or divide the urban space through fear and insecurity.[4] This is not a coincidence, as it points to the original paradox highlighted just above: cities are broadly understood as places of cooperative social interaction, democratization, and industrialized economic development,[5] but prosperous areas can exist side by side with sites of intense violence. The occurrence of intense or protracted armed violence is a problem that is not sufficiently explained by the urban studies field, given its tendency to look at urbanization as an "a-political process."[6] Among the most prolific fields of recent urban violence research has been that focusing on the multiple local orders managed by nonstate armed groups, with relations to the central state and local populations ranging from collaborative to conflictive.[7] These violent actors and the security they claim to provide are often seen as legitimate, or at least legitimate enough to challenge the state's monopoly on legitimate violence, undermining state authority from the local level but ultimately contributing to "national state fragility."[8] Fragmentation of the urban space contains unique local political dynamics and broader national (and potentially international) implications.

This fragmentation points to what Emma Elfversson, Ivan Gusic, and Kristine Höglund have called the "spatiality of violence": the influence of spatial and political dynamics of urban areas in the shape and impact of armed violence. Central to this spatiality is the unequal distribution of violence among and within cities: political struggles tend to focus on control of key urban areas, whereas violence is unevenly distributed among microlocalities within each city.[9] The urban political space in contexts of armed violence comprises areas within the same municipal or metropolitan continuum with disparate experiences of vulnerability to violence—with some informal settlements, for instance, being exposed to oppressive forms of criminal governance or repressive policing while neighboring areas enjoy much safer environments.[10] It also involves the multiple state and nonstate actors competing or collaborating for the provision of security, rules, and services (from which profitable rents are extracted).

Urban fragmentation, especially in cities affected by protracted armed violence, involves the formation or intensification of boundaries, which is part of the aforementioned paradox—the urban coalescing tendency seemingly interrupted by the division of space reminiscent of national borders and sometimes enforced through violence by gangs, militias, insurgents, or parties to interstate wars. Drawing from a brief overview of the academic literature, this chapter identifies exclusionary boundaries linked to the urban space as a key mechanism of protracted urban violence, underpinning the separation between communities, security providers, and governance regimes. Accompanying this boundary activation mechanism is the separation of residents across political identities, which is sometimes implicit but carries life-or-death implications for people trying to access certain areas or living in pockets of exclusion from rule-of-law or democratic institutions. The chapter argues that boundary activation is a key mechanism through which violence infiltrates the urban space, producing long-lasting divisions, clustering criminal economies and armed actors, and making some areas safe and others profoundly vulnerable.

Departing from the volume's reflection on the specific formats of identity-based mass violence in cities, this chapter explores the meaning and roles of identity in the formation of boundaries, with a particular focus on the concept of political identity. The focus here is on what has been termed, in the context of this volume, "acute violence," defined as direct, overt acts of aggression that are intended to harm others (mostly in a physical form). This is a broad category, so the aim here is not to provide universally applicable theories or explanations. Instead, we draw from a methodological approach on specific mechanisms of social events (rather than broad universal causes) to reflect on how the urban space and its local forms of governance and political identities contribute to drivers of armed violence. The chapter later identifies one specific urban mechanism of armed violence: the intensification of intra-urban boundaries and political identities, which provide a critical enabler for the involvement of armed actors. This comprises an extreme format of the urban fragmentation that has come to characterize contemporary cities and that we discuss below in the context of a growing academic literature.

Identifying the mechanisms specific to urban forms of violence is a crucial step to support policies to prevent or reduce violence and measures to address the unequal distribution of vulnerability among communities, with some areas of extreme violence and predation by armed actors (including the state) coexisting side by side with prosperous cosmopolitan spaces. International organizations and policy frameworks on peace and security have not (yet) developed dedicated workstreams on cities. This is partially because conflict prevention and resolution processes have been designed by and for national states in the international system.[11] But this is also partially because of a lingering sense that the urban environment is a minor manifestation of much bigger problems—despite research (some of which is cited below) showing the specific drivers and implications of urban violence. National governments' approaches vary, but the overreliance on repressive and militarized police operations in low-income communities of Latin America, for instance, shows that urban violence is often understood superficially as a temporary anomaly that can be resolved through quick crackdowns. As Andrea Pavoni and Simone Tulumello have noted, "the *urban* in urban violence" has often been reduced to a neutral container, whereas violence in the city has been considered an "exogenous anomaly to be eradicated" rather than a "spatial process."[12] Peace and security practitioners and scholars have largely drawn from a concept of cities and urbanization as an "a-political process," as Karen Büscher argues, focusing instead on administrative, logistical, and economic angles often disconnected from political processes "central to dynamics of state formation and power contestation."[13]

One benefit of better understanding the deeply political processes at play in various aspects of urban violence is that it unveils mechanisms that can be acted on through public policy or nonstate actors such as civil society related to spatial inequalities, distribution of resources across urban areas, population density, and the unique mixing of multiple social groups in relatively compressed areas.[14] Understanding of urban mechanisms of violence provides valuable entry points for policymakers. This is, of course, not lost on practitioners and scholars working on urban violence reduction or prevention, especially in Latin America, where policies such as the improvement of gang-affected hillside areas of Medellín and the controversial "pacification" strategy of Rio de Janeiro's favelas engaged with better urban integration through public transport and common spaces.[15] But comprehensive urban interventions have remained limited in time and space, with repressive policing or national conflict resolution processes that bypass the urban question remaining much more common.

Urban Mechanisms of Armed Violence and Boundary Activation

These urban mechanisms of violence are profoundly political and spatially unequal. These mechanisms tend to activate forms of identity boundaries, akin to the ones identified by Charles Tilly in his ambitious theory of collective violence, but in this case with the strong influence of spatial-political (or geopolitical) elements such as streets (sometimes serving as borders between gangs or combatants), ethnic enclaves, and symbolic sites such as religious buildings. Tilly posits that political identities "offer public, collective answers to the questions 'Who are you?', 'Who are we?', and 'Who are they?'," providing crucial boundaries between "us" and "them" in situations of armed violence. In Tilly's example, the identity boundaries of Hutus and Tutsis were a matter of life and death during the Rwandan genocide of 1994.[16] Operating around these political identities, Tilly identifies the actions of "political entrepreneurs" (e.g., national leaders and militias) who garner resources (human and otherwise) for violence by activating boundaries reinforcing "deeply felt identities and age-old hatreds."[17] In cities, these political identities and mechanisms of us-them separations gain a spatial-political dimension that is potentially even more powerful because of the tangible and visible presence of structures, buildings, streets, and walls that can serve as boundaries and totems of separate communities.

The relevance of such differences and identities fluctuates over time as tensions, broader conflict, or political actors activate them. Boundary activation consists of "a shift in social interactions" making people identify increasingly according to us-them boundaries, making certain identities that had long been "relatively insignificant" dominant frames of interaction.[18] This chapter argues that the activation of exclusionary political boundaries in densely inhabited areas by an armed group is a crucial urban mechanism for armed violence. This is an extreme but unfortunately recurring form of political fragmentation of the urban space between state and sub-state armed actors and between competing communities or armed groups.

This chapter examines the role of political identities in boundary activation for urban violence. The chapter provides an initial and nonexhaustive review of key points in the recent literature on urban violence to examine the different dimensions of this mechanism at play—which is just one among many that can be identified by further research on this topic. It is a policy-oriented discussion using prominent theoretical frameworks. Its aim is not to be a literature review or a comprehensive theoretical discussion but merely to spark further discussion and to identify applications of these theoretical frameworks to resolve certain policy challenges linked to urban violence.

One key takeaway for policymakers and civil society at all levels (local, national, global) is that better understanding mechanisms of urban violence helps in identifying areas or communities disproportionately vulnerable to large-scale violence, thereby helping in the building of early warning systems and prevention strategies. The concentration of violent dynamics in certain areas can be described as *clustered vulnerability*, to express the clustering of victims, homes, and predatory actors or practices in communities where exclusionary boundaries have increased the risk of victimization by armed violence. Local leaders, national governments, and civil society should take into consideration this specifically urban form of boundary activation when devising preventative and reactive measures to armed violence.

The section below serves as a nonexhaustive discussion of the main analytical streams on political violence in cities, identifying key lines of thought on the relationship between the urban space, political fragmentation, and armed violence. Following that, the chapter expands on Tilly's conceptual theories around mechanisms and processes for violence, drawing conceptual ideas on the role of the urban space in such theories.

The Political Fragmentation of Urban Space and the "Urban Geopolitics"

Urban violence amounts to a breakdown in the social flows that normally characterize urban life, especially when it involves prolonged clashes between armed groups (as opposed to one-off fights or brawls). Plurality is, as one prominent academic on urban conflicts has put it, "sine qua non" for modern cities: "for a city to be a city, it must be seen in such terms."[19] Literature on political violence in cities identifies the breakdown in plurality—or the "collapse of customary and complex reciprocities"—as a prominent marker of conflict escalation.[20] But when we look at a broader range of urban violence types—and of academic literature on the topic—the problem of breakdown in plurality seems to be a more widespread tension at the heart of contemporary cities worldwide. Contemporary cities outside of armed conflict or postconflict settings have also been extensively shaped by segregation and division, in instances such as hypersecuritization of certain areas as part of counterterrorism measures, enhanced forms of political polarization in Western democracies, and different types of borders.[21] Diane Davis has argued that the insecurity and lawlessness that historically tended to concentrate in interstate border areas has been replicated in many cities, as urbanization changed the social makeup of human settlements into increasingly dense conglomerations defying government control of illicit economic practices.[22]

Many nation-states face myriad local armed competitors in providing rules, security, and even public services, and the resulting gaps in governments' control in even some of the largest cities in overtly democratic countries erode societal trust in nation-al states. This is partially a symptom of a broader hybridity in forms of governance and security provision in our world that goes further than the urban environment. But this is also a particularly acute challenge in cities due to population density and the geographical proximity between these local armed competitors.

Various settings of armed violence and types of armed groups illustrate a breakdown of the idealized version of the state as a political authority exerting the monopoly of legitimate use of force across its national territory. Thomas Risse summarizes this trend neatly by stating that "in the twenty-first century, it is increasingly clear that conventional modes of political steering by the nation-states and international intergovernmental organizations (IOs) are not living up to global challenges such as environmental issues, humanitarian catastrophes, and new security threats," making way for "areas of limited statehood" that defy decisions taken by central authorities.[23] The classic view of armed conflict protagonists as states and rebels has often been scaled down to forms of "multi-layered governance" with "various armed groups opposing states, and as well cooperating with or opposing each other."[24] This important academic debate showed that armed groups operating separately from the state are linked to state actors and other influential political figures (e.g., warlords, candidates in elections, and wealthy business people) in complex webs of uneasy alliances seeking the "construction of alternative paths to the acquisition of power."[25]

Hybridity of governance practices and fragmentation of political power has affected cities in ways that are not merely replication in smaller scale of these broader global trends. Moritz Schuberth points out that states' inability to provide security across their vast territories, for instance, is not equally felt by all citizens: "those living in the most affluent parts of the main cities often enjoy functioning protection by police and private security firms, while those living in neglected areas are denied access to formal security systems."[26] Furthermore, armed groups that have shown a predilection for urban areas, such as militias, vigilante groups, and gangs, tend to fight either for economic enrichment or parochial political interests linked to local strongmen or as armed wings of political parties.[27]

Indeed, frequent protagonists of urban violence in settings as diverse as Brazil and Libya are militia groups. The term "militia" is commonly mentioned in media reports on conflict-affected settings (and some nonconflict ones such as Brazil) and, perhaps precisely because of that, tends to be vaguely and broadly applied. But recent scholarship has shed light on the role of militias as local security providers linked to political actors.[28] This linkage to relatively parochial political interests and local security provision has important implications to cities, as I argued elsewhere, since cities contain both valuable resources for ambitious political entrepreneurs and areas of tenuous state presence.[29] The recent conflict between the Sudanese Armed Forces and a paramilitary militia known as Rapid Support Forces, for instance, has heavily concentrated in the capital Khartoum and other cities and towns.[30] The expulsion of civilians of certain ethnicities from certain areas and the destruction of homes was a frequent tactic of Arab militias, including through breaking into people's homes to kill male residents and loot. An Amnesty International report on this is titled *Death Came to Our Homes*, reflecting the deliberate targeting of urban residential areas.[31] This is further evidence that cities are not just inert receptacles or neutral stages for violence.

The urban manifestation of this growing fragmentation of political authority is marked by geographical proximity between clashing interests, with the frequent availability of small arms and illicit economies adding fuel to the fire. As they exploit economically and politically valuable resources in urban areas, armed groups implement forms of social control or governance that have been described as "new imagined communities of allegiance" separate (but geographically close to) the central state.[32] Civil wars and broader societal tensions in central and eastern Africa, for instance, have had specifically urban "translations" in "(ethnically) fragmented urban neighborhoods or violent struggles over urban public space" between rival groups living side by side.[33] These local manifestations of conflict, societal tensions, and economic struggles (in the case of criminal violence) are far from localized concerns. Armed conflicts "erode states in the local level," furthering sectarian, ethnic, or broader societal tensions and reducing trust in national state authorities.[34] Organized crime, through gangs, mafias, and transnational smuggling networks, has profound political implications in urban territories where their social rules and informal economic structures prevail, as they "negotiate (sometimes violently) with the state over not just the control of the drug trade or access to illicit markets but over who is the dominant authority on a local level," as per Nicholas Barnes's "criminal politics" concept.[35]

Even more crucial, if darker, connections between the urban space and the process of political power in our world came from the analysis of urban destruction as the combined violence against people and spaces, taking the dramatic form of elimination of places with emotional meaning for people's identities and histories—urbicide, the deliberate destruction of buildings or structures "as a condition of possibility of being-with others."[36] In other words, violence and even killings can victimize not only human beings but also the environment where the "being" takes place: homes, communities, heritage, and the *civitas* (city) that provide humans with their sense of civilization.[37] This reminds us of the deliberate targeting of specific areas with certain ethnic majorities in Sudan mentioned above, with the invasion of homes exemplifying in horrific tones how spaces become linked—at least in combatants' perspectives—to the politics of the fighting.

In the wake of the destruction of the twin towers of New York's World Trade Center on 9/11, this field of work expanded to account for the conduct of war and terror through violence against urban, local sites—which became popularized as urban geopolitics.[38] Recently this concept has received a valuable reconceptualization from cities as targets of large-scale destructive firepower to the (much more frequent) political dynamics of segregation and mixing of populations in today's cities.[39]

Going back to where we started this section, contemporary cities' role as melting pots of diverse communities provides a uniquely urban flare to armed violence and conflict. Proximity and mingling can suddenly give way to enmity and violence, as we will explore in examples in the following section. The activation of borders between political identities so closely and casually intertwined in mixed neighborhoods poses unique challenges: for civilian residents, how to reinterpret your home environment from that of peaceful and even economically advantageous coexistence to one of "living with the enemy." For governments and international organizations, how this fragmentation of urban space into rival turfs for armed actors can be prevented or countered. I argue that an important first step is to understand specific urban mechanisms of armed violence. I explore below key features of these mechanisms tied to urban space and politics, inspired by the conceptual theories of Charles Tilly.

Activation of Exclusionary Boundaries in Cities

Cities are hosts to a bewildering range of violent events and processes. This section proposes a reflection on a mechanism of activation of political identities and their respective boundaries splintering the urban space into the sorts of areas of alternative governance arrangements, armed groups' turfs, and rival ethnic groups discussed above. Developing better understanding of mechanisms of urban violence can help policymakers and civil society target their specific triggers and processes with the aim of preventing or reducing violence. It can also help in developing early warning when activation of potentially destructive cycles of violence are starting.

Mechanisms and Processes Behind Boundary Activation in Cities

Mechanisms are a methodological instrument to understand, as Jon Elster argues, frequently occurring causal patterns that are triggered in association with certain events—not universal laws, but links in a chain of causation.[40] Tilly emphasizes that mechanisms are different from the much broader causes of violence that scholarly research tends to focus on, such as poverty, societal grievances, ideology, and so on. Mechanisms are more specific—for instance, the set of events, some guided by political entrepreneurs, that caused the shift in how Hutus and Tutsis viewed each other at the lead up to the Rwandan genocide.[41] It is particularly useful to look at urban patterns of violence, given it shifts focus from grand causes such as ideology or poverty to smaller scale—and therefore potentially more *local*—triggering events of violence. In fact, Tilly described mechanisms as "causes on the small scale," similar events that trigger the same effect in a wide range of contexts.

Mechanisms can comprise decisions made by certain armed groups (especially their leadership)—for instance, to scratch an alliance with another armed group and fight them instead.[42] A more complex set of mechanisms comprises changes in relations between social groups, such as when two religious or sectarian groups with a long history of peaceful cohabitation start supporting rival militias and moving into single-sect neighborhoods.

A key mechanism involved in such stark separations is boundary activation. Boundaries are almost universally available, especially in socially diverse cities, but are activated in specific times, usually, as Tilly mentions, with the help of political or armed actors that intensify such divisions. For Tilly, boundary activation consists of a shift in social interactions such that they increasingly (a) organize around a single us-them boundary and (b) differentiate between within-boundary and cross-boundary interactions. Hence us-them boundaries such as male–female, Hutu-Tutsi, cowboy outfit A versus cowboy outfit B, or landlord-peasant, although always available in certain settings, shift from being relatively insignificant to absolutely dominant for current interactions.[43]

The case of Baghdad provides a striking example of boundaries forming along both symbolic and physical lines. Bouts of sectarian violence rocked the neighborhoods of Washash and Iskan after the US invasion in 2003, escalating in 2005 when Sunni insurgents increasingly targeted Shia and the Shia-majority government while Shia militias, especially the Badr Corps, reportedly took part in several detentions and executions of Sunni men.[44] The situation escalated in mixed areas after the February 2006 bombing of a holy site for Shia Islam, with Shiite militias erecting checkpoints in Sunni or mixed areas and Sunni residents either arming themselves or fleeing toward more homogeneous areas.[45] Baghdad moved in the span of little more than three years from a city of cohabitation between Sunni and Shia Muslims to one of extreme segregation violently enforced by militias claiming to represent each side as they expelled residents of the "rival" community to take control over previously mixed communities.[46] As a *New York Times* article from 2007 put it: "Baghdad has become a capital of corrosive and violent borderlines.[47] Streets never crossed. Conversations never started. Doors never entered." This is illustrative of how broader intercommunity tensions can lead to specifically urban violence, in which urban geography and sectarian identities became intertwined and jointly relevant for residents to make calculations about their safety, their involvement in armed collectives, or whether to flee.

Sometimes the urban segregation precedes—and contributes to—the boundary activation and violent clashes. A recent example comes from a new city, of all places: the planned city of Gurugram, a cluster of gleaming skyscrapers nicknamed "Millennium City" located not far from the Indian capital of Delhi. As is increasingly common in rapidly growing cities, Gurugram hosts a low-income settlement for construction workers and other non-white-collar professionals—in this case, Tigra, a majority Muslim shanty town in a majority Hindu city. After a tense Hindu procession through a majority Muslim community in a nearby town resulted in violent clashes, Tigra residents witnessed attacks on a mosque, and Muslims in the city's mixed communities were forced out by landlords and even illegally by local councils.[48] Housing, real estate, and planning politics can be leveraged as instruments of separation and intimidation, contributing to the tensions fueling armed violence.

The joining of political identities to physical living spaces such as streets, communities, neighborhoods, and informal settlements is therefore an important element of urban boundary activation. When this space becomes exclusionary, the potential for violence becomes greater, and the existence of armed groups purporting to defend certain communities from others—such as in the Sunni-Shia schism in Baghdad—is often a powerful trigger for violence. Fortunately, not all cities have specialists in violence organized into militias or vigilantes, but intercommunity clashes can still take place, as the case of India's Millennium City shows.

Political identities can be associated with places in various ways, sometimes drawing from historical events, sometimes from their ethnic, sectarian, or national composition. In urban environments, meaning-loaded places abound and overlap, with different groups laying competing claims to legitimate control of certain spaces—sometimes with violence, sometimes not, but such competition always results in a divided urban space.[49] The intensity of division and the propensity for violence is heavily affected by the broader political contexts of the city in national or international distributions of violence—for instance, in cases of wars. An estimated 2.5 million Syrians are thought to have been affected by sieges by armed actors during the Syrian civil war, used "to punish towns, neighborhoods, and cities where they had lost control."[50]

In these cases, urban location determined access to humanitarian aid, restrictions of movement, and attacks on civilian targets, including hospitals, intended to inflict suffering.[51] In Aleppo, the consolidation of armed groups opposed to the regime of President Bashar al-Assad in areas of the city and its suburbs was considered "a critical threat and unacceptable challenge to its sovereignty" because of the proximity to the national capital, Damascus.[52] The city's geopolitical role has thus been seen as an important factor determining the government's military tactics, such as indiscriminate bombing of opposition-held areas and later evictions and demolitions.

Political identities need not be shared homogeneously across certain areas for residents to be affected by their violent implications. As in the case of Tilly's example of "cowboy outfit A versus cowboy outfit B," two or more armed groups can perceive themselves as part of fiercely rival entities with security implications for residents who do not share these identities. One such case was reported to me during a visit in 2018 to the Maré complex of favelas in the northern area of Rio de Janeiro, a city renowned for its strictly territorial and highly violent criminal organizations. Whereas many favelas in Rio are located on steep hills and are dominated by one single criminal organization or militia, Maré is horizontally sprawling and divided along different factions; historically, the main ones have been the Red Command (Comando Vermelho, or CV) and Third Pure Command (Terceiro Comando Puro, or TCP). Maré residents have a live-and-let-live arrangement with the gangs most times, as long as they respect some rules, usually with regard to outsiders entering the community or to relations with the police. The main hotspot of conflict concentrated on the street separating the two drug-trafficking factions. This was a tense area where gunfights could erupt at any moment and locals needing to cross faced an inevitable risk. The area became known as "Gaza Strip," in reference to the frequent armed conflicts registered in the eponymous region in the Middle East.[53] Other gang-enforced borders have existed (and shifted locations) over the years in Rio, gaining war-alluding nicknames such as "Vietnam" and others.[54]

The joining of political identities to physical living spaces such as streets, communities, neighborhoods, and informal settlements is, therefore, an important element of urban boundary activation. When this space becomes exclusionary, the potential for violence becomes greater, and the existence of armed groups purporting to defend certain communities from others—such as in the Sunni-Shia schism in Baghdad—is a crucial trigger for targeted violence on a specific social group.[55] This boundary activation can also be enacted and enforced entirely by nonstate armed groups such as the CV and TCP in Rio, with consequences for anyone whether or not they even have an opinion on the groups.

Be it as part of a larger identitarian conflict or a specific gang turf clash, the assignment of an exclusionary political meaning to densely inhabited areas by an armed group is a crucial urban mechanism for armed violence. The process or moment of this assignment comprises a critical boundary activation that is accompanied by explicit or implicit threat or use of force: Rio's invisible borders separating rival gangs, India's Muslim-Hindu tensions, Baghdad's sudden loss of urban mixing between sects. It has immediate and often lethal consequences for hundreds or thousands of local residents and amounts to violence not only against people but also against the city (or town) as an urban environment in the deepest sense of its contemporary use: a space of plurality, heterogeneity, and encounters.

Understanding this crucial urban mechanism of armed violence can help identify early signs of potential violence escalation. Civil society groups and governments willing and able to help or, when possible, intervene with preventative tools can look for such boundaries and political identities. Whereas they are complex mechanisms that cannot be deactivated easily or quickly, they can be an important indicator for identifying vulnerable populations around boundary sites and prioritizing long-term prevention and/or security programs.

It is important to highlight, however, that many government interventions relying on repressive policing tend to strengthen urban boundaries or form new ones. An example, cited in a paper on identity-based mass violence that served as initial research for this volume, is that of Kenya's response to terrorist attacks by the Somali violent Islamist group al-Shabaab in 2012.[56] Police used heavy-handed interventions in Nairobi's Eastleigh area, with its high concentration of Somalis, harassing and arresting several community members. Research from 2016 found that

10 percent of the population of the South Eastleigh administrative area had experienced police violence.[57] In Rio de Janeiro, operations by the military police usually involve entering areas known to be controlled by a certain gang in order to arrest or eliminate a certain suspect, resulting in gunfights amid extremely high-density areas and the frequent deaths of bystanders—444 deaths by state security forces in Rio in 2022, to be specific.[58] From 2020 to 2022, Rio registered nine so-called megamassacres in which eight or more people died during a police operation.[59] These interventions are usually momentary raids after which officers withdraw, local civilians are left to deal with the bloody aftermath, and criminal groups return to their borders, armament, and a renewed sense of enmity toward the police.

Boundaries and Clustering of Vulnerable Populations

This shift from "we" to the "us-them boundary" is potentially disastrous for urban areas and their residents. Such a situation in a densely inhabited neighborhood can escalate into mass violence relatively quickly, given that the perceived rivals are not just side by side but often mixed in the same residential complexes or areas. This is not to say that such community boundaries are not worrying in rural areas, but the scale and speed of violence escalation is potentially greater in cities.

The interruption of plurality in urban life—such as the everyday interactions between neighbors, the mingling of diverse people in the workspace, the encounters in public transport—triggered by extreme forms of boundary activation represent security risks for minority or persecuted groups. When exclusionary political identities are triggered and boundaries become matters of life and death, insecurity impregnates urban space and violence reaches not only individuals but homes, streets, routes to work or study, social relations, and trust. The positive roles that cities have historically had for human civilization (a word deriving from the Latin *civitas*, or "city") are harmed: economic productivity, the benefits of agglomeration for firms, the security of trade hubs, and political and social security, especially in countries where large cities have represented shelter from nearby wars.[60] This clustered vulnerability in spaces is tied to the place-based character of urban life: homes, work, routes, and the unequal distribution of insecurity, security provision (by state or nonstate actors), and other public goods.

If in cases of sudden intercommunity conflicts or internal wars this clustered vulnerability can emerge in a matter of days, certain communities have experienced clustered vulnerability for long periods. One of the cross-cutting lessons from recent research on urban violence is how frequently it concentrates in certain areas; this is highly visible in Latin America, where intense bouts of armed violence are registered in low-income settlements involving police and rifle-wielding gangs.[61] Clustering is also a visible—and highly volatile—phenomenon in the urban geopolitics of cities split according to fiercely felt ethnic or sectarian separation lines between competing social groups—the case of Palestinians and Israelis in Jerusalem.[62]

This vulnerability of particular social groups to violence points to the importance of the issues discussed in this chapter to security, humanitarian, and developmental policies among local and national authorities and international organizations. The analysis of urban mechanisms of violence, specifically the activation of exclusionary boundaries and political identities in densely inhabited areas, can help governments, civil society groups, and international humanitarian or aid organizations identify physical areas and communities vulnerable to mass violence. Human rights organizations in settings as varied as Nairobi's sprawling informal settlements and Brazil's hillside favelas have consistently raised concerns about disproportionate use of force or unfair treatment to their communities. On the other end of the spectrum of violence, in situations of war, the International Committee of the Red Cross has conducted campaigns about the increasing humanitarian impact of armed conflict in cities.[63] The analysis of how exclusionary boundaries are formed can further aid in identifying early warning signs of crises and vulnerability and, it is hoped, aid in the development of prevention tools and policies.

Conclusion

This chapter provided a discussion on mechanisms of armed violence linked to spatial politics inherent to cities, in view of the growing body of research examining the fragmentation of political authority and hybrid security-provisions arrangements involving nonstate (and state-linked) armed groups. Its core contribution has been to identify the activation of exclusionary political boundaries in densely inhabited areas by an armed group as a key mechanism in processes of urban violence. This boundary activation amounts to an interruption of the plurality that, to varying degrees, characterizes contemporary urban life. Therefore, the dynamics of urban violence examined here impede some of the core (mostly positive) roles that contemporary cities have had in national economic growth, social cohabitation, and in many cases shelter from rural-based wars.

The identification of urban-specific mechanisms of armed violence—with one of them laid out in the chapter and potentially more to explore—does not mean that other mechanisms, not urban-specific, do not apply to cities. Rather, it is important to examine the relationship between the urban spatial politics increasingly identified by recent scholarship and some important theories regarding the mechanisms leading to armed violence. This chapter attempted a reflection on this relationship by drawing heavily from Charles Tilly's theories.

Another implication of the discussion here, hopefully with a more positive implication, is that further study of urban mechanisms of armed violence can help identify communities at risk of exposition to armed violence escalation. Research on urban geopolitics, urbicide, and local orders involving armed and frequently predatory groups have shown that violence can affect places as well as people: it can involve destruction or invasion of homes, the interruption of urban mobility, urban displacement, or even the intentional targeting of areas as an attempt to destroy communities' symbolic (and actual) places. Further study on spatial mechanisms of urban violence can help expand the avenues for policy and civil society action on this crucial challenge for humanity in our urban century.

Notes

1. Jo Beall, Tom Goodfellow, and Dennis Rodgers. 'Cities and Conflict in Fragile States in the Developing World'. *Urban Studies* 50, no. 15 (November 2013): 3065–83. https://doi.org/10.1177/0042098013487775.
2. Scott Bollens, 'Cities, Nationalism and Democratization'. London: Routledge, 2007, p. 1.
3. Jo Beall, Tom Goodfellow, and Dennis Rodgers. 'Cities, Conflict and State Fragility—Working Paper No. 85–Cities and Fragile States | ALNAP'. Cities and Fragile States Working Paper Series. Crisis States Research Centre, January 2011, p. 1. https://library.alnap.org/help-library/cities-conflict-and-state-fragility-working-paper-no-85-cities-and-fragile-states.
4. Caroline Moser and Cathy McIlwaine. 'New Frontiers in Twenty-First Century Urban Conflict and Violence'. *Environment and Urbanization* 26, no. 2 (2014): 331–44. P. 3.
5. Eduardo Moncada, 'The Politics of Urban Violence: Challenges for Development in the Global South', *Studies in Comparative International Development*, 48, no. 3 (1 September 2013): 217–39.
6. Karen Büscher, 'African Cities and Violent Conflict: The Urban Dimension of Conflict and Post Conflict Dynamics in Central and Eastern Africa'. *Journal of Eastern African Studies* 12, no. 2 (3 April 2018): 193–210.
7. Moncada, "Politics of Urban Violence," 229.
8. Beall, Goodfellow and Rodgers. Cities, Conflict and State Fragility. P. 17.
9. Emma Elfversson, Ivan Gusic and Kristine Höglund, 'The Spatiality of Violence in Post-War Cities', *Third World Thematics: A TWQ Journal* 4, no. 2–3 (Nov. 19, 2019): 83.
10. For an overview of the criminal governance concept, see Benjamin Lessing, "Conceptualizing Criminal Governance," *Perspectives on Politics* 19, no. 3 (September 2021).
11. Antônio Sampaio, 'Before and after Urban Warfare: Conflict Prevention and Transitions in Cities', International Review of the Red Cross, 15 April 2016.

12. Andrea Pavoni, and Simone Tulumello. 'What Is Urban Violence?' Progress in Human Geography 44, no. 1 (1 February 2020): 49–76, pp. 49-50.
13. Büscher, "African Cities," 201.
14. Elfversson, Gusic, and Höglund, "Spatiality of Violence."
15. On the controversies surrounding Rio de Janeiro's pacification, see Antônio Sampaio. 'Illicit Order: The Militarization Logic of Organized Crime and Urban Security in Rio de Janeiro'. Global Initiative Against Transnational Organized Crime, September 2019. https://read-me.org/more-global-crime/2024/9/19/illicit-order-the-militarization-logic-of-organized-crime-and-urban-security-in-rio-de-janeiro.
16. Charles Tilly, *The Politics of Collective Violence* (Cambridge: Cambridge University Press, 2003), 32.
17. Ibid., 34.
18. Ibid., 21.
19. Wendy Pullan and Britt Baillie, "Introduction," in *Locating Urban Conflicts: Ethnicity, Nationalism and the Everyday*, ed. by Wendy Pullan and Britt Baillie (London: Palgrave Macmillan, 2013), 3.
20. Wendy Pullan, "Spatial Discontinuities: Conflict Infrastructures in Contested Cities," in *Locating Urban Conflicts: Ethnicity, Nationalism and the Everyday*, ed. by Wendy Pullan and Britt Baillie (London: Palgrave Macmillan, 2013), 19.
21. Jonathan Rokem, Sara Fregonese, Adam Ramadan, Elisa Pascucci, Gillad Rosen, Igal Charney, Till F. Paasche, and James D. Sidaway. 'Interventions in Urban Geopolitics'. Political Geography 61, November 2017, pp. 253-254.
22. Davis, Diane E. 'Irregular Armed Forces, Shifting Patterns of Commitment, and Fragmented Sovereignty in the Developing World'. *Theory and Society* 39, no. 3/4 (2010), p. 232.
23. Thomas Risse, 'Governance in Areas of Limited Statehood', in *The Oxford Handbook of Governance*, edited by David Levi-Faur, 0. Oxford University Press, 2012.
24. G.E. Frerks, N.M. Terpstra, and Nelson Kasfir. 'Introduction: Armed Groups and Multi-Layered Governance'. *Civil Wars* 19, no. 3 (2017): 257–78.

25. Augustine Ikelegbe and Wafula Okumu. 'Introduction: Towards Conceptualisation and Understanding of the Threats of Armed Non-State Groups to Human Security and the State in Africa'. In *Militias Rebels and Islamist Militants: Human Insecurity and State Crises in Africa*, edited by Augustine Ikelegbe and Wafula Okumu. Pretoria: Institute for Security Studies, 2010, p. 27.
26. Moritz Schuberth, "The Challenge of Community-Based Armed Groups: Towards a Conceptualization of Militias, Gangs, and Vigilantes," *Contemporary Security Policy* 36, no. 2 (2015): 304.
27. Ibid., 298.
28. David J. Francis, "Introduction," in *Civil Militia: Africa's Intractable Security Menace?*, ed. David J. Francis (Abingdon, UK: Routledge, 2005), 4.
29. Antônio Sampaio. 'The Militia Challenge in Cities'. *Urban Violence Research Network*, 19 January 2021. https://urbanviolence.org/the-militia-challenge-in-cities/.
30. Brandon Bolte. 'Why Militia Politics Is Preventing Democratization and Stability in Sudan'. *Political Violence at a Glance*, 26 April 2023. https://politicalviolenceataglance.org/2023/04/26/why-militia-politics-is-preventing-democratization-and-stability-in-sudan/.
31. Amnesty International, 'Death Came to Our Home: War Crimes and Civilian Suffering in Sudan', 3 August 2023. https://www.amnesty.org/en/latest/news/2023/08/sudan-war-crimes-rampant-as-civilians-killed-in-both-deliberate-and-indiscriminate-attacks-new-report.
32. Davis, 'Irregular Armed Forces'.
33. Büscher, "African Cities," 199.
34. Beall, Goodfellow and Rodgers, 'Cities, Conflict and State Fragility', p. 17.
35. Nicholas Barnes, 'Criminal Politics: An Integrated Approach to the Study of Organized Crime, Politics, and Violence', *Perspectives on Politics* 15, no. 4 (December 2017): 967–87.
36. Martin Coward, 'Urbicide: The Politics of Urban Destruction'. London: Routledge, 2009, pp. 14-15.

37. 'Civilizations', National Geographic. https://education.nationalg eographic.org/resource/civilizations/.
38. Stephen Graham, 'Postmortem City: Towards an Urban Geopolitics', *City* 8, no. 2, July 2004, p. 170.
39. Rokem et al., 'Interventions in urban geopolitics', pp. 254-254.
40. Jon Elster, *Explaining Social Behaviour: More Nuts and Bolts for the Social Sciences* (Cambridge: Cambridge University Press, 2007), 32-36.
41. Tilly, The Politics of Collective Violence, pp. 20-21.
42. Ibid., 20.
43. Ibid., 21.
44. Patrick Gaughen, 'Baghdad Neighborhood Project: Washash and Iskan', The Institute for The Study of War, Pp. 2-3. https://www.understandingwar.org/sites/default/files/reports/Backgrounder13.pdf.
45. Sudarsan Raghavan, 'Distrust Breaks the Bonds of a Baghdad Neighborhood', *The Washington Post*, 26 September 2006. https://www.washingtonpost.com/archive/politics/2006/09/27/distrust-breaks-the-bonds-of-a-baghdad-neighborhood-span-cla ssbankheadin-mixed-area-violence-defies-peace-effortsspan/7a4 dcdae-a681-465e-9e72-9738e590c205/.
46. Mahbub Rashid, and Dhirgham Alobaydi. 'Territory, Politics of Power, and Physical Spatial Networks: The Case of Baghdad, Iraq'. *Habitat International* 50 (1 December 2015): 180–94.
47. Damien Cave, 'In Baghdad, Sectarian Lines Too Deadly to Cross', *The New York Times*, 4 March 2007. https://www.nytimes.com/2007/03/04/world/middleeast/04baghdad.html.
48. Philip Sherwell, Economic boom and sectarian violence in India's 'millennium city', *The Times*, 27 August 2023. https://www.the times.co.uk/article/economic-boom-and-sectarian-violence-in-ind ias-millennium-city-qbk5zm20k.
49. Büscher, "African Cities," 200.
50. Pax, 'Siege Watch: Out of Sight, Out of Mind: The Aftermath of Syria's Sieges', p. 8. https://paxforpeace.nl/wp-content/uploads/sites/2/import/import/pax-siege-watch-final-report.pdf.
51. Ibid., 8.

52. Sawsan Abou Zainedin and Hani Fakhani, 'Syria's Urbicide: The Built Environment As a Means to Consolidate Homogeneity', The Aleppo Project, July 2019. p. 5. https://www.thealeppoproject.com/wp-content/uploads/2019/07/SyriasUrbicideSawsanAbouZainedinHaniFakhani2019.pdf.
53. Eduardo Ribeiro, Luiz Eduardo Soares and Miriam Krenzinger, 'Tipos de governança criminal: Estudo comparativo a partir dos casos da Maré', Dilemas, no. 4, 2022, p. 576. https://www.scielo.br/j/dilemas/a/hrVDFTrYck5zBF9P8dxP9tt/?format=pdf&lang=pt.
54. Mario Hugo Monken, 'Medo faz rua ser chamada de "faixa de Gaza"', Folha de São Paulo, 15 January 2004. https://www1.folha.uol.com.br/fsp/cotidian/ff1501200413.htm.
55. Ariana Markowitz, 'Big Events on a Small Scale: Exploring Identity-Based Mass Violence in Cities', December 2020, p. 3.
56. Ibid., 8.
57. Peter Kiama, Catrine Christensen, Steffen Jensen and Tobias Kelly, 'Violence Amongst the Urban Poor in Nairobi', Independent Medico-Legal Unit, August 2016, p. 24. https://torturedocumentationproject.files.wordpress.com/2014/05/violence-amongst-the-urban-poor-in-nairobi.pdf.
58. Instituto de Segurança Pública, ISP Visualização. http://www.ispvisualizacao.rj.gov.br/Letalidade.html.
59. Daniel Hirata, Carolina Christoph Grillo, Renato Coelho Dirk and Diogo Azevedo Lyra, 'Chacinas Policiais no Rio de Janeiro: Estatização das mortes, mega chacinas policiais e impunidade', GENI: Grupo de Estudos dos Novos Ilegalismos, April 2023. https://geni.uff.br/2023/05/05/chacinas-policiais-no-rio-de-janeiro-estatizacao-das-mortes-mega-chacinas-policiais-e-impunidade/.
60. Paul Swinney and Olivia Vera, 'Office politics: London and the rise of home working', Centre for Cities, 24 May 2023. https://www.centreforcities.org/reader/office-politics/the-impact-of-agglomeration-on-the-economy/.

61. Robert Muggah. 'Researching the Urban Dilemma: Urbanization, Poverty and Violence'. International Development Research Centre, 2012, p. 30.
62. For a comprehensive review of urban geopolitics, see "Interventions in Urban Geopolitics," ed. Jonathan Rokem et al., *Political Geography* 61 (November 2017).
63. International Committee of the Red Cross, 'Urban Warfare and Violence'. https://www.icrc.org/en/what-we-do/war-in-cities.

Antônio Jacinto Sampaio recently led a research team on cities and illicit economies at the Global Initiative Against Transnational Organized Crime. He has worked at the International Institute for Strategic Studies and has advised NATO on urban warfare. He has published in peer-reviewed journals and news outlets on organized crime, urban conflicts, an Brazilian politics. Sampaio is currently pursuing a PhD at the School of Security Studies, King's College London.

Open Access This chapter is licensed under the terms of the Creative Commons Attribution-NonCommercial-NoDerivatives 4.0 International License (http://creativecommons.org/licenses/by-nc-nd/4.0/), which permits any noncommercial use, sharing, distribution and reproduction in any medium or format, as long as you give appropriate credit to the original author(s) and the source, provide a link to the Creative Commons license and indicate if you modified the licensed material. You do not have permission under this license to share adapted material derived from this chapter or parts of it.

The images or other third party material in this chapter are included in the chapter's Creative Commons license, unless indicated otherwise in a credit line to the material. If material is not included in the chapter's Creative Commons license and your intended use is not permitted by statutory regulation or exceeds the permitted use, you will need to obtain permission directly from the copyright holder.

Tearing the Seams: Cycles of Structural and Acute Violence in Aleppo

Alhakam Shaar

Introduction[1]

My hometown of Aleppo, Syria is at once synonymous with revolution, civil activism, and pride in cultural heritage, as well as with urban division, destruction, and forced displacement. Until 2011, many around the world and in Syria had looked at Aleppo as a beacon of stability and economic productivity and were taken by surprise by the eruption of violence following the Arab Spring uprisings in 2010.[2] However, half a century of systemic but not immediately visible violent practices and power arrangements had laid the foundation for subsequent instability and violence in Aleppo.

This chapter was completed before the fall of the Assad regime in the last weeks of 2024. Opposition forces captured the city of Aleppo on November 29. On December 8 Bashar al-Assad fled Damascus, signaling the end of 54 years of the Assads' rule and 61 years of rule by the Baath Party.

A. Shaar (✉)
The Aleppo Project, Tübingen, Germany
e-mail: shaar@thealeppoproject.com

In this chapter, I draw on examples from Syria's modern history to argue that various forms of violence used on and in Aleppo were an intentional tool and tactic embedded in state institutions dominated by the Assad regime to consolidate power in Syria. The regime's use of physical and psychological violence was intended to infiltrate and establish uncontested control over social, political, and economic networks. In Aleppo, this manifested in the silencing of opposition, the cleaving of communities, and the separation and displacement of its residents. Levers of government such as legislation, policy, urban planning, and security forces that could have been used to develop a dynamic and thriving city were instead corrupted and reoriented to perpetrate violence of various forms and intent.

Two forms of violence, structural and acute, become evident in the cycles discussed below. I provide brief definitions and, following a contextual grounding of Aleppo's political and social dynamics, proceed with examples in the body of the chapter. Structural violence is the harm systematically inflicted on groups of people who, through enforced power differentials, are left behind in society in terms of economy, health, and other aspects of life, while acute violence as approached in this volume emphasizes the explicit and immediate nature of violence, where harm is inflicted directly on individuals or groups, whether in a single event or as part of a larger group of incidents.[3] The two kinds of violence, while not always co-present, are co-constitutive. In Aleppo, they are mutually reinforcing cycles of harm, decimating the city and its people's ability to thrive within it.

A Brief History

The Ba'ath Party's military coup of 1963 established it as the sole "legal political party in Syria."[4] In 1970, Ba'athist General Hafez al-Assad, from the Alawite minority group who was part of the 1963 junta, orchestrated a coup that further consolidated his and the party's political and patrimonial power in Syria. Under Hafez al-Assad (ruled 1970–2000), Article 8 of the 1973 constitution installed the Ba'ath Party as the "Leader of Society and State." The same constitution gave the president the right to "declare a state of emergency" under which Syria was run for most of the Ba'athists rule. Their rule was also defined by its staunch secularism and a process of redistributing military and political positions from majority Sunnis to Alawites. This shift introduced identity politics into Ba'ath Party and government practices. In an absolute quest for complete control, the Syrian government and the Ba'ath Party built systems of patronage, doling out government and military positions and economic benefits based on loyalty or sectarian ties. Paradoxically, with absolute control came insecurity, and in the last fifty years, the Assads initiated cycles of structural and acute violence to maintain their privilege and influence and to protect their interests.

Over time, the government of Syria became synonymous with the Assad family, introducing a dynastic form of leadership passed from father to son. As the Assads consolidated control over the economy, military, and government they elevated identity politics, heightening competition between the minority Alawites, to which they belong, and the Sunnis. These dynamics were evident in Aleppo and are profiled in this chapter. They are a grim reminder of how unchecked power can destroy the social, physical, and economic life of a city and its people.

A Sociopolitical and Economic Geography of Aleppo

Historically built east of the Quweiq River, Aleppo is among the oldest continuously inhabited cities in the world.[5] The Aleppo Governorate—comprising one quarter of the Syrian population (roughly 5.5 million of Syria's 23 million residents lived in Aleppo in 2010) and serving as the country's economic capital—had limited political influence in Syria.[6] As the main trading hub in the eastern Mediterranean, Aleppo, once considered a cosmopolitan city, hosted diverse cultural, ethnic, and religious groups who lived and worked in harmony.[7] Until the civil war in 2011,[8] Aleppo was an economic production center for the country, its prosperity stemming from an alliance of financial expedience between the city's business elite in western Aleppo, who employed rural migrants who had settled in eastern Aleppo.

In the nineteenth century, as populations grew and the ruling Ottomans adopted modern municipal practices, new neighborhoods, such as Azizieh, Jamilieh, and Ismailieh were planned on private lands astride the river, to the west of the city. They included gridded streets, apartment buildings, high schools, and police stations. Affluent Aleppians, mostly families of merchants and clerks, left their traditional Old City houses in eastern Aleppo for modern apartments in the newly developing western portion of the city. The appeal of modern houses and multistory buildings encouraged urban development nearby, which could only expand west toward the river, with the Old City to the east. The Old City housed middle- and low-income families, and lands farther east were largely used for olive and pistachio orchards until the second half of the twentieth century.

Prior to 1963, the distinctions between eastern and western Aleppo occurred gradually, as a result of formal planning decisions in some instances, the absence of planning in others, and the informal reactions to these dynamics. By the time of the Ba'ath Party's 1963 coup, demand was growing for affordable housing in Aleppo. However, red tape, including new restrictions for building on agricultural land, curtailed the development of new neighborhoods in eastern Aleppo. With few alternatives, Aleppians built on agricultural land without municipal approval in what became known as *sakan ashwai* ("random housing"), with each individual structure referred to as *binaa mukhalef* ("contravening building"). These buildings engulfed Aleppo from the north, east, and south, creating a distinct contrast to the more intentionally planned developments of western Aleppo. East Aleppo's residential areas appeared less structured and organized; out of necessity, residents in the east, largely working-class migrants from rural areas, bypassed official regulations and constructed unsanctioned, informal housing and buildings on "protected" agricultural lands.[9]

Informal building in dense neighborhoods in eastern Aleppo continued to intensify in the 1970s and '80s, as formal plans to expand the city did not meet the scale of demand.[10] A socioeconomic cleavage was now becoming entrenched between those who could afford to live in western Aleppo's better-built, planned, and serviced districts and those who could not, in eastern Aleppo. As will be discussed below, this divide went beyond class. Over time, the two halves of the city were further differentiated by the degree of participation in the political and civic institutions of the state and city.

A joke I remember from my childhood, which has resurfaced on social media, captures this cleavage well: A man was downtown and wanted to take the bus to his home in Bab al-Nairab in eastern Aleppo. By mistake he boarded a bus going to al-Muhafaza in western Aleppo. Before the bus took the wrong turn, he asked a fellow passenger, "Where's this bus headed?" The fellow passenger replied, "To al-Muhafaza." The man screamed to the driver, "Drop me off here!" before he complained, "I knew them folks were not our folks!".[11]

When I was 10, my family moved from the centrally planned Hamdaniyyeh neighborhood in western Aleppo to Qadi Askar on the eastern edge of Old Aleppo. I was struck not only by the beauty of the white stone houses but also the shabby state of the streets. The main street connecting our alleyway to the rest of the city, Sharea al-Mazbah, was paved through houses demolished in a 1958 project aiming to create a car axis running east to west. That project left behind dozens of half-demolished houses, cutting through bedrooms that were left exposed to the public and the elements. Residents were told not to repair and rebuild as there would be a complementary beautification plan, the Qadi Askar Beautification Project.

This would have included our house, which bordered one of the half-demolished houses. Despite the project remaining on the municipal government's agenda for over 60 years, it has yet to be completed. According to municipal engineers with whom my father inquired about the project, "every six months we send the plan to the Ministry of Public Works and Housing in Damascus, who sends it back to us with requests for minor corrections and modifications, before we send it back again." This bureaucratic turpitude, along with the disinterest of the national government in Aleppo's most basic functions and needs, combined with waves of violence, gradually reshaped and delineated the city into two.

In her paper *Big Events on a Small Scale: Exploring Identity-Based Mass Violence in Cities*, Ariana Markowitz refers to the enclaving of cities and the creation of two cities in one, which is evident in Aleppo's urban cleaving.[12] I argue that the lack of formal planning and investment in eastern Aleppo was intentional, a form of structural violence wherein the state fails to serve locals, who then organize to protect themselves from real and perceived threats. In response, citizens developed processes and networks to fill gaps created and maintained by those in power. These gaps, including public services, security, and permits, can be viewed as intentional forms of punishment, exclusion or suppression in response to challenges to existing power structures. In Markowitz's telling, the elite disengage and disembed from the rest of the city, enclaving themselves to form another identity around status, proximity to power, and influence. The bifurcation of the city in Aleppo had serious ramifications for its residents and topography.

As I discuss, each cycle of violence served to further segregate and distinguish the city as two distinct entities, one an alliance of convenience with the regime in the west and the other in opposition to it in the east; the former an area largely protected from violence, the latter subjected to repeated and varied manifestations of it. In a 2016 paper, Robert Templer and I argued that what Aleppo lived through during the war—from 2012 to 2016—amounted to urbicide, or city killing.[13] Dean Sharp argues that the violence perpetrated on the city is intended to rearrange the social and economic networks to more effectively control the urban settings.[14] Stephen Graham proposes three outcomes of urbicide: systematic destruction, exclusion of certain groups from cities, and exclusionary reconstruction frameworks, each of which are evident in Aleppo.[15]

Aleppo's Waves of Violence

In the past 60 years, we can see clear phases and methods of violence in and on Aleppo that fluctuated in its acuteness. However, even when not immediately subject to obvious violence, Aleppo and its population continued to experience a high level of structural violence inflicted by the Assad regime.

The Assads' long-term vision was of absolute control with minimal tolerance for opposition.[16] This was often achieved through structural violence—the approval or withholding of permits to develop infrastructure and plan new neighborhoods—which allowed the regime to shape the physical features and inhabitation of the city. Additionally, the infiltration of life by an assortment of intelligence agencies (at one count 15 under the rule of Hafez al-Assad)[17] instilled fear, curtailing discourse and movement to such an extent that the violence pervaded daily life in the city. Merchant industrialists in western Aleppo, in an effort to survive, aligned themselves with the regime. In turn, the regime rewarded adherents with new housing developments, jobs, and political appointments. Those viewed as detractors were punished through material neglect, arrests, and detention.

The power struggle in Aleppo was one for control as well as survival. As the elite consolidated their grip over the city, they reshaped its landscape and composition of its residents. Waves of violence cycled between violence on the city and violence in the city as the pendulum of harm swung between subjugation of Aleppians and control over Aleppo's urban form and function.

Acute violence was used to enforce acquiescence or silence, the staccato to the symphony of structural violence the Assads have conducted for half a century. The protracted episodes of acute violence (specifically the "Eighties Events," and then from 2011 to 2016) have signaled the willingness of the Ba'athists since the 1963 coup, and the Assads since 1970, to deploy whatever means necessary to maintain control and power. By analyzing the cycles of acute and structural violence perpetrated by the Assads, I show how they empowered the Alawites, the minority group to which they belong, and managed to shift alliances and leverage the positions of Alawites in the military, internal security, and government. This strategy had multiple purposes with specific consequences on the city of Aleppo, which will be explored in the following pages.

1963–1976: Monopoly of Politics: Identity and Structural Violence

The 1963 Ba'athist coup ushered in a new era of military governance that also shifted the composition of the Syrian army and security forces.[18] Through intimidation, arrests and other forms of coercion, the

Ba'ath Party monopolized politics. One of the most durable pillars of the Ba'ath regime was the change in the status of the Alawite religious minority, which transformed from a relatively small rural farming population to dominating the military and political classes. Sunni officers were sacked en masse in the 1960s and replaced by Alawite officers at all levels of the military. The mass replacement of officers was rooted in distrust of Sunni officers traditionally from the main cities of Damascus, Aleppo, Hama, and Homs, who were more often part of the urban, merchant, and landowner classes. Hafez Assad's strategic positioning of fellow Alawites into senior army and security positions, described by Yassin al Haj Saleh as "coup-proofing," facilitated his military, political, and personal control of Syria.[19] His "neo-patrimonial" regime granted authority, privileges, and access not on the basis of merit and political representation but on the basis of loyalty to the leader. Although, as Raymond Hinnebusch argues, some degree of cross-sectarian alliance building remained important for the regime to co-opt opposition, "an informal but widely understood 'ethnic arithmetic.'" But even then, Assad valued religious, tribal, and kinship ties over loyalty based on political, class, and other identities.[20]

This boosted the Alawites' standing over Sunnis in the military and political spheres. Alawite affiliation with the Assads provided leverage over the majority Sunni population, reconfiguring the balance of power and delivering a launch pad for future dissent and conflict between the groups. As the Assad regime tightened its grip on Syria's political, economic, and cultural life, it moved from a vision of a pan-Syrian community to a more fractured, identity-based configuration. The Assad family's efforts to align themselves (and the Alawites) with the Twelver Shia denomination and to be seen as a protector of other religious minorities (Christians, Druze, Ismailis) created fissures among the main religious groups in Syria, who had until this period coexisted relatively peacefully.

Assad's tactics risked reducing perceptions of Alawites to a hegemonic political elite, aligned with the destructive and chauvinistic regime. Many Alawites, however, opposed the Assads and did not share in or benefit from this power distribution in Syria.[21] In a book chapter titled "Violence in Identity," Indian economist and philosopher Amartya Sen warned that reducing identity to only one of its constitutive elements contributes to committing violence against this group.[22] By positioning itself as a force primarily concerned with promoting the interests of Alawites at the expense of other identity groups in Syria (via, for instance, initially sacking the majority of Sunni officers and later promoting only Alawites to leadership positions), the Assad regime contributed to the perception, by the majority Sunnis, of Alawites not as another ingredient of Syria but as the source of domination in army and civil life. This segmented Syrian society and further entrenched the insecurity of Alawites, who felt the need to monopolize their control of Syrian institutions and society. This again further augmented the resentment and sense of injustice among other Syrians, especially in Sunni working-class areas, such as eastern Aleppo neighborhoods, where levels of education and enrolment in the Ba'ath Party were low. While membership of the Ba'ath Party without Alawite affiliation did not elevate citizens to positions of high power in Syrian military, security, and civil institutions, it enabled them to reach mid-level positions, such as appointment as state employees. For instance, it was mandatory for school teachers to be members of the Ba'ath Party.

The subsequent social and political exclusion of the Sunni majority was structural violence, as elaborated on by Peter Uvin: the distribution of government positions and economic privileges at both the national and city scales to specific groups on the basis of religious sect and personal connections.[23] This favoritism has since been thoroughly reinforced by measures including community proximity to the president (being Alawite) and Ba'ath Party membership. The latter is a lower hurdle than the former. Decades of student cohorts, including myself and virtually all of my high school classmates, were coerced to enroll in the Ba'ath Party. As an acquired and actively encouraged identity, Ba'ath Party membership served the purpose of weeding out dissenters but was never as important as belonging to the Alawite community.

The Assads and the Alawite elite gradually shifted Syria's power center farther toward Damascus, away from Aleppo. Until 1963, Aleppians were often elected and served in Syria's parliament. With the coup, new generations of Aleppians felt they did not matter on the pan-Syrian political landscape. Traditional Aleppian elites, Sunnis and Christians alike, through historical family prestige and control over economic production, retained tenuous links to the regime. Despite their role as laborers contributing to the country's and western Aleppo's economic strength, eastern Aleppians, largely drawn from rural Sunni areas, reaped few of the political and economic benefits. The political, social, and cultural isolation of Aleppo, with its elites holding onto whatever relics of power was left by the Ba'ath Party and the Assads, were precipitating factors that shaped the fight in, for, and against Aleppo during the "Eighties Events" and from 2012 to 2016.

1976–1982: The "Eighties Events": The City as a Terrorists' Den (Acute)

From 1976 to 1982, Syria was engulfed by widespread protests and civic strikes by leftist parties, the conservative Sunni Muslim Brotherhood, as well as civic institutions such as the doctors' and engineers' syndicates that demanded the return of political and civic life to Syria. These manifestations soon spiraled into an armed fight between the Muslim Brotherhood and the Syrian regime under Hafez al-Assad. A faction of the Muslim Brotherhood carried out terrorist attacks and assassinations of suspected regime loyalists, primarily Alawite Ba'athists. Most infamously, in 1979, Colonel Ibrahim al-Youssef, a Sunni who was formally a Ba'ath Party member but secretly a member of the Tali'a extremist faction of the Muslim Brotherhood, called his cadets at the Aleppo Artillery Academy to a Ba'ath Party meeting. He then opened fire on them, killing 79, most or all of whom are thought to have been Alawite.[24]

The regime responded violently through mass arrests of communists, Muslim Brotherhood members, and anyone rumored to have expressed disagreement. The Syrian parliament outlawed the Muslim Brotherhood, imposing capital punishment on its members. Among those swept up in the crackdown were teenage university students who were found with anti-regime leaflets or publications, such as Aleppian writer and researcher Muhammad Berro, whom I met in 2015 in Istanbul. He was 17 when he was arrested and spent 13 years in the infamous Tadmor Prison, a few kilometers from the Palmyra (Tadmor in Arabic) Historical site. Berro remained in Syria after his release but now lives in exile because of his support for the 2011 Syrian Revolution.

Protests occurred predominantly in the cities of Aleppo and Hama. Thousands of young Aleppian men were disappeared in regime prisons, including Tadmor prison in Palmyra, by the early 1980s. Most of those who survived were only released in the late 1990s. In campaigns in the cities against "terrorists' dens," as referred to by commanders according to a veteran conscript, the regime conducted armed raids in civilian neighborhoods, rounding up civilian men, often at random, and then summarily executing them. Growing up, it was not unusual to see bullet holes on the exteriors of buildings in Old Aleppo, such as the Al-Bakraji Mosque in Qadi Askar. These bullets dated from the early 1980s.

The "events," as they are called in Aleppo, culminated in 1980, when an estimated 2,000 people were killed in security operations and 8,000 to 10,000 people were arrested.[25] In one such instance, following a Muslim Brotherhood operation on regime points in Aleppo, the Syrian Special Forces besieged the Masharqah neighborhood on the morning of Eid al-Fitr holiday (August 11), detained an unknown number of civilians (estimated at 80), and summarily executed and buried them in a mass grave in neighboring Hanano Cemetery.[26] While the fate of some of the disappeared was never known, a minority were released with signs of torture and deprival; others were found dead in the Queiq River.

The regime's violence during the "Eighties Events" instilled fear of protest in Syrians. Although demands for reform by a small number of intellectuals and human rights lawyers continued with the ascendance of Hafez al-Assad's son, Bashar al-Assad, to power in 2000, Syrians would not protest or gather in masses to revolt until March 2011, a generation after the "Eighties Events." The legacy of those events has entrenched a sense that the regime was willing to deploy violence to instill fear, oppress, and silence opponents in order to hold on to power. By some accounts, this modus operandi also intended to protect Alawites from future persecution or reprisals.[27]

The acuteness of the violence was both targeted and random, physical and psychological. The regime's deployment of structural violence for the purpose of retaining power at any cost sanctioned the use of these various forms of violence. This included intelligence services whose brutality reflected both long- and short-term strategies of violence. Their methods are imprinted on the bodies of the detainees imprisoned and tortured and the psyches of the population who witnessed the pain imposed on released prisoners and felt the absence of the many men (for the most part) who went permanently missing.

1980s–March 2011: A "Stable" Aleppo (Structural)

The late 1980s were an interlude of relative calm; opposition groups and bystanders alike were violently silenced, quelling dissent and establishing the absolute power of the Assad government and military. The oppression preceding this period was continued through various forms, less overt, but just as deadly and insidious for Aleppo's people. As an overwhelmingly non-Alawite city, Aleppo was deprived of its agency in national as well as local decision-making. In civic life, the Damascus-appointed governor of Aleppo Governorate and the Ba'ath Party leader in Aleppo each played a more powerful role than the locally elected president of the municipal council of Aleppo, whose role was reduced to technical service provision, rather than shaping a vision for the city.[28]

Before the Syrian Revolution ignited in 2011, the Assad regime monopolized power through a dual informal-formal approach to governance. Formally, extraordinary powers were granted to the ruling party through a 44-year state of emergency that upheld martial law and placed restrictions on freedom of association and speech. Additional laws and regulations followed in subsequent decades, limiting basic human rights, silencing critics, and curtailing civil society work under the guise of preserving national security. Under the state of emergency, civilians could be referred to the Supreme State Security Court (Mahkamat Amn al-Dawla al-`Uliyya), which was "exempted from the rules of procedure followed by regular Syrian courts."[29]

Informally, the plethora of secret service forces (locally known as *mukhabarat*) across the country used beatings and other forms of torture to coerce unyielding citizens. The mandatory military service for males, which was reduced before the 2011 revolution from 2.5 to 1.5 years, forcibly pooled Sunni manpower in the hands of Alawite officers, who exclusively occupied the highest echelons of the Syrian army and the numerous secret service administrations.

The informal-formal duality is important for understanding violence, structural and acute, in Syria. In February 2012, a year after the start of the Syrian Revolution, a new constitution was approved that formally removed Article 8 and the state of emergency, a cosmetic procedure aimed at appeasing the revolting population and giving the impression that the regime was reforming. Informally, detentions continued, most often without a prosecutor's warrant. Systematic torture in *mukhabarat* dungeons continued, now on a mass scale. According to the Syrian Network for Human Rights, no fewer than 120,000 Syrians are documented to have been forcibly disappeared in regime prisons.[30] Many of them have died while imprisoned and as a result of torture; the Syrian regime started to update civil registries of disappeared persons as "dead" years after their detention and enforced disappearance. As Bourgeois and Scheper-Huges write, violence is "mediated between the legitimate and illegitimate," between what is considered official or sanctioned, as when led by the state, or by a violent mob. In this case, the formal and legitimate structures of power orchestrated both.[31]

July 2012–December 2016: Revolution and War (Acute)

Inspired by the Arab Spring protests that started in late 2010 in Tunisia, masses across Syria's regions took to the street in March 2011. This was a rare show of defiance of the Syrian regime. The protests were peaceful, but the regime met them with brutal force, deploying snipers on rooftops, regime-recruited thugs (*shabbeeha*), and plainclothes *mukhabarat* officers who often were at the scene of protests before they even started, ready to beat and arrest whoever dared start the first chant. In Aleppo, the memory of previous episodes of violence by the Assad regime, particularly the "Eighties Events," was powerful. The general population was too cautious to join the revolution, fearing the repeat of past traumas. My brother told me how at one of the very first attempts at protesting in Aleppo in March 2011, at Amneh Mosque in Saif al-Dawleh, he was beaten with slippers, not by *shabbeeha* or *mukhabarat*, but by ordinary Aleppians who feared a repeat of the 1980s events. Until the fighting reached Aleppo in July 2012, Syrians in other parts of the country often mocked Aleppo for its denialism and reluctance to join the revolution, such as by the song mimicking the Aleppian word *tawel* (which means "at all"), titled "Nothing Is Happening Here at All."[32]

But by 2012, as the idea of revolution took hold across Syria and the regime escalated its violent crackdown on dissenting regions, Aleppo's protests grew louder, larger, and more frequent. However, daily student protests at the University of Aleppo and in neighborhoods across the city such as Hamdaniyeh, Salahaddin, Sakhour, Sukkari, Ashrafiyeh, and Bustan al-Qasr were never allowed to converge in the central square of Saadallah al-Jabri. All streets leading to the square were heavily guarded by security forces that shot at any demonstrators marching toward it. This deprived Aleppians of their moment of collective expression in the most communal space of the city.

The socioeconomic cleavages in Aleppo were etched in its geography in July 2012, when Liwa al-Tawhid, a coalition of armed rebels commanded from the northern countryside of Aleppo, advanced into the city and captured its eastern half in days. The regime was able to stop the rebels from occupying western Aleppo, where the elite lived, but had little interest in fighting for the more impoverished half of the city that hosts most of Aleppo's informal settlements. Its retreat from eastern Aleppo, however, brought battles to the geographic heart of the city. Initially, after its capture by the rebels, eastern Aleppo, free from the control of the Assads for the first time since 1970, bustled with social, political, and economic activity. The Free Aleppo City Council and neighborhood councils soon formed.

From 2012 to 2016, rebels controlled eastern Aleppo. Choosing to fight a war of attrition from a distance rather than engage in street battles in dissentious urban areas, the regime responded with sustained and targeted bombardment; it dropped thousands of barrel bombs, displacing the majority of the estimated 1.5 million population.[33] Although most casualties and urban destruction resulted from the relentless bombing (mostly aerial) by the Syrian regime and its Iranian and Russian allies, thousands others were forcibly disappeared at regime checkpoints erected across Aleppo and at roads leading into and out of the areas of regime control.[34]

As the faction that advanced onto Aleppo in 2012 numbered in the low thousands and was minimally equipped,[35] the retreating regime forces left a military vacuum in eastern Aleppo that was soon filled by sundry rebel groups of various leanings and allegiances. Transnational Sunni Islamist fighters (whom the Syrian regime had sent to undermine the Americans in Iraq in the mid-2000s)[36] re-emerged in 2013 in rebel-held Syria as the terrorist group the Islamic State of Iraq and Syria (ISIS), initially sharing control with Syrian rebel groups. In Aleppo, ISIS, though few in number and lacking popular support, taunted other groups and kidnapped and disappeared Aleppo's secular and religious activists. For example, Wael Ibrahim, who went by the alias Abu Mariam, organized near daily protests in his neighborhood of Bustan al-Qasr, where he made impassioned speeches on democracy, freedom, and dignity and invited others to speak, offering the back of his truck as a podium. After he had removed a banner bearing the words "an Islamic State" in a video-recorded protest, he was disappeared by ISIS.[37]

The presence of ISIS in Aleppo did not last long. By the end of 2013, rebel groups had launched a campaign to root out the terror group from rebel-held Syria. While the campaign failed catastrophically in Raqqa, which ISIS soon declared the capital of "the Caliphate," Aleppo and Idlib became free from ISIS by January 2014. That's when the Syrian regime intensified its war, not on ISIS-held Raqqa, but on Aleppo and Idlib.

The Syrian army perfected the manufacture and use of barrel bombs, crude explosives that can be ignited with a cigarette lighter and dropped from the back of a helicopter over urban areas.[38] Quickly, eastern Aleppo was depopulating.

I left Syria in April 2012 and have since only managed to visit my family's home in the Old City and eastern Aleppo neighborhood of Qadi Askar once, in October 2014. The bombing had caused serious damage to our house, with window glass broken and wooden ceiling beams and doors blasted down. Eastern Aleppo was transformed. Most of the population had left, and the city felt like a ghost town. Two years later, our neighbor sent us photos showing half of our house reduced to stones by a barrel bomb that fell in the middle of our street, a cul-de-sac alleyway. Two days after that, he was among the last fleeing Aleppo before the regime took full control of the city at the end of December 2016. He joined his family, who had left for their safety years earlier, in the Turkish city of Antakya. The last remaining residents, totaling 34,000 people, were bused out of eastern Aleppo through a deal brokered by Turkey and Russia. They joined the nearly 1.5 million residents of eastern Aleppo displaced mostly in rebel-held northwestern Syria and Turkey.

This cycle of acute violence came to an end around December 2016. Once bustling neighborhoods, mostly in formerly rebel-held eastern Aleppo and the Old City, were emptied. Some were killed, some expelled for their political views, and others still unable to return. In this void a new reality appeared where long-term and structural violence continues to suppress and deny hopes for renewal and meaningful reconstruction in eastern Aleppo.

Unlike in the aftermath of the eighties when Aleppo's civic life was manipulated mostly through state control, the power consolidation efforts that followed the regime's reconquest of Aleppo in 2016 featured neoliberal tools. This included manipulating the city's reconstruction efforts and cultural heritage management. For example, a local pro-Assad businessman, Hussam Katerji, whose wartime profits came from transporting oil from ISIS-held areas in northeastern Syria to Assad-controlled areas, was rewarded with a 50-year lease on land in the upscale New Aleppo district in the city's west.[39] More recently, the president's wife, Asma Assad, who has been increasingly active in controlling business in Syria, reportedly claimed Katerji's assets as part of her redevelopment efforts in Aleppo.[40]

Such takeovers are purported to benefit Asma Assad's projects, such as the Syria Trust for Development, and are conducted using the highest levels of government power. One of these mechanisms is, according to multiple reports, a special *mukhabarat* force reporting to the presidential palace.[41] It is also noteworthy that Asma Assad used the pretext of heritage management to advance the Assads' influence in an area where the local elite had previously enjoyed some autonomy. As an example, the Syria Trust for Development made an agreement with Aleppo's municipal Directorate of the Old City, potentially under pressure, to share its offices in the historical Saif al-Dawleh Palace with Asma Assad's Manaret Halab ("Aleppo's Minaret," a project of the Syria Trust), as outlined in a news report by Syria's official news agency, SANA.[42]

The post-2016 structures of violence have transitioned from the state's repressive apparatus to the use of nonstate actors such as businesspeople and NGOs. This new arrangement serves two purposes. First, it moves away from the more violent, illegitimate uses of state power and offers a veneer of legitimacy and civic mindedness. Second, it redistributes power and profit among the ruling elites[43] while continuing to suppress the Aleppo population's right to its city. The irony of cultural institutions being denied to those communities they are intended to serve, and instead being ostensibly protected by the wife of the same president who killed and displaced members of these same communities, is highly symbolic and will have lasting effects on the city's life.

Are Aleppo's Times of Acute and Structural Violence a Reflection of Its Identities?

The practices of the Assad regime during the 2012–2016 episode of acute violence pitted Aleppians not only against the state but also against each other. The violence exacerbated the existing social divisions in the city, where people on both sides of it felt antagonized and victimized by the other. The regime weaponized Aleppo's spatial-identity split when it positioned its artillery in western Aleppo from 2012 to 2016. While the artillery was intended to protect the west, it instead created a shelling target for rebel-held eastern Aleppian troops. In turn, western Aleppo's residents lost sympathy for their eastern neighbors, as they realized the defeat (including by annihilation) of eastern Aleppo would bring an end to the barrage of attacks.

Whether inflicted through mass bombing from the sky or detentions and forced disappearances on the ground, violence in Aleppo's post-1963 history has been largely identity-based. Although both halves of the city are Sunni majority, with a significant Christian minority in central-western Aleppo, other identity markers were used to distinguish one's "right to the city." This included the right to work, access to services, or even the right to exist in the city.[44] Identity framed through a complex set of factors including class, geography, and religion could result in the perpetration of violence. Being from eastern Aleppo, a rebel-held area, or being a member of a conservative Sunni Muslim sect were equated with antagonism toward the liberal Alawite elite. One's address on their identity card, the heaviness of an Aleppian accent, or one's perceived religiosity—be it a beard or a head or face covering—also resulted in arbitrary treatment and targeting. As Antonio Sampaio discusses in this volume, these identity boundary activations served to distinguish between those deserving protection or services and those intended for elimination, exclusion, or extraction from the city.

It is important to note that the identity fractures along which violence in the city occurred did not originate in Aleppo but in Damascus. The key cleavage in Aleppo for the past 60 years has been one deepened by support for the regime; allegiance to the regime has often trumped sectarian ties. For example, some of the *shabbeeha* suppressing the 2011 protests in Aleppo were paid for by the local Sunni Berri clan, which had long been aligned with the regime.[45] At the same time, it is indisputable that the regime has actively fostered the creation of sectarian identities. As Raymond Hinnebusch suggests, the ascent of Alawites can be seen both as a product and a strategy of maintaining the Assads' regime in power, creating a dominant sectarian identity out of a previously irrelevant one. Yassin al Haj Saleh calls the Alawite sectarian identity "sculpted" by giving the group political and economic privileges, making group identification attractive, while suppressing political dissent within the group.[46] Both agree that a Sunni Islamic opposition identity has emerged in part as a reaction to the privileging of sectarian ties among the Alawites and has been facilitated by a sense of being denied opportunities—in other words, the structural violence of social exclusion.

Nearly half of Aleppo's 2011 population, estimated at around three million, have been displaced or forced out of the city, an exile that was politically expedient for the Syrian regime.[47] Most of them are from the eastern half of the city.[48] Half of them live less than 100 kilometers from home in internally displaced person (IDP) camps in Idlib and the western and northern regions of Aleppo Governorate and in Turkey. Despite dire living conditions in the camps, displaced Aleppians do not believe that returning to their homes is an option. They fear persecution, arrests at checkpoints, and mandatory military service (for males) in the very army that destroyed their homes and killed their families and neighbors.[49]

This forced extraction created new "out groups" of displaced Aleppians. Some of those displacements were of existing IDPs, reinforcing a sense of exclusion and decimating any sense of belonging and home.[50] The remaining population of Aleppo were those most closely aligned with the Assad regime. These displacements can be viewed as a form of structural violence, made possible by the targeted atrocities of the regime. The displaced are a new identity group—a consequence of the violence, presently enclaved in camps, and subjected to ongoing forms of exclusion. The IDPs' location in rural areas creates yet another contrasting identity to the cosmopolitan western Aleppian. A keen observer will note the irony that many of those displaced were originally rural migrants who moved to Aleppo in the 1980s, contributing to the city's economic growth and the country's productivity.

Conclusion

There are no military battles being fought in Aleppo today. However, as of the writing of this chapter (early 2024), the Syrian regime and its allies, Russia and Iran, continue to bombard swathes of Aleppo and Idlib governorates held by forces opposed to the Syrian regime. This spate of violence has spawned new identity groups, increasingly vulnerable and subjected to the types of structural violence—including discrimination, exclusion, and geographic isolation—that are difficult to overcome without substantial political and economic evolution.

The Assad regime's response to the Syrian Revolution in 2011 ushered in a period of acute violence, including deadly battles between the state and resistance forces as well as armed nonstate groups. The enduring conflict is a continuation of decades of structural violence perpetrated against Syria's communities and cities. In Aleppo, government, rebel, and Islamist groups used the city as a staging ground. Each deployed its own forms of violence with lasting impacts on the demographics, skyline, and infrastructure of the city. These physical reminders take the shape of bullet holes, dilapidated buildings, and of the dispersion and absence of its residents. They are poignant markers of the duality of acute violence—brief interludes of intense violence that can leave permanent scars. The Syrian government neglected its formal responsibility to protect Aleppo and its population; rather than rebuild, it left eastern Aleppo in ruins, enforcing its own brand of structural violence, a more insidious, lingering, and intentional practice. It maintains control through urbicide: targeted destruction of the built environment as well as the deprivation of services and assistance.[51]

The most recent period of acute violence (2012–2016) was not an isolated event and can be considered part of a playbook of an intentionally perpetrated condition of violence built into the structure of state and society. Past episodes of acute violence, and the structurally violent "peaceful" interludes they left behind—such as the nonchalant neglect of the economically disadvantaged and politically nonenmeshed eastern Aleppo—have created a pattern that remains visible in the population's response to more recent events. Unlike in Hama in 1982, where the entire city was collectively punished by the regime for its resistance, the response in Aleppo was conditional, gauged by a spatialized identity created and institutionalized by politics and sectarianism. The extent to which the regime's response in Aleppo had been spacialized in the 1980s would necessitate separate research. However, the entrenchment of violence and urban destruction in the most recent conflict is today evident in the Syrian urban landscape beyond Aleppo. In Damascus, for instance, well-off neighborhoods were largely spared the urban fighting. In contrast, the former Ghouta orchards surrounding Damascus that had turned into densely populated informal settlements have borne the brunt of fighting, urban destruction, and mass displacement since 2011.[52] This dynamic is of course not specific to Syria. Identity-based mass violence in cities around the world, such as Baghdad and Delhi, has been highly spatialized, further enclaving identity-assigned communities.[53]

Aleppians' cautious engagement during the early days of the Syrian Revolution, as well as the inability of IDPs to return to the city, reflect the trauma of a violent history and the legacy of distrust and inequality it has created. Regime-led reconstruction and heritage-protection efforts reflect a strategy of domination, a usurping of identity by seemingly legitimate means to maintain control that continue to divide the city. Peace in Aleppo is relative, it is an interlude during which physical, armed, and targeted battles give way to forms of neglect, oppression, and control that benefit few. Ultimately, the scars of violence are borne by the city and its people in an ongoing struggle for autonomy and self-reliance.

Notes

1. This chapter benefited immensely from lengthy discussions, recommendations, and reviews by Ioli Filmeridis, Rachel Locke, and Olga Löblová. Without their Ayyub-like patience as well as the unrelenting support of this volume's editorial team, this chapter would not have seen the light of day. I also acknowledge the sharp insights I gained from the participants and advisers at each of the volume's workshops, as well as from Zafer Nahhas and Mohammed Ateek.
2. "Protesters Want Changes to Syria's Power Structure," NPR, April 27, 2011, https://www.npr.org/2011/04/27/135760793/protests-disrupt-syrias-power-structure.
3. Johan Galtung, "Violence, Peace, and Peace Research," *Journal of Peace Research* 6, no. 3 (1969): 167–91.
4. The Baath Party in Syria. Harvard Divinity School. Religion and Public Life. https://rpl.hds.harvard.edu. The al Ba'ath Arab Socialist Party was founded in Syria on the basis of secular Arab nationalism, socialism, and militarism.
5. Nick Compton, "What Is the Oldest City in the World?," *The Guardian*, February 16, 2015, Cities, https://www.theguardian.com/cities/2015/feb/16/whats-the-oldest-city-in-the-world.
6. Syria is geographically composed of 14 administrative units called governorates. A governorate is analogous to a province in Turkey or a county in the United Kingdom.

7. Keith David Watenpaugh, "Cleansing the Cosmopolitan City: Historicism, Journalism and the Arab Nation in the Post-Ottoman Eastern Mediterranean," *Social History* 30, no. 1 (February 1, 2005): 1–24, https://doi.org/10.1080/03071024200337260.
8. Although protests in Syria, including Aleppo, started in March 2011 and developed into an armed conflict by late 2011, Aleppo only became a military battleground in July 2012. In this text, I sometimes refer to 2011 and other times to 2012 as the relevant starting point of the latest conflict in Aleppo.
9. Zeido Zeido and Nura Ibold, "The Division of Aleppo City: Heritage and Urban Space," in *Urban Heritage in Divided Cities*, ed. Mirjana Ristic and Sybille Frank, 1st ed. (New York: Routledge, 2019), 87–104, https://doi.org/10.4324/9780429460388-6.
10. Ibid.
11. Mohamad Khayata, "حلبية أنتيكا | بزمناتو كان بالمنشية القديمة موقف باص حي | السبيل ووراه مباشرة موقف باص باب النيرب," Facebook, January 15, 2021, https://www.facebook.com/groups/aleppo.antika/posts/3480050192220588.
12. Ariana Markowitz, *Big Events on a Small Scale: Exploring Identity-Based Mass Violence in Cities*, Stanley Center for Peace and Security and Impact:Peace, December 2020.
13. Alhakam Shaar and Robert Templer, "Urbicide or an Elegy for Aleppo," *Tvergastein Interdisciplinary Journal of the Environment* 7 (August 2016): 108–19.
14. Sharp, Deen. 'Urbicide and the Arrangement of Violence in Syria'. In *Beyond the Square: Urbanism and the Arab Uprisings*, edited by Deen Sharp and Claire Panetta, 118. Urban Research. New York City: Terreform, Inc., 2016.
15. Hani Fakhani and Sawsan Abou Zainedin, *Syria's Urbicide: The Built Environment as a Means to Consolidate Homogeneity*, July 2019, 1, accessed January 3, 2024, https://www.thealeppoproject.com/wp-content/uploads/2019/07/SyriasUrbicideSawsanAbouZainedinHaniFakhani2019.pdf.
16. Yassin al Haj Saleh, "Assad's 'Eternal Rule': The Long Prelude to Genocide," *Crisis Magazine*, October 1, 2019, https://crisismag.net/2019/10/01/assads-eternal-rule-the-long-prelude-to-genocide/.
17. "The Inquiry: Aleppo under the Assads," BBC Sounds, accessed December 22, 2023, https://www.bbc.co.uk/sounds/play/p04f0x8b.

18. The 1963 Baath Party coup was initiated by three Alawite army officers: Muhammad Umran, Salah Jadid, and Hafez Assad. Umran was sidelined in the 1966 intra-Baathist coup, leaving Jadid and Assad competing over absolute dominance, until Assad led the 1970 coup that he dubbed the "Corrective Movement," which landed Jadid in Mezzeh Prison in Damascus until his death in 1993.
19. Haj Saleh, "Assad's 'Eternal Rule.'".
20. Raymond Hinnebusch, "Syria's Alawis and the Ba'ath Party," in *The Alawis of Syria*, ed. Michael Kerr and Craig Larkin (Oxford: Oxford University Press, 2015), 107–24, https://doi.org/10.1093/acprof:oso/9780190458119.003.0005.
21. Ibid.
22. Amartya Sen, "Violence in Identity," in *Values and Violence: Intangible Aspects of Terrorism*, ed. Ibrahim A. Karawan, Wayne McCormack, and Stephen E. Reynolds, Studies in Global Justice (Dordrecht: Springer Netherlands, 2008), 3–13, https://doi.org/10.1007/978-1-4020-8660-1_1.
23. Peter Uvin, "Global Dreams and Local Anger: From Structural to Acute Violence in a Globalizing World," in *Rethinking Global Political Economy* (Milton Park, UK: Routledge, 2004), 157–72.
24. Salwa Ismail, *The Rule of Violence: Subjectivity, Memory and Government in Syria*, 1st ed. (Cambridge: Cambridge University Press, 2018), 83, https://doi.org/10.1017/9781139424721.
25. Human rights watch-Middle East, ed. *Syria Unmasked: The Suppression of Human Rights by the Asad Regime*. Human Rights Watch Books. New Haven: Yale University Press, 1991.
26. Syrian Human Rights Committee, "Thirty-Five Years on the Mashariqa Massacre: Blood Which Hasn't Yet Dried," August 1, 2015, https://www.shrc.org/en/?p=25565.
27. Hinnebusch, "Syria's Alawis."
28. Even though the municipal council is chosen in local elections, these elections were cosmetic, with the regime approving its members, based on party membership and other considerations.
29. 'No Room to Breathe: State Repression of Human Rights Activism in Syria'. Human Rights Watch, October 2007, Footnote 26. https://www.hrw.org/report/2007/10/16/no-room-breathe/state-repression-human-rights-activism-syria.

30. Syrian Network for Human Rights, *SNHR's 12th Annual Report on Enforced Disappearance in Syria on the International Day of the Disappeared: Enforced Disappearance Is an Ongoing Crime in Syria*, August 30, 2023, https://snhr.org/blog/2023/08/30/snhrs-12th-annual-report-on-enforced-disappearance-in-syria-on-the-international-day-of-the-disappeared-enforced-disappearance-is-an-ongoing-crime-in-syria.

31. Pearce, Jenny V. 'Violence, Power and Participation: Building Citizenship in Contexts of Chronic Violence.' Working Paper. Institute of Development Studies, 2007. https://bradscholars.brad.ac.uk/handle/10454/3802.

32. اسأل الحلبي حاول (واقع أهل حلب خلال الثورة السورية), 2011, https://www.youtube.com/watch?v=tENAaUw3aEk.

33. Anna Costa and Michele Macmillan, *From Rebel to Regime: Barriers of Return to Aleppo for Internally Displaced People (IDPs)*, The Aleppo Project, July 2018.

34. "Syria: A Stream of Bodies in Aleppo's River," Human Rights Watch, June 4, 2013, https://www.hrw.org/news/2013/06/04/syria-stream-bodies-aleppos-river.

35. Armenak Tokmajyan, "Aleppo Conflict Timeline—2012," The Aleppo Project, May 10, 2016, https://www.thealeppoproject.com/aleppo-conflict-timeline-2012.

36. Michael Weiss and Hassan Hassan, *ISIS: Inside the Army of Terror*, updated ed. (New York: Simon and Schuster, 2016).

37. Liz Sly, "How the Syrian Revolt Went So Horribly, Tragically Wrong," *Washington Post*, March 12, 2016, https://www.washingtonpost.com/world/middle_east/how-the-syrian-revolt-went-so-horribly-tragically-wrong/2016/03/12/4aba6c86-d979-11e5-8210-f0bd8de915f6_story.html.

38. "What's a Barrel Bomb?," BBC News, 2015, https://www.youtube.com/watch?v=OmJI0DTI1Lo.

39. Karam Shaar, "نص عقد استثمار القاطرجي لأرض المشفى العسكري في حلب لمدة 50 عامًا- نيسان 2021," accessed January 2, 2024, https://www.karamshaar.com/qaterji-investment-alepoo-tourism.

40. "Oil Trader and Militia Leader Hossam Qaterji Escapes; Asma al-Assad Seizes His Property," *Syrian Observer* (blog), October 17, 2023, https://syrianobserver.com/features/85707/oil-trader-and-militia-leader-hossam-qaterji-escapes-asma-al-assad-seizes-his-property.html.

41. Raya Jalabi, "Syria's State Capture: The Rising Influence of Mrs Assad," *Financial Times*, April 2, 2023, https://www.ft.com/content/a51c6227-0c93-4fe1-aca7-25783a43708f.
42. "اتفاقية لتأسيس وإطلاق منارة حلب ضمن مدرسة سيف الدولة في حلب القديمة," Syrian Arab News Agency—SANA, August 5, 2023, https://sana.sy/?p=1944420.
43. AlHakam Shaar, "Reconstruction, but for Whom? Embracing the Role of Aleppo's Displaced," in *Reconstructing Syria: Risks and Side Effects* (Berlin, Adopt a Revolution, 2018), https://adoptrevolution.org/wp-content/uploads/2019/01/Reconstruction_Web-EN_Final.pdf.
44. "Syria: A Stream of Bodies in Aleppo's River."
45. Salwa, *Rule of Violence*, 83.
46. Haj Saleh, "Assad's 'Eternal Rule.'".
47. ElSayed Mahmoud ElSehamy, "The World as an Exiling Political Structure: Yassin al-Haj Saleh's Conceptualisation of Exile," in *Refugees and Knowledge Production* (Milton Park, UK: Routledge, 2022).
48. While no official figures exist, thousands of residents left western Aleppo to escape the war, persecution (including some of my closest friends who joined the protests in 2011 and 2012), and the regime's mandatory military service. Residents of eastern Aleppo, on the other hand, were gradually forced out of their homes from mid-2012 to the end of 2016, first by the mass bombing by the regime and their allies and eventually as they closed in on the city, forcibly evicting the last remaining 34,000 residents. Since 2016, when Assad took back control of eastern Aleppo, only a minority of the displaced have felt safe to return. According to the UN High Commissioner for Refugees' "Return Perception and Intention Survey among Syrian Refugees," 1.1 percent of Syrian refugees surveyed in 2023 said they intended to return to their homes in the next 12 months, even though 56 percent expressed their wish to return to Syria one day. (See UN OCHA's *Humanitarian Needs Overview: Syrian Arab Republic*, February 2024, p. 30).
49. Costa and Macmillan, *From Rebel to Regime*, 15.
50. Sharp, "Urbicide."
51. Shaar and Templer, "Urbicide or an Elegy for Aleppo."
52. Anna Costa, *The Barriers and Limitations of the Modern Approach to Recognizing Genocide in Syria: A Case Study of the Sieges of Eastern Aleppo and Eastern Ghouta*, The Aleppo Project, Central European University, April 2021, https://www.thealeppoproject.com/wp-content/uploads/2021/04/Costa_Genocide_Syria_TheAleppoProject.pdf.

53. Harith Hasan Al-Qarawee, *Iraq's Sectarian Crisis: A Legacy of Exclusion*, Carnegie Middle East Center, April 2014, https://www.jstor.org/stable/pdf/resrep12876.pdf.; "Jahangirpuri: Shock and Anger in Delhi after Religious Violence," BBC News, April 18, 2022, India, https://www.bbc.com/news/world-asia-india-61137974.

References

Al-Qarawee, Harith Hasan. *Iraq's Sectarian Crisis: A Legacy of Exclusion*. Carnegie Middle East Center, April 2014. https://www.jstor.org/stable/pdf/resrep12876.pdf?acceptTC=true&coverpage=false&addFooter=false.

Compton, Nick. "What Is the Oldest City in the World?," *The Guardian*, February 16, 2015, Cities. https://www.theguardian.com/cities/2015/feb/16/whats-the-oldest-city-in-the-world.

Costa, Anna. The Barriers and Limitations of the Modern Approach to Recognizing Genocide in Syria: A Case Study of the Sieges of Eastern Aleppo and Eastern Ghouta. The Aleppo Project, Central European University, April 2021. https://www.thealeppoproject.com/wp-content/uploads/2021/04/Costa_Genocide_Syria_TheAleppoProject.pdf.

Costa, Anna, and Michele Macmillan. *From Rebel to Regime: Barriers of Return to Aleppo for Internally Displaced People (IDPs)*. The Aleppo Project, July 2018.

ElSehamy, ElSayed Mahmoud. "The World as an Exiling Political Structure: Yassin al-Haj Saleh's Conceptualisation of Exile." In *Refugees and Knowledge Production*. Milton Park, UK: Routledge, 2022.

Galtung, Johan. "Violence, Peace, and Peace Research." *Journal of Peace Research* 6, no. 3 (1969): 167–91.

Haj Saleh, Yassin al. "Assad's 'Eternal Rule': The Long Prelude to Genocide." *Crisis Magazine*, October 2, 2019. https://crisismag.net/2019/10/01/assads-eternal-rule-the-long-prelude-to-genocide.

Hani Fakhani and Sawsan Abou Zainedin, *Syria's Urbicide: The Built Environment as a Means to Consolidate Homogeneity*, July 2019, 1, accessed January 3, 2024, https://www.thealeppoproject.com/wp-content/uploads/2019/07/SyriasUrbicideSawsanAbouZainedinHaniFakhani2019.pdf.

Hinnebusch, Raymond. "Syria's Alawis and the Ba'ath Party." In *The Alawis of Syria*, edited by Michael Kerr and Craig Larkin, 107–24.

Oxford: Oxford University Press, 2015. https://doi.org/10.1093/acprof:oso/9780190458119.003.0005.

Human rights watch-Middle East, ed. *Syria Unmasked: The Suppression of Human Rights by the Asad Regime*. Human Rights Watch Books. New Haven: Yale University Press, 1991.

Ismail, Salwa. *The Rule of Violence: Subjectivity, Memory and Government in Syria*. 1st ed. Cambridge: Cambridge University Press, 2018. https://doi.org/10.1017/9781139424721.

"Jahangirpuri: Shock and Anger in Delhi after Religious Violence." BBC News, April 18, 2022, India. https://www.bbc.com/news/world-asia-india-61137974.

Jalabi, Raya. "Syria's State Capture: The Rising Influence of Mrs Assad." *Financial Times*, April 2, 2023. https://www.ft.com/content/a51c6227-0c93-4fe1-aca7-25783a43708f.

Karam Shaar. "نص عقد استثمار القاطرجي لأرض المشفى العسكري في حلب لمدة 50 عامًا- نيسان 2021." Accessed January 2, 2024. https://www.karamshaar.com/qaterji-investment-alepoo-tourism.

"نص عقد استثمار القاطرجي لأرض المشفى العسكري في حلب لمدة 50 عامًا- نيسان 2021," Karam Shaar, accessed January 2, 2024, https://www.karamshaar.com/qaterji-investment-alepoo-tourism.

Khayata, Mohamad. "حلبية أنتيكا | بزمناتو كان بالمنشية القديمة موقف باص حي السبيل- وراه مباشرة موقف باص باب النيرب." Facebook, January 15, 2021. https://www.facebook.com/groups/aleppo.antika/posts/3480050192220588.

Markowitz, Ariana. *Big Events on a Small Scale: Exploring Identity-Based Mass Violence in Cities*. Stanley Center for Peace and Security and Impact:Peace, December 2020.

'No Room to Breathe: State Repression of Human Rights Activism in Syria'. Human Rights Watch, October 2007, Footnote 26. https://www.hrw.org/report/2007/10/16/no-room-breathe/state-repression-human-rights-activism-syria.

Pearce, Jenny V. 'Violence, Power and Participation: Building Citizenship in Contexts of Chronic Violence.' Working Paper. Institute of Development Studies, 2007. https://bradscholars.brad.ac.uk/handle/10454/3802.

"Protesters Want Changes to Syria's Power Structure." NPR, April 27, 2011. https://www.npr.org/2011/04/27/135760793/protests-disrupt-syrias-power-structure.

Sen, Amartya. "Violence in Identity." In *Values and Violence: Intangible Aspects of Terrorism*, edited by Ibrahim A. Karawan, Wayne McCormack, and Stephen E. Reynolds, 3–13. Studies in Global Justice. Dordrecht: Springer Netherlands, 2008. https://doi.org/10.1007/978-1-4020-8660-1_1.

Shaar, Alhakam. "Reconstruction, but for Whom? Embracing the Role of Aleppo's Displaced." In *Reconstructing Syria: Risks and Side Effects*. Adopt a Revolution, 2018. https://adoptrevolution.org/wp-content/uploads/2019/01/Reconstruction_Web-EN_Final.pdf.

Shaar, Alhakam, and Robert Templer. "Urbicide or an Elegy for Aleppo." *Tvergastein Interdisciplinary Journal of the Environment* 7 (August 2016): 108–19.

Sharp, Deen. 'Urbicide and the Arrangement of Violence in Syria'. In *Beyond the Square: Urbanism and the Arab Uprisings*, edited by Deen Sharp and Claire Panetta, 118. Urban Research. New York City: Terreform, Inc., 2016.

Sly, Liz. "How the Syrian Revolt Went So Horribly, Tragically Wrong." *Washington Post*, March 12, 2016. https://www.washingtonpost.com/world/middle_east/how-the-syrian-revolt-went-so-horribly-tragically-wrong/2016/03/12/4aba6c86-d979-11e5-8210-f0bd8de915f6_story.html.

"Syria: A Stream of Bodies in Aleppo's River." Human Rights Watch, June 4, 2013. https://www.hrw.org/news/2013/06/04/syria-stream-bodies-aleppos-river.

Syrian Human Rights Committee. "Thirty-Five Years on the Mashariqa Massacre: Blood Which Hasn't Yet Dried," August 1, 2015. https://www.shrc.org/en/?p=25565.

Syrian Network for Human Rights. SNHR's 12th Annual Report on Enforced Disappearance in Syria on the International Day of the Disappeared: Enforced Disappearance Is an Ongoing Crime in Syria, August 30, 2023. https://snhr.org/blog/2023/08/30/snhrs-12th-annual-report-on-enforced-disappearance-in-syria-on-the-international-day-of-the-disappeared-enforced-disappearance-is-an-ongoing-crime-in-syria.

Syrian Observer. "Oil Trader and Militia Leader Hossam Qaterji Escapes; Asma al-Assad Seizes His Property," October 17, 2023. https://syrianobserver.com/features/85707/oil-trader-and-militia-leader-hossam-qaterji-escapes-asma-al-assad-seizes-his-property.html.

"The Inquiry: Aleppo under the Assads." BBC Sounds. Accessed December 22, 2023. https://www.bbc.co.uk/sounds/play/p04f0x8b.

Tokmajyan, Armenak. "Aleppo Conflict Timeline—2012." The Aleppo Project, May 10, 2016. https://www.thealeppoproject.com/aleppo-conflict-timeline-2012.

UN Office for the Coordination of Human Affairs. *Humanitarian Needs Overview: Syrian Arab Republic*. February 2024. https://reliefweb.int/report/syrian-arab-republic/syrian-arab-republic-2024-humanitarian-needs-overview-february-2024.

Uvin, Peter. "Global Dreams and Local Anger: From Structural to Acute Violence in a Globalizing World." In *Rethinking Global Political Economy*, 157–72. Milton Park, UK: Routledge, 2004.

Watenpaugh, Keith David. "Cleansing the Cosmopolitan City: Historicism, Journalism and the Arab Nation in the Post-Ottoman Eastern Mediterranean." *Social History* 30, no. 1 (February 1, 2005): 1–24. https://doi.org/10.1080/03071024200033760.

Weiss, Michael, and Hassan Hassan. *ISIS: Inside the Army of Terror*. Updated ed. New York: Simon and Schuster, 2016.

"What's a Barrel Bomb?," BBC News, 2015. https://www.youtube.com/watch?v=OmJI0DTI1Lo.

Zeido, Zeido, and Nura Ibold. "The Division of Aleppo City: Heritage and Urban Space." In *Urban Heritage in Divided Cities*, edited by Mirjana Ristic and Sybille Frank, 1st ed., 87–104. New York: Routledge, 2019. https://doi.org/10.4324/9780429460388-6.

"اتفاقية لتأسيس وإطلاق منارة حلب ضمن مدرسة سيف الدولة في حلب القديمة." Syrian Arab News Agency—SANA, August 5, 2023. https://sana.sy/?p=1944420.

(واقع أهل حلب خلال الثورة السورية اسأل الحلبي حاول), 2011. https://www.youtube.com/watch?v=tENAaUw3aEk.

Alhakam Shaar is a linguist and urban sociologist. He is a researcher at The Aleppo Project (Central Eueopean University, 2015–2020; independently, 2020 -), and currently contributes to research on preserving Aleppian cultural heritage Facebook groups, as part of the Modern Endangered Archives Program at the Unversity of California at Los Angeles. He holds master's degrees in Applied Linguistics (University of Aleppo, 2012) and Sociology and Social Anthropology (CEU, 2021). His thesis used ethnographic methods to study placemaking by Aleppian migrants and refugees in Berlin. He is now training in computational linguistics, aiming to contribute to the documentation of Aleppo's linguistic heritage. Shaar also enjoys interpreting at conferences and workshops.

Open Access This chapter is licensed under the terms of the Creative Commons Attribution-NonCommercial-NoDerivatives 4.0 International License (http://creativecommons.org/licenses/by-nc-nd/4.0/), which permits any noncommercial use, sharing, distribution and reproduction in any medium or format, as long as you give appropriate credit to the original author(s) and the source, provide a link to the Creative Commons license and indicate if you modified the licensed material. You do not have permission under this license to share adapted material derived from this chapter or parts of it.

The images or other third party material in this chapter are included in the chapter's Creative Commons license, unless indicated otherwise in a credit line to the material. If material is not included in the chapter's Creative Commons license and your intended use is not permitted by statutory regulation or exceeds the permitted use, you will need to obtain permission directly from the copyright holder.

Nourish You
A Mother Searches for Her Son, Arrested During President Bukele's State of Emergency in El Salvador

Juan Martínez d'Aubuisson and Sarah Meléndez

J. M. d'Aubuisson (✉) · S. Meléndez
Dromomanos, San Salvador, El Salvador
e-mail: juanjosemartinez.rds@gmail.com

S. Meléndez
Dromomanos, San Salvador, El Salvador

At my house many years ago, we caught a baby bird. It was a baby pigeon and did nothing but cry during the day and snuggle into itself, depressed, at night, but it didn't die. One day we discovered a large bird in the window with something in its beak. It was the baby bird's mother sneaking it food. She stuck her beak through the metal bars on the window and put worms within reach of her baby. She repeated this procedure several times a day, with the tenacity of one who has no alternative.

Nourish You   **235**

> Thank god they took the cans out of the windows.

Says Eva when we got close to the biggest prison in the capital of El Salvador, where her nineteen-year-old son has been held for the past year.

The prison complex is big, old, and in the middle of the city. Outside, just a few meters from the building's cells and bars, buses, cars, and people rush by. The "cans", in reality, were metal sheets that the security forces put over the street-facing windows so that the prisoners couldn't communicate with their families or anyone else from inside their cells. They put them up one month after the mass raids, when the regime filled the country's prisons with tens of thousands of Salvadorans.

During the first days the men yelled for hours...

> How's my mom?

> Lupeeeee!

> Send the combined cream!

..then the metal sheets arrived..

...now, nobody yells.

Outside is a sort of encampment. The dozens of stalls that have been set up for selling food and prison uniforms, white shorts, white T-shirts and white rubber-soled shoes are crammed together like the town's marketplace. An evangelical pastor shouts with the help of a portable megaphone, "This is a message of surrender, of love." And then he talks about David and some problem he had with another biblical figure. He knows that the men inside can hear him, and he tells them that this is an opportunity to change, to let God into their lives; he tells them that maybe they don't understand it now but that's what's happening.

Eva gets out of our pickup truck (usually she comes by bus) and heads toward one of the stalls of this makeshift market.

Her son, Jonas, like approximately 70,000 Salvadorans, was arrested by the security forces during the state of emergency put in place by President Nayib Bukele at the beginning of 2022, after an agreement with the Maras, the mafias of gang origin that have ruled a good part of the country for two decades, went sour, and the gang's network began to almost indiscriminately assassinate Salvadorans. The viciousness of the Maras after the rupture of the agreements with the Bukele regime was so intense that March 26, 2022, was the day with the highest number of registered killings in El Salvador's history since the end of the civil war 32 years ago. At least 62 Salvadorans lost their lives that day. The president's response was to implement a state of emergency regime in an attempt to destroy the Maras' power in one fell swoop. The government organized mass raids, wich were as indiscriminate as the gang members' bullets, and once again powerless Salvadorans paid the price for the poorly managed agreements between powerful Salvadorans.

Eva cannot see or speak to her son. No one can see those who are being detained, not even human rights organizations or their designated lawyers. However, feeding 70,000 people, in addition to the 40,000 prisoners that already made up the Salvadoran prison population, isn't easy, and above all, isn't cheap. Bukele's regime opted for an easy out: let their families feed them.

238   J. M. d'Aubuisson and S. Meléndez

Among the list of articles that can be sent to prisoners, one stands out. The combined cream. It's a mix meant for fungal infections and many other skin problems. Including it on the list is the government's way of saying that inside prisoners could have health problems. The truth is that it's more than a problem, it's become an epidemic of scabies. More than six sources who have recently left the prison system still have the scars on their skin left by scabies, and they talk about an out-of-control epidemic, of entire bodies infected by the digging parasite that causes it.

The seller takes a tube of this cream and empties it into a plastic bag. In El Salvador the idea has spread that by adding some ground amoxicillin, ibuprofen, and just about any pills they can get their hands on into the cream will increase its potency.

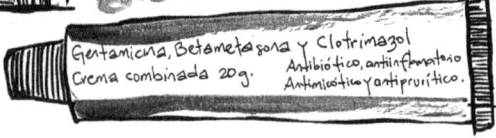

He asks Eva if she wants the enhanced cream and recommends amoxicillin. It's minor contraband, and likely has no medical effect.

Nourish You   **239**

Although Eva can't see or talk to her son, she has to travel every 15 days, or whenever money permits, to leave him a package of food at the prison.

How lucky, today it's empty.

Before turning over the package, Eva stands in a long line to confirm that Jonas hasn't been moved somewhere else.

045738
Jonas
Sector 9
Cell 5

INFORMATION
↓ HERE ↓

Another line, just as long, is for those who prefer to pay cash so that the government will take care of delivering the packages.

Paquetes para hombre

Descripción	Valor
Paquete 1 nutrición	$ 95.00
Paquete 2 misceláneos	$ 70.00
Paquete 4 Higiene	$ 15.00
Paquete 5 Vestimenta	$ 30.00
Paquete 7 Limpieza de área	$ 20.00

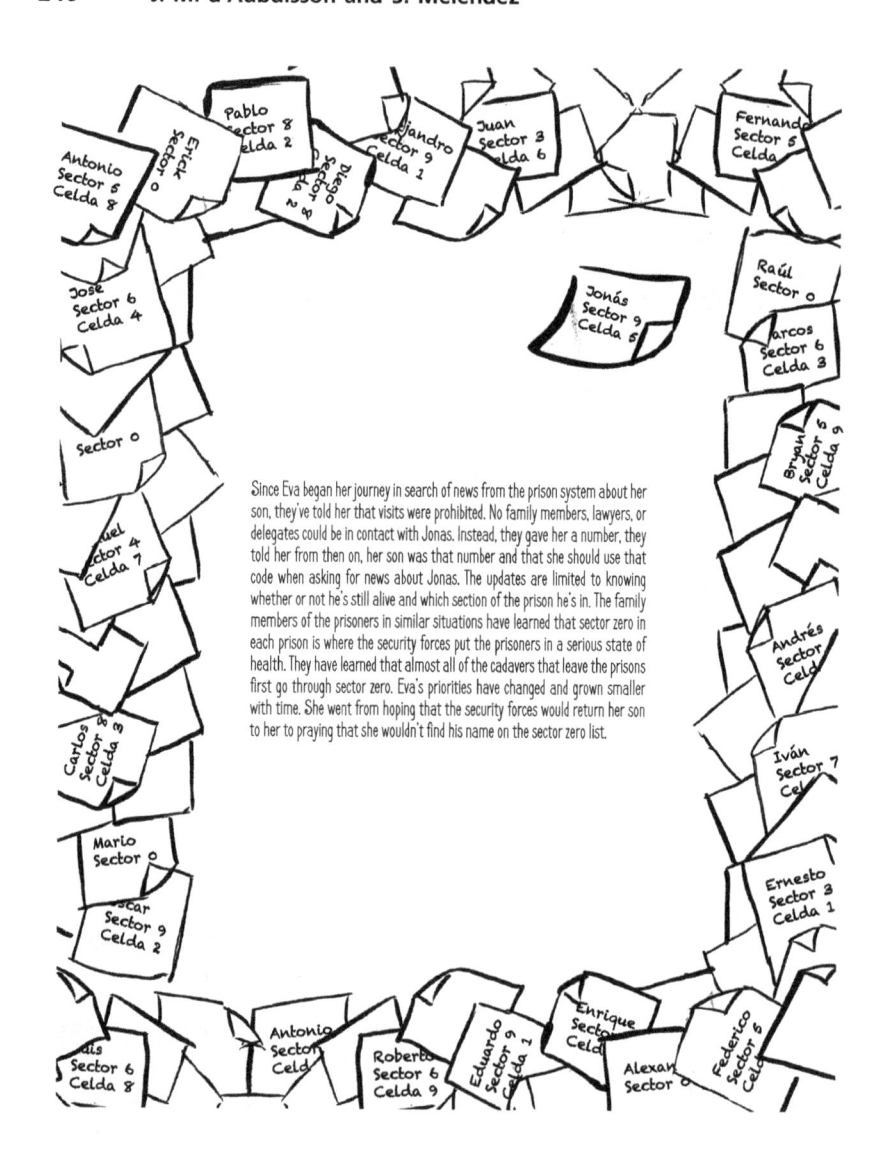

Since Eva began her journey in search of news from the prison system about her son, they've told her that visits were prohibited. No family members, lawyers, or delegates could be in contact with Jonas. Instead, they gave her a number, they told her from then on, her son was that number and that she should use that code when asking for news about Jonas. The updates are limited to knowing whether or not he's still alive and which section of the prison he's in. The family members of the prisoners in similar situations have learned that sector zero in each prison is where the security forces put the prisoners in a serious state of health. They have learned that almost all of the cadavers that leave the prisons first go through sector zero. Eva's priorities have changed and grown smaller with time. She went from hoping that the security forces would return her son to her to praying that she wouldn't find his name on the sector zero list.

A WORD, A SIGN, A CALL

The mountain town where Eva lives, and where Jonas lived until a short time ago, we'll call it Roca Alta, is in western El Salvador. It's a peaceful place. In theory it was a place under the influence, but not dominion, of the Mara Salvatrucha 13, one of the three gang mafias that the president is looking to exorcise from El Salvador using the state of emergency regime. In Roca Alta, people are largely farmers, although they also sell a resin which they extract in pretty much the same way as they did 200 years ago, from the balsam tree. It's not a violent place, it never has been. At least not by Central American standards. There would occasionally be, of course, someone wounded with a machete in a heated drunken exchange during a town party, or young guys beat up after the soccer games in the cow pastures.

Eva and Goyo, her husband, are the caretakers of a balsam tree plantation, and there they've raised their 10 children; Jonas is the fifth. The police patrol assigned to the area often passed by the property and would stop to drink water at Eva and Goyo's house. The chief of police of the area, a young, severe officer named Espada, would joke with Eva's boys and more than once ate with them during some festivity.

At the end of 2021, a neighbor known as Burro entered the property that Goyo and Eva caretake without permission, filled up some barrels of water at a spring, and left. Two days later he returned with several men and filled up more barrels, and a week later he came in with a medium-sized truck and long hoses. Goyo told him that a few barrels were fine, but that he couldn't just take a truck filled with barrels whenever he wanted. Burro invoked a superior force to intimidate his farmer neighbor. He made the universal sign of the Mara Salvatrucha 13.

He told him that he had the gang members of the "MS" backing him up, that it wasn't a good idea to deny him anything he asked for. It was sufficient for Goyo to leave him alone. It had been rumored for a few years that Burro and his brother-in-law were connected to the MS13, and the rumor, true or not, protected them and helped them quickly settle any argument with their neighbors.

I've received information about that kid, but unfortunately nothing can be done without proof, and since the people around here are really resistant to reporting anything, they leave us with our hands tied.

Nourish You   243

One day after the slaughter of Salvadorans at the hands of the Maras, President Bukele, with the approval of a deferential Legislative Assembly and a judicial system at his service, announced the state of emergency. In simple terms, at a distance and free from any technical descriptions, we could say it consists of turning off some constitutional rights for a time and giving judicial power to the police and the military in the street to arrest people, without any proof beyond mere suspicion, the anonymous call, or knowledge of local police about who is and isn't a gang member.

"The first rotten apples have just fallen. I got Burro and his group a few days ago."

Agent Espada told us at the end of April 2022. Burro, his brother-in-law, and others close to him were arrested during the first days of the state of emergency, accused of "unlawful assocation," the ambiguous crime for which tens of thousands of people are held in prison today.

Eva didn't see Burro and his ilk's arrest with her own eyes. They weren't the only ones; several of her neighbors were arrested arbitrarily, and during all of 2022, their whereabouts were unclear. Eva has seven children around the age of those being targeted, and the crusade of hooded police officers, taking people at night without letting families know their location, didn't sit well with them. It reminded them of wartimes.

"Here they passed through, often, the mass of police and soldiers. They arrived at the house and were asking endless questions about gang members and where they were hiding out. We didn't tell them anything because we don't know anything."

Eva told us weeks before the arrest of her son Jonas.

THE ARREST

> They took him to a bar called The Stable. That day, Jonas had worked the entire day, he came home to change and then he went to watch a soccer match that his friends had invited him to, and he didn't come home again.

After finding out about the arrest, Eva took it upon herself to reconstruct her son's last day of freedom. She told us that Jonas worked from seven in the morning on a neighbor's small farm harvesting green chili peppers. It was Saturday, he arrived home tired and dirty, he left her the week's pay of $10, changed, and left to watch a soccer match in a neighboring town whose name we won't mention. Eva has put together the puzzle time and time again, and after speaking with every person who saw or was with her son that day, she was able to determine that Jonas left after the game with four friends and they had a beer at the bar called The Stable, a saloon with a cowboy-style bar and an enormous wagon wheel in the entrance for decoration. They ordered 10 beers. "He hadn't eaten breakfast, and that was why he got drunk so quickly," says Eva. She and her family are Evangelical Pentacostals, one of the most conservative Protestant denominations. For them, alcohol is prohibited, as is soccer. For this reason, there's shame in her words; this is why she lowers her gaze while she tells us this. His friends told Eva that Jonas, enlivened after having a few beers, danced and made a fool of himself in front of his friends. That was when a group of soldiers and police entered. The boys said that Jonas got hostile, and when they asked him if he lived in Roca Alta, he responded with a word commonly used among gang members and outlaws: *simón* (yes). He was immediately handcuffed and put into a pickup truck.

In reality, he'd been reported. Someone told us that on two occasions Jonas had thrown the Salvatrucha gang sign. We know who the person is, but we can't say because the call they made was anonymous.

Agent Espada told us, a few months after Jonas was taken. He told us that it wasn't him but one of his colleagues who had arrested him.

I saw him when he was already at the police station. Look how stupid you are, I told him, you are dumb for what you got yourself into...and your whole family are working people.

That's one of the prerogatives that the state of emergency gives to the security forces in charge of maintaining order, the ability to arrest anyone without any explanation. They can say there was a call, or that someone came to them in secret to accuse a neighbor, or simply say that they saw someone acting suspiciously. If what officer Espada says is true, then someone accused Jonas of using the same sign that Burro used to threaten his family.

Nourish You   **247**

They let me know in the afternoon. One of my daughters came to tell me that the security forces had taken Jonas. I left in what I was wearing and went down to town.

When Eva arrived, there was a tumult of local farmer women at the town hall, in the center of the town. A police officer recognized her: "There comes Jonas's mom", he said. When she went in, another police officer said out loud: "Yes, there goes the mom of that gang banger." Eva looked for Espada, the officer who had eaten and napped in the hammock of her house.

He was brought down by a complaint, Doña Eva, they reported him. I can't say who, but they accused him of doing the same thing that Burro did to you all.

Because of their friendship, Espada told her to bring food and that he would give it to him, a privilege that not everyone there had. Then Eva saw Jonas. He was embarrassed, and he gave her his wallet and his belt with his head hanging and eyes downcast. It was the last thing this woman could do for her son before losing him to the entrails of the system.

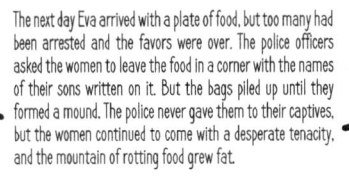

The next day Eva arrived with a plate of food, but too many had been arrested and the favors were over. The police officers asked the women to leave the food in a corner with the names of their sons written on it. But the bags piled up until they formed a mound. The police never gave them to their captives, but the women continued to come with a desperate tenacity, and the mountain of rotting food grew fat.

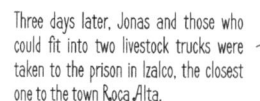

Three days later, Jonas and those who could fit into two livestock trucks were taken to the prison in Izalco, the closest one to the town Roca Alta.

"From there I didn't know where to go but I asked and asked and went with a group of women in search of a place called Human Rights", says Eva.

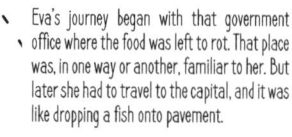

Eva's journey began with that government office where the food was left to rot. That place was, in one way or another, familiar to her. But later she had to travel to the capital, and it was like dropping a fish onto pavement.

HUMAN RIGHTS?

This place might have been the Attorney General's Office in Defense of Human Rights, a body created after the end of our civil war. It collects complaints and makes recommendations, but it has no enforcement capabilities, especially after it was co-opted by Bukele's regime. But it also could have been the nonprofit Cristosal, a private entity that maintains a detailed registry of all the arrests and human rights violations. It's difficult to know what place Eva is referring to.

That's all she says about the first place she went. For her, Human Rights is a place, an office where a woman took her statement while they cried together. That woman told her that for the moment that was the only thing she could do for her: take her statement, listen to her, cry.

"Human Rights" didn't give her as much as a piece of paper, and the only thing we know about its location and function is that it's in San Salvador and that a woman there cried with her.

After a while the baby bird died. He didn't get enough food, and we weren't able to keep him warm like we should have. But the bigger bird continued coming every day with worms in her mouth, chirping diligently. After a while she left, but a few hours later she'd be at the window again, food dangling from her beak, as if insistence alone would wake up her baby, as if it would bring him back.

Next Eva went to the Attorney General's Office. But there they were even more blunt. The government official she met with told her that this was a state of emergency that had to be carried out. That after a year there would be an initial hearing, and that, if he remained behind bars, after a year there would be another one. These events are merely a formality. The prosecutor's office holds mass hearings, bringing together 500 people and bringing identical charges against them. This modality allows the prosecutor's office to sentence thousands of detainees in one day, without providing any conclusive evidence or individualizing the cases. The charges are for unlawful association, which means belonging in some way to the Maras. President Bukele's regime has opted for casting a giant net over the population. They know that gang members will be caught in the net, and it doesn't seem to matter to them if thousands of innocent people down there too.

The only information of value for Eva, after her journey through the government institutions, were the instructions to take food to her son.

Next Eva traveled to the prison in Izalco. It's one of the facilities designated a decade ago for gang members. She arrived there together with a large group of mothers, daughters, sisters, and wives. A military blockade made them form a line a kilometer (about two-thirds of a mile) away from the prison. They walked under the sun until they arrived at the doors of the prison. There some of the prison guards gave them a piece of paper with a number on it and told them to leave their packages on some tables. They told them there wouldn't be visits and that those who'd been arrested couldn't make any calls or see their lawyers. One of the officers told Eva that it would be better not to waste her money on lawyers because there was absolutely nothing they could do. It would be like throwing her money away. That day, May 10th, the day they moved her son to that facility, Mother's Day was celebrated in El Salvador.

Two months later, in June 2022, Jonas was moved, together with hundreds of other detainees, to a prison in the capital. But even though El Salvador is the smallest country in the Americas and the distances are very short, the true distances can't be measured in kilometers. For Eva it was very difficult to understand the streets and bus routes in San Salvador. She had never felt so lost in her entire life. Weeks later, in one of the worship services of her evangelical church, she met another woman in a similar situation, with her husband and her brother held in the prison in the capital, taken in the first days after the state of emergency was declared. It was Burro's wife. They started to travel together every week. Their old quarrels over river water were left behind; they were united by the urgency of feeding their loved ones in the huge prison where President Bukele had locked them up.

In the Roca Alta region, the people celebrate the arrest of Burro, of the gang members and their collaborators who devastated the area, but they also lament the arrest of Jonas, of Guillermo the ice cream vendor, of Pedro the carpenter and his two sons. This is the same duality that El Salvador finds itself in. People celebrate the downfall of the Maras at the hands of "Bukelism" and hope that their innocent family members will one day be freed. Mothers teach their adolescent children strategies to avoid being arrested, and at the same time breathe easier now that they don't have to live under the crushing yoke of the Maras. The country now lives without Maras, and its population is trying to adjust as it can to living under an authoritarian regime led by the caprice of a single man who controls everything. After 40 years of living with a democracy, imperfect and corrupt as it was yet at the end of the day a democracy, the déjà vu of the dictatorship has returned. The curse never left this land.

President Bukele, in a flagrant violation of the Salvadoran Constitution, has been crowned president once again. In June 2024 his second term began. More than 75,000 people have now been arrested, and the state of emergency has become the new normal for life in El Salvador. It's a threat that we Salvadorans carry with us constantly, a sort of sleeping indictment that weighs on each one of us and that could materialize in an arrest at any moment.

Eva hopes, with growing conviction, that the Salvadoran government will come to its senses and realize that her son isn't a criminal. She hopes that when she arrives at the prison, they won't inform her that the number that her son has become hasn't been assigned to sector zero, the step before prisoners leave as cadavers. She continues gathering up coins, asking her other children for money to be able to take a bag each month with food and combined cream to the prison. It's the stubbornness of life. This is her way of beating death at this game. Feeding that number is, in essence, her way of continuing to be Jonas's mother.

Juan Martínez d'Aubuisson is an anthropologist and journalist from El Salvador. His work has appeared in *Gatopardo, El Faro, and the Washington Post*. He has researched gangs and gang violence extensively in El Salvador since 2008.

Sara Meléndez has a degree in graphic design from the Universidad Tecnologica de El Salvador. She also studied in Madrid at the Istituto Europeo di Design, has collaborated on projects with the Studio GrandeGraphix and the Studio Franchise, and manages the graphic direction and communication of Melro y Asociados S.A. de C.V.

Open Access This chapter is licensed under the terms of the Creative Commons Attribution-NonCommercial-NoDerivatives 4.0 International License (http://creativecommons.org/licenses/by-nc-nd/4.0/), which permits any noncommercial use, sharing, distribution and reproduction in any medium or format, as long as you give appropriate credit to the original author(s) and the source, provide a link to the Creative Commons license and indicate if you modified the licensed material. You do not have permission under this license to share adapted material derived from this chapter or parts of it.

The images or other third party material in this chapter are included in the chapter's Creative Commons license, unless indicated otherwise in a credit line to the material. If material is not included in the chapter's Creative Commons license and your intended use is not permitted by statutory regulation or exceeds the permitted use, you will need to obtain permission directly from the copyright holder.

Reimagine, Reclaim, and Repurpose Urban Space for Justice and Healing

Kerry Whigham

When considering identity-based mass violence (IBMV), we often first focus on the manner in which this violence is exacted on the bodies of members of targeted groups—and rightly so. The mass violation of the physical integrity of individuals—what this volume refers to as "acute violence"—is the most visible and immediately traumatic form that such violence takes. But IBMV also plays out in other spheres and takes many other forms that are often more obscure(d) than the horrific acts of acute, physical violence most associated with mass atrocities. This includes "structural violence" that, as the editors of this volume explain in Chapter 1, "is the consequence of decisions that value certain identity groups over others and is embedded within social, political, and economic systems and institutions." Even if this violence is less visible, however, it can be tremendously detrimental; because it may not be perceived as violence, it can often endure long after the physical acts of torture and killing come to an end. Elsewhere, I call this capacity for

K. Whigham (✉)
Binghamton University, Binghamton, New York, USA
e-mail: kwhigham@binghamton.edu

violence to radiate outward, impacting all spheres of a society, "resonant violence."[1]

The resonating nature of large-scale violence is what leads to structural violence—the aspects of IBMV that endure in governmental institutions, public policy, economic practices, and even daily social interactions. Likewise, enduring structural violence increases the risk that persecuted groups will experience episodes of acute violence. One aspect of both acute and structural violence that is often overlooked, however, is the actual structures it produces, that is, the built environment that surrounds us. Perpetrating regimes, which can include both state and nonstate actors, often use space as a key tool for control and repression. These regimes often totally transform urban space, in particular during processes of IBMV, as perpetrators restrict access to and redesign space to facilitate the oppression of certain groups. But the transformation of urban space and the ways that people engage with and in it are also byproducts of the repressive tools that perpetrators use. As populations adapt to violence, they adjust the ways they encounter and inhabit public space. They may transform their homes into private fortresses—harbors of relative safety compared to the dangers of the public sphere. Certain areas of the city may become "off limits" while others become spaces for "their" community. In their examination of memory spaces in the urban landscape of Buenos Aires, Argentina, the authors of *Memorias en la ciudad* (Memories in the city) write, "Urban space has always been a terrain for the expression of social conflicts, and the state has intervened on numerous opportunities, seeking to design it as a means of control and discipline, from structuring not only the space itself, but also the forms in which it is used, consequently regulating the practices and means of inhabiting it."[2]

For this reason, urban space must be a central consideration when determining how to transform societies in the midst and aftermath of IBMV. Transitional justice measures and public policy responses are essential, of course, but if, in the process of dealing with present and past violence, stakeholders do not also engage with the urban landscape itself, the "geographies of domination," to use geographer Steven Pile's term, remain in place.[3] According to Pile, geographies of domination describe the way authorities use public space to maintain control over populations. As I write elsewhere, geographies of domination "manifest in any number of ways, including the parceling or breaking apart of public space, the regulation and control of borders, the use of architectural scale to assert authority over subjects, and the management of how bodies are allowed to move through physical space."[4] When the acute forms of IBMV come to an end, it is essential that societies attend to public space, especially in urban settings, asking how it has been shaped by IBMV, how it was used as a tool for perpetuating IBMV, and how it can be redesigned to counter the acute violence that has occurred and dismantle the structural violence that remains.

One tool that has emerged in numerous societies for the transformation of these geographies of domination into spaces for justice and healing is art. The power of art to engage people on both intellectual and emotional levels can serve as a forceful response to the dangerous strength of resonant violence. If, as Michel de Certeau argues, strategies are the tools of the strong, while tactics are the tools of the weak,[5] art stands out as an invaluable tactic, particularly for groups that have been the direct targets of identity-based violence. It provides a measure through which victim groups can rally themselves and generate empathy in others who have not been directly impacted by violence, consequently building alliances of solidarity that can and indeed have led to large-scale social and political change.

This chapter focuses on three cases in which art has been used as a tool for transforming public space and, as a result, the social and political environment in the aftermath of IBMV. These cases demonstrate the flexibility of art and its potential to be a reparative tool for victim groups, allied populations, and even the state itself. The chapter begins by looking at Argentina in the period following the military dictatorship of 1976–83, outlining two ways art has played a vital role in transforming public space and dismantling geographies of domination. Next, the chapter turns to Colombia, where an art project in the urban center of Bogotá was formally written into the peace agreement designed to bring an end to decades of armed conflict. Finally, the chapter ends with a transnational art project designed by a single artist-activist relating to the 1995 genocide in Srebrenica, Bosnia and Herzegovina, that highlights how even temporary interventions in public space can generate lasting impacts.

Argentina: Transforming the State by Transforming Public Space

From 1976 to 1983, Argentina lived under one of the most repressive dictatorships of the twentieth century, during which the right-wing military junta sought to destroy opposition to its regime and, in particular, all left-wing ideology. As part of its so-called Process of National Reorganization, as many as 30,000 Argentinians were forcibly disappeared and imprisoned in one or more of the 500-plus clandestine detention and torture centers across the country. After being tortured, many of the disappeared were murdered, though the military kept these practices secret from the public. Many of the family members of the disappeared are still seeking the remains of their lost loved ones to give them a proper burial.

As with most oppressive regimes, the military dictatorship used public space as a tool for exercising its authority. Entire neighborhoods were destroyed to make way for a new interstate highway, leading directly to the creation of *villas miserias*, or slums, on the outskirts of Buenos Aires.[6] Public conversations of more than a few people were suppressed. Many public squares and parks were physically altered to turn them into spaces that people walked through rather than lounged in. Benches and green spaces were often removed, for instance, to prevent the congregation of groups.[7] In fact, the famed human rights group Mothers of the Plaza de Mayo, who met (and continue to meet) every Thursday afternoon in the square in front of the presidential palace to demand the return of their disappeared children, began their famous circular march around the square because the police would not allow them to stand still.[8]

In perpetrating regimes, public space becomes at once a battlefield and a weapon. It is a place where the "war" is waged, as well as a tool used to wage it. For this reason, any effort to bring an end to the violence and its resonating effects must also consider public space, how it has been used, and how it should be altered to produce less-violent ends. In the case of Argentina, art has been a key tool in this process, both during the dictatorship and in its aftermath. Two specific examples demonstrate this reality.

In September 1983, the power of the military dictatorship was waning. In the previous year, the junta had lost a war against the United Kingdom over control of the Falkland Islands/Malvinas, and public support of the dictatorship was at an all-time low. As a light began to appear at the end of the tunnel, human rights activists took action to hasten the fall of the dictatorship. One such action was El Siluetazo, an intervention developed by three visual artists: Rodolfo Aguerreberry, Julio Flores, and Guillermo Kexel. On September 21, 1983, these artists, in collaboration with other human rights organizations, convened a workshop near the Obelisk, a central landmark in Buenos Aires. Using butcher block paper and paint, people laid down on the paper while others traced the outlines of their bodies, with the goal of creating 30,000 individual silhouettes to plaster across the cityscape. The idea, according to Ana Longoni and Gustavo Bruzzone, who wrote a book-length study of the project, was to create "a work that alludes to the quantitative dimension of the disappearance of persons, the physical space that would be occupied by the sum total of those thirty thousand bodies violently ripped away from us."[9] In the face of the inherently invisible crime of enforced disappearance, this artistic intervention reappeared those bodies in the public sphere, visually representing the scale of the crimes that had been committed and making the absence of the disappeared present and perceptible.

Several months after El Siluetazo, in December 1983, democracy officially returned to Argentina when Raul Alfonsín was elected president. Immediately, Alfonsín began to institute an impressive array of measures to deal with the abuses of the dictatorship. First, he formed the National Commission on the Disappearance of Persons (CONADEP, for its initials in Spanish), which many regard as the world's first truth commission.[10] In 1985, Argentina also became one of the first countries in the world to put its former leaders on trial.[11] But several new attempted coups and the continued threat of the military pushed Alfonsín and his administration to put the brakes on further actions.

Several laws were swiftly passed to bring an end to prosecutions, and in 1990, new president Carlos Menem issued a full presidential pardon to all the perpetrators of the dictatorship. Argentina had entered what is typically referred to as its era of impunity.[12]

Even as the state was failing in its responsibilities to prosecute human rights violations, civil society remained active in turning the tide. Joining the mothers and grandmothers of the disappeared in their activism, the children of the disappeared came of age during this era of impunity and began their own vibrant activist practices. The best-known example of this activism was developed by H.I.J.O.S. (Sons and Daughters for Identity and Justice against Oblivion and Silence), a human rights group formed by the children of the disappeared, who created the public demonstration known as the *escrache*. From the Argentine Spanish slang verb *escrachar*, meaning "to uncover or bring to light," *escraches* were vibrant street demonstrations in front of the houses of known perpetrators of atrocity crimes. Their goal was to make the entire neighborhood aware that torturers and genocidaires were living free and unpunished among the rest of society, thus encouraging the state to resume trials against these perpetrators.[13] H.I.J.O.S. worked closely with various art collectives to support the *escraches*, recognizing the power of visual and performing arts in achieving their quest for justice. Street theater, puppetry, and other visual art forms all made appearances in the carnivalesque demonstrations.[14]

An art group that made one of the biggest marks on the *escraches* and the city of Buenos Aires was Grupo de Arte Callejero (literally, Street Art Group), or GAC, for short.[15] GAC is a woman's art collective that developed a unique artistic practice that transformed public space to achieve the goals of the *escraches*. They started creating what looked like official street signs. Instead of providing directions or alerting drivers to warnings, however, these signs described the locations and crimes of perpetrators during the military dictatorship. Some signs simply listed the name and address of a perpetrator, warning that he lived 100 meters distance from the sign. Others included iconographic images that represented specific crimes relating to the dictatorship. For instance, a sign with the outline of a pregnant woman behind bars represented the 500-plus women who were disappeared while they were pregnant. Those women were kept alive in captivity until they gave birth. They were then murdered, and their children were given to military families and their allies to raise as their own.

The street signs of GAC are particularly compelling because they used one of the tools of the state to critique that government for not fulfilling its responsibility to maintain the rule of law and apply it equally to all citizens. Although each *escrache* lasted only a few hours as a physical demonstration, the artistic interventions of GAC stuck around much longer—at least until they were discovered and taken down. Because they looked so similar to official street signs, however, many of them stayed in place for long periods. In the same way that the aforementioned silhouettes made visible the 30,000 victims who were disappeared during the dictatorship, the street signs of GAC did the same thing for the perpetrators and their crimes, giving them a visual representation so they could not be ignored or forgotten. By reshaping public space in this way, they reminded Argentinians of the unprosecuted crimes and of their responsibility to demand justice. Ultimately, because of the continued activism of human rights groups like H.I.J.O.S., GAC, and many others, the Argentinian government reopened trials against perpetrators in 2005. To date, over 1,200 individuals have been brought to justice through formal legal mechanisms.

Colombia: Considering Public Spaces During Periods of Political Transition

In 2016, the Colombian government of President Juan Mañuel Santos signed a peace agreement with the Revolutionary Armed Forces of Colombia—People's Army, or the FARC-EP (its Spanish acronym), the principal paramilitary group the government had been fighting. This landmark accord was intended to bring an end to the armed conflict that wracked Colombia for decades. The peace accord laid the groundwork for a comprehensive transitional justice process to deal with the country's difficult past. It established a variety of new mechanisms, including a national truth commission to clarify the harms experienced by victims across the country; a complex new plan for land development and redistribution; a new Special Jurisdiction for Peace, which oversees criminal justice and reparations proceedings; and a detailed plan for the disarmament, demobilization, and reintegration (DDR) of former paramilitary and guerrilla fighters.

Many aspects of the 2016 Colombian peace accord are groundbreaking, but one aspect in particular stands out with respect to this chapter. Every DDR process raises countless questions, among them what to do with all the weapons that have been gathered through the disarmament process. In the case of Colombia, the FARC and many Colombians did not want their weapons going directly to the Colombian military, which they had been fighting for decades (and who had perpetrated its own share of atrocity crimes).[16] A compromise needed to be reached. And so, as a component of the disarmament process, the accord stipulates that "the FARC-EP weapons will be used to build three monuments: one at the headquarters of the United Nations, one in the Republic of Cuba, and one on Colombian soil." This phrase likely demonstrates the first time that the transformation of public space through an artistic intervention was written into a peace agreement.

At the time of writing this chapter, decisions were still being made about the monument that will be erected in Havana, Cuba—the site of the signing of the peace accord. The monument at the United Nations was unveiled in 2019. Titled *Kusikawsay*, which is Quechuan for "peaceful and happy life," this statue representing an Indigenous canoe was designed by Chilean artist Mario Opazo, who won an open call for proposals following the signing of the peace agreement.[17] While the symbolism of having this monument constructed from the weapons of war on the grounds of the United Nations is powerful, *Kusikawsay* is a much more traditional take on public art that does not transform public space in the same way that the Bogotá memorial does.

President Santos commissioned internationally renowned Colombian artist Doris Salcedo to design and craft the Bogotá monument. Her canvas was the grounds of a fallen colonial building in a historic neighborhood of the capital city. Her materials were 37 tons of weapons gathered from 13,049 ex-combatants. The piece she produced was inaugurated in 2018, and she calls it *Fragmentos: Espacio de Arte y Memoria* (Fragments: Space of Art and Memory).

Salcedo's *Fragmentos* disrupts traditional approaches to monumentalization in a way that recognizes their power to transform societies through changing public space. Fragmentos is built around the ruins of a seventeenth-century colonial building. Rather than starting from a clean slate, however, Salcedo left the crumbling architecture present and visible, building her monument around it. In doing so, the symbolism of building a new Colombia out of the ruins of the past is clear.

Fragmentos includes none of the traditional tropes associated with monuments: stone, water, an eternal flame, a list of the names of victims, etc.[18] Instead, *Fragmentos* is a building that includes three rooms of different sizes, connected by a single glass hallway. Throughout, the floor of the structure consists of 1,296 square tiles formed from the melted metal of the weapons obtained through the disarmament process. To form the molds for the floor tiles, Salcedo brought together a group of women, all of whom were victims of sexualized violence at the hands of the military and paramilitaries during the armed conflict. Together, these women used hammers and other tools to beat the sheets of metal that would become the molds for the tiles. As they beat the metal, many of them spoke of it as a cathartic experience—an opportunity for them to beat their pain and trauma into the metal, in the company of other women who had experienced similar pain. One woman who participated in creating *Fragmentos* described the experience: "I start to get the poison out of my system, you could say. I find an outlet for my anger, and I have all those thoughts about what happened. Then you go on hammering and beating, get rid of that poison and start to feel a little bit of relief."[19] The act of participating in the construction of the monument, then, was itself a reparative act for these victims.

But *Fragmentos* was not only built for the victims. Salcedo designed it to be a space for art and dialogue for all Colombians—a place where groups can come together to discuss and even argue difficult subjects, but in a democratic space and without resorting to violence. Salcedo describes her intent:

What I meant to do in this space is build something new with these weapons, 53 years on, so that other artists might come after me, with their own notions of what war is, whatever those may be. Their ideas might be different from mine, might even conflict with me, but that doesn't matter. The important thing is to continue this extraordinary dialogue, which saw combatants from both sides reach the Havana agreement, within this space. These discussions between former enemies and opposing forces aren't easy, but this is the idea, and it's the only thing that matters, nothing else is important.[20]

Traditional monuments are tools of the state to intervene on public space with clear messages that reassert the authority of the state itself.[21] *Fragmentos* offers something else. It is a gathering space. It is a crucible for public discussion, and as such it is a microcosm for what the whole of Colombian society could become.

But *Fragmentos* has yet to fulfill this beautiful, ambitious vision. Under the administration of the National Museum of Colombia, it is mostly used as a space to exhibit art rather than a space for organizing meetings and facilitating dialogue. The potential of the space, however, is enormous. The very notion of discussing strategies for building peace and democracy on the literal weapons of war that tore Colombia apart for so many years demonstrates the impact that reimagining public space can have in the aftermath of IBMV. The fact that such an initiative came out of the peace negotiations that brought an end to decades of conflict will hopefully inspire others to recognize the absolute necessity of considering public space and its transformation as a constituent part of peacebuilding and postatrocity regrowth.

Bosnia and Herzegovina and Beyond: Reuniting and Building Communities

It can be easy to think of IBMV as being constrained to the very specific localities where physical violence is manifested. In truth, the full impact of the violence is rarely limited to a single city or even a single country. Its effects resonate outward, and one of the clearest ways one can see this is through the groups of people who are displaced by mass violence.

According to the UN High Commissioner for Refugees (UNHCR), as of June 2023 there were at least 108 million forcibly displaced people in the world—the highest number in history. Of those, 40.7 million were refugees and asylum seekers who had been forced to flee their home countries, many because of IBMV and mass atrocities. For instance, over half of them came from just three countries: Syria, Ukraine, and Afghanistan.[22] Each of those countries is experiencing ongoing atrocities and IBMV. These groups are never wholly free of the effects of IBMV, even when they leave their homes to flee it. These individuals must often deal with the trauma that comes from witnessing and/or experiencing violence, along with the trauma of being away from one's home, one's culture, and/or one's language. But refugees are also targets of further discrimination and identity-based violence in their new homes, as they are frequently labeled as an "other" who is taking resources or jobs from the host country. How can we consider reimagining, reclaiming, and repurposing urban space for justice and healing for communities that may not even think of that space as "home"? How can host communities reframe the public sphere to make it as inclusive as possible for those who have migrated there because of IBMV they have experienced elsewhere?

One beautiful answer to these questions comes from Bosnian American artist Aida Šehović. Šehović is herself a refugee, forced to flee her native Bosnia and Herzegovina when she was a child during the atrocities that ravaged the country in the early 1990s. Around 100,000 people were killed during this conflict, 80 percent of whom, like Šehović, were Bosnian Muslims. Between 2 million and 3 million others were displaced by the conflict.[23] Years later, in the early 2000s, Šehović started thinking about an artistic intervention that could speak to the IBMV she experienced and honor the memory of those who were lost, most especially in the 1995 genocide in the UN Safe Area of Srebrenica. On July 11, 1995, Bosnian Serb military forces entered this small city that was supposed to be protected by Dutch peacekeepers, separated the men and boys from the women and girls, loaded the women and girls onto busses to be carried to the front lines, and then systematically murdered the remaining 8,372 Bosnian Muslims over about a week and a half.

As Šehović pondered how best to respond to and represent this atrocity through art, she had many conversations with the women who lost their husbands and sons in the genocide. In her conversations, the women often told her that they most miss their loved ones when they drink their coffee alone in the morning. Coffee plays a central role in Bosnian culture, as it is always a social affair. Rather than taking their coffee "to go," Bosnians approach coffee drinking as a ritual that is always done with others. Based on these stories, Šehović developed *ŠTO TE NEMA* (Bosnian for "Why are you not here?"), which she describes as a "nomadic monument." Just as Šehović and the millions of other refugees were forced to travel in the midst of mass violence, this monument was also designed to travel as a means of reimagining public space for the Bosnian diaspora and for a global community who could stand in solidarity with them and others facing IBMV now and in the future.

Šehović began collecting *fildzani*, the small, handleless, porcelain cups used to drink coffee in Bosnia, with the goal of collecting one for each of the 8,372 Bosnian Muslims who died in the genocide in Srebrenica. Starting in Sarajevo on July 11, 2006, Šehović and a team of volunteers met in a public square and spent the day brewing coffee. That first year, Šehović herself poured the coffee into the *fildzani* and left them in the square, undrunk, in memory of those who died and are no longer able to have coffee with their loved ones. As the monument continued each year, however, members of the victim community and passersby began to help her pour. From that point on, *ŠTO TE NEMA* became a fully participatory monument. Each year, on July 11, Šehović traveled with her cups to a new city around the world that had a Bosnian diaspora population. Thousands of people met her in the public square to help brew and pour coffee throughout the day. At day's end, the monument was disassembled, packed away, and put into storage until the next year, when it would travel to a new city. Between July 2006 and July 2019, the monument was constructed in Sarajevo, UN headquarters in New York City; Tuzla, Bosnia and Herzegovina; The Hague, Netherlands; Stockholm, Sweden; Burlington, Vermont; Istanbul, Turkey; New York City; Toronto, Canada; Geneva, Switzerland; Boston, Massachusetts;

Chicago, Illinois; Zurich, Switzerland; and Venice, Italy. Its final installation took place on the 25th anniversary of the genocide, July 11, 2020, in Srebrenica itself, where the cups now remain.

ŠTO TE NEMA is nothing if not a perfect example of how a simple, creative intervention in public space can have resounding impacts. The key goal of all forms of IBMV is to destroy communities. What better way to respond to that violence, then, but by creating a project that reconstitutes the communities that it once tore asunder? Each year, as the nomadic monument arrived in the public square of a new city, members of the Bosnian community who had been ripped apart by atrocity violence came together to perform a collective act of remembrance. But *ŠTO TE NEMA* was not only built by the Bosnian diaspora. Many others, including strangers and random passersby would stop to see what was going on, begin a conversation with Šehović or any of the others who were there, and learn about Srebrenica and the lives that were lost. New communities of solidarity were built over the course of a day. People who may never before have considered the impacts of IBMV occurring elsewhere around the world or the power of art to intervene on it had their minds transformed. Such an interaction had the potential to lead to an even more lasting change of behavior in the future. This art project, over the course of one day per year, transformed a simple public square into a space for collective repair and inclusion, providing a restorative salve to the wounds of IBMV, which, however much time passes, may never fully heal. On the topic of healing, Šehović has said:

Healing from genocide and persecution cannot be completed. You don't heal from it completely. But I now recognize and see my own transformation from the beginning of this project as a very, very angry and frustrated person with a lot of rage toward the whole world. I think it's important to call it for what it is. Because that place of rage and anger is not only negative. It can also make you courageous and brave and creative, and enable you to imagine things that seem unimaginable.[24]

To reimagine, reclaim, and repurpose urban space for justice and healing requires all these things: courage, bravery, and creativity. But perhaps most of all it requires the will to push oneself and one's community to imagine the unimaginable—to move beyond the traditional "tools" in the "toolbox" and forge new ones that may not yet exist. A tall task, to be sure, but one that is without doubt owed to those who have experienced the unimaginable horrors of IBMV.

Conclusion

Public space is the arena in which IBMV is carried out, just as it is a tool used to execute it. Given its essential nature in the perpetration of violence, it must also be a central consideration in the violence's aftermath. Public officials and civil society must consider how to reimagine, reclaim, and repurpose public space so it is no longer a battlefield and a weapon but a place for justice, healing, and rebuilding community.

As the three cases explored in this chapter demonstrate, art is one key means through which state and civil society actors can engage with the past and positively transform public space in the present. Argentina shows us how the use of art in public space can be a tool for civil society activists to demand social and political change. Colombia illustrates how art is increasingly being recognized as a fundamental mechanism for dealing with the past—so much so that it can be written into peace agreements alongside mechanisms like truth commissions, judicial proceedings, and reparations processes. And *ŠTO TE NEMA* exemplifies both the necessity to consider public space in a broader, transnational sense, particularly in cases where IBMV leads to displacement, and the possibilities that emerge through such consideration. Urban cityscapes have the potential to be spaces for violence and spaces for community, reconciliation, and healing. Artistic interventions offer a clear opportunity to transform these spaces from the former into the latter.

Notes

1. Kerry Whigham, *Resonant violence: Affect, memory, and activism in post-genocide societies* (New Brunswick, NJ: Rutgers University Press, 2022).

2. Memoria Abierta, *Memorias en la ciudad: Señales del terrorismo de estado en Buenos Aires* (Buenos Aires: Eudeba, 2009), 67 (translation by the author).
3. Steve Pile, "Introduction: Opposition, political identities, and spaces of resistance," in *Geographies of resistance*, ed. Steve Pile and Michael Keith (London: Routledge, 1997), 1–32.
4. Whigham, *Resonant violence*, 166.
5. Michel De Certeau, *The practice of everyday life*, trans. Steven Rendall (Berkeley: University of California Press, 1984).
6. Javier Auyero, *Poor people's politics: Peronist survival networks and the legacy of Evita* (Durham, NC: Duke University Press, 2001).
7. Memoria Abierta, *Memorias en la ciudad*.
8. Marguerite Guzman Bouvard, *Revolutionizing Motherhood: The Mothers of the Plaza de Mayo* (Wilmington, DE: Scholarly Resources, 1994).
9. Ana Longoni and Gustavo Bruzzone, *El Siluetazo* (Buenos Aires: Adriana Hidalgo, 2008), 24.
10. Priscilla B. Hayner, *Unspeakable Truths: Transitional Justice and the Challenge of Truth Commissions*, 2nd ed. (New York: Routledge, 2011).
11. Kathryn Sikkink, *The Justice Cascade: How Human Rights Prosecutions Are Changing World Politics* (New York: W. W. Norton, 2011).
12. Andrea Gualde, "Reparations for Crimes against Humanity as Public Policy: Argentina's Relationship with the Past, from the Individual to the Collective as a Tool for Prevention," trans. Kerry Whigham, AIPR's Policy Papers in Prevention Series (New York: Auschwitz Institute for Peace and Reconciliation, 2015).
13. Susana Kaiser, "Escraches: Demonstrations, Communication and Political Memory in Post-Dictatorial Argentina," *Media Culture Society* 24 (2002): 499–516; Benedetta Calandra, *La Memoria Ostinata: H.I.J.O.S., i Figli Dei Desaperecidos Argentini* (Rome: Carrocci editore, 2004); Brian Whitener, "Introduction," in *Genocide in the Neighborhood* (Oakland, CA: Chainlinks, 2009), 11–32; Kerry Whigham, "Acting across Violence: H.I.J.O.S., Practices of Trans-Action, and Biopoetics in Post-Dictatorship Argentina,"

Journal of Latin American Cultural Studies 25, no. 2 (2016): 179–98.
14. Whigham, "Acting across Violence."
15. Grupo de Arte Callejero, *GAC: Pensamientos, Prácticas, Acciones* (Buenos Aires: Tinta Limón, 2009).
16. Comisión de la Verdad, *Hay futuro si hay verdad: Informe Final de la Comisión para el Esclarecimiento de la Verdad, la Convivencia y la No Repetición* (Bogotá: Comisión de la Verdad, 2022), https://www.comisiondelaverdad.co/.
17. "Kusikawsay," United Nations Gifts, United Nations, accessed June 24, 2024, https://www.un.org/ungifts/content/kusikawsay-UNNY328G.
18. James E. Young, *The stages of memory: Reflections on memorial art, loss, and the spaces between* (Amherst: University of Massachusetts Press, 2018).
19. Doris Salcedo, *Fragmentos*, documentary (Museo Nacional de Colombia, 2020), https://www.youtube.com/watch?v=d7rAb2O0JV8.
20. Ibid.
21. Whigham, *Resonant violence*.
22. "Figures at a Glance," UNHCR US, accessed January 29, 2024, https://www.unhcr.org/us/about-unhcr/who-we-are/figures-glance.
23. Martin Mennecke, "Genocidal violence in the Former Yugoslavia: Bosnia Herzegovina," in *Centuries of genocide: Essays and eyewitness accounts*, ed. Samuel Totten and William S. Parsons (New York: Routledge, 2013), 477–512.
24. Kerry Whigham, "Activist voices: Nomadic monuments—Interview with Aida Šehović," in *The Routledge Handbook of Memory Activism*, ed. Yifat Gutman and Jenny Wüstenberg (London: Routledge, 2023), 370.

Kerry Whigham is Assistant Professor of Genocide and Mass Atrocity Prevention at Binghamton University and Director of Research and Online Education at the Auschwitz Institute for the Prevention of Genocide and Mass Atrocities. With a PhD in performative studies from

New York University, specializing in postgenocidal studies, he is the author of *Resonant Violence: Affect, Memory, and Activism in Post-Genocide Societies* (New Brunswick, NJ: Rutgers University Press, 2022) and has published a broad range of peer-reviewed articles.

Open Access This chapter is licensed under the terms of the Creative Commons Attribution-NonCommercial-NoDerivatives 4.0 International License (http://creativecommons.org/licenses/by-nc-nd/4.0/), which permits any noncommercial use, sharing, distribution and reproduction in any medium or format, as long as you give appropriate credit to the original author(s) and the source, provide a link to the Creative Commons license and indicate if you modified the licensed material. You do not have permission under this license to share adapted material derived from this chapter or parts of it.

The images or other third party material in this chapter are included in the chapter's Creative Commons license, unless indicated otherwise in a credit line to the material. If material is not included in the chapter's Creative Commons license and your intended use is not permitted by statutory regulation or exceeds the permitted use, you will need to obtain permission directly from the copyright holder.

From the Jungle to the City: Asha's Journey

Mariana Medina Barragán, Luz Adriana López Medina, and Alejandra Medina Barragán

M. M. Barragán (✉)
Coalico, Bogotá, Colombia
e-mail: observatorio@coalico.org

L. A. L. Medina
Activist, Santa Marta, Colombia

A. M. Barragán
Freelance Graphic Design, Bogotá, Colombia

© The Author(s) 2026
R. Locke et al. (eds.), *Identity-Based Mass Violence in Urban Contexts*, Palgrave Studies in Victims and Victimology, https://doi.org/10.1007/978-3-031-98068-8_14

FROM THE JUNGLE TO THE CITY,
Asha's Journey

ALTHOUGH THIS STORY IS NOT AN OFFICIAL TESTIMONY, IT IS BASED ON THE ACCOUNTS OF GIRLS AND BOYS WHO WERE RECRUITED AND USED BY ARMED GROUPS THAT HAVE PLAYED A LEADING ROLE IN THE ARMED CONFLICT COLOMBIA HAS BEEN SUFFERING UNDER FOR MANY DECADES.

ACCORDING TO THE COMMISSION FOR THE CLARIFICATION OF TRUTH, COEXISTENCE AND NON-REPETITION, IN THE PERIOD OF TIME BETWEEN 1990 AND 2017 AT LEAST 27,101– AND AS MANY AS 40,828– GIRLS, BOYS AND ADOLESCENTS WERE VICTIMS OF RECRUITMENT IN THE COUNTRY.

IN COLOMBIA, ON A FARM SITUATED ON A COUNTRY ROAD, SET APART FROM THE URBAN AREAS AND THE REGIONAL CAPITAL, LIVES ASHA, A TWELVE-YEAR-OLD GIRL, WITH HER MOTHER, HER GRANDMA AND HER UNCLE. THERE THEY GROW A VARIETY OF CROPS FOR FOOD.

Road closed

Good afternoon! As you know, we need your collaboration for the cause. How many chickens can we take with us today?

Coca plants

From the Jungle to the City: Asha's Journey   275

SINCE THERE WAS ONLY ONE SCHOOL ON THEIR ROAD, WHEN ASHA FINISHED ELEMENTARY SCHOOL SHE HAD TO GO TO A BOARDING SCHOOL FAR FROM HER FAMILY IN ORDER TO CONTINUE HER STUDIES.

EDUCATION IN THE RURAL AREAS OF COLOMBIA IS CHARACTERIZED BY LIMITED GEOGRAPHIC REACH AND A LACK OF QUALITY AND RELEVANCE, WHICH LEADS TO THE IMPOVERISHMENT OF THE POPULATION AND THE VIOLENCE THAT THE COUNTRY SUFFERS FROM.

ONE DAY, THEY TOLD HER THAT A YOUNG MAN WAS AT THE DOCK ASKING FOR HER.
Should we go? My mom must have sent a package for me.
Are you Asha?
Yes.
You need to come with me.
Come with me, don't leave me here by myself.

From the Jungle to the City: Asha's Journey 277

TRAINING BEGAN VERY EARLY.
4:00
Prrriiiiii
Fasteeeer! This isn't your mother's house.
If you don't hurry up, you won't get any breakfast!

THEY TRAINED FOR HOURS WITH A STICK SIMULATING A GUN, EVEN WHEN THE EXERCISES WERE SO PHYSICALLY DEMANDING THAT THEY PASSED OUT AND VOMITED DURING TRAINING.

From the Jungle to the City: Asha's Journey 279

ASHA AND HER FRIEND FOUND IT UNBEARABLE TO GET UNDRESSED IN FRONT OF EVERYONE IN ORDER TO BATHE, AND THEY WERE PUNISHED FOR THIS SEVERAL TIMES.

If you don't get undressed and quickly take a bath you're not going to make it on time.

Girls, once again you're going to have to carry these heavy tree trunks.

DISOBEYING ORDERS WASN'T AN OPTION. THE GIRLS AND BOYS WHO TRIED TO ESCAPE WERE KILLED IN FRONT OF THE OTHERS TO INSTILL FEAR IN THE ENTIRE GROUP. COMMITTING OTHER OFFENSES MEANT THEY HAD TO DIG TRENCHES OR CARRY VERY HEAVY FIREWOOD.

THE NIGHTS WERE TRUE NIGHTMARES.
It's going to hurt more if she doesn't stay still.
NO MOOOORE, PLEASE, LET ME GO!
FOR ASHA, AS WAS THE CASE FOR ALL THE WOMEN AND GIRLS, SHE WAS ORDERED TO UNDERGO A MEDICAL INSPECTION WHERE THEY INSERTED AN INTRAUTERINE DEVICE INSIDE HER THAT CAUSED HER A LOT OF PAIN. THOSE WHO BECAME PREGNANT UNDERWENT FORCED ABORTIONS.

From the Jungle to the City: Asha's Journey 281

ONE DAY THEY DECIDED TO MOVE ASHA, TOGETHER WITH HER FRIEND AND THE OTHER GIRLS AND BOYS, TO A NEW CAMP.

You will all be charged with strengthening the Catatumbo zone.
It will be the new Arturo Ruiz Column.
Timochenko
Mono Jojoy

From the Jungle to the City: Asha's Journey   283

*A MILITARY OPERATION UNDERTAKEN BY THE NATIONAL ARMY BETWEEN THE END OF 2000 AND THE BEGINNING OF 2001 IN PÁRAMO BERLIN. 94 PEOPLE DIED, 74 OF WHOM WERE MINORS RECRUITED BY THE FARC-EP. THE COLOMBIAN JUSTICE SYSTEM HAS GATHERED EVIDENCE ABOUT THE CRIMES THAT WERE COMMITTED AGAINST THESE CHILDREN DURING OPERATION BERLIN.

From the Jungle to the City: Asha's Journey   285

They had to go to countless government institutions.
Another line? Last time we had to wait for three hours and they didn't resolve anything.
Friend! Do you know how to use firearms?
Well, yes, I learned with the guerrilla fighters.
Then you're the one for this job.
This is the guy that can help us with these runs.
Of course, boss, I'll help with whatever you need.

From the Jungle to the City: Asha's Journey

Lookout

Narcotics distribution

"Did you get the money together? You know what'll happen if you don't give it to me right now."

Calls to extort money

With time, and depending on the "skills" they acquired, they were given weapons.

And they even learned how to drive motorcycles and cars in order to carry out robberies, kidnappings, and homicides.

MEANWHILE ASHA
Why did your parents let you join the guerrillas?
How many people did you kill?
Did you prefer to join the guerrilla fighters instead of continuing your studies?
...THEY WENT TO AN ENDLESS NUMBER OF INSTITUTIONS...
Hi! It's good to see you all again.
Here they only let us go out in the sun for an hour.
I was at another one where they just teach manners and yell at us all the time.
I'm leaving for Bogota.
Now you're ready to hit the streets.
...WHERE CRISTIAN ENDED UP INVOLVED IN CRIMINAL ACTIVITIES.

From the Jungle to the City: Asha's Journey

WHILE ALL OF THIS WAS GOING ON, ASHA'S MOM...
Mija, they took Asha...
...and they took her too.
How? Who?
Some minors were found.
Look, there they are, it's them.
ASHA TRIED TO CALL THEM BUT..
Hi! This is Asha, could you tell my mom that I'm ok?
Of course, I'll tell her.
HER MOTHER DIDN'T RECEIVE THE MESSAGE.

From the Jungle to the City: Asha's Journey

THE MOMS TRAVEL TO BOGOTA.

I would like to be able to hug you, but they won't let us go in.

Mom, get me out of here.

Do you know where my daughter is?

It's not that easy.

I know, they separated us.

ON THEIR WAY BACK TO THEIR TOWN...

Do you know who those strange men are?

They say they are paramilitaries.

...THE WOMEN WERE DISPLACED.

YEARS LATER, WHEN ASHA WAS ABLE TO RETURN HOME, HER GRANDMA HAD DIED AND HER MOTHER WAS LIVING IN AWFUL CONDITIONS.

In 2016, the guerrilla group FARC-EP and the federal government signed a peace accord, through which the Special Jurisdiction for Peace was created, a tribunal that brings to light the crimes committed during the armed conflict that occurred before December 1, 2016, to which transitional justice must be applied. It was created to provide redress for the rights of the victims to truth and justice and to contribute to reparations for them.

One of the macro-cases opened by this jurisdiction is case 07, which centers on the recruitment of girls and boys into the armed conflict.

In September of 2019, together with 23 other victims of recruitment, accompanied by Benposta Nation of Youth and the Coalition against the involvement of girls, boys, and young people in the armed conflict in Colombia - COALICO - Asha presented a report of all the mistreatment they suffered under during their time involved in the war and gave testimony in front of the judges, raising her voice to claim her rights and those of the others. She has helped many young people gain accreditation with the Special Jurisdiction of Peace, who like her, were ripped from their families to form part of the ranks of armed groups. She is committed to this process for as long as it takes to find out the truth about what happened and to repair the damage that was caused.

She has also offered to support the reconstruction of life projects for girls, boys, and youth who were able to return to the places from which they were taken after the signing of the accord.

In addition, she accompanies families in their search for victims of recruitment whose whereabouts have been unknown since they were taken by the FARC-EP, and are demanding to know what happened to them so that they can either embrace them once again or give them a dignified farewell.

From the Jungle to the City: Asha's Journey 293

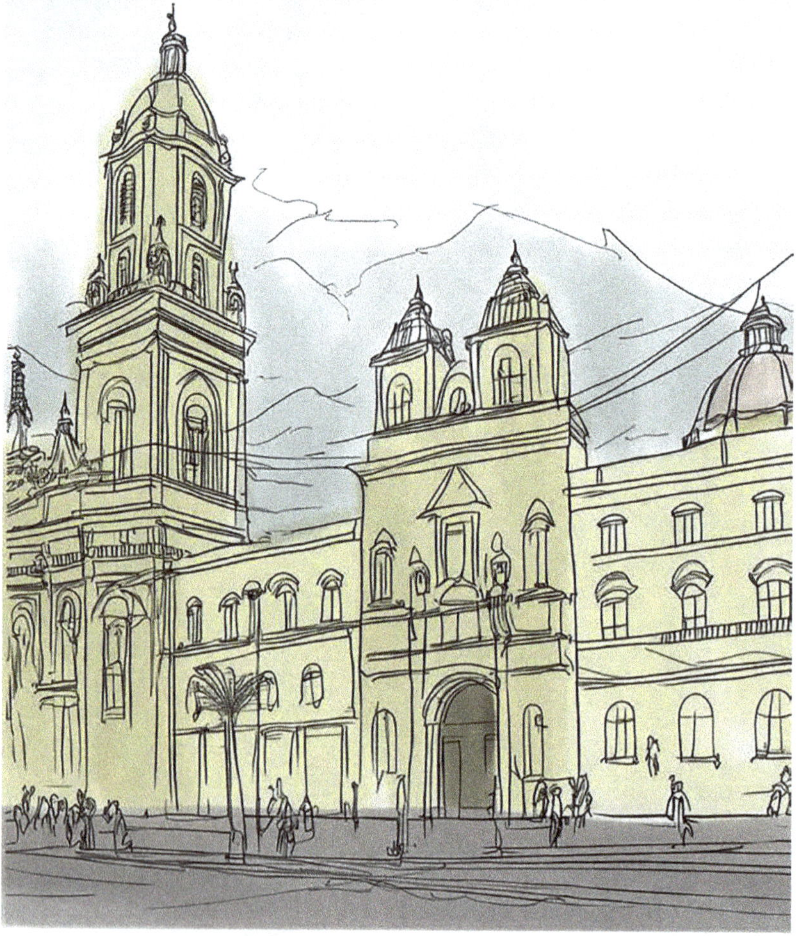

From the Jungle to the City: Asha's Journey

Despite the signing of the Peace Accord with the FARC-EP guerrillas, since 2016, at least 8,000 minors would continue to be victims of this abuse, committed by the different actors that make up the armed, social and political conflict that this country suffers from.

Although there is a robust normativity regarding the subject which attempts to prevent this from happening again, provide support for those who have been victimized and penalize the perpetrators, there are still many challenges to the understanding that the girls and boys who have been involved with armed groups are principally victims and require specific measures to address what they've gone through, even after they've become adults.

It's especially urgent to concentrate efforts to prevent their re-capture by armed groups with infrastructures present in cities, and that see in these individuals an opportunity to expand their criminal activities. On the one hand, they consider their experience living with armed groups an advantage for their participation in criminal groups, and on the other hand, the structural conditions of the contexts that led them to be linked with armed groups in the first place persist—lack of educational and work opportunities, violence, and, among others, the possibility of being recruited and used again. In addition to that is the fact that once they turn 18, their social inclusion and protection becomes limited.

Mariana Medina Barragán is a human rights lawyer and specialist in public policies and gender justice. Her work includes serving as a researcher and adviser to civil society organizations, international cooperation agencies, and state entities. She has a law degree and MA in constitutional rights from the National University of Colombia and a postgraduate degree in human rights from the University of Chile.

Luz Adriana López Medina is a nurse and former child victim of recruitment by the Colombian FARC-EP guerrilla group. Through her work and activism, she continues to search for children who are still considered missing after being recruited by armed groups.

Alejandra Medina Barragán is a graphic designer who has been honored several times for her work. In each of her projects, she seeks to capture the essence of the narrative and translate it into a visual language that inspires, moves, and transcends borders.

Open Access This chapter is licensed under the terms of the Creative Commons Attribution-NonCommercial-NoDerivatives 4.0 International License (http://creativecommons.org/licenses/by-nc-nd/4.0/), which permits any noncommercial use, sharing, distribution and reproduction in any medium or format, as long as you give appropriate credit to the original author(s) and the source, provide a link to the Creative Commons license and indicate if you modified the licensed material. You do not have permission under this license to share adapted material derived from this chapter or parts of it.

The images or other third party material in this chapter are included in the chapter's Creative Commons license, unless indicated otherwise in a credit line to the material. If material is not included in the chapter's Creative Commons license and your intended use is not permitted by statutory regulation or exceeds the permitted use, you will need to obtain permission directly from the copyright holder.

Toward Urban Violence Prevention: Committing to a Multisite Ethics of Care

Friederike Bubenzer

Introduction

In 2024, the World Bank estimated that by 2050, nearly 70% of the world's population will live in urban areas.[1] Most of this urban growth will occur in the world's least-developed countries, where poor economic and political governance as well as environmental pressures will force people to seek opportunities in cities. Research suggests that people living in urban areas are more likely to experience mental health and psychosocial problems than people living in rural areas. This is compounded in conflict-affected and low-income communities where legacies of oppression, such as colonialism, as well as the impacts of direct and structural violence contribute to high levels of stress. And where systems are too weak to adequately respond to the needs of immigrants, whether from other (conflict-affected) countries or due to rural impoverishment and

F. Bubenzer (✉)
Peacebuilding, Mental Health, and Psychosocial Support, Johannesburg, South Africa
e-mail: friederikebubenzer@gmail.com

forced urbanization, climate change and other contemporary challenges, thereby adding social and economic pressure on already tenuous social dynamics.

Public transport that is dangerous, expensive, and unreliable; unequal service delivery; high levels of pollution; overcrowding; the constant fear of crime; and noise have a corrosive effect on the well-being of individuals and communities. Mental health problems, especially when left untreated or poorly managed, can negatively impact social relationships, impede community participation, and, in some cases, increase the likelihood of violent behavior. This confluence of often long-standing factors—especially structural violence—influences how identity-based mass violence (IBMV) occurs in cities. Identity-based mass violence refers to widespread, systemic, or large-scale acts of violence that target individuals or groups based on their perceived identity characteristics, such as race, ethnicity, religion, gender, sexuality, or political affiliation.

For centuries, cities have also been at the center of human innovation and development, of culture and tradition, making space and being a home for people from all walks of life and creating bustling, dynamic, and unique melting pots of human existence. It is in cities around the world where trends in fashion, design, and architecture are born, where musicians and artists find audiences, where culture and tradition defy time, and where narratives are shaped and molded before they become history. And cities are adaptable ecosystems that are continually evolving, shaped by constant social, economic, environmental, and political changes, pressures, and challenges. So how can cities become more resilient, equitable, just, and responsive to the needs of their citizens, thereby contributing to the prevention of IBMV? How can cities celebrate and build on those foundations that positively contribute to human development and flourishing? What is needed to create public spaces and infrastructure that ensure safety, bring people together, and cultivate joy and connection rather than division and segregation—that model care-full spaces and places?[2]

This chapter looks at why life in many cities around the world has a particularly negative effect on its citizens' well-being and how, despite this, we might develop more-resilient cityscapes that can proactively sow an equitable ethics of care as part of identity-based urban-violence-prevention efforts.

Life in the City

Around the world, people are drawn to cities in search of opportunities, often leaving behind trusted and familiar social, cultural, and economic systems. They are forced to adapt to a new, faster-pace life that can be invigorating and exciting, as well as foreign and hostile. Many cities around the world are associated with poor mental health of the people living in them. Research by the Center for Urban Design and Mental Health has found that preexisting risk factors, as well as social and environmental factors,[3] are the main reasons people in cities face mental health problems and psychosocial challenges, often more so than in rural areas. Some of the push factors that drive people to migrate to cities and that may influence their adaptation there include poverty, unemployment, experiences of violence, homelessness, and personal and family crises. The push factors driving people into cities can also be risk factors for mental health problems, resulting in a population group particularly predisposed to mental disorders as well as psychosocial challenges. These realities are disproportionately experienced by historically oppressed and marginalized groups in which intergenerational trauma is also prevalent.[4] These factors also tend to predispose people to encounter real hardship as they embark on life in the city, such as living in informal neighborhoods that are characterized by poverty and crime, poor service delivery, and infrastructure and where feelings of hopelessness, fear, and isolation are pronounced and affect their well-being. In combination with experiences of poverty and marginalization, this can fuel resentment, social tensions, and a sense of exclusion that increases vulnerability to xenophobia and other harmful ideologies. Cumulatively, this causes what Donna Hicks calls "primal insults to dignity" to people, many of whom have already endured severe hardship and suffering.[5]

Because of their size and density, many cities emit multiple competing sensory stimuli that can overload people's baseline of arousal. Noise, light, smells, air pollution, and population and building density, which are pronounced in low-income urban neighborhoods (Konrad Miciukiewicz and Geoff Vigar) can significantly increase stress levels.[6] The lack of protective factors—such as characteristics in individuals and communities that cushion and nurture people, helping them deal more effectively with stressful events and mitigating risk—can lead to more stress. In many cities, access is limited to natural resources that can contribute to alleviating stress and provide space for leisure time such as parks, forests, playgrounds, and beaches. The absence of well-resourced public spaces—such as community centers, which can offer vocational training, relationship building, networking opportunities, and free internet and/or libraries, where children in unsafe communities could spend afternoons—erodes people's sense of self-worth and can deprive them of access to information and the internet, shelter, and public bathrooms.

The symptoms related to mental health problems that are common among people who lived and/or live in a violent environment are well studied and can include feelings of grief, sadness, flashbacks, intrusive thoughts, avoidance, emotion-regulation difficulties, and substance abuse. For most people, experiencing disruptive events does not automatically lead to trauma or to mental health problems. Psychological distress is a normal reaction to an abnormal situation, and in most cases, adverse mental health problems are a temporary response to difficult circumstances. However, for a small group of people, the symptoms can become chronic if they are not adequately managed. "If unaddressed, these symptoms can have longer-term effects on individual and collective well-being. This can create obstacles to positive social engagement, social cohesion, and social justice, thus increasing the risk of anti-social behaviour and ongoing stressors"[7] (UNDP, 2022). And since trauma is not the only mental health concern stemming from violence, it is also important to consider here the "daily stress" of living in a constant state of fear and alertness. Kenneth Miller and Andrew Rasmussen define daily stress as the material and emotional conditions of everyday life that are often considered just as problematic in eroding well-being as traumatic experiences, if not more so, given their pervasive and insidious nature.[8]

In a rapidly urbanizing world, multidisciplinary and multistakeholder efforts are needed to address the root causes of identity-based violence in cities as part of prevention efforts. Scalable and affordable solutions are needed to turn cities into safety nets of care and dignity, rather than propellers of violence and indignity. In *The Caring City*, British architecture professor Juliet Davis makes the case for an ethics of care in the spatial, material, and experiential aspects of urban design. She argues that "design can support people in their everyday lives, enabling them to meet needs and develop capabilities key to well-being and flourishing. It can pattern the giving and receiving of care between people, fostering awareness of others' needs across lines of cultural and generational difference. It can help maintain bonds between people and places, acting as a repository for memories that people hold dear."[9] In their book *Restorative Cities*, Jenny Roe and Layla McKay make the first ever appeal for what they call "restorative urbanism": "a 'quieter' approach that puts mental health, wellness and quality of life at the forefront of city planning and urban design."[10] Could these intentional, human-centered models that are underpinned by the notion of interdependence and care contribute to human flourishing and IBMV prevention?

Defining Ethics of Care

There is no single, short definition of ethics of care. In its simplest form, it is a feminist moral framework that regards the care of individuals and communities as the highest moral obligation. It emphasizes individual responsibility as well as collective responsibility that must be shared by families, communities, and society as a whole. The most widely cited definition of this ethics of care was developed by Joan Tronto and Berenice Ficher, who explain it as a "species activity that includes everything that we do to maintain, continue, and repair our 'world' so that we can live in it as well as possible. This world includes our bodies, ourselves, and our environment, all of which we seek to interweave in a complex, life-sustaining web."[11]

The recognition of the interconnectedness and interdependence of social and ecological systems is a central feature of the ethics of care. Indeed, our social interdependence as it relates to caring and being cared for is, as Daniel Engster explains, fundamental to a functioning society.[12] Ethics of care value relationality and the centrality of healthy relationships as a conduit for strong social fabric. Like Engster, Miriam Williams maintains that we are dependent on others for our care and limited by our bodily capacity to care, which, through illness, exhaustion, and trauma can be dramatically curtailed.[13] This underscores the importance of intentionally and consciously putting in place systems and services that facilitate equitable caregiving and care receiving, especially for vulnerable and historically marginalized and oppressed communities.

Trauma-Transformative and Restorative Approaches

Applying the ethics of care lens to the promotion of well-being and identity-based-violence prevention in cities suggests the importance of an all-of-society and interdisciplinary approach that is both trauma transformative and restorative in nature. By situating the care of individuals and communities as the highest moral obligation, equitable mechanisms are put in place that are conflict sensitive and acknowledge legacies of violence and pain, while also being reparative and addressing the harm done in the past.

Cordula Reimann and Sarh Habibi define trauma-transformative approaches as those that "create enabling conditions for deep individual and collective healing as a cornerstone for ending cycles of violence, including shifting narratives, identities and social conditions, as a basis for enabling new foundations and approaches for the future of individual and collective health, wellbeing, and resilience." Trauma-transformative approaches to violence prevention recognize the impact that unaddressed trauma and intergenerational trauma can have on individuals and communities (i.e., trauma-informed) but go further to empower individuals and communities to transform drivers of stress, insecurity, and injustice to build resilience.[14]

Restorative approaches use dialogue, accountability, and community involvement to acknowledge legacies of structural inequality and injustice, and they seek to repair and rebuild what has been damaged in an empathetic way. Roe and McKay argue for a "salutogenic"—or health-promoting—approach to urban design that focuses on well-being while also applying a systems perspective that recognizes the many intersectionalities within the system that comprises the city. Dignity and its restoration must be a central feature of restorative and trauma-transformative urban design: "extending care and attention to those who had endured unspeakable atrocities, helped them recover their sense of self-worth. Offering care and attention is [...] at the heart of treating people with dignity" (Hicks, 2011:xii).

So what steps can cities take to enable the well-being and thriving of the entire social, political, and environmental ecosystem? And how can cities develop care-based spaces and infrastructures that respond to the full spectrum of needs of people across the city, cultivating constructive relationships among citizens and between government and citizens?

Imagining Urban Care Ethics in Practice

Ensuring that urban design and development are based on inclusive and participatory processes aimed at establishing community needs must go hand-in-hand with ethics of care to prevent "solutions" from failing or further disadvantaging and excluding the most vulnerable. This was evidenced in Bogota, Colombia, where much of the historical neighborhood of Santa Inéz, deemed by the ruling party as a "symbol of chaos and government impotence" was razed (including tens of thousands of people being displaced without compensation) to make room for a park that, failing to address the underlying root causes of the chaos, was soon occupied by unhoused people who—rightfully—demanded better public housing. The notion that spaces and places can be "wounded," (Davis, 2022; Till, 2012), resulting in the rupturing of place-based attachments and the socioecological ecosystems that existed there, can still be seen in places like South Africa's District Six.[15] There, more than 50 years after the neighborhood was declared a whites-only area by the apartheid regime and more than 60,000 people were forcibly evicted, most of the land lies barren and unoccupied. Time, politics, and resources have not been kind to land redistribution in South Africa, where millions of people of color who were disenfranchised under apartheid continue to hope that land taken from them will be returned. In South Africa and Colombia, as well as in other similar contexts, sincere, inclusive, and deliberate dialogue and consultation processes are the most effective way of ensuring disadvantaged people feel seen and heard and that urban development is humancentric.

Public Transport

Research by Kenzie Latham-Mintus, Keith Miller, and others suggests that safe, affordable, and widely accessible public transport is a significant enabler of participation in social activities such as visiting friends/family, attending religious services, participating in organizations, and visiting parks, beaches, and mountains for enjoyment.[16] These activities in turn play a positive role in people's individual and collective well-being. These social and recreational interactions that are enabled by freedom of movement contribute to more-meaningful relationships and lifestyles and the ability to engage in activities that contribute to individual and collective well-being. Konrad Miciukiewicz and Geoff Vigar's notion of the "splintered city" points to increasing polarization where poor mobility results in individuals as well as whole neighborhoods exhibiting problems of connectedness in relation to employment, consumption, leisure, and social life. Their research suggests that mobility exclusion correlates with social isolation and estrangement and thus undermines all forms of sociability, including participation in civil organizations, local associations, and family life. Miciukiewicz and Vigar point to multiple potential opportunities embedded in urban mobility, which is not only a key to access to work, education and health, and the social mobility of all individuals, but also provides "a channel" to social interaction, the integration of urban society, and the political activation of citizens across urban space. In this way, communities come together and contribute to and participate in finding solutions.

Public Spaces

Inclusive, free, and safe public spaces that are accessible and welcoming to citizens across the city have been noted by countless authors and research projects around the world as critical to the well-being of individuals and communities and an important cog in the multipart wheel of urban-violence prevention. This is particularly true for women: safe public spaces that enable women to move freely without fear of violence and harassment are essential because they promote women's independence and participation in work and community life.

> **Box 1. WHO Healthy Cities Checklist** Increasingly, urban designers and architects are integrating an ethics of care into the way spaces are developed, collaborating with other sectors such as public health, safety, and education to ensure integrated solutions to reduce crime, poverty, inequality, and violence. A widely consultative process gave rise to the WHO Healthy Cities checklist:
>
> - A clean, safe physical environment of high quality (including housing quality).
> - An ecosystem that is stable now, sustainable in the long term.
> - A strong, mutually supportive and nonexploitative community.
> - A high degree of participation in and control by the citizens over the decisions affecting their lives, health, and well-being.
> - The meeting of basic needs (food, water, shelter, income, safety, and work) for all the city's people.
> - Access by the people to a wide variety of experiences and resources, with the chance for a wide variety of contact, interaction, and communication.
> - A diverse, vital, and innovative economy.
> - Connectedness with the past, with the cultural and biological heritage of city dwellers, and with other groups and individuals.
> - Form that is compatible with and enhances the preceding characteristics.
> - Optimum level of appropriate public health and sickness care services, accessible to all.

> – High health status (high levels of positive health and low levels of disease).
>
> World Health Organization. "Healthy City Vision." April 5, 2018. https://www.who.int/europe/news-room/fact-sheets/item/healthy-cities-vision.

Perhaps the most important question to ask relating to the development of cities that practice an ethics of care as a basis for the prevention of IBMV and the promotion of human flourishing is how people and vulnerable groups in particular feel in the spaces they occupy and whether that feeling is conducive to their mental and social wellbeing, to the fostering of relationships, and thus to violence prevention. The UN Women's Safe Cities and Safe Public Spaces for Women and Girls initiative has made significant strides in creating a sense of safety for women and girls by creating safer urban environments in cities around the world, based on extensive research and consultation. Using a holistic approach, the initiative focuses on identifying local interventions, developing legislation and policies, investing in safe public spaces, and changing social norms. Several cities have implemented new policies or amended existing ones to address sexual harassment in public spaces. For example, Quito, Ecuador, amended a local ordinance to strengthen action against sexual harassment. In Egypt, the Ministry of Housing adopted women's safety audits to ensure a gender approach to urban planning. Rwanda's Gender Monitoring Office launched training on preventing sexual harassment against women in public transportation. The initiative emphasizes grassroots involvement, engaging women, men, and youth in community-mobilization activities to transform social norms.

In the Khayelitsha Township of South Africa, UN Women partnered with local government in 2011 in a physical upgrading project aimed at addressing the extremely high levels of rape that had been reported. The physical upgrading took into account the "triangle of violence," covering urban renewal strategies to reduce risks of violence, criminal justice measures to discourage potential violators, and public health and conflict-resolution interventions to support victims of violence. Lights and closed-circuit television systems were installed, alongside public telephone systems, improved public transport, and safe walkways. Communities were invited to be involvement in providing safety hubs in dangerous areas. A number of specific anti-rape strategies were introduced that included establishing rape crisis centers and counseling services, self-defense training, and community awareness raising. Police received training, and their presence was increased in dangerous locations. Finally, jobs and services were brought closer to residents, meaning less time, energy, and money had to be spent on accessing them and allowing for these limited resources to be spent in more-meaningful ways. Between April 2008 and March 2009, there was a 20% reduction in violent crime (UN Women, 2020).[17]

Public spaces that invite individuals, families, and communities to socialize, exercise, and spend leisure time, as well as libraries, parks, community centers, beaches, and sports facilities, "channel" social interaction in similar ways as does public transport. Roe and McKay argue that such "restorative environments" in which people can walk, jog, play games, and picnic can have significant mental health benefits by fostering recovery from mental fatigue, depression, stress, and anxiety (2021: 9).

A rapidly growing body of research is providing evidence for the health benefits of spending time in nature, including the benefits of listening to birdsong, gardening and "bathing in forests." A 2015 cross-sectional study on urban street tree density in London that found that fewer antidepressants were prescribed in areas with more trees.[18]

In Los Angeles County, Jesse Owens Park is today a hub of peaceful physical activity and socializing rather than the grim and violent area it was before 2010. The park was rejuvenated as part of the Los Angeles County Department of Parks and Recreation's Parks after Dark program, which was run in conjunction with the county administration, the county Department of Public Health, and law enforcement. J. A. Jacob writes: "Three nights a week during the summer in the designated parks, children swim in pools and chase soccer balls across fields, teenagers play basketball, and people stroll through the park in organized walking groups and attend exercise classes. Deputy sheriffs on duty ensure the safety of visitors and participate in the activities too"[19] (Jacob, 2015).

Everyone needs a garden. This is our soil. When you work with it, things grow. It's nature, life. I am a poor man, sometimes my family and I only eat once a day, but I can live without food; I couldn't live without seeing green leaves and flowers. They come from heaven.

Snow, L. War Gardens: A Journey through Conflict in Search of Calm. London: Quercus, 2018.

Equitable access to safe and green public spaces designed using an ethics of care play a vital role in promoting dignity and enhancing the psychosocial well-being of city residents. By enabling physical exercise and making spaces available for recreational activities, celebrations, and community meetings, safe public spaces play a vital role in reducing stress, promoting health, and positively influencing behavior, thereby contributing to the reduction of violence.[20]

Sites of Conscience

"People need recognition for what they have suffered," explains Donna Hicks in her book about dignity, adding that nameless and unvoiced indignities are a missing link in our understanding of what keep conflicts alive (Hicks, 2011: xiii). Acknowledgment can take many forms. Museums, memorials, and other sites of conscience are important ways cities can use inclusive and consultative processes to publicly acknowledge and honor local histories and narratives of injustice and oppression. Such spaces and the events and activities they enable can simultaneously play a preventive role for young people and society at large by hosting intentional and targeted civic education, dialogue, and cultural events that provide alternative spaces for young people to engage with.

Perhaps the most pertinent example of a city that acknowledges and remembers openly and widely is the German capital Berlin. There it is difficult not to stumble over the world famous Stolpersteine (stumbling stones)—a ten-centimeter concrete cube inserted into the paved ground outside the homes of victims of Nazi extermination or persecution, bearing a brass plate inscribed with their name and life dates.

Initiated by artist Gunter Demnig, these small, decentralized memorials foster personal connections to history and encourage public reflection. And a tourist's schedule is incomplete without visiting memorials such as the Memorial to the Murdered Jews of Europe; the stunning neoclassical Neue Wache Memorial that serves as a memorial to war and tyranny (and that houses, in its bare center, a sculpture by Käthe Kollwitz titled *Mother with Her Dead Son*); or Checkpoint Charlie, the checkpoint between East and West Germany during the Cold War, which remains today as a monument and a reminder of the city's divided past.

More recently, sites of conscience are being constructed in more-deliberate and intentional ways, enabling the public (especially students) to visit educational exhibits, watch videos, and dialogue with volunteer storytellers as part of their prevention efforts. This is the case in Johannesburg, South Africa, where the first Constitutional Court was established in 1993. As a major symbolic gesture of transformation and after an extensive public consultation process, the court was built on the site of and using bricks from a former prison. Among many other striking and inspiring gestures of inclusivity and transparency, the imposing wooden doors to the court have the 27 rights of the South African Bill of Rights carved into them, written in all 11 of the country's official languages. The court is open to the public at no cost and is a sought-after experiential learning destination for local schools and scholars from around the world.

Trauma-Informed Education

Increasingly, education institutions around the world are teaching and using trauma-informed pedagogies to create school communities centered on empathy and safety, aspects of community life that tend to be less freely available to learners from low-income communities in dense urban settings. Given that many children spend the majority of their time in school, school-based care programs are essential to promoting socioemotional development while also fostering understanding, respect, and appreciation for diverse identities, cultures, and perspectives, thereby helping to counter narratives of "us versus them" that can fuel identity-based conflicts. Using this approach positions the school/learning environment as a model microcosm where safety is paramount and staff understand the impact of stress and trauma on learners' brains. In this way, schools and all their staff (from teachers to cleaning and security staff) are trained to be attuned to the learners' needs and model for learners the kind of behavior and social relationships that are conducive to a healthy society and social cohesion. Safe and supportive learning environments that provide counseling to students who have experienced violence or traumatic events, helping them process their experiences and build resilience, can contribute to a reduction in learners dropping out, resorting to substance abuse, or developing mental health problems.[21] Using participatory theater as a violence-prevention tool in inner-city American schools with high levels of community violence, Bessel van der Kolk found significant positive responses among participating learners, including fewer fights and angry outbursts, more cooperation and self-assertion with peers, and more attentiveness and engagement in the classroom.[22] Samantha De Silva adds that after-school programs, extracurricular activities, and mentorship opportunities can give youth positive outlets and alternatives to violence or extremism.[23] Shantel Crosby et al. argue that trauma-informed teaching is also an act of social justice education, explaining that "these models equip school staff with skills and tools to reflect on and challenge their responses to students that perpetuate disempowerment through harsh school discipline."[24]

Public Health

Public health has long been regarded as a vital cog in the wheel of violence prevention. The World Health Organization (WHO) defines a public health approach to reducing violence as one that "seeks to improve the health and safety of all individuals by addressing underlying risk factors that increase the likelihood that an individual will become a victim or a perpetrator of violence."[25] Public health is fundamentally focused on maximizing benefits for the greatest number of individuals. Programs aimed at the primary prevention of violence, grounded in a public health framework, are crafted to reach a wide segment of the population. These initiatives seek to implement prevention strategies that effectively reduce and prevent violence on a community-wide scale. Public health methodologies are both interdisciplinary and collaborative in nature. By analyzing and seeking to understand the factors that increase or decrease the likelihood of violence and their impact on health care, public health approaches contribute often-rare data to violence-prevention efforts. By addressing modifiable risk factors such as socioeconomic conditions and community disorganization, alongside enhancing protective factors like strong family ties and community cohesion, cities can embody the ethics of care in their governance. This approach emphasizes the importance of nurturing relationships and collective responsibility, ultimately contributing to the reduction of violence while fostering supportive urban environments.

In Zimbabwe, the Friendship Bench, a local nongovernmental organization (NGO), has trained *mbuya* (local grandmothers) as lay health workers in response to research that pointed to high levels of trauma. By providing free therapy on widely available public park benches, the Friendship Bench bridges the professional healthcare gap by providing accessible healing and listening spaces where people can come to seek help. Friendship benches are available in 288 primary health-care facilities across Zimbabwe. There are more than 1,000 benches in Zimbabwe's capital Harare alone, and the *mbuya* have seen more than 160,000 people in a two-year period.[26]

The Global Health and Peace Initiative (GHPI)[27] of the WHO aims to strengthen the role of the health sector in contributing to the prospects for peace. It advocates for the delivery of health-care services that are provided in a conflict-sensitive and peace-responsive way. The GHPI contributes to "positive peace," which relates to the attitudes, institutions, and structures that create and sustain peaceful societies (rather than simply the absence of conflict or violence, known as "negative peace"). That is to say, the initiative focuses on how health activities can be designed and implemented in a way that better contributes to outcomes such as increased social cohesion and trust, decreased exclusion and marginalization, and improved resilience to the impact of armed conflict and the effects of violence. The initiative also seeks to contribute to reducing or preventing community violence by designing health activities for groups at risk of violence to support their social and economic integration into society. Collaboration and partnerships are core tenets of the GHPI. "By working on improving citizen–state cohesion through health equity, by facilitating collaboration in health governance with all parties to a conflict and by promoting community healing through dialogue and inclusion, health programmes can deliver peace dividends in addition to health benefits."[28]

From 2019 to 2021, WHO partnered with the United Nations Children's Fund, International Organization for Migration, and the Peacebuilding Fund to strengthen support for mental health and psychosocial needs of conflict-affected young men and women in Somalia to advance peacebuilding and reconciliation in the country. The project integrated the care and treatment of mental illness into primary health services delivered at local health facilities and strengthened community-based supports for addressing mental health and psychosocial needs. In this way, health facilities doubled up as meeting places for young people to participate in dialogue and trust-building processes.

The Building Blocks of Urban Well-Being

The following approaches constitute some of the most urgent components of a city that prioritizes the well-being and flourishing of the urban system as part of its contribution to violence prevention:

1. **Incorporating care ethics into policy development and implementation**

    Care ethics should be integrated into the framing, implementation, and monitoring of planning policies to ensure that inclusive and equitable actions are developed and implemented in a way that prioritizes care and well-being. This includes enacting laws and regulations that prioritize the well-being and safety of all residents, regardless of ethnicity, sexual orientation, gender, class, and other such identities. Policies should be informed by community input and address the social determinants of violence, such as poverty, inequality, and lack of access to essential services.

2. Fostering social connection and community building

To ensure that policies are responsive to the needs of the community, violence-prevention policies that are premised on an ethics of care should be developed with input from community members, particularly those who are most affected by violence. Creating and maintaining spaces and events where vertical and horizontal trust can be cultivated is critical to establishing relationships able to resist the challenges implied in addressing and adequately responding to violence. Building strong social connections and communities is essential for promoting care and empathy within urban environments. Cities should establish accessible platforms for dialogue and active participation, where community members can discuss their concerns, share experiences, and collaborate on solutions. This creates a sense of belonging and encourages collective responsibility for preventing violence.

3. Creating and sustaining public spaces that nurture care

Designing and maintaining accessible, safe public spaces is an important aspect of promoting well-being, fostering connection and creating spaces for vulnerable groups to engage in meaningful activities. Cities should prioritize the creation of well-lit, inclusive, and accessible public spaces, ideally in such a way that people from different social, political, and religious groupings can come together to engage in shared activities. Libraries, playgrounds, sports fields, and outdoor gyms that encourage social interaction—enabling low-cost leisure activities and a sense of community and belonging—can contribute to enhancing well-being and overcoming difference. Ethical placemaking can promote health justice by creating places that allow for bodily integrity, mobility, and autonomy, and that promote care.

Simple mechanisms can be used to ensure that a wide and diverse variety of people feel accommodated, safe, free, and welcome in urban spaces. Linguistic, spatial, cultural, and religious accommodations should be made to turn theories of inclusion into practical realities for all citizens.

Creating safe and accessible infrastructure for walking, cycling, and public transport is essential for reducing pollution, promoting physical activity and health, and reducing the dominance of cars in urban environments. This in turn promotes physical and mental well-being as well as stress reduction in crowded, loud, and busy urban spaces. Strategies for prioritizing nonmotorized transportation include creating protected bike lanes, improving public transit systems, and redesigning streets to prioritize pedestrians.

4. Availing care-full support services

Having access to affordable, nearby support services is essential for individuals affected by violence. Cities can invest in accessible and affordable counseling services, trauma-informed care, and victim-support programs. Support groups can provide ongoing spaces for sharing and reflection among survivors of violence while also sharing coping and stress-management mechanisms.

5. Seeking collaboration and building partnerships

Local and sub local governments, municipalities, and administrations should collaborate with local organizations, NGOs, and community groups to develop comprehensive violence-prevention strategies. By partnering with diverse stakeholders, including social workers, educators, law enforcement agencies, and health-care professionals, cities can leverage their collective expertise to address the root causes of violence and promote a culture of care.

6. Incorporating green infrastructure

Integrating green infrastructure into urban design can help mitigate the negative impacts of urbanization on the environment and public health while also creating opportunities for community engagement and involvement. Green infrastructure includes parks and community gardens that have been shown to reduce community violence. Supporting local and sustainable food systems can include promoting urban farming, supporting farmers markets and localized, community-supported agriculture programs, and investing in food-waste-reduction and composting initiatives.

Conclusion

Cities have endless opportunities to be places where identity-based mass violence can be prevented, and human connection and flourishing can be cultivated. While political will, financial investment, and good governance must be central tenets of realizing these opportunities, so must the ethics of care and the belief in the inherent dignity of every human being. Where people's basic human rights and most immediate needs are met in an equitable way—allowing for a balance between meaningful, gainful employment and time for social connection—human flourishing can give way to more-peaceful communities.

Notes

1. World Bank. *Urban Development*. 2024. https://www.worldbank.org/en/topic/urbandevelopment/overview.
2. Miriam Williams defines care-full cities as those in which every day spaces receive diverse forms of care. Williams, M. J. "The Possibility of Care-Full Cities." *Cities* 98. (March 2020). https://www.sciencedirect.com/science/article/abs/pii/S0264275119306493.
3. The Center for Urban Design and Mental Health is a global think tank working to understand how better mental health can be designed into cities. Data analysis by Layla McCay and Todd Litman underpins the quoted information and is available on the website of the Center for Urban Design and Mental

Health at https://www.urbandesignmentalhealth.com/facts-and-figures.html.

Preexisting risk factors are conditions that increase an individual's likelihood of experiencing an adverse health outcome and that are present before occurrence of the adverse event. These may include financial stress, mental health problems such as anxiety and/or depression, and social isolation.

Social and environmental factors impacting poor mental health in cities may include having too little time or energy to socialize, having to commute long distances using expensive transport to travel to places of work and to socialize, and limited access to recreational places where well-being may be nurtured, such as parks, forests, mountains, and beaches.

McCay, Layla and Litman, Todd. "Facts and Figures," Centre for Urban Design and Mental Health, n.d., https://www.urbandesignmentalhealth.com/facts-and-figures.html.
4. Williams, M. J. "The Possibility of Care-Full Cities." *Cities* 98. (March 2020). https://www.sciencedirect.com/science/article/abs/pii/S0264275119306493.
5. Hicks, D. *Dignity: Its Essential Role in Resolving Conflict*. New Haven, CT, and London: Yale University Press, 2011.
6. Miciukiewicz, K., and G. Vigar. "Mobility and Social Cohesion in the Splintered City: Challenging Technocentric Transport Research and Policy-Making Practices." *Urban Studies* 49, no. 9 (June 15, 2012): 1941–1957. https://doi.org/10.1177/0042098012444886.
7. United Nations Development Programme. *Integrating Mental Health and Psychosocial Support into Peacebuilding*. Guidance Note, May 5, 2022. https://www.undp.org/publications/integrating-mental-health-and-psychosocial-support-peacebuilding.
8. Miller, K. E., and A. Rasmussen. "War Experiences, Daily Stressors and Mental Health Five Years On: Elaborations and Future Directions." *Intervention: Journal of Mental Health and Psychosocial Support in Conflict Affected Areas* 12, no. 4 (Dec. 2014): 33–42. https://pmc.ncbi.nlm.nih.gov/articles/PMC9161635/.

9. Davis, J. *The Caring City: Ethics of Urban Design.* Bristol, UK: Bristol University Press, 2022. https://doi.org/10.2307/j.ctv2jtxrfc.
10. Roe, J., and L. McKay. *Restorative Cities: Urban Design for Mental Health and Wellbeing.* London: Bloomsbury, 2021.
11. Tronto, J. C., and B. Fisher. "Toward a Feminist Theory of Caring." In *Circles of Care*, edited by E. Abel and M. Nelson, 36–54. Albany, New York: SUNY Press, 1990.
12. Engster, D. "Rethinking Care Theory: The Practice of Caring and the Obligation to Care." *Hypatia* 20, no. 3 (Summer 2005): 50–74.
13. Williams, M. J. "The Possibility of Care-Full Cities." Cities 98. (March 2020). https://www.sciencedirect.com/science/article/abs/pii/S0264275119306493.
14. Reiman, C., and S. Habibi. (Nov. 28, 2023). "The Trauma-Awareness Spectrum in Humanitarian, Development and Peacebuilding Interventions." Published at https://www.linkedin.com/pulse/trauma-awareness-spectrum-humanitarian-development-cordula-reimann-7xtnf/?trackingId=3KYcbsFDRMix68CjOCjsyg as part of a forthcoming work on trauma-responsive peacebuilding to be published by Routledge in 2025.
15. Till, K. E. "Wounded Cities: Memory-Work and a Place-Based Ethics of Care. *Political Geography* 31, no. 1 (January 2012): 3–14. https://mural.maynoothuniversity.ie/id/eprint/9005/1/KT_wounded%20cities%202012.pdf.
16. Latham-Mintus, K., and K. Miller. "Social Cohesion, Transportation, and Participation in Social Activities among Older Adults." *Innovation in Aging* 3, supplement 1 (Nov. 2019): S215. https://doi.org/10.1093/geroni/igz038.788.
17. UN Women. *Safe Public Spaces.* 2020. https://www.endvawnow.org/en/articles/1990-safe-public-spaces.html.
18. Taylor, Mark S., Benedict W. Wheeler, Mathew P. White, Theodoros Economou, and Nicholas J. Osborne. Research Note: Urban Street Tree Density and Antidepressant Prescription Rates—A Cross-sectional Study in London, UK. Landscape and

Urban Planning 136, (2015): 174–179. https://doi.org/10.1016/j.landurbplan.2014.12.005.
19. Jacob, J. A. "Exercise and Gardening Programs as Tools to Reduce Community Violence." *Journal of the American Medical Association* 314, no. 14 (Oct. 13, 2015): 1435–1437. https://doi.org/10.1001/jama.2015.9002.
20. Snow, L. *War Gardens: A Journey through Conflict in Search of Calm*. London: Quercus, 2018.
21. For more information about the initiative, see 'Creating safe and empowering public spaces with women and girls' at https://www.unwomen.org/en/what-we-do/ending-violence-against-women/creating-safe-public-spaces.
22. Van der Kolk, B. The Body Keeps the Score: Mind, Brain and Body in the Transformation of Trauma. London: Penguin Books, 2014.
23. De Silva, S. "Role of Education in the Prevention of Violent Extremism." Working paper for the World Bank. Oct. 1, 2017. https://documents.worldbank.org/en/publication/documents-reports/documentdetail/448221510079762554/role-of-education-in-the-prevention-of-violent-extremism.
24. Crosby, S. "Social justice education through trauma-informed teaching." Middle School Journal, no 49 (4, 2018):15–23.
25. "Violence Prevention Alliance Approach." World Health Organization. https://www.who.int/groups/violence-prevention alliance/approach.
26. "Creating Safe Spaces and a Sense of Belonging in Communities to Enhance Quality of Life," Friendship Bench Zimbabwe. https://www.friendshipbenchzimbabwe.org/.
27. World Health Organization. "Global Health for Peace Initiative," third draft of the roadmap. March 2023. https://cdn.who.int/media/docs/default-source/campaigns-and-initiatives/health-and-peace/ghpi-roadmap-v3.pdf?sfvrsn=73ab4141_1.
28. Coninx, R., K. Ousman, M. Boddaert, and Hyung-Tae Kim. "How Health Can Make a Contribution to Peace in Africa: WHO's Global Health for Peace Initiative (GHPI)." *BMJ Global Health* 7 (Oct. 2022): e009342. https://doi.org/10.1136/bmjgh-2022-009342.

Friederike Bubenzer is an independent South African peacebuilding practitioner and holds an MPhil degree in development studies and social transformation from the University of Cape Town. She is coeditor with Pumla Gobodo Madikizela and Marietjie Oelofsen of *These Are the Things That Sit With Us* (Johannesburg: Jacana, 2019) and coeditor with Orly Stern of *Hope, Pain and Patience: The Lives of Women in South Sudan* (Johannesburg: Jacana, 2011).

Open Access This chapter is licensed under the terms of the Creative Commons Attribution-NonCommercial-NoDerivatives 4.0 International License (http://creativecommons.org/licenses/by-nc-nd/4.0/), which permits any noncommercial use, sharing, distribution and reproduction in any medium or format, as long as you give appropriate credit to the original author(s) and the source, provide a link to the Creative Commons license and indicate if you modified the licensed material. You do not have permission under this license to share adapted material derived from this chapter or parts of it.

The images or other third party material in this chapter are included in the chapter's Creative Commons license, unless indicated otherwise in a credit line to the material. If material is not included in the chapter's Creative Commons license and your intended use is not permitted by statutory regulation or exceeds the permitted use, you will need to obtain permission directly from the copyright holder.

We Want to Learn! Restorative Justice to Protect Black Girls in Education

Barbara Sherrod

I never leave the building when I run out of class and run around the building, so why would I do that now?

None of the nine adults in the circle had the answer for eight-year-old Kelly, a Black girl in the third grade who, from the perspective of building staff, had a problem with respecting adults and bullying her peers. In the days prior to this impromptu conference, I was in the planning phase of a restorative conversation between Kelly and her classmates responsible for some of the school-based violence Kelly experienced that caused her to leave the classroom. Forty-five minutes before this impromptu restorative circle occurred, Kelly ran through the three-story school, evading her classroom teachers, principal, and the elementary administrator. Fifteen minutes into the school staff's chase, a distraught message on the walkie said Kelly had grabbed her backpack and planned

---

B. Sherrod (✉)
Baltimore, MD, USA
e-mail: barbara.sherrod@icloud.com

© The Author(s) 2026
R. Locke et al. (eds.), *Identity-Based Mass Violence in Urban Contexts*, Palgrave Studies in Victims and Victimology, https://doi.org/10.1007/978-3-031-98068-8_16

to leave the building and go off campus. The school was placed on code yellow, and her mother, Ms. Hall, was called to the school. The principal, aware of my rapport with Kelly, asked me to lead a circle process to help address what happened between Kelly, her mother, and the staff involved in the chase to help address what happened.

As I tell Kelly's story and how restorative circles saved her life and school career, you should know that she had experienced three years of racial abuse from four white male classmates before I entered the school community and Kelly's life. Kelly's school contacted my organization, Restorative Response Baltimore, seeking a partnership to support restorative justice implementation. Restorative Justice Implementation in schools focuses on providing training, coaching, and facilitation services to an identified school community's staff, caregivers, and youth, shifting from punitive responses to youth misbehavior to more connective and communal approaches. Kelly was one of 1,400 students in her Baltimore City Public School, serving students from prekindergarten to eighth grade. I met Kelly at the beginning of the 2017–2018 school year in my first assignment as a full-time restorative practices specialist. I was assigned to her school three days a week; I facilitated restorative circles with staff, students, and families; asked restorative questions to students and staff who were involved in a conflict; facilitated professional development; and supported school administration in adopting restorative approaches codified by the school system's student handbook.

Kelly experienced both structural violence from the school staff and acute violence from her classmates, with her first experience beginning in pre-K. The boys would physically assault her anytime adult supervision was lacking, particularly during recess and lunch. The boys would take Kelly's classwork or threaten to destroy her items to upset her. Rather than acknowledging the harm being done to Kelly, the primarily white and few Black teachers at the school seemed to only catch Kelly in the act of retaliating or defining what was taking place by blaming Kelly for "stirring up trouble."

> Your safety is not a priority, and you do not have the right to protect yourself or seek safety.

In an exchange between Kelly's mother and a resource teacher, Ms. Bolt, a white woman, I witnessed Kelly's mother, Ms. Hall, advocating for her child's safety while being told that Kelly was "a smart girl who can convince people to see things her way, and once she sets her mind to do something to someone, she does it." I intervened with a hand to the resource teacher as she attempted to hug Kelly's mother without permission after accusing her daughter of malicious intent. She missed Kelly's mother's look, which held disgust, sadness, and disbelief. Her mother later shared with me an incident that changed Kelly forever. Once, in kindergarten, the boys had bullied her so harshly that she sought safety underneath a classroom chair. She would not come out until her mother picked her up after dismissal. Hearing the sadness and anger in her mother's voice confirmed that the event is a memory both Kelly and her mother will hold onto forever.

During our first exchange, Kelly's mother shared how the school community had criminalized them both for speaking up. Kelly's mother worked the overnight shift and was often unavailable during school hours, evoking negative comments or questioning from staff about her capability to be a present parent for Kelly and her three siblings. To cope with the school-based violence from her peers, Kelly ran out of the classroom or away from her class whenever she felt stressed, angry, or unsafe. In response to Kelly's coping mechanisms, her teachers would write referrals, detentions, loss of privileges, etc., citing "disruption," "defiance," or "disrespect" as the reason for the disciplinary action. Without considering the consequences of their actions, the school community sent a clear message to Kelly and her mother: "Your safety is not a priority, and you do not have the right to protect yourself." This message rings familiar for many Black women and girls in the American education system.

For Black girls who experience trauma—whether gendered, racialized, or even sexual—their responses to the violent conditions they experience are often criminalized by surrounding adults. By criminalizing Black girls' responses to trauma, adults reinforce the school-to-prison pipeline and carceral practices imposed on Black children often codified in the same student handbooks that promote the use of restorative justice practices, strengthening systems of identity-based inequality and reinforcing harm (Haynes, Stewart, and Allen 2016; Kaba 2021; Morris

2016; Wadhwa 2016; Yahwon 2019). Further, when Black girl/femme students are criminalized for protecting themselves, mistrust is cultivated between the institution, community residents, and the students, reinforcing a matrix of mistrust and extending the initial harm (Haynes et al. 2016; Kaba 2021; Toliver 2022; Young 2021).

In this case, Kelly had experienced bullying from her peers and the school community. Addressing Kelly's experiences with different forms of violence in the school building from her classmates, teachers, and school staff was only a tiny portion of the harm that needed to be addressed to implement restorative justice. The broader imperative was to build stronger connections among individuals within the school community, reimagine responses to disruptive behavior, and reduce the disproportionality of discipline, which was oriented around the race and gender of the school's youth. Understanding this broader context was important to fully realize the ambitions of the restorative justice response. The school's principal, Principal H, acknowledged that the school building is housed in a neighborhood historically known for its white wealth and redlining practices. This historical reality influences the present-day context.

The racial tension in the neighborhood permeates throughout the school building, influencing how the Black students, staff, and other Black community residents are received by their non-Black peers and teachers. Even as an educator within the community, I was not exempt from the effects of this racial tension. I recall being asked by a middle-aged white woman standing in line at the neighborhood Starbucks if I was looking for a nanny position while minding my Black ass business. The Asian woman ahead of me in the queue turned around with a stunned look upon hearing the question. We held each other's eyes to communicate like Black and non-Black women of color do when our existence has been muddled to one suitable for the caretaking of white people. "I am here alone. What makes you think I care for children?" I asked the white woman in response. She justified her question by saying she saw the children across the room in the stroller and thought to ask. I saw the woman again that afternoon, collecting her two children from my assigned school during dismissal. I wondered what racist values and beliefs she consciously and unconsciously bequeathed to her children—moreover, the racist values and beliefs they inherited and carried into the school community. I asked myself that evening, what effect does white supremacist ideology have on the Black children in the school community and our attempts to use restorative justice here? How do we address the harm Black and Brown children and their families experience in this school community?

During the back-to-school night, the Black and Brown parents did not question restorative justice's effectiveness in supporting their students and providing opportunities to make amends. Rather, they were concerned that the proposed dialogue processes were another approach for their children to be criminalized by the school community. The structural racism in the school community led to distrust and even physical withdrawal of nonwhite students for their mental, physical, emotional, and spiritual well-being. I learned from Kelly that she and her siblings had been withdrawn once before for their protection and their mother's exhaustion with poor treatment from the school's community. Returning to the school community, her mother hoped this time would be different.

What happened?

Two weeks into the 2017–2018 school year, however, on the third floor of the school, I met Kelly while she was evading the support staff and administrators chasing her. Kelly mistakenly ran into my classroom, assuming it was unoccupied. As she burst in, she took one look at me and began to back away. "Are you all right baby?" I asked. She gave no response, but remained in my room. A few seconds later, there was a frantic knock at my classroom door. Kelly, wide-eyed, moved closer to me; she was terrified. I hustled to my classroom door, grabbed the knob, and looked through the window.

Ms. Rose, one of the school's therapists, was on the other side asking to come in. I looked at Kelly; her eye roll told me enough. I permitted Ms. Rose to enter. Just as Ms. Rose situated herself in the center of the room, Kelly positioned herself to make a run out of the classroom. I declared, "I don't know you; I don't know what happened, but you can talk to me. I can't give you a consequence. That ain't my job here, I promise." Ms. Rose quickly affirmed my offering to Kelly; she offered to walkie the rest of the search crew, halting the search only if Kelly agreed to talk with me.

We gave Kelly a minute to decide what she wanted to do. She decided to sit at a student desk in the circle I had set up earlier that day. Ms. Rose asked if she could stay, and Kelly shook her head no. Ms. Rose shared with me where Kelly was scheduled to be, and we all agreed I would walk her back to her classroom in thirty minutes.

In *Justice on Both Sides* (Winn 2018), Dr. Maisha Winn asserts that restorative justice in education provides "transformative learning communities offering unique opportunities to practice freedom, justice, and democratic engagement that transforms participants' ways of engaging and relating to other participant stakeholders." Could a school community bogged down by harmful behavior from unjust practices and beliefs grounded in race, gender, socioeconomic status, disability/abilities convert into a transformative learning community using restorative justice circles and asking restorative questions?

Ms. Rose left, and I went to the circle where Kelly was seated. As I sat down, she began to cry. I started with the question all restorative justice practitioners are trained to ask: "What happened?".

In our twenty-minute conversation about what happened, I introduced myself and my role at the school. After my introduction, I learned Kelly had experienced physical and emotional violence from four white male classmates since pre-K and would no longer tolerate their behavior. These four classmates would initiate the adverse action and would seek "safety" in adult presence when Kelly went to retaliate. I asked Kelly how she felt about the situation, and she said she often felt angry and annoyed with coming to school because she knew "the boys would start stuff, and she would get into trouble." She felt negative emotions about school because the adults she worked closely with in the building believed the boys and labeled her a bully. Kelly noted many of the adults who took every opportunity to discipline her. Especially Ms. Kurt, one of the school's resource teachers, and Mr. Goodwin, one of the three third-grade teachers. I asked what her friends thought about her actions. I learned that her classmates and friends point out to Kelly her constant anger. "But no one ever holds the boys responsible," she said.

Kelly was aware of hostility expressed by several teachers who had taken issue with her behavior. With 10 minutes left, I probed her to think about how the boys, her classmates, and the adults around her impacted her. Kelly shared that physically leaving the space when she felt angry helped because she needed space to calm down. She is constantly denied permission to leave the classroom and is instead forced to either remain in a space where she feels unsafe and left unable to learn or decide to run out of the room toward safety, even against her teachers' instructions. She evades the staff dedicated to finding her until she is tired of running or is unsuccessful in her attempt to seek sanctuary.

What if they lie like they always do?

I asked her what she wanted to do next. Kelly asked me what her options were based on my role in supporting the school's implementation of restorative justice. I asked Kelly if she would consider a restorative conversation between her and the boys. I explained that before the circle, I needed to meet with each student and ask if they were open to a restorative conversation. "I'm gonna ask them restorative questions and see if they will admit their behavior." Kelly did not hesitate to ask, "What if they lie like they always do?" I assured her that if none of the boys accepted responsibility, I would hold a healing circle for her. The healing circle would comprise her friends, adults in the building she felt safe and connected with, as well as her mama. During the healing circle, we support a codeveloped plan with her friends and supportive adults at home and school to prioritize her right to learn in a safe environment. I told her we could do both processes and did not have to decide on one.

Kelly agreed to participate in a school-based restorative justice process we call "restorative conversations." Restorative conversations are a tier 2 approach (focusing on community and relationship restoration) to identify conflicts' nuclei and promote accountability(Curtis et al. 2020; Parker-Shandal 2022). I explained the opportunity to talk directly with the boys about the harm, its impact on her safety, school life, community, and what she needed from the boys to move forward. Kelly was willing to meet with all of the boys except for one—the one who gave marching orders to the other boys. I asked Kelly what she needed to feel safe while we went through the preparation steps for a restorative conversation. Kelly asked if I could check on her when I am scheduled to visit her school. I told her I would coordinate with her classroom teachers to identify the best time to meet while we prepare for the restorative conversation.

I believed Kelly when she told me that some adults perceived her as a bully and an aggressor. I met Kelly's homeroom/English language arts teacher, Ms. Doug, while dropping Kelly back to class. After helping Kelly transition back into the classroom with the support of her table group mates and her aide, Ms. Doug and I debriefed in the hallway.

Ms. Doug, a white woman with twenty-plus years of classroom teacher experience, shared her perception and experience of Kelly. "Kelly is such a sweet girl and has been through a lot," she said. "Her entire family has. She is having difficulty adjusting to the school community, and I want to see her succeed. What can I do to help?" I was relieved to hear that Ms. Doug, even in the difficulty of maintaining a safe learning environment for more than twenty-five students, remained invested in Kelly's safety and well-being. I told her about the plan that Kelly and I developed together to address the harm using restorative conversations and a healing circle. Ms. Doug was excited to hear about Kelly's willingness to participate in a restorative justice circle to be heard and seen. She added, "I think it would be a good idea for the adults to have a circle too." It was clear from my interactions with Kelly, Ms. Doug, and Ms. Rose that they were open to finding out together if restorative justice and practices in schools provided an opportunity for change to happen within the individual, throughout the school community, and systemically.

Ms. Doug shared from her perspective the level of frustration and hostility of some of the adults in their learning community toward Kelly. Ms. Doug was worried that those adults would resist the proposed restorative processes, choosing the traditional punitive practices (out-of-school suspension, in-school suspension [complete assignments in behavior interventionist office for the day], school-based arrest, etc.). Ms. Doug recognized the opportunities restorative justice processes provided the adults in the building to come together, discuss and work through their feelings around the student's behavior, and develop a plan that suits the student's needs. A restorative circle for adults would allow them to strengthen their emotional-management tools to feel more equipped to disrupt the violence students experience and work together to engage in conflict dialogue without bias and adult-centered power. "Who else do you think will support using restorative approaches to disrupt the harm, discuss our options for mending the disconnect, and how to move forward?" I asked. Ms. Doug cited herself; Kelly's aide, Ms. Turner; Ms. Strings, a third-grade resource teacher; and Ms. Room, whom she recognized as the adults supporting Kelly during challenging moments.

Ms. Doug and I planned a time for my next site visit where I would meet with each of the boys individually to discuss what happened, the impact of the ongoing harm, and how to move forward. Ms. Doug shared that the ongoing conflict had become so severe between Kelly and the fourth boy that his parents and Kelly's mom had gone to the school district to file "bullying incident reports" against one another. She was uncertain if the student would admit to his role and, in agreement with Kelly and me, did not want to engage him in the process without his acknowledging the behavior or harm caused to Kelly.

I met briefly with Ms. Bolt, the resource teacher in charge of the third-grade-level meetings, to discuss the background of the conflict impacting the entire third-grade community. She also thought it was a good idea for the adults to participate in a circle to discuss their frustration with the ongoing conflict and plan a way to support the students. To prepare the adults, I shared articles on bullying, racial implicit bias, and the adultification of Black girls. These articles were assigned as prereading to disrupt harmful thoughts and beliefs about Kelly, which led to barriers in their relationships and encouraged them to discipline Kelly while excusing the boys' behavior.

They always do it when they know you all aren't looking.

On the morning of my second site visit for the week, before I had a chance to meet with the boys, an announcement was made that the school was on lockdown under "code yellow." Kelly and one of the boys argued; the conflict physically escalated, and she left the room. The staff believed she was attempting to leave the school grounds, and her mother had been contacted. Determined to set the school on a restorative pathway, the principal asked if I could facilitate a restorative circle for the staff, Kelly, and her mama to discuss what had just occurred.

On site with me that day, my supervisor agreed to be the lead facilitator in this impromptu restorative conference at the principal's request. In this conference, my supervisor and I took turns during the discussion to remind the adults of the adult–child power imbalance present in the circle—one youth to eight adults can lead to the adults centering their emotions and expectations over listening to the youth's voice and emotions and collaborating for a way forward.

Despite Kelly feeling overwhelmingly angry after a physical altercation with one of her classmates, Ms. Rose, one of the school's therapists, centered her own emotions on the ordeal and believed Kelly should be disciplined for making the staff worried that she intended to leave the school property. My supervisor asked Ms. Rose to repeat what she heard Kelly say was happening and how she felt. Ms. Rose began to double down on her answer.

Before she could finish her sentence again, Kelly interrupted and asked, "I never leave the building when I run out of class and run around the building, so why would I do that now?" The adults familiar with Kelly's situation noticed that she never grabbed her book bag, and they were worried she would leave the building and end up somewhere unsafe. Kelly's mother, Ms. Hall, said Kelly was already unsafe because of what she was experiencing daily with four boys in her grade, with insufficient action being taken to stop the boys' behavior.

The circle space was so quiet you could hear each participant breathing. Ms. Turner, who supervised third-grade recess, asked Kelly if she was sure the boys were picking on her because she never saw them interact when they were on the blacktop or playground. Kelly was sure of her interactions and added, "They always do it when they know you all aren't looking." Principal H expressed remorse that Kelly and her mother had been silenced for so long. In addition to expressing remorse, Principal H shared that he did not believe a suspension for Kelly was appropriate and believed strongly the suspension would not address the ongoing conflict. He acknowledged the racial and gender differences of the students and told the staff to consider how racial and gender bias can influence how they respond to student behavior. Kelly asked to go home for the day, and her mother agreed.

I met with each boy as planned with Ms. Doug for the afternoon. For 90 minutes, I listened as each boy admitted his role in harming Kelly. Two of the three boys said they thought Kelly could be fun to hang with but lost her cool over little things. The third student thought she was smart but could be mean. In response to their perception of Kelly, I asked them what Kelly did to deserve being taunted, poked, and hit. The boys shared in private that they felt pressure to be mean to Kelly from the same boy Kelly did not wish to meet with. I was curious why his approval required his friends to prove their friendship with acts of violence toward other students, specifically Kelly. Tyler, one of the boys, shared, "He just doesn't seem to like her that much." Each of the boys accepted responsibility for his behavior toward Kelly. Each agreed to meet with Kelly in the circle to discuss the impact of their actions and how to repair the harm and move forward. I asked them how they would engage with Kelly until our restorative conversation. In different ways, the boys offered a commitment to honor Kelly's physical safety and not fall under pressure from their "friend" to cause her harm.

> Children have never been very good at listening to their elders, but they have never failed to imitate them.—James Baldwin

The following week, I kicked off our planned restorative circle for the adults impacted by the ongoing conflict, as discussed with Ms. Doug. The adult support circle occurred in my classroom, so the teachers and support staff were in a "neutral" space. The circle comprised 10 staff members, not including myself and my cofacilitator. I cofacilitated the restorative justice circle process with my colleague Meredith, a white woman graduate student studying social work. Meredith and I opened the circle with a quote from James Baldwin, "Children have never been very good at listening to their elders, but they have never failed to imitate them." Citing how children learn from adults' socializing behavior is essential in supporting adult mindset shifts. This mindset shift helps adults reflect on their awareness of accountability and how they see themselves in transferring skills to the school community's youth outside of content instruction.

We introduced ourselves as the facilitators and the circle process. This circle, we explained, would focus on how the adults were processing the conflict and violence happening with the five students and to plan as a community a prevention and intervention method for Kelly's safety. We introduced the talking piece, which holds ultimate authority in the restorative circle process. The talking piece can be a picture, book, or stuffed object. The talking piece in a restorative circle process highlights who is speaking and demands those without the piece to listen without interruption and with understanding. It also serves as a connector between the participants of the circle. Used in both proactive and reactive restorative processes, the talking piece can aid in cultivating a circle site that can hold the demands of individuals and collectives experiencing harm and unjust conditions influenced by power imbalances.

We asked the adults to check in and share their feelings for the day when they experienced or engaged in bullying behavior that led to violence. After check-in, we asked each participant to share a value they believed was needed to engage in authentic dialogue and a guideline that promotes conversation in the circle and action beyond the circle site. Values are elemental to the circle process and promote mutual accountability and collective understanding about desired behavior. To make good use of the 70 minutes, we asked the staff members to answer questions that guided our dialogue. The first question addressed the challenges and concerns: What do you believe about the student's behavior? The second and third questions focused on restorative support: What can we do to support Kelly? How can we rebuild trust with Kelly? The final question of the circle was an opportunity for the circle of staff to reflect together: After listening to your colleagues' thoughts and feelings and learning new information about the conflict and harm among the student group, what do you wish to do differently?

By the end of the adult support circle, the staff had learned that everyone in the circle had an experience with being bullied or engaging in bullying behavior that led to violence—or a combination of the two. All the adults in the circle acknowledged that they eagerly filled the role when allowed to bully their youths. In the first round of the circle, just as Kelly and Ms. Bolt shared, some teachers, especially Mr. Goodwin, Kelly's math teacher, felt hostility and frustration with Kelly because of her "constant attitude" and "attention seeking." He made a connection between his thoughts and feelings about Kelly and the perception of the adults in the assigned readings who dehumanized Black girl children by robbing them of their innocence by expecting them to "know better" and "needing less comfort." (Morris 2016; Park 2017) Several adults agreed with Mr. Goodwin's reflection, connecting some of his own childhood bullying behavior and actions toward Kelly when she reacted to the boys' behavior. Through reading, reflection, and group dialogue, the adults in the circle recognized that in their efforts to stop the violence and conflict among the students, they perpetuated structural violence with controlling and punitive classroom-management practices that left Kelly without any support or safety. Several of the teachers asked in the circle how to support Kelly and rebuild trust with her; many of the adults noted that Kelly had opened up in the days since our initial run-in and asked me if she shared what she needed from them. I encouraged them to listen to Kelly when she needs a break and keep a close eye on the boys when they are in her vicinity. The group agreed that Kelly could come to my room for 10 minutes when she needs a break from her learning environment to focus on her emotional management. At the closing of the circle, Ms. Rose said she was committed to working to earn Kelly's trust after realizing that her desire to discipline Kelly while ignoring the boys' behavior contributed to the racial and gendered inequities in the school community.

In the circle, we scheduled the restorative conversation between Kelly and the boys for my following site visit. I offered a piece of wisdom to the circle of adults eager to support Kelly and the boys: "It took years for Kelly to get to this point with her behavior, and we will have to keep creating an environment together every day where she feels safe to learn. Our circle today does not mean Kelly will show up ready to stay in the classroom tomorrow, or the boys will keep from harming her." There was an echo of agreement from the circle participants. Kelly remained in the classroom without any issues with the boys that day. Before I left the school building, I checked in with all four students to see if they were still interested in a restorative conversation. All four were prepared to come together in a circle to discuss what had taken place.

Word spread throughout the school that circles had been successful for Kelly and the boys.

On my next site visit, I collected the four students and made our way to my classroom on the third floor. As I had discussed with them individually, we would start by sharing what happened, how it impacted especially Kelly, and a plan to move forward. I asked the group who would like to begin by sharing what happened. Tyler, one of the three boys, agreed to share what happened. After he recounted the incidents from the current school year, I asked each student if they wanted to add anything else to what Tyler shared. Kelly then shared that the incidents made her feel sad and isolated, and the teachers always taking the boys' side made her believe she was not a good student. Michael, the second boy, did not know that Kelly was so hurt by their actions. He took an opportunity to ask Kelly why she always pinched him in the hallway. Kelly said it was because he kept taking her pencils and her classwork, causing her to become distracted. Michael apologized, and Kelly said she would not pinch him if he respected her things. I asked the students if I could write Michael's apology and Kelly's agreement points, and they agreed. Kevin, the third boy, offered to write Kelly an apology and promised not to poke or kick her during recess anymore. Using the restorative conversation agreement sheet, I wrote down the students' agreements to respect each other's personal space, to be kind, and to intervene whenever the fourth boy attempted to harm Kelly or distract her. I committed to checking in with each student weekly for the first 30 days, then monthly, if they could follow what they agreed on in the circle. I asked the students if they felt their conflict with one another had been resolved. Kelly said yes, and the boys nodded in agreement. "Are you all sure? If so, we will each sign the agreement form, and I will let your teachers know the conflict has been resolved and the agreement points you'll need support with." They expressed certainty and permitted me to pass the agreement form around so each student could sign their name (Fig. 1).

With the cooperation of the students, staff, and school leadership, we pushed a school community to reimagine new ways to respond to conflict, violence, and disruption of learning time. School buildings

Fig. 1 Illustration by Octavia Ink, Pretty in Ink Press (1)

are not always a sanctuary for learning and girlhood for Black girls. When restorative justice processes honor the importance of history, race, language, justice, and the future, we provide a new way forward with one another. Circles initiated to support one student in Kelly's school community have expanded into circle opportunities for hundreds of students there. Third graders in Kelly's school began their day in a circle site with their teachers, checking in emotionally and, sometimes, learning in a circle. The adults continued to reflect on their beliefs and teaching practices.

In the weeks following the restorative circles, I ran into Ms. Turner. She told me that while out at recess, she watched the boy who did not want to participate and was not allowed in the restorative conversation approach Kelly. Before she could verbally intervene, she saw the student kick Kelly. She pulled him from the playground and escorted Kelly to the nurse to check for any injury. She clarified during our conversation that Michael, Tyler, and Kevin were not involved and that she would pull Kelly aside and apologize for not believing her sooner.

Fig. 2 Illustration by Octavia Ink, Pretty in Ink Press (2)

Word spread throughout the school that circles had been successful for Kelly and the boys. By remaining consistent in all of our efforts and responses to support the third-grade community members in conflict and experiencing structural violence, the school community began to take actual steps to repair the harm caused by the school's use of exclusionary practices labeled as discipline (Fig. 2).

Implementing restorative justice processes in the school community was not perfect. However, by the end of the 2017–2018 school year, 15 Black girls (which included Kelly) in third grade met weekly in a circle with me to discuss home, Black girlhood, and navigating their school community. These weekly circles increased their self-esteem, gave them a positive approach to conflict, and helped the girls feel a sense of belonging in a school located in a white neighborhood known for its historical redlining practices. Further, by the end of November 2017, the staff had gone through two trainings: an introduction to restorative practices and cultivating a restorative mindset. The latter training focused on teaching the school staff about restorative justice and restorative tools to disrupt implicit bias, white supremacy, and punitive practices detrimental to building justice-centered relationships with students and a restorative pedagogy that disrupts academic and social inequities. Restorative justice processes are not *the* answer to preventing and intervening in structural violence; they are *an* answer. Every week, 15 Black girls and I, sometimes 17 if we invited a guest, made the best of this answer in a circle in my room.

When violence and harm occur, disrupting the immediate threat of violence is necessary. It must be done in a way that brings individuals together to engage in dialogue about the violence and how to move forward to prevent further violence. In Kelly's case, by responding to the immediate threat of violence in a way that brought in the voices of the other students and sought reflection from the adults in the building, we were able to draw a through line between Kelly's experience and the broader culture in the building. The school staff, teachers, I, Kelly, her classmates, her mama, and supporting community members committed to the restorative justice processes. Even when it was difficult, we maintained our commitment to come together as a community in a circle and name the structural violence that Kelly experienced. Using a community-centered approach to restorative justice mitigated the long-term consequences of structural violence felt by Kelly. Six years later, Kelly is in her first year of high school and doing well. Kelly remains close to most girls who participated in the Black Girl Support Circle series. Kelly knows six years later from that experience that she can ask restorative questions when experiencing conflict, communicate the impact of people's behavior toward her, then state her need, and when all else fails... *run*!

References

Curtis, Denise, Fania E. Davis, Franklin Hysten, Komoia Johnson, Sangita Kumar, Tanya Mayo, Barbara McClung, and David Yusem. 2020. "Oakland Unified School District Restorative Justice Implementation Guide A Whole School Approach." Implementation Manual. Oakland, California:

Oakland Unified School District. https://www.seattleschools.org/wp-content/uploads/2023/02/OUSD-Implementation-Guide.pdf.

Haynes, Chayla, Saran Stewart, and Evette Allen. 2016. "Three Paths, One Struggle: Black Women and Girls Battling Invisibility in U.S. Classrooms." *The Journal of Negro Education* 85 (3): 380. https://doi.org/10.7709/jnegroeducation.85.3.0380.

Kaba, Mariam. 2021. "There Are No Perfect Victims." In *We Do This 'til We Free Us*, 206. Abolitionist Paper Series. Chicago, IL: Haymarket Books.

Morris, Monique. 2016. *Pushout : The Criminalization of Black Girls in Schools*. New York: The New Press.

Park, Jenny. 2017. "Report: Adults View Black Girls as 'less Innocent' than Their White Peers." *The Nation's Health* 47 (7): 6.

Parker-Shandal, Crystena A.H. 2022. *Restorative Justice in the Classroom: Liberating Students' Voices Through Relational Pedagogy*. Palgrave Macmillan.

Toliver, S.R. 2022. "Preface." In *Recovering Black Storytelling in Qualitative Research: Endarkened Storywork*, xvi–xix. Futures of Data Analysis in Qualitative Research 3. New York, New York: Routledge Taylor & Francis Group.

Wadhwa, Anita. 2016. *Restorative Justice in Urban Schools : Disrupting the School-to-Prison Pipeline*. Routledge Research in Educational Leadership Series. New York: Routledge.

Winn, Maisha T. 2018. *Justice on Both Sides: Transforming Education through Restorative Justice*. Race and Education Series. Cambridge, Massachusetts: Harvard Education Press.

Yahwon, Bilphena. 2019. "Affective Statements and the Adultification of Black Girls in Schools." *Akoben Blog* (blog). 09 2019. https://akobenllc.org/affective-statements-and-the-adultification-of-black-girls-in-schools.

Young, Alexis Morgan. 2021. "Witnessing Wonderland: Research with Black Girls Imagining Freer Futures." *English Teaching: Practice & Critique* 20 (4): 420–39. https://doi.org/10.1108/ETPC-04-2021-0029.

Barbara Sherrod recently served as Director of Programs for Restorative Response Baltimore. She received her EdD from Morgan State University, studying urban educational leadership. Her writing has been featured in *Colorizing Restorative Justice: Voicing Our Realities* (Saint Paul, MN: Living Justice Press, 2020) and in the online publication *Juvenile Justice Information Exchange*.

Open Access This chapter is licensed under the terms of the Creative Commons Attribution-NonCommercial-NoDerivatives 4.0 International License (http://creativecommons.org/licenses/by-nc-nd/4.0/), which permits any noncommercial use, sharing, distribution and reproduction in any medium or format, as long as you give appropriate credit to the original author(s) and the source, provide a link to the Creative Commons license and indicate if you modified the licensed material. You do not have permission under this license to share adapted material derived from this chapter or parts of it.

The images or other third party material in this chapter are included in the chapter's Creative Commons license, unless indicated otherwise in a credit line to the material. If material is not included in the chapter's Creative Commons license and your intended use is not permitted by statutory regulation or exceeds the permitted use, you will need to obtain permission directly from the copyright holder.

Identifying, Amplifying, and Learning from Local Peacebuilders: A Transformative Journey

Prince Charles Dickson

This contribution examines the complex tapestry of conflict in Plateau State, Nigeria, focusing on the lived experiences of local peacebuilders in Riyom and Bassa, two local government areas within the state. These regions have been deeply impacted by intercommunal clashes, religious tensions, and farmer-herder conflicts, leaving deep scars on the social fabric. This work delves into the complexities of these conflicts, exploring their historical roots, the devastating impact on communities, and the limitations of traditional peacebuilding efforts. It emphasizes the critical role of local voices and the power of Indigenous wisdom in fostering healing and reconciliation.

The narrative centers on individuals like Gyang Bhuba and Danlami Madaki, who, despite witnessing and participating in violence, embarked on extraordinary journeys of redemption and reconciliation. Their stories, amplified through community engagement and dialogue, offer

---

P. C. Dickson (✉)
The Tattaunawa Roundtable Initiative TRICentre, Jos, Nigeria
e-mail: pcdbooks@gmail.com

invaluable lessons for sustainable peacebuilding. Analyzing the experiences of Gyang, Danlami, and other local peacebuilders, this chapter aims to identify key lessons for sustainable peacebuilding. This is not an academic analysis but rather a reflection on the resilience of the human spirit and the enduring hope for peace in the face of adversity.

Plateau State, nestled in the heart of Nigeria's Middle Belt, has tragically become synonymous with cycles of violence. For decades, the state has grappled with a devastating cocktail of intercommunal clashes, religious tensions, and escalating farmer-herder conflicts. These deep-seated grievances, rooted in disputes over land, resources, and identity, have fueled a spiral of violence that has claimed thousands of lives and shattered the social fabric of countless communities.

The human cost of this conflict is immeasurable. Countless families have been displaced from their homes, their livelihoods destroyed, and their lives irrevocably altered by the trauma of violence. The specter of fear hangs heavy over the state, where communities live in constant apprehension, their daily lives disrupted by the threat of the next attack.

Riyom and Bassa exemplify the devastating impact of these conflicts. These once-peaceful regions have been torn apart by a complex web of historical, social, and political factors, leaving them scarred by cycles of violence and mistrust. The erosion of trust, the breakdown of social cohesion, and the displacement of entire communities have created a humanitarian crisis, leaving thousands vulnerable to poverty, hunger, and the long-term psychological trauma of violence.

The state has 17 local government areas, of which only 4 have been spared in the conflicts and clashes. According to the *Tattaaunawa Policy Brief*, a paper that provides concise peace and conflict policy analysis for decision-makers, this region has witnessed more than 43 major confrontations, and more than 10,000 lives have been lost, depending on who is providing the figures.

The tranquility, peace, and stability of Riyom and Bassa, 2 of the 17 local government areas that shared boundaries within the Plateau State Northern Senatorial District, have been profoundly disrupted by intercommunal and interfaith tensions as well as confrontations between farmers and herders. These conflicts have emerged from an intricate intermingling of historical, social, economic, and political elements, intensifying the strains among diverse ethnic, religious, and vocational segments within these regions.

This volatile environment has led to a pervasive climate of fear and insecurity, where communities live in constant apprehension of the next attack. The cycle of violence has eroded trust, shattered social cohesion, and hindered any meaningful development. Women and children are particularly vulnerable, facing increased risks of sexual violence, displacement, and psychological trauma. The ongoing conflict has created a humanitarian crisis, with thousands displaced and living in precarious conditions, further exacerbating poverty and inequality.

Intercommunal Conflicts

In Riyom and Bassa, intercommunal clashes have arisen among diverse ethnic groups, especially those originating from distinct tribes or cultural heritages. These confrontations are frequently due to the rivalry over land ownership, access to resources, and the influence wielded in political spheres. Imagine, for example, that Bassa alone has over 100 villages and 15 different distinct languages. This linguistic diversity underscores the deep-rooted cultural differences that can contribute to misunderstandings and conflict.

Long-standing disputes over land ownership, the competition for limited resources, and the strategic manipulation of ethnic and tribal affiliations by political entities have acted as catalysts for these conflicts. From 2018 to 2022, Riyom and Bassa each saw four major clashes, averaging one per year.

These clashes are often characterized by extreme brutality, with reports of massacres, mutilations, and the destruction of entire villages. The use of sophisticated weaponry, including AK-47s, highlights the intensity and deadliness of these conflicts. Women and children are frequently targeted, suffering sexual violence, abduction, and forced displacement. The cycle of violence and reprisals has created a deep-seated culture of fear and mistrust, making reconciliation and peacebuilding efforts even more challenging.

Interfaith Conflicts

In Plateau State, interfaith conflicts are prominent and play a big role in the Indigenous and settlers' narratives of who owns the land. Conflicts of an interfaith nature usually encompass strained relations among diverse religious factions, with a predominant focus on the Christian and Muslim communities. It is also not a coincidence that natives or indigenes are largely Christians, and settlers Muslims.

These religious discrepancies have been harnessed by various stakeholders to foment unrest, frequently culminating in the destruction of religious landmarks and residences and the forced migration of communities. Political and economic factors, along with deep-rooted historical grievances, can further aggravate these tensions because of the nature of retail politics that is played in these communities.

This religious dimension adds a dangerous layer of complexity to the conflict, as it can be easily manipulated to incite violence and deepen divisions. Extremist elements within both Christian and Muslim communities exploit religious rhetoric to justify attacks and demonize the "other." Places of worship, once sanctuaries of peace, have become targets of violence, with churches and mosques desecrated or destroyed.

This not only fuels religious intolerance but also undermines efforts to foster interfaith dialogue and reconciliation. The politicization of religion further exacerbates tensions, as politicians often exploit religious differences to mobilize support and consolidate power, leaving communities vulnerable to manipulation and further violence.

Farmer-Herder Clashes

Riyom and Bassa have become battlegrounds for a long-familiar conflict: the struggle between farmers and herders. Competition for land and resources has intensified in these regions, fueled by a complex web of factors. Farmers, primarily Indigenous communities, accuse nomadic herders of encroaching on their ancestral lands, disrupting their livelihoods, and destroying their crops. Herders, in turn, argue that their traditional grazing routes are being blocked by expanding farmland, leaving them with nowhere to go.

This struggle is further complicated by the harsh realities of climate change. Drought and desertification are shrinking grazing lands, forcing herders to migrate farther in search of pasture, often leading to clashes with farmers. The government's failure to effectively address these issues were exacerbated by insensitive remarks from a former governor in the state, who, in justifying his office's placement on a former grazing route, spoke dismissively of traditional land use patterns and lacked empathy for herder livelihoods. These actions fueled resentment, inflamed tensions, and deepened the divide between these communities.

Adding to this already volatile mix is the overlay of religious and ethnic identities, which can be easily exploited by those seeking to sow discord. The farmers are predominantly Christian, while the herders are largely Muslim. Even within the Indigenous communities, there are further divisions along denominational and political lines, creating a complex and fragmented landscape where conflict can easily ignite. This intricate web of grievances, competing claims, and identity politics makes finding a lasting solution all the more challenging.

Impact and Consequences

These conflicts have had severe repercussions on communities in Riyom and Bassa. Lives have been extinguished, properties lay in ruins, and families have been uprooted from their homes. These clashes have disrupted the fabric of social unity, strained the connections between various groups, and impeded economic undertakings. The displacement of communities has wrought the forfeiture of means of sustenance, an escalation in poverty rates, and the erosion of trust among the disparate factions. The psychological scars of violence run deep, leaving communities traumatized and vulnerable to further conflict. Children have been orphaned and women widowed, and entire generations bear the burden of loss and displacement.

Peacebuilding Efforts

Initiatives aimed at tackling these conflicts and advancing peace have encompassed a blend of high-handed government-led endeavors, grassroots interventions, and active involvement of civil society. To foster reconciliation and encourage connections between diverse factions, efforts have been directed toward mediating discussions, convening dialogues, and orchestrating conversations centered on nurturing peace.

Moreover, bolstering law enforcement, enhancing governance, and confronting fundamental socioeconomic disparities stand out as pivotal components in the pursuit of establishing enduring foundations for peacebuilding, but as long as suspicions remain on the role of state actors, then local peacebuilders, more often than not, are best suited to anchor the efforts.

However, these efforts have often had limited success. Top-down peacebuilding initiatives imposed by the government are often viewed with suspicion by local communities, who feel excluded from the process. Grassroots efforts, while well-intentioned, often lack the resources and coordination to achieve lasting impact. Furthermore, the deep-rooted mistrust among communities, coupled with the ongoing cycle of violence and reprisals, makes reconciliation a daunting task.

The lack of accountability for past atrocities and human rights abuses further fuels grievances and undermines trust in the peacebuilding process. Without addressing these fundamental issues, any attempts at peace will remain fragile and susceptible to collapse.

To conclude, the clashes among different communities, varying faiths, and herders/farmers in Riyom and Bassa illuminate the complex weave of elements that fuel conflicts within societies. Resolving these disputes necessitates an all-encompassing strategy that factors in historical resentments, the equitable distribution of resources, effective governance, and the intricacies of cultural interactions.

By nurturing open dialogues, advocating for inclusiveness, and tackling underlying triggers with the help of local peacebuilders, the path toward achieving enduring tranquility and steadiness in these communities becomes attainable.

The Revival Springs of Riyom and the Healing Winds of Bassa

In the elevated terrains of Plateau State, where the winds cradle ancient tales, the serene town of Riyom finds its abode. Once celebrated for its lush foliage and harmonious coexistence, this local government area has weathered years of intercommunity and interfaith strife. The hills that once reverberated with laughter and melodies now bear the scars of resentment and suffering. Yet from the heart of this town, a hamlet—or village—emerges a tale of hope and transformation, a narrative of a local peacebuilder who, along with others, has breathed restoration into the land.

Similarly, in the lush valleys of Bassa, a story of metamorphosis unfolds. This territory, once a symbol of unity, has been marred by the bitter discord between the Irrigwes, Rukubas, and Fulani communities. Once-bonded communities now find themselves torn apart by the relentless intercommunal and herder-farmer conflicts. Amid the embers of these clashes, a story of optimism rises, centered on the local peacebuilders who bear the torch of healing.

The cycle of turmoil in Riyom has taken a toll on its residents. Profound animosity has taken root, dividing neighbors and families along faith lines. Yet amid the chaos, a few discerning individuals glimpsed the potential for transformation. Gyang Bhuba's Berom by ethnicity; he refers to himself as a repentant combatant who bore witness to the havoc wrought by violence. Gyang understood that true healing was necessary, and if anyone could do so, it had to be those responsible and the victims amplifying their voices of change.

Gyang said it was a painful realization for him. He had witnessed his mother killed alongside two of his siblings and vowed to take revenge. Ten years have passed since that night. "I have not found the revenge, and I could not continue like this," he admitted.

In the case of Bassa, the echoes of violence had etched deep wounds in the hearts of the Irrigwe, Rukuba, and Fulani communities. Bitterness and distrust replaced the unity that once bound them. Nevertheless, amid the ruins of discord, a few souls recognized the power of change. Among them were Danlami Madaki and his sister, their story a strong one of resilience. Danlami and his sister are Fulani. She was married to an Irrigwe man who was killed by the Rukuba Militia group. They had witnessed the devastation caused by conflicts. The two siblings grasped, much like Gyang, that genuine reconciliation required using their own stories as catalysts for change.

Recognizing the Local Advocates of Peace: Gyang's Odyssey and Danlami's Path

Gyang's journey wasn't just about turning his own life around; it was about transforming an entire community. He had been deeply involved in the violence that plagued his region, and the weight of his actions pressed heavily on his conscience. But instead of succumbing to guilt and despair, he used his remorse as fuel for change. Gyang recognized the futility of endless conflict, the cycle of revenge that only perpetuated suffering. He understood that true healing required acknowledging the pain of those he had harmed and actively working to repair the damage.

Danlami, too, had witnessed the devastating consequences of conflict. He and his sister had both lost loved ones in the violence, and they were determined to break the cycle of hatred and revenge. They understood that true reconciliation meant not only acknowledging their pain but also empathizing with the suffering of others, even those they perceived as enemies. They committed themselves to fostering understanding and healing, recognizing that lasting peace required a shift in narratives, a move away from blame and toward shared responsibility.

These two men, Gyang and Danlami, represent the power of individual transformation to spark wider change. They show us that even those who have been deeply involved in violence can become powerful advocates for peace. Their journeys remind us that healing and reconciliation are possible, even in the most deeply divided communities. But they require courage, empathy, and a willingness to confront the past to build a better future.

Their stories also highlight the importance of acknowledging the interconnectedness of suffering. Gyang and Danlami understood that true healing could only occur when both victims and perpetrators were willing to confront their shared history and work together toward a common goal. This recognition of shared humanity, even in the face of immense pain and loss, is essential for breaking cycles of violence and building a foundation for lasting peace.

Amplifying the Local Narratives: The Circles of Healing and Rebirth

In the heart of Riyom, a remarkable transformation was taking root. Gyang, alongside other peacebuilders, created safe spaces where the raw wounds of conflict could be exposed and healed. They called these gatherings "healing circles," and they were unlike anything the community had ever seen. Victims and perpetrators, once separated by fear and anger, came together in an atmosphere of vulnerability and shared humanity.

Within these circles, stories unfolded that pierced the heart of the conflict. A widow shared the devastating loss of her husband, her voice trembling with grief. Gyang, with tears in his eyes, confessed his role in the violence, acknowledging the pain he had inflicted on innocent people. He spoke of how he had once believed his actions were justified but now recognized the deep harm he had caused.

These honest and heartfelt confessions, amplified by the collective witness of the community, began to mend the shattered bonds of trust. Gyang's message was clear: violence and hatred have no place in a community built on shared humanity.

Meanwhile, in Bassa, Danlami was also working to create a space for healing and reconciliation. He brought together members of the Irrigwe, Rukuba, and Fulani communities, who had long been locked in a cycle of violence and revenge. In these gatherings, pain was acknowledged, and forgiveness was sought. A soldier, his voice thick with emotion, shared the story of how he lost his arm in the conflict. Danlami, with tears streaming down his face, expressed his remorse, not for the soldier's injury directly, but for his failure to prevent the escalation of violence that led to the attack. These shared stories of loss and regret resonated deeply, rekindling the embers of empathy and understanding.

The healing circles in Riyom and Bassa were more than just gatherings; they were transformative experiences that challenged deeply ingrained narratives of hatred and division. By creating a space for vulnerability and shared humanity, these initiatives allowed communities to confront their painful past and begin the difficult but essential work of rebuilding trust and reconciliation.

Learning from Indigenous Wisdom: Seeds of Metamorphosis and Evolution

These gatherings were more than just talk. They were a place where wisdom was shared, passed down from those who had lived through the very heart of the conflict. Gyang's story, though personal, resonated with everyone. It showed that even those who had been part of the violence could change and could become forces for peace. Danlami's journey, too, offered a glimmer of hope, proving that forgiveness and understanding were possible, even after immense suffering.

Through these shared stories, the communities began to see the conflict from different perspectives. They realized that the grievances that fueled the violence were often shared and that everyone had experienced loss and pain. This understanding became a powerful catalyst for change. It allowed them to begin to let go of the anger and resentment that had held them captive for so long.

These gatherings were like a school for peace, where everyone was both a student and a teacher. They learned to unlearn the old ways of thinking, the us-versus-them mentality that had caused so much bloodshed. They began to see the humanity in each other, to recognize that they were all part of the same community, sharing the same hopes and dreams for a better future.

This process of unlearning and relearning was not easy. It required courage, humility, and a willingness to challenge deeply held beliefs. But the rewards were immense. As communities began to see the conflict through a wider lens, they opened themselves up to the possibility of forgiveness, reconciliation, and a future free from the cycle of violence.

Constructing Bridges for a Serene Tomorrow: Unity in Diversity

Something incredible began to happen as the healing circles grew and spread throughout Riyom and Bassa. It was like watching a flower bloom in the desert. Where once there was only suspicion and hostility, now understanding and empathy were taking root. People who had seen each other as enemies were starting to see each other as human beings with shared experiences and common dreams.

The old barriers that had divided people—ethnicity, religion, and land—were slowly dissolving. Diversity, once a source of fear and conflict, was now being recognized as a strength. Gyang, in Riyom, worked tirelessly to nurture this transformation, ensuring that it wasn't just a fleeting moment of peace but a lasting foundation for harmony. He understood that true peace required ongoing effort and a constant commitment to dialogue and understanding.

In Bassa, Danlami's leadership inspired a similar shift. Suspicion gave way to empathy, and distrust melted into understanding. The communities, once bitterly divided, were beginning to celebrate their differences, recognizing that their diversity was a source of richness, not conflict. The local peacebuilders, inspired by Danlami's example, worked tirelessly to ensure that this newfound unity would endure.

This transformation was not just about changing hearts and minds; it was about changing the very fabric of society. It was about creating a new narrative, one that embraced diversity, celebrated shared humanity, and rejected the old patterns of violence and division. It was a testament to the power of local leadership, community engagement, and the unwavering belief in the possibility of a better future.

The Steadfastness of Riyom and Bassa

The stories of Riyom and Bassa are powerful reminders of the resilience of the human spirit. These communities, once torn apart by conflict, have shown the world that healing and reconciliation are possible, even in the face of deep-seated divisions and historical wounds. Through the tireless efforts of local peacebuilders like Gyang and Danlami, the seeds of forgiveness and understanding have been sown, and a new era of hope is dawning.

These peacebuilders, who themselves have often experienced the pain of conflict firsthand, have become beacons of hope, guiding their communities toward a future free from violence. Their journeys demonstrate that transformation is possible and that even those who have been involved in perpetuating violence can become powerful advocates for peace. They have shown that the wounds of the past can be healed through compassion, empathy, and a shared commitment to building a better future.

As Riyom and Bassa continue their journey toward lasting peace, they offer inspiration to other communities struggling with conflict. They demonstrate that even in the darkest of times, the human spirit can prevail and that through collective action and a shared vision for a better future, even the deepest wounds can heal. The people of Riyom and Bassa understand that the path to peace is not always easy, and there will be setbacks along the way. But they are resolute in their commitment to building a future where diversity is celebrated and peace prevails.

Their stories also serve as a powerful reminder that peacebuilding is not just the absence of conflict; it is an active and ongoing process that requires constant nurturing and commitment. It is about transforming relationships, rebuilding trust, and creating a society where everyone feels safe, respected, and valued. The journeys of Riyom and Bassa are a testament to the power of human agency to overcome adversity and build a more peaceful and just world.

Identifying Local Peacebuilders and Walking in Their Shoes

The beauty of local peacebuilders is that they often emerge from the very communities that have been scarred by conflict. They carry with them an understanding that goes beyond the surface, as they've personally experienced the pain, loss, and consequences. Local peacebuilders are individuals who take it upon themselves to bridge the gaps, heal wounds, and rebuild relationships within their communities.

These individuals might not possess political influence or global recognition, but they know the story. It is their story, their conflict, their dedication, empathy, and understanding that make them indispensable forces in promoting reconciliation and healing. And when peace returns, they are the first beneficiaries. Their work is especially vital in areas where long-standing conflicts have eroded trust and unity, leaving communities divided and vulnerable. They are the history, and they are either rewriting or painstakingly scripting a new story of victory over their long-held differences.

In my work on peacebuilding and conflict transformation, I've consistently witnessed the remarkable capacity for change within individuals, even those who have been deeply involved in perpetuating violence. Whether in Riyom or Bassa, the stories of individuals transitioning from victimizers to peace advocates demonstrate the potential for profound personal transformation. These individuals, once caught in the cycle of violence, have not only embarked on journeys of personal redemption but have also become catalysts for healing and reconciliation within their communities.

Furthermore, the experiences of victims themselves highlight the resilience of the human spirit. Despite the trauma they have endured, many individuals demonstrate a remarkable capacity to heal and actively participate in the process of rebuilding their communities. Their willingness to engage in dialogue, forgiveness, and reconciliation is essential for creating a holistic psychosocial process of transformation and renewal. These individual journeys of change, both by those who have caused harm and those who have been harmed, are crucial for breaking cycles of violence and fostering sustainable peace.

Local Voices Are Telling Stories for Transformation

As a researcher and practitioner in the field of peace and conflict studies, I've witnessed firsthand the transformative power of these inclusive dialogues. When we create spaces for victims and perpetrators to share their stories, we open up possibilities for empathy, understanding, and ultimately, forgiveness. These encounters challenge the dehumanizing narratives that often fuel conflict, allowing individuals to reclaim their agency and participate in the process of healing and reconciliation. By amplifying these voices, we not only contribute to building sustainable peace but also affirm the inherent dignity and resilience of the human spirit.

True reconciliation can only happen when we listen to the voices that are often silenced—the voices of those who have been hurt and those who have caused harm. It's about creating spaces where both victims and perpetrators can step forward, share their stories, and acknowledge their roles in the conflict. This is not easy. It requires courage, vulnerability, and a willingness to confront painful truths. But it is essential for breaking the cycle of violence and building a foundation for lasting peace.

Healing circles and community dialogues become powerful tools in this process. They provide a safe and supportive environment where people can speak their truth without fear of judgment or reprisal. In these spaces, we begin to see the human faces behind the conflict, the individuals who have been wounded, both physically and emotionally. We hear stories of loss, grief, and regret but also stories of resilience, hope, and forgiveness. These shared narratives help to break down the barriers that divide us, fostering empathy and understanding.

The stories of local peacebuilders like Gyang and Danlami are particularly powerful in this regard. They demonstrate that transformation is possible and that even those who have been deeply involved in violence can become agents of peace. By amplifying these stories through community gatherings, media platforms, and other channels, we can inspire others to follow their lead. These narratives humanize the struggles, making it easier for people to connect with the peacebuilding process and see themselves as part of the solution.

Moreover, amplifying these voices challenges the dominant narratives that often perpetuate conflict. It disrupts the cycle of blame and victimhood, creating space for new narratives of shared responsibility and collective healing. By giving voice to the marginalized and silenced, we can create a more inclusive and equitable peacebuilding process, one that recognizes the dignity and humanity of all involved.

Learning Lessons for Sustainable Peace

In my years of working as a peacebuilder in conflict zones, I've come to appreciate the invaluable lessons that local peacebuilders offer. Their insights, often rooted in deep cultural understanding and lived experiences, provide a critical lens for crafting sustainable peacebuilding strategies. These lessons challenge us to move beyond theoretical frameworks and engage with the realities on the ground, bridging the gap between "town and gown," as we say.

One of the most powerful lessons I've learned is the importance of inclusive dialogue. By bringing together victims and victimizers, communities can gain a deeper understanding of the grievances that fuel conflict. This awareness paves the way for cooperative initiatives that address the root causes of violence and promote development, economic growth, and social cohesion. The narratives shared in healing circles, often infused with Indigenous wisdom, offer profound insights into the historical, social, and economic factors that contribute to conflict.

These stories—whether from individuals like Gyang who have transformed from perpetrators to peacebuilders or from those like Danlami who have navigated the complexities of intercommunal conflict—provide valuable perspectives on conflict dynamics and potential solutions. They highlight the transformative power of empathy and forgiveness, demonstrating that even those deeply involved in violence can become champions of peace.

The lessons gleaned from these narratives, often told through multiple lenses and diverse voices, become seeds of rebirth, guiding communities toward a future free from animosity. By integrating these local perspectives into our peacebuilding efforts, we can develop more-effective strategies that address the root causes of conflict and prevent its resurgence. Ultimately, it is through learning from those most affected by conflict that we can build a more sustainable and just peace.

Building Bridges for a Peaceful Future Through Collaboration

The journey of local peacebuilders is not without challenges. They face skepticism, threats, and the daunting task of convincing others to join them on the path of reconciliation. We do not forget that they are embedded in a vengeful circle of revenge, payback, retribution, retaliation, and punishment. However, the seeds they plant and the bridges they build ultimately lead to a more peaceful future. Collaborative efforts involving state actors like local authorities, nonstate actors in civil society organizations, and national institutions can amplify the impact of their initiatives.

In conclusion, supporting local peacebuilders is not merely a strategy, but a vital journey. It demands recognizing and addressing the intricate interplay of power, inequality, and, most profoundly, the deeply felt wounds of identity. Through this holistic approach, local initiatives offer the most promising path toward a truly transformative peace, one built on understanding and lasting partnership.

Understanding these intersections is crucial for collaboration that formulates effective strategies for conflict resolution, peacebuilding, and fostering a more just and peaceful society.

Amplifying Peacebuilders by Sharing Stories of Change

Amplification involves the skill of expanding the reach of local peacebuilders' work beyond their immediate sphere of influence. It encompasses illuminating their endeavors, recognizing their significant contributions, and mobilizing support for their mission.

Amplifying the voices and impact of local peacebuilders involves several strategic approaches.

Media and Communication: Leveraging media platforms like radio, television, and, in some cases, social media to disseminate success stories, testimonials, and narratives about the challenges confronted by local peacebuilders can significantly enhance the visibility of their work. This approach not only raises awareness but also broadens the audience reached by their message, contributing to a more extensive support base. Many of these peacebuilders want their stories told.

Advocacy Campaigns: Advocacy campaigns can be potent tools for mobilizing public opinion. Such campaigns can apply pressure on governments, institutions, and international organizations to acknowledge and provide support for local peacebuilders. By galvanizing public sentiment, these efforts can facilitate increased recognition and backing for the vital work of peacebuilders within communities.

Networking: Establishing connections between local peacebuilders and regional and global networks can offer a range of benefits. It provides access to valuable resources, specialized expertise, and collaborative opportunities that can significantly amplify the impact of their endeavors. Through networking, local peacebuilders can tap into a wealth of knowledge and support, further strengthening their capacity to effect positive change.

We can play a pivotal role in elevating the work of local peacebuilders, ensuring that their efforts resonate far beyond their immediate surroundings and garnering the recognition and backing them rightfully deserve.

Gaining Insights from Local Peacebuilders: A Reciprocal Exchange of Wisdom

An essential part of this journey entails acquiring knowledge from the wisdom and firsthand experiences of local peacebuilders. Their perspectives provide invaluable lessons that extend beyond academic textbooks and theoretical frameworks, informing the development of impactful peacebuilding strategies.

Cultural Insight and Nuanced Understanding: Local peacebuilders offer invaluable insights into the intricate fabric of cultural, social, and historical contexts that underpin conflicts. Their deep-rooted contextual understanding enables outsiders to comprehend the nuances of the situation, fostering a more comprehensive approach to conflict resolution. Additionally, their heightened cultural sensitivity minimizes the inadvertent exacerbation of tensions that might otherwise occur. They help in terms of a practical understanding and application of the do-no-harm concept. In other instances, local peacebuilders' advantage is as simple as overcoming language barriers.

Trust Cultivation: Engaging with local peacebuilders serves as a foundational step in nurturing trust between external organizations and the community. This trust-building process is paramount, as it lays the groundwork for more-productive and meaningful collaborations. As trust is cultivated, it paves the way for enhanced communication and cooperation, which are pivotal components of effective peacebuilding efforts. This helps in the ongoing conversation around the decolonization of aid and local ownership of interventions.

Adaptability and Integration: The strategies employed by local peacebuilders exhibit a remarkable degree of adaptability. These locally derived approaches can seamlessly integrate into broader peacebuilding frameworks, enriching and enhancing their overall effectiveness. The ability to draw from the wisdom of local peacebuilders empowers organizations to tailor their strategies to specific contexts, thereby increasing their impact.

Community Ownership and Sustainable Peace: For peace to truly take hold and endure, it must be organically cultivated from within the community itself. This truth resonated deeply with figures like Gyang and Danlami, and countless other local peacebuilders who found profound comfort and effectiveness in participatory processes. Local NGOs echoed this sentiment, emphasizing the vital importance of contextual relevance and community-driven design for programs to not only succeed, but to be genuinely owned and sustained by the very people they are intended to serve.

Conflict Prevention at the Grassroots: Addressing conflicts at the local level holds significant promise for preventing their escalation into larger-scale violence. Local peacebuilders possess an acute awareness of the early warning signs and triggers that can lead to conflict. By intervening and mediating at this level, they play a crucial role in averting the catastrophic consequences of full-scale conflict, thereby safeguarding the well-being of communities and regions.

Challenges, Recommendations, and Suggestions: A Beacon of Hope

To achieve success, it is imperative to begin by identifying individuals who are actively fostering peace within their communities. These local peacebuilders possess a profound understanding of the intricacies of their surroundings. They are well versed in recognizing the underlying tensions, historical context, and cultural nuances that play a role in conflicts. Recognizing these individuals necessitates a compassionate ear, sharp observation, and a receptive mindset.

However, challenges do exist in supporting local peacebuilders, and these challenges can be categorized into several key areas.

Resource Constraints: One significant challenge local peacebuilders face is the limitation of resources. They often lack the necessary funding and support to expand and sustain their peacebuilding initiatives effectively. Gyang says that much of what they achieved has been done as a result of community effort and that given the right resources they could do more.

Security Risks: Engaging in peacebuilding activities can entail considerable security risks, particularly in conflict-affected regions and sometimes even the communities themselves during the dialogues. Danlami spoke of occasions when, as a result of his intimate knowledge of the conflict dynamics, he faced personal security threats as a result of his involvement.

Limited Recognition: Another challenge lies in the recognition of the invaluable work undertaken by local peacebuilders. Often, their efforts remain unnoticed on the global stage, which can undermine their potential for broader impact and support. Efforts must be made to amplify the work they do.

Addressing these challenges is crucial to enabling the impactful work of local peacebuilders and advancing peace and stability within communities. Several essential considerations that come into play when seeking to identify these key contributors to peace and conflict resolution within a community include:

Community Engagement: A fundamental step involves engaging deeply with the community itself. This entails forging meaningful connections with local leaders, respected elders, and grassroots organizations. Often, these community figures possess valuable insights into individuals who are actively committed to reducing conflicts and fostering a sense of harmony.

Listening: A vital aspect of this process is active and attentive listening. By lending an ear to the stories and experiences shared by members of the community, one can unveil the unsung heroes who mediate disputes, organize dialogues, and unite factions that may have been divided.

Mapping Networks: Another crucial strategy involves mapping the intricate networks that exist within the community. This approach allows for the recognition of the interconnected web comprising individuals and organizations dedicated to peacebuilding efforts. By understanding these networks, it becomes possible to identify those who play pivotal roles in promoting peace and resolving conflicts at the local level.

Together, these methods empower individuals and organizations to effectively pinpoint and support those who are instrumental in driving positive change and harmony within their communities.

Conclusion

In Danlami's words, "The solutions to our conflicts are not easy in any way. *White people* say that it is not easy, and they are bringing money and will teach us how to stop fighting ourselves, but I say we are the solution, they should come and learn how to help us."

The journey of recognizing, amplifying, and learning from local peacebuilders resonates universally, transcending diverse cultures and regions affected by conflict. Their stories act as beacons illuminating the path toward healing, reconciliation, and lasting peace. While their vital contributions may not always garner international attention, it is these individuals who nurture the very essence of peace.

Communities around the world can find inspiration in the narratives of local peacebuilders like Danlami. By creating platforms where both victims and those who bear responsibility for the conflict and its violence can share their experiences, societies can foster empathy, reduce the likelihood of recurrent conflicts, and pave the way for unity and harmony. The journey toward transformation begins with acknowledging the pivotal role played by these often-unsung heroes and amplifying their voices as they guide communities toward a brighter and more peaceful future.

The stories of Gyang and Danlami serve as compelling symbols of hope, illustrating that even in the face of deeply entrenched conflicts, the potential for transformation remains within reach. Local peacebuilders, particularly those who have personally grappled with the dual roles of victim and perpetrator, embody the qualities of resilience and reconciliation. Their narratives convey a profound message that genuine healing begins when we actively listen, seek understanding, and collaborate to create a world where animosity yields to empathy and scars are replaced by unity.

Understandings

Plateau State, located in the central region of Nigeria, is a land of striking contrasts, where breathtaking beauty and vibrant cultural heritage coexist with the harsh realities of conflict and insecurity. Known as the Home of Peace and Tourism, Plateau State boasts a diverse landscape of highlands, plateaus, hills, and valleys, offering stunning vistas and a pleasant climate that once attracted vacationers from across the country. However, the state's tourism potential has been tragically undermined by persistent conflict, leaving its economy and communities struggling to thrive.

Plateau State is home to a diverse population of approximately 4.5 million people, representing over 48 ethnic groups, including the Berom, Hausa, and Fulani. This rich diversity of cultures and languages contributes to the state's unique identity but has also become a source of division and conflict. Competition for land, resources, and political power, often exacerbated by religious and ethnic differences, has fueled intercommunal tensions and violent clashes.

Agriculture remains a significant contributor to Plateau State's economy, with fertile lands supporting the cultivation of crops like potatoes, maize, and yams. Historically, mining, particularly tin mining, played a major role in the state's economic development, earning it the nickname The Tin City. However, the decline of the mining industry and the persistent conflict have hampered economic growth, leaving many communities facing poverty and limited opportunities.

Despite the challenges, Plateau State boasts a strong commitment to education, with several institutions of higher learning, including the University of Jos and Plateau State University. The state is also rich in cultural traditions, with various festivals and celebrations showcasing its diverse heritage. The Nzem Berom festival, for example, celebrates the Berom culture, while the annual Jos Carnival brings together communities from across the state to showcase their music, dance, and art.

The Tattaaunawa Policy Brief

The *Tattaaunawa Policy Brief* is a comprehensive policy document produced by the Tattaaunawa Roundtable Initiative, TRICentre, it addresses the complex issue of conflicts in Nigeria, with a particular focus on Northern Nigeria. "Tattaaunawa" is a word from the Hausa language, widely spoken in the region, which translates to "dialogue" or "peaceful coexistence." The brief provides a structured and informed approach to understanding, managing, and resolving conflicts in this region, which has experienced various forms of violence and instability over the years.

Key Components of the *Tattaaunawa Policy Brief*: conflict analysis, impact assessment, and policy recommendations. They cover areas such as security and law enforcement, governance and institutional Reforms, community engagement, youth and women empowerment, and interfaith and interethnic dialogue.

Riyom Local Government Area

Riyom Local Government Area (LGA), located in the central highlands of Plateau State, Nigeria, is a region of striking contrasts. Renowned for its picturesque landscapes and rich cultural heritage, Riyom is also a microcosm of the complex challenges facing communities grappling with persistent conflict. With a population exceeding 300,000 people spread across over 50 villages, Riyom LGA is home to a diverse range of ethnic groups, including the Berom, Fulani, and Hausa. This diversity, while a source of cultural richness, has also become a fault line for conflict, as different groups compete for land, resources, and political power.

Agriculture forms the backbone of Riyom's economy, with fertile lands supporting the cultivation of crops like potatoes, maize, and yams. Livestock farming, particularly cattle rearing, is also prevalent, contributing to the livelihoods of many families. However, this reliance on land and natural resources has also become a source of tension, as competition for grazing land and water resources has fueled clashes between farmers and herders.

Riyom LGA has been particularly affected by security challenges, including intercommunal conflicts and farmer-herder clashes. These conflicts have not only resulted in the tragic loss of life and displacement but have also disrupted economic activities, hindered development, and eroded trust among communities. Despite these challenges, efforts are underway to address the root causes of conflict and promote peace and coexistence. Community dialogues, peacebuilding initiatives, and government interventions are all playing a role in fostering reconciliation and building a more harmonious future for Riyom LGA.

Bassa Local Government Area

Bassa Local Government Area (LGA), situated in the heart of Plateau State, Nigeria, embodies the region's rich culture, traditions, and challenging realities. Characterized by a diverse landscape of flatlands and hills, Bassa is a microcosm of the ethnic and religious complexities that shape Plateau State. With a population exceeding 298,000 people, Bassa LGA is home to over 100 villages, each with its own unique cultural practices and traditions. This vibrant mix of ethnicities, including the Irrigwe, Rukuba, Berom, and Fulani, contributes to the area's rich heritage but also presents challenges for social cohesion and peace.

Agriculture plays a vital role in Bassa's economy, with fertile lands supporting the cultivation of staple crops such as yams, maize, and potatoes. Livestock farming is also prevalent, contributing to the livelihoods of many families. However, competition for land and resources, coupled with environmental challenges, has fueled tensions between farmers and herders, leading to intercommunal conflicts and farmer-herder clashes.

Despite these challenges, Bassa LGA remains a place of resilience and cultural vibrancy. Its diverse communities celebrate their heritage through various festivals and traditions, showcasing traditional dances, music, and art forms. Efforts are underway to address the security challenges and promote peaceful coexistence, recognizing the importance of unity and understanding in building a prosperous future for Bassa LGA.

Irrigwe, Rukuba, Berom, and Fulani

Plateau State, Nigeria, is a microcosm of ethnic diversity, with over 48 distinct groups, each possessing its own unique language and cultural practices. Among these are the Irrigwe, Rukuba, Berom, and Fulani people, who have long inhabited the region and contributed to its rich culture.

The Irrigwe, Rukuba, and Berom, predominantly agrarian communities have traditionally held strong ties to the land and maintained their unique cultural practices, including traditional leadership structures and belief systems. While they have historically adhered to Indigenous religions, the influence of Christianity and Islam has grown in recent years, adding another layer of complexity to their identities.

The Fulani, renowned for their pastoralist lifestyle, are traditionally nomadic cattle herders with a distinct language, Fulfulde. While maintaining their cultural heritage, many Fulani have also engaged in farming and other economic activities, contributing to the region's agricultural landscape. The Fulani people primarily adhere to Islam, which has played a significant role in shaping their identity and interactions with other communities in Plateau State.

The coexistence of these diverse ethnic groups has been marked by both cooperation and conflict, reflecting the complexities of navigating cultural differences, resource competition, and historical grievances in a dynamic and evolving society.

References

Crocker, Chester A., Fen Osler Hampson, and Pamela R. Aall, eds. *Turbulent Peace: The Challenges of Managing International Conflict*. Washington, D.C.: United States Institute of Peace Press, 2001. https://www.usip.org/publicati ons/2001/turbulent-peace-challenges-managing-international-conflict.

Donais, Timothy, ed. *Local Ownership in International Peacebuilding*. London: Routledge, 2008. https://www.routledge.com/Local-Ownership-in-Internati onal-Peacebuilding/Donais/p/book/9780415456775.

Human Rights Watch. "Leave Everything to God: Accountability for Inter-Communal Violence in Plateau and Kaduna States, Nigeria." New York: Human Rights Watch, December 2013. https://www.hrw.org/reports/nigeri a1213_reportcover_webUpload.pdf.

International Crisis Group. "Nigeria." Brussels: International Crisis Group, 2025. https://www.crisisgroup.org/africa/west-africa/nigeria.

Jenkins, Robert, ed. *Peacebuilding: From Concept to Commission*. London: Routledge, 2018.

Kriesberg, Louis. "From the Ground Up: Assessing the Record of Promoting Local and National Conflict Resolution Initiatives." *Publication details are not available.*

Mac Ginty, Roger. *Local to Global Peacebuilding: Local Peacemaking in the International Arena*. New York: Palgrave Macmillan, 2011.

Mac Ginty, Roger, and Oliver Richmond. "Local Peacebuilding and National Peace: Interaction Between Grassroots and Elite Processes." *International Peacekeeping* 14, no. 5 (2007): 558–572. https://doi.org/10.1080/13533310701658371.

Peace Direct. *Amplifying the Voice of Local Peacebuilders: Opportunities and Challenges*. London: Peace Direct, 2019. https://www.peacedirect.org/publications/amplifying-the-voice-of-local-peacebuilders-opportunities-and-challenges.

Ramsbotham, Alexander, and Kwame Akonor. "Local Voices in Measurement and Evaluation: The Missing Link in UN Peace Operations." *International Peacekeeping* 17, no. 1 (February 2010): 15–34. https://doi.org/10.1080/13533310903484697.

Reychler, Luc, and Thania Paffenholz. *Peacebuilding: A Field Guide*. Boulder, CO: Lynne Rienner Publishers, 2001.

Vanguard News. "Insecurity: 60,000 Lives Lost in Farmers-Herders Clashes." January 22, 2024. https://www.vanguardngr.com/2024/01/insecurity-60000-lives-lost-in-farmers-herders-clashes-nextier.

Woodhouse, Tom, and Robert Bruce, eds. *Contemporary Peacebuilding: Conflict Resolution Systems in Transition*. London: Frank Cass Publishers, 2003.

Prince Charles Dickson is a peace-policy analyst based in Nigeria. He holds a PhD in psychology from Georgetown University and has decades of expertise in media, public policy, and development practice. In addition to his work in advocacy, peacebuilding, and psychology, he has been a reporter, editor, and syndicated columnist in Nigeria.

Open Access This chapter is licensed under the terms of the Creative Commons Attribution-NonCommercial-NoDerivatives 4.0 International License (http://creativecommons.org/licenses/by-nc-nd/4.0/), which permits any noncommercial use, sharing, distribution and reproduction in any medium or format, as long as you give appropriate credit to the original author(s) and the source, provide a link to the Creative Commons license and indicate if you modified the licensed material. You do not have permission under this license to share adapted material derived from this chapter or parts of it.

The images or other third party material in this chapter are included in the chapter's Creative Commons license, unless indicated otherwise in a credit line to the material. If material is not included in the chapter's Creative Commons license and your intended use is not permitted by statutory regulation or exceeds the permitted use, you will need to obtain permission directly from the copyright holder.

Mending the Fabric: Healing Communities Through Trauma Resilience and Awareness

Rose Mbone

My journey, like many other women in informal settlements of Nairobi, began with a deeply personal transformation after a traumatic life in my teenage years. In 2012, tragedy struck my life when my elder brother became a victim of extrajudicial execution after spending eight years in prison (Fig. 1).

Extrajudicial killings frequently occur in informal settlements in Kenya due to the inefficiency of the criminal justice system. When young men commit crimes, they are taken to court and later released, often repeatedly engaging in crime without being held accountable, sometimes even harming or killing police officers. In response, sometimes the police shoot young men who repeatedly engage in crime, without going through the due process of the law to remove them from society. Unfortunately, some of the youths caught up in these police shootings are innocent and fall victim because of mistaken identity.

R. Mbone (✉)
The Legend Kenya, Nairobi, Kenya
e-mail: roseroundtheworld@yahoo.com

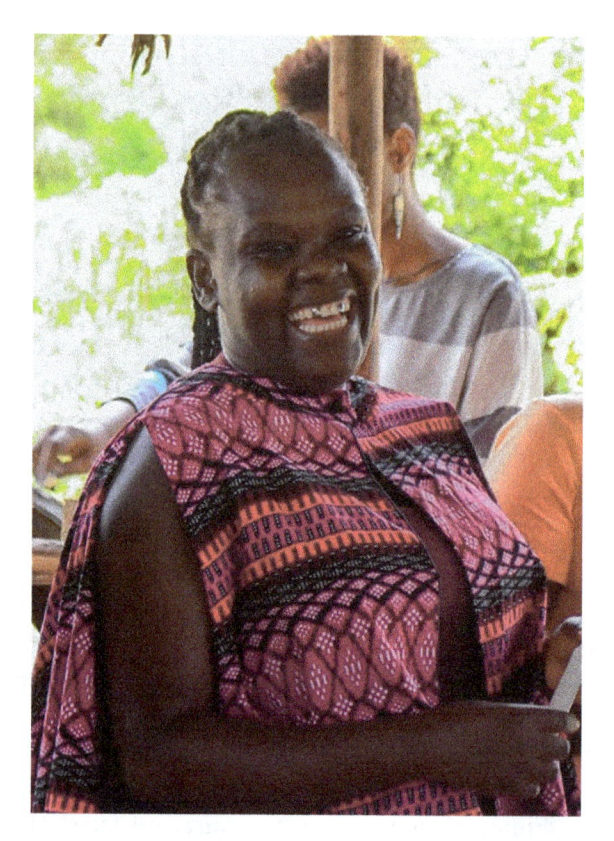

Fig. 1 The author, Rose Mbone, during an event with young women and men who have been directly affected by extrajudicial killings. Photo by Francis Namaba

The devastating loss of my brother broke my heart as well as our family. The death of a loved one is painful and shocking, and we were devastated by the loss of our brother, whom we looked to as the head of our family since our dad was never there. I loved my brother so much; we were very close. The loss left a painful psychological wound in my heart that is still healing thanks to various interventions I have undergone.

Two years after my brother's death, I experienced a transformative intervention that positively changed the course of my life. One of my mentors, Mrs. Seline, had recommended that I attend trauma-awareness and resilience-learning sessions that were being held by her colleague.

Mrs. Seline understood my experience; she could see and understand my mental state and pain. Her recommendation to attend this five-day training was beyond fortunate and found me at a time when I needed it most.

After learning about psychological trauma and resilience and practicing the tools learned in this training, I felt relieved of the pain and anger toward police that I had been carrying. On one of the days, I cried the whole night during the learning period. My transformation journey was quickened, and I was equipped with tools for processing trauma and building resilience for myself, but also in relation to and with others in the community. This experience was profound and eye-opening to me and became a catalyst for change in me and my community.

A healed individual cannot stay in a sick community and thrive. As I healed, I felt a fierce passion ignite within me to champion psychosocial trauma healing, justice, and peace in our communities that have been plagued by cycles of violence and injustice, and to transform our pain to positive energy for the peace of individuals and our community.

One of my commitments at the training was that when I returned to my community, I would reach out to as many youths as possible who are carrying pain and anger toward police as a result of their traumatic experiences with the message of resilience to break the cycles of violence and trauma (Fig. 2).

The challenges we face in informal settlements are daunting and painful. We have high rates of poverty, insecurity, and violence, including the rape of women of all ages, glorification of youth gangs and crime, and the cycle of school dropouts leading to early, often violent, marriages. All of these cause pain and suffering to our community and paint a grim picture of the informal settlements. Yet amid these trials, I witness daily a remarkable display of resilience and hope for a better future. Our community refused to surrender to despair despite the adversity it faced daily.

My colleagues and I founded The Legend Kenya, a community-based organization, to be a vehicle for implementing initiatives addressing violence and trauma, especially building healthy relationships between youths and parents and youths and security agencies. Due to our consistent activism for good relationships with the local police, we have

Fig. 2 A site in Mathare, an informal settlement in Nairobi, that has been reclaimed by youth and transformed into a people's park, providing a safe space for young people to gather. Photo by Francis Namaba

been able to have allies in the police service who now understand that extrajudicial killings are not the only solution to youth violence, but trauma-informed dialogue is also necessary. We have held trauma-awareness and resilience-learning sessions with the security agencies. They have been able to learn that when you use violence, it breeds hatred and revenge among the youths who vow to avenge and kill police, and the cycle of violence between police and youth does not end. But if they can understand the pain of trauma and have open and honest conversations, they can have some level of understanding and build positive relations where they share the responsibility of preventing violent crime. And they can inspire young individuals to make positive, life-changing choices to leave behind the path of crime and violence, opting instead to lead impactful lives (Fig. 3).

Fig. 3 A circle process during a trauma-healing session led by the author and her organization, The Legend Kenya. Photo by Francis Namaba

Fostering Healing: Pamoja Mtaani

Since 2015, we have led the Pamoja Mtaani Initiative, loosely translated as "Together in the Streets Initiative," through which we empower youth leaders to support disengagement and reintegration in the community. This is a process in which youth involved in violence using small arms are transformed and reintegrated back into the community as reformed and productive citizens after going through healing and reconciliation, learning and practice. I've seen many young people heal and transform after going through the process; they are able to go back to their families and resume a normal, healthy life. Others rejoin communities they had been ostracized from and are welcomed back.

The trauma-awareness and resilience-building approach we use is not just a program; it's a lifeline and transforming process for those enduring the pain of trauma. It is overwhelming to see that The Legend Kenya has become a sanctuary for healing wounded souls, offering a place of open dialogue, devoid of judgment or prejudice.

Trauma deals with you at a personal level. To deal with trauma, you work to unpack your pain, you unpack your frustration, you unpack some of the challenges. And if a person has healed, they cannot transfer pain. If a person has gone through this process, there is a level of awareness. That is why we don't just say trauma healing; we say trauma healing, awareness, and resilience. We are creating this awareness so that we are able to deal with it, we're able to manage it, and this directly impacts the community.

Recently, during an interview with women in the community, I received feedback that grabbed my attention:

> Rose you are our symbol of hope. I have never understood how you went through so much pain and while processing your own stress you thought of supporting us [to] overcome some of our most disturbing, unhealed wounds in our hearts. Anytime I see you I say a silent prayer of protection because I know you are spreading hope and love to our community and beyond.
>
> Rose I am so afraid of losing my grandson because it's almost 15 years since his father was shot dead, but anytime I think I am still raising another generation here I feel sad and frustrated. I also don't think a lot has changed, because I still see drug dealers living amidst us, and this makes me so worried about breaking this sad chain of events.

The process offers a safe space for individuals to embark on their healing journey to recognize that they are psychologically wounded by their terrible experiences and that the wounds they carry are hurting them. After, they are equipped with tools to process the wounds, find healing, and build resilience to withstand future bad experiences. It's a healing path, a path that comprises five transformative days.

Trauma awareness and resilience learning are focused on meeting the needs of learners and equipping them with skills and tools that enable them to heal from their trauma and resume an active, normal life, and well-being. The model is inspired by the STAR program of Eastern Mennonite University (EMU). I have had the opportunity to attend various short trainings conducted by EMU alumni. The model is also inspired by various trainings held by the Life & Peace Institute. Day one starts with acknowledgment, exposing the complexity of trauma, while

Fig. 4 The author and her team from The Legend Kenya, briefing before a session with young women and men directly impacted by extrajudicial killings. Photo by Francis Namaba

days two and three delve into understanding and healing. Resilience is cultivated on day four, and the workshop concludes with empowerment on day five. Participants emerge not just healed but also as agents of change, a community of healers ready to break the cycle of violence (Fig. 4).

Curriculum and Process of The Legend Kenya's Five-Day Trauma and Resilience Program

1. Understanding trauma. This is done on day one, and it helps participants understand what trauma is, its causes, and its impact on our bodies and well-being. Participants are guided to be able to relate to their own situation and context and find their own trauma, its cause,

and how it has impacted them. It's a journey of self-discovery and awareness.
2. Justice and trauma healing. On day two, participants learn about different strategies and tools they can apply in their own context for healing and post-traumatic growth and well-being. In the case of trauma caused by violent conflicts, the subject of how to achieve justice and forgiveness is discussed, as are various options that are available for pursuit of healing and reconciliation.
3. Resilience and self-care. On day three, participants learn about available support structures and systems they can draw from to enhance their posttraumatic growth and prevent recurrence of events that may cause trauma. They also learn about their inner strength and resources they have and can apply to withstand the impact of trauma in case they experience it again.
4. Action planning. On day four, participants are guided to come up with a realistic action plan for how they will apply the knowledge, skills, and tools learned to help themselves and others in healing and posttraumatic growth in their own context and life.
5. Follow up/referral. On day five, a follow up of participants' progress in implementing their plans is done by the trainers, and mentors are identified and paired with each participant. Support, such as resources, are offered to participants to enable them to implement their actions and find healing. A referral is made for those whose cases require further professional care that is beyond the capacity of the training.

The Impact of Trauma Healing, Resilience, and Awareness Training

What we find in these programs is that people are often going through similar challenges, for example, extrajudicial executions, gender- and sexual-based violence, and structural violence. These are some of the issues that we can look at with a resilience aspect of the community level.

Trauma really impacts women and children in the informal settlements. By reaching out and creating a community of women who have taken part in these trauma-healing programs, we're seeking to dilute the intensity of trauma and pain in homes, where children spend most of their time with their mothers. It is more often women who have gone through some level of pain, for example, by losing their kids to drugs. Some are in prison, some have been shot dead. And for some of these mothers, the pain is too much, and we see levels of posttraumatic stress that require medication. These are women who we really target in most of our sessions. While we cannot support children directly, we are able to work with their mothers, and by doing so, this is our way of trying to support the community at a larger scale.

We also work with ex-offenders. When they come back to the community, they're often not very welcome. And where they're coming from—the prisons—they are also not welcomed there. The Legend Kenya has had an opportunity to invite some of them and give them platform to just talk to the community and also have a chance to feel like they served their sentence. "So, here you are—you are a new person." We work to help ex-offenders see that they aren't tagged to their challenges forever; that was just a phase in their lives.

The relationships between ex-offenders, youth, and the police are very important and are something we work to support through our process of trauma healing and resilience. We realized early on that inviting the police to a trauma-healing session is not enough. Instead, we found that by seeking conversations with leadership, we were able to both understand and create environments that fostered a joint effort beneficial to us all, both the community and the police. Normally when there is an insecurity at the community level, the police are the first responders. Yet their mental health has not really been looked into properly, because before you are anything, you are a human being. It doesn't matter if you are a police officer, if you are a youth. If you are a woman or a young person or a child, you are a human being. You are you, and you are alive. And that is something that really is important with regard to police and the community and trauma work.

The trauma process has been able to support all of these groups in their understanding of ways of communicating, including that it's possible to criticize but still maintain dignity. We can work together, and we still maintain respect for each other. Many of the police leadership we've had in the informal settlements understand that they are part of a police *service* rather than police *force*, and they are working to shift the narrative further away from *force*, guiding the junior police and calling out where responses may have been too extreme. We also have seen the police come out and join forces with the community to participate in outdoor activities, football tournaments, community cleanups, sharing meals at the police station, and a beautification project of the police station. We have had an opportunity to plant trees. When we were planting these trees, I said, "We need fruit trees in this station. When this tree grows, the fruit will not be for police alone. It'll be for community and them." So we now have a police station in the informal settlement with fruit trees. Later, I realized that these trees did not just grow on their own. The youths have been watering these trees every evening (Fig. 5).

Fig. 5 Tree planting along the creek embankment. This location was the site of an effort by the government to remove housing. Community healing includes healing the land as well. Photo by Francis Namaba

Although mental health challenges are still not always taken seriously, so many people across the globe are doing at least something with regard to mental health. It gives us hope to know that we are not alone, and the process of trauma healing and resilience keeps spreading across the globe. And I believe that with time, people will begin to appreciate that their mental health challenges are not insurmountable. Someone is not mad—we never conclude that this is a mad person. We look at it with an empathetic lens, and we look to imagine if this was happening to someone who is close to me or someone I loved dearly.

Trauma work is a process that you can do for a whole year and not see results. Let us not give up. Let us keep soldiering on, because if those who came before us gave up, where would we be now? Let us always, always, always continue to water it. One day, it will shoot up and sprout. And that, that is a solution.

My call to action is clear: Let's prioritize mental well-being to prevent suffering and violence. A world that embraces mental stability is one step closer to a better future. As United Nations Secretary General António Guterres said: "Peacebuilding, mental health and psychosocial support are deeply interconnected. People who have suffered losses, attacks, family separation and gender-based violence carry grievances and wounds that can perpetuate repetition and cycles of violence."[1]

My journey is a testament to the strength of the human spirit, and I call on everyone to join me in the pursuit of sustainable peace and justice. We need to heal wounds to prevent the recurrence of conflicts, violence, and destruction of the environment.

Notes

1. "Secretary-General's Message to High-Level Event on Mental Health Interventions for Peacebuilding in Conflict and Humanitarian Settings Secretary-General." United Nations, September 8, 2021. https://www.un.org/sg/en/content/sg/statement/2021-09-08/secretary-generals-message-high-level-event-mental-healthintervent ions-for-peacebuilding-conflict-and-humanitarian-settings.

Rose Mbone is a peace and justice advocate in Nairobi, Kenya. She was among the first cohort of the Inspiring African Women Leaders in Peace and Security Program at the Kofi Annan International Peacekeeping Training Center in Ghana. She is currently coordinating trauma-awareness and resilience campaigns in Nairobi with support from the Daima Initiatives for Peace and Development.

Open Access This chapter is licensed under the terms of the Creative Commons Attribution-NonCommercial-NoDerivatives 4.0 International License (http://creativecommons.org/licenses/by-nc-nd/4.0/), which permits any noncommercial use, sharing, distribution and reproduction in any medium or format, as long as you give appropriate credit to the original author(s) and the source, provide a link to the Creative Commons license and indicate if you modified the licensed material. You do not have permission under this license to share adapted material derived from this chapter or parts of it.

The images or other third party material in this chapter are included in the chapter's Creative Commons license, unless indicated otherwise in a credit line to the material. If material is not included in the chapter's Creative Commons license and your intended use is not permitted by statutory regulation or exceeds the permitted use, you will need to obtain permission directly from the copyright holder.

Urban Planning with Identity: Exploring Alternative Methods and Possibilities for Preventing Identity-Based Mass Violence

Natalia Garcia Cervantes

Introduction: Identity, Place, and Planning

The relations between identity, violence, and urban planning are complex and intertwined. Identity, encompassing personal and collective perceptions of individuals and communities, is deeply connected with the sense of place. As places carry cultural, historical, and social significance, they shape and influence individual and group identities, providing a sense of belonging, attachment, and rootedness.[1] Melanie has argued that "phenomenological approaches understand place to be constitutive of human identity."[2] In this context, planning plays a crucial role in this interrelation by shaping processes and physical environments and holding the potential to create the conditions for social interaction and community development that foster identity and an environment for identity/identities to thrive.[3]

N. G. Cervantes (✉)
School of Architecture, Art and Design, Tecnologico de Monterrey, Monterrey, Mexico
e-mail: nataliagcervantes@tec.mx

N. Ujang and K. Zakariya have argued that planners should be conscious of the meanings that inhabitants attach to a place, since planners might be at risk of focusing on appearance and imageability of the physical elements but "fall short in integrating place meanings."[4] Place is about identity and is thus imbued with social meaning.[5] In this regard, the distinction between place and space has been debated extensively in the geography and urban realms.[6] Indeed, Hague argues that places *are* places "because they have identity." Identity of place is formed through a mix of meanings, experiences, actions, memories and socialization;[7] in a way, identity is imprinted *in a place* through the *uses* of that space, or by how "identities are relational" or "formed in relation to other people, other places and other identities for that place."[8] Thus, identity of place speaks of how individual and community power relations are reflected in the environment and how power is disputed in the territory.[9] Planning holds the potential to mediate this relation, but planning is rarely neutral.[10]

Effective planning must take into account the diverse identities and needs of the people who inhabit a place, with the potential to create inclusive, livable, and sustainable environments that reflect and respect the cultural and social fabric of a community. There are a few good practice examples for this. For instance, in the city of Quebec, a neighborhood-identity assessment was conducted in order to shape and guide urban renewal strategies in the area of Saint-Roch.[11]

Yet inadequate or insensitive planning can lead to marginalization, exclusion, and erasure of identities, perpetuating inequalities and social divisions.[12] Therefore, planning can potentially exert structural identity-based mass violence over certain communities or groups within a city based on the construction of an identity assigned to a group in a territory. This can be illustrated by the case of the relocation of the Plan Cabanes plaza, a central space for the North African community in Montpellier, France, since the 1970s, where "memories of migration and resettlement...have been erased from a key public space...and the urban landscape purposefully reordered to reflect a homogeneous vision of French heritage and history."[13]

Understanding the relations between identity, violence, and planning is essential for creating cities and communities that celebrate diversity, promote equity, and facilitate meaningful human experiences while inhibiting factors that may lead to exclusion, oppression, and violence. All manifestations of violence, urban violence, and identity-based mass violence have impacts that are reflected on the urban space. Violence generally tends to be mirrored on the one hand in the built environment and on the other hand on perceptions and inhabitants' uses and conceptions of space. Thus, planning that is inclusive and aware of its potential pitfalls can be key in mediating these interactions. Identity-based mass violence has been documented to have specific impacts, reflected on the conditions of the built environment—for example, segregation, displacement of communities or groups, damage to property, or through areas with graffiti or signs of physical incivility associated with these violent manifestations—which are, in turn, precursors and indicators of identity-based mass violence[14] (see Fig. 1).

Fig. 1 Graffiti-covered "Peace Wall" in Belfast, Northern Ireland, marking physical and symbolic segregation between Protestant and Catholic communities. Photo by Kirk Fisher—http://stock.adobe.com

While structurally exerted, identity-based mass violence has roots based on personal and collective identity. This showcases the importance of understanding, systematizing, and incorporating individuals' perspectives on (1) how identity is reflected in the territory and (2) how planners might implement strategies that prevent identity-based mass violence and help communities address and recover from these events. This chapter explores the multilayered relations between planning, identity, and identity-based mass violence, arguing that planning practices can play a crucial role in addressing, preventing, or mitigating such violence by moving beyond identity preconceptualizations of communities and through the use of alternative grounded methods such as participatory visual tools.

Participatory visual methods emphasize participants' production of "inclusive accounts using their own words and frameworks of understanding" through a variety of techniques, such as mental and community mapping, timelines, matrices, and photography.[15]

The study of Campana-Altamira in Monterrey, Mexico, presented here was conducted in 2021 during the COVID-19 pandemic used a qualitative approach that involved various methods. Semi-structured interviews and participatory mapping exercises were organized within the community, and autophotography (photos by participants) was implemented. Participatory visual methods involved four community members: three women who had lived in the community for over 30 years and a young man approximately 16 years old. Following these activities, we conducted semi-structured interviews with community members to gather more insights. Due to the COVID-19 restrictions, data collection methods had to be adapted. Participants shared their photographs with us via WhatsApp, and for the mapping exercise, we distributed maps among participants, asking them to mark their contributions. In the upcoming section, we will delve deeper into the application and results of the methodology, providing a more comprehensive explanation of the rationale and advantages of these approaches.

The next section of this chapter briefly builds on the themes presented in this introduction, particularly manifestations of identity-based mass violence in urban contexts linked to planning. Section "Official and Unofficial Planning Responses" explores the double-edged nature of planning, analyzing how its processes can have unintended consequences that might promote the appearance of identity-based mass violence at community and individual levels.[16] This is linked to structural violence, which is exerted through the marginalization and revictimization of certain areas within a city.

Presenting the case study of Campana-Altamira, an informal settlement in the city of Monterrey, Mexico, this section delves into the potential for planning as a response to these issues through the use of participatory visual methods to achieve a better understanding of place and identity. Section "Closing Comments" presents a discussion and conclusions for the chapter.

Identity-Based Mass Violence and Planning: Power and Intersections at Community and Individual Levels

Identity-based mass violence can have a significant impact on the built environment in a number of ways. One of its first impacts on space is the creation of segregated and isolated communities, with members of different groups living in separate areas for safety reasons. This can result in the physical separation of communities and the creation of physical barriers between groups. An example of this is Northern Ireland, where religious, ethnic, and political conflict had tangible and noticeable repercussions in the built environment through so-called peace walls, establishing no-go areas, and limited uses of spaces for communities[17] (see Fig. 1).

Other manifestations of identity-based mass violence at community levels might also be destruction of property, including businesses, and public infrastructure that can result in a loss of vital community assets and resources, as well as a decline in the overall quality of the built environment and perceptions of security. In this regard, the implications of domicide, or the loss of one's home, are explored in more depth in chapter 2 by Ammar Azzouz. In other extreme cases, identity-based mass violence can force individuals and communities to flee their homes and seek refuge elsewhere. This can result in the displacement of large numbers of people, leading to overcrowding and strain on infrastructure and resources in host communities. Identity-based mass violence can also involve the destruction of symbolic sites and landmarks that hold cultural, historical, or religious significance for particular communities, resulting in a loss of cultural heritage and a diminished sense of community identity.[18] Indeed, it has been debated and documented how violence and insecurity might reinforce divides while constructing otherness, through planning. Examples of this are found in Kabul[19] and Karachi,[20] where perceptions of insecurity, otherness, and official planning further segregate communities and increase perceptions of insecurity, which illustrate how those with power make planning decisions that further reinforce these perceptions of insecurity and otherness.

In this sense, identity-based mass violence might be exercised at individual and community levels. Communities with high crime rates are often stigmatized at the city level, resulting in what Abello-Colak refers to as "territorial stigmatization" ("the attachment of stigma to place"), which "has fostered and reproduced fear of certain groups or places." In some cases, territorial stigmatization occurs in addition to multiple stigmatization of communities suffering from poverty, racial discrimination, and/or other forms of structural violence.[21] The importance of these preconceptualizations of communities lies in the fact that stigmatization might seem like a justification for harsh measures that seek to reduce or respond to violence from a territorial approach, or for perpetuating existing identity-based mass violence in certain spaces. When a community with shared traits inhabits a stigmatized urban area, it may be more likely to experience structural violence through planning, or lack thereof. This could include receiving limited resources for education, infrastructure, or services. Neglect and abandonment of these areas then amplifies the territorial stigmatization, entrenching violence dynamics.

This is particularly relevant for the case of informal communities in Latin America, where—whether referred to as *favelas*, Villas Miseria, or *tugurios*—through planning policy and discourse, certain predominantly negative identities are attached to these places. The importance lies in the fact that these negative identities are then used to victimize neighborhoods in two ways. First, and as it was mentioned above, these negative identities serve as justification for harsh antiviolence prevention and reduction measures, and second, residents carry what has been referred to as "the social marking" of the settlement they inhabit, which "constitute[s] an experience made of discrimination and identification struggles that take away from its population the right to a positive self-interpretation."[22] Not only might stigmatization of communities based on their identity represent systemic and structural violence, but the ideological and discourse components leading to such stigmatization should also be scrutinized, since these then tend to materialize in policy or concrete actions.

Indeed, as Amartya argues, a sense of identity can totally exclude many people even as it warmly embraces others.[23] In other words, by actively or passively planning, emphasis is placed on the role of urban development institutions in mediating this interrelation through deliberate actions or omissions.[24] These scenarios are found in many contexts, such as in Mexico and Brazil, and, more importantly, they can be more inconspicuous and insidious. Territorial stigmatization implemented through passive planning might be manifested as less investment in infrastructure or services, or as unwillingness of the state to respond to communities' needs. For this reason, the double-edged nature of planning should be critically examined.[25] At its extreme, planning can be viewed as part of interlocking systems of oppression. It has the negative potential to undermine a person's sense of belonging, privilege one group or community over others, and exert identity-based mass violence. This violence is often manifested as limited access to employment, education, and other opportunities. The following section explores how planning might represent structural violence and how other alternatives are possible, as well as responses to identity-based mass violence that might stem from better, more-grounded and accessible planning practices.

Official and Unofficial Planning Responses

Recognizing the complex spatial impacts of identity-based mass violence opens possibilities as to how planning could mediate its repercussions on the built environment, and broadly, on urban space. Louise looked at the links between identity, space, and power, arguing that "to feel or know a space as enclosing or expansive, comforting or alien, empowering or oppressive, depends upon power relationships that are established both in and around that place."[26] Following this premise and building on the fact that power is contested in space,[27] this implies that "territory becomes [a] resource that is used to assert ethnic control, collective identity, and economic superiority."[28] For example, with regard to planning processes, certain groups have historically been excluded from city-making based on identity, specifically in informal or irregular settlements. This refers to everyday manifestations of urban life and geography shaped by class, which is one of the most evident yet often overlooked dimensions of identity-based structural violence. The concept of class—and, in some cases, gender—adds a critical layer to understanding how structural violence is experienced. It highlights disparities in access to resources, spatial exclusion, and the lived experiences of marginalized groups. This perspective also offers a more universal lens to examine how urban planning and spatial organization contribute to these issues, as well as the ways in which responses are shaped by explicit and implicit understandings of identity.

Structural violence may target a specific community directly, while more subtly, "governments [might] use their planning powers to manipulate ethnic spatial relations in order to protect the dominant ethnic group."[29] However, these dynamics are not limited to ethnic considerations alone. They can also manifest through planning decisions that inadvertently or deliberately result in regressive and manipulative outcomes, driven by the interests of powerful, narrow groups. Approaches to addressing such consequences may emerge from either official or unofficial planning responses, but particular attention must be given to the "gray space" that exists between these two spheres.[30] Gray spaces refer to areas that exist in a state of ambiguity between legality and illegality, formal and informal, planned and unplanned, like a space in between space. These are "positioned between the 'whiteness' of legality/approval/safety, and the 'blackness' of eviction/destruction/death. They are neither integrated nor eliminated, forming pseudo-permanent margins of today's urban regions."[31] These gray spaces refer to settlements with an assigned informality status, but they also allow us to think and plan beyond established methods in order to understand more deeply the complexities of planning *with* identity and planning beyond established structures. The concept of gray space is used here in two ways: first, to analyze the case study of an informal settlement in the city of Monterrey, and second, to illustrate the methods that, while removed from these official planning structures, might enable us to plan more closely with communities.

Official Planning Responses (Participatory Planning)

Planning responses to identity-based mass violence are crucial in addressing the complex challenges it poses to communities, and these responses can encompass official and unofficial measures aimed at mitigating the impacts of violence on the affected areas. Official planning institutions can devise strategies and policies to enhance safety, promote social cohesion, and restore a sense of security and well-being. Official responses may involve targeted interventions, such as applying crime prevention through environmental design principles or addressing situational risk factors like insufficient lighting and poor public area maintenance. These responses can also include creating new public spaces, improving existing ones, expanding public transportation to reach previously excluded populations, and promoting socially-conscious urban development that considers how planning decisions can either contribute to or mitigate identity-based mass violence.[32]

Other contentious official responses to identity-based mass violence include the use of "peace walls" like in Northern Ireland. Initially constructed from barbed wire and later replaced with concrete, these physical barriers were designed to separate neighboring communities, ostensibly to maintain "peace" amid extreme political and religious violence. At first, "the physical lines of demarcation provided safety and a sense of security and gave communities a mechanism for identifying 'friendly territory'."[33] But some argue that these walls ended up reinforcing differences between communities, consolidating the construction of "the otherness," and preventing the restoration of community interactions.[34]

In terms of other official planning mechanisms, land use and the built environment play a crucial role in the occurrence and patterning of criminal activities and violence directed at specific groups or communities. Land use and changing patterns in individual neighborhoods can significantly impact residents. Various activity choices—such as how a space is used, when, and by whom—reshape the landscape and influence perceptions of how space is designed and managed, and for whom. These patterns can also include the possibility of spaces being used for criminal activity, as understood from a situational perspective. The physical forms such as buildings and placement of windows or vantage points might enhance natural surveillance and improve perceptions of safety. This influences residents' routine activities and the presence or absence of guardians watching over the users, which may inhibit or promote incidences of violent behavior in a neighborhood. Other, more generic planning responses include urban upgrading and providing infrastructure, although it should be noted these have been criticized for stemming from Global North contexts, considering in a limited way the contextual characteristics of the sites where these are implemented.[35]

Planning responses should emphasize community engagement facilitating community interactions and participatory approaches, involving residents in decision-making processes to ensure their voices are heard and their specific needs and concerns are addressed. Faranak[36] has referred to this as "invited spaces," or institutional spaces where communities are invited to participate in planning decisions. In this context, participatory approaches emerge as an official planning response to identity-based mass violence, building on the gray spaces that might bring official planning closer to inhabitants in violence contexts considering individual identities, perceptions, and uses of space.[37]

Particularly, instruments like community transect walks allow a view of neighborhoods through the perspective and experience of community members, and they become crucial in understanding the territory in a nuanced, grounded manner. Other methods of data collection, such as participatory visual exercises, allow "the individuality of direct and indirect experiences and perceptions of violence and insecurity to be captured, as well as the spatiality of violence" and aid in understanding perceptions at the local, community, and street levels, and the dynamics of identity-based mass violence in urban space.[38] These types of tools might help bridge the gap between the abstractions and inaccessibility of official planning and the phenomenological daily experiences of people in the territory by deconstructing preconceptualizations of these communities' identities and needs by the state.

There are, however, caveats in participatory planning; it has been widely recognized and documented that communities are heterogeneous, and participation risks representing only a privileged few or reinforcing unequal power dynamics among communities, even in low-income communities.[39] Therefore an inclusive, representative participation must be context sensitive and recognize a spectrum of identities within communities. Other risks are related to tokenistic participation, where it is reduced to mere consultation and only tangentially linked to centers of power, rather than enabling citizen control.[40] In this sense, participatory visual methods, such as community maps and autophotography, used within a top-down approach, aim to address the blind spots that planners might have. These methods promote a broader view of knowledge, challenging traditional epistemological approaches and creating channels of communication between planners and communities that go beyond verbal and written methods. Once these channels are established, they can evolve into spaces of recognition, visibility, and negotiation for communities that would otherwise be ignored or excluded from planning processes. Through inclusive planning practices, communities can reclaim their spaces, fostering a sense of ownership, empowerment, and identity.

Though responses to identity-based mass violence from a planning perspective are often discussed as separate or contrasting, in reality, these interventions tend to have blurred lines when it comes to community participation and official interventions. This will be elaborated on in the conclusion.

Unofficial Planning Responses (Community-Based Interventions)

Driven by grassroots initiatives and community-led efforts—or as invented spaces[41]—unofficial planning responses may involve community patrols or policing, the establishment of safe zones or neighborhood watch groups, and the revitalization of public spaces by the community in order to create environments that promote community identity and discourage violence. However, community-driven reclamation of space should not be considered a panacea. Community policing and self-protection groups can be benevolent forms of democratized participation or sinister forms of vigilantism. These approaches and structures of participation may therefore serve preventive or remedial purposes in relation to identity-based mass violence, or they could potentially aggravate them.

There are many examples of best practices linked to successful community-based interventions. For example, in Colombia, it was found that "central to reducing violence and building intracommunity support and relations, eroded by violence, is the construction of scenarios in which communication within communities and between the state and citizens can build on existing social connections and promote positive interactions."[42] This particularly refers to making formerly "invisible citizens" visible by acknowledging their presence, needs, and contributions through approaches that go beyond traditional planning frameworks. In the case of Medellín, Colombia, the neighborhood Comuna 13 has gained significant attention for achieving a balance between institutional interventions and community-led efforts in violence prevention.

Comuna 13 was once known for high levels of violence, gang activity, social instability, and deprivation.[43] However, through community-based violence reduction strategies met by institutional efforts to respond to violence and decades of neglect, the neighborhood has undergone significant transformation over the years.[44] Planning initiatives to respond to violence in Colombia were targeted at providing cultural and educational infrastructure in deprived neighborhoods and focusing on improving transportation while building on and increasing social cohesion.

Some key elements of the approach taken in Comuna 13 included investment in infrastructure, specifically focused on building schools, parks, community centers, and public spaces, which helped create a more vibrant and welcoming environment for residents. Similarly, public transportation and urban integration were enhanced through the implementation of an escalator system that improved mobility for residents. This system reduced physical barriers between different areas of the community, connected them to the city center, and facilitated access to education and job opportunities.[45] Community-based measures included community policing where local police worked closely with community members to build trust and ensure a better understanding of the neighborhood's specific challenges. The focus shifted from solely punitive actions to a problem-solving approach.[46] Similarly, youth engagement was pursued through the implementation of various social programs, including education initiatives, vocational training, and after-school activities. Engaging young people was crucial to steer them away from violence and gang involvement. Additionally, the introduction of art and culture played a vital role in transforming Comuna 13. Murals and graffiti produced with and by the community were used to express identity, unity, and resilience. Some similarities to this approach are found in the case study presented below of Campana-Altamira in Monterrey, Mexico.

The case of Medellín shows that the divisions between official and unofficial responses to violence might be more diffuse than what has been previously acknowledged, echoing the concept of O. Yiftachel's gray spaces. In order to grasp the potential of these spaces, other mixed initiatives are explored, adapting bottom-up planning practices, for example, where participatory visual methods are employed to analyze and systematize residents' perceptions, uses, and conceptions of space. This might help bridge the gap between planning policies, how space is configured, and how people actually live in such space, considering individual and community identities. In this regard, unofficial forms of place-making become essential, as they are often shaped by official practices, to involve vulnerable and excluded groups in planning processes where their identities might otherwise lead to their neglect.

Participatory Visual Methods

Participatory research methods and visual methods have been around for some time. R. Pain and P. Francis differentiate between participatory research approaches and participatory diagramming and methods.[47] Participatory research approaches are "not so much the methods and techniques employed, but the degree of engagement of participants within and beyond the research encounter." Rather than a set of techniques, these approaches are "a process by which communities can work towards change."[48]

Using participatory visual methods can unravel identitarian preconceptions associated with specific groups and strengthen urban planning processes if planners spend enough time on the ground to achieve an understanding of context and people's perceptions of space, identity, and insecurity that is as close to reality as possible. For example, what official planners perceive as a worthwhile initiative to respond to violence in a given neighborhood—such as investing in infrastructure like green spaces, pavements, or improved services like lighting—might differ significantly from what residents believe would make them feel more secure.

Some simple guidelines for these exercises included asking community members for photographs of their favorite places, disliked places, places they avoid, and representative places (linked to community identity). This allows grasping an understanding of contextual characteristics of places that might be more or less pleasant, and places more closely known by participants. Similarly, if there are instances of victimization or unpleasant past experiences in those spaces, these are likely to come up through photographs. Participatory visual methods often require pre- or post=interviews where the participants explain and expand on their decisions regarding the photographs they included in the exercise. In follow-up interviews, respondents might be asked about their feelings for certain spaces and what factors cause them to put certain ones in the "preferred" or "avoided" categories. Importantly, autophotography can enable participants to open up about their daily routes and familiar or representative places.

Similarly, community mapping is an ethnographic tool used for the study and social analysis of the behavior of a specific community or group represented by means of graphic and visual instruments such as maps. The main objective of this tool is to identify and graphically represent areas of opportunity to achieve comprehensive development based on what the citizens perceive as necessary.

The following section presents an example of the use of these methods in an informal settlement in Monterrey, Mexico, during the COVID-19 pandemic. Participants produced rich ethnographic data through mapping and autophotography, illustrating how Campana-Altamira's strong community identity is unique in the city, even though that identity has at times been used to the settlement's disadvantage.

Planning, Identity, and the Impacts of Violent Events in an Informal Settlement: Campana-Altamira

Campana-Altamira is in the south-central area of Monterrey. It comprises fourteen neighborhoods and about 19,000 residents. The settlement has a privileged location in the city, being a few kilometers from San Pedro Garza Garcia,[49] and it hosts elite universities such as Tecnologico de Monterrey. From 2009 to 2014, a surge in violence impacted the whole city, while being particularly insidious in Campana-Altamira (Fig. 2).

The neighborhood was victimized in two ways. First, due to the complex topography of the site and lack of state and police presence, criminal actors settled on the top parts of the Campana-Altamira hill (Fig. 3), increasing perceptions of insecurity among inhabitants and victimizing the community through the coercion of youth, indiscriminate acts of violence against inhabitants, and other actions. Second, the community is perceived from the outside in a negative way. This justified the absence, neglect, and omissions by the state that first created the conditions for criminal actors to settle in the area, and then served to cement the perceptions inhabitants of Monterrey had of Campana-Altamira: the identity of *los malitos* (criminal actors) who settled on the top parts of the hill merged indiscriminately with the community identity of Campana-Altamira.

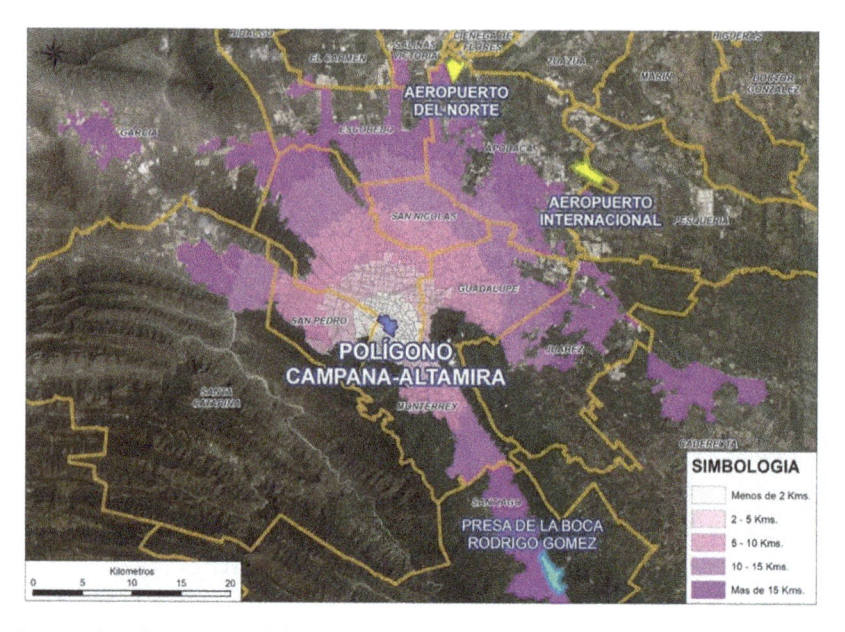

Fig. 2 The location of Campana-Altamira in the Metropolitan Area of Monterrey, Mexico (*Source* Gaceta Municipal of the Government of Monterrey, Volume 27, "Proyecto del Programa Parcial de Desarrollo Urbano 'Distrito Campana-Altamira 2020–2040'", 2021. https://www.monterrey.gob.mx/pdf/gacetas/2021/GacetaEnero2021EspecialDistritoCampanaAltamira.pdf)

As a result, the community was largely left unattended, witnessing increased structural violence such as neglectful urban planning, refusal to provide services, and limited access to employment and education opportunities despite a privileged location, as even top parts and specific areas of the hill did not have a census recording until very recently as a result of territorial stigmatization. Inhabitants resent this labeling of the settlement from outsiders within the city, as Blanca, a resident for over forty years in the area, argues:

> And yes, it hurts, it personally hurts me when they say: "Oh, La Campana is very dangerous." Or simply the taxis, you say, "Where are you going?" "To La Campana." "Ah, no, I'm not going." "Hey, why?" "No, no, I'm not going, I'm not going." That is, you don't go and the taxi picks you up. But…I, right now, I can tell you, you can come without any problem.

Urban Planning with Identity: Exploring Alternative ... 397

Fig. 3 Green dots mark the locations of familiar/locally-representative places and red dots of insecure places in Campana-Altamira, from participants' perspective. Photos by authophotography exercise participants, collage by the author. Map data from OpenStreetMap openstreetmap.org/copyright

> If you know that there is a risk, you...well, I'm not going to bring a person when they say, you know what....Like for example, when there was insecurity I wasn't going to tell you, "Hey, come, no problem," when I knew that I live here myself and I'm afraid, even less am I going to bring other people who are not from here, who don't know them or what they do to them. I know something is going to happen to them, no, no, no. Um, eh, but well, I don't know, unfortunately it is like that, people are sometimes very cruel.[50]

The interview illuminates the complexity of residents' own perceptions of the settlement, recognizing insecurity existed (and arguably still does, as in the rest of Monterrey). But insecurity seeped into the conceptualization of the territorial identity of the settlement, and residents resent being associated with negative identitarian connotations based on the settling of external criminal actors in the site. This is juxtaposed with the strong sense of identity that exists in the community, derived from the area's informal development process. Inhabitants proudly recognize their identity, in terms of strong social cohesion and artistic manifestations such as music and murals, even when this might be subject to stigmatization in the rest of the city. There are murals in several parts of Campana and Altamira hills that show how collective identity is illustrated, turning it into a tangible manifestation of a cultural expression. The largest mural in Campana-Altamira, *Ave de los Sueños*, was an effort to change the preconceptions outsiders might have of this space, and it is accompanied by a poem that emphasizes the hardworking nature of inhabitants and their strong sense of identity in spite of (or due to) the informal development of the neighborhood:

> We were the birds that flew through the skies looking for opportunities, looking for sustenance. We fly, sometimes against the wind, to achieve our dreams and we take flight despite all the adversity, like a pilgrim bird in search of identity. Our will carved stone and our feet climbed the hill in search of a home. We were the ones who arrived.
> We are the ones who stayed, through effort, in these streets that now tell our story. We are those birds that made a home out of nothing and that now go out, day after day, in search of food with our gaze always forward. We are the ones who sing, dream and live a better tomorrow.

We fly in search of improvement. With our past accounted for, we guide those who follow us. "We build community and harmony because we are one of the birds that strengthens its nest day by day."[51]

Certain characteristics of the case of Campana-Altamira echo those of informal settlements in Latin America and the Global South more broadly. As Melanie and Ananya have argued, one must be wary of attaching a deterministic informal "identity" to informal settlement residents, as these are heterogeneous, complex, and beyond the dichotomy of formal/informal.[52] One of the advantages of the use of participatory visual methods is that, if implemented with sensitivity to the site, they might allow us to grasp a more nuanced understanding of collective and community identity as it is attached to place, bridging the gap between community understanding of place and broader planning processes. In Campana-Altamira, one of the main findings is that, in spite of the negative connotations associated with the neighborhood, residents inhabit the area proudly, building on a strong sense of identity, belonging, and community cohesion.

This dichotomy, how residents inhabit the area and perceive themselves versus outsiders' views from policy or planning perspectives, is illustrative of the sense of belonging and cohesion experienced by insiders and the sense of fear and trepidation that informs the perspectives of those from outside, which is not mutually incompatible. The use of participatory methods in the area and the tools presented here—the mapping exercise in particular—allows participants to graphically locate and find convergence of opinions over some problematic areas in the community, such as alleys or narrow streets, or the lack of lighting in central areas, which were considered insecure or unpleasant.

These areas negatively impacted inhabitants' feelings of security, causing them to feel unsafe while moving through the community. One of the main issues, linked to passive planning, is the lack of maintenance to infrastructure, since participants said lighting was one of the most deficient aspects of the built environment, followed by pavements and streets maintenance, which causes some areas to be perceived as dangerous at night (see Fig. 3).

The second activity relates to manifestations of identity in the built environment. Participants included photographs of the hill featuring the *Ave de los Sueños* mural, graffiti in the neighborhoods with the word "Campana," and other parts of the hill. These included pedestrian bridges overlooking the Cerro de la Silla, a natural landmark in Monterrey, and Arroyo Seco, a stream that borders the neighborhood. These images graphically represent and locate identity manifestations in space.

The exercise conducted in Campana-Altamira sheds light on two important issues. First, it illustrates how a story of community cohesion, collaborative work, dignity, and identity converges to transform collective spaces in ways that go beyond the tangibleness of the built environment. Second, it highlights a contradiction inherent in proudly inhabiting, owning, and claiming spaces despite the structural violence and identity-based violence expressed in myriad ways that neighborhoods like Campana-Altamira have witnessed.

Closing Comments

This chapter has explored the multiple ways identity-based mass violence impacts spaces and how differentiated planning might cement dynamics of structural violence into the built environment. As this chapter has discussed, territorial struggles based on identity have specific manifestations, such as segregation, fragmentation, and the way identity is reflected in the built environment. In this sense, institutionalized ways of urban planning play a key role, but individual practices also are important to consider. These have been referred to as "ordinary" forms of place-making and are often overlooked in official planning systems.[53] They have potential for bridging the gap, addressing and lessening the physically manifested impacts of identity-based mass violence.

Overall, planning responses to identity-based mass violence require a collaborative and comprehensive approach that involves multiple stakeholders and addresses the immediate causes and underlying social and economic factors that contribute to structural violence. The examples shown here involving participatory visual methods might aid in bridging the gap between institutionalized planning and how identity is imprinted in place, gathering and focusing input to planning from the uses, activities, and perceptions inhabitants have of the different places in their communities.

Effective planning responses to identity-based mass violence require a comprehensive understanding of the local context, active collaboration among stakeholders, and a commitment to creating safe, inclusive, and resilient communities, underscoring the fact that communities are not homogeneous and that individual and collective identity and perspectives matter. By recognizing and valuing different identities, planners can foster a sense of ownership and pride among residents, promote social cohesion, and enhance the overall well-being of individuals and communities. The division of official and unofficial responses might be more blurred than acknowledged, for example, in Colombia, while the situation has improved and Medellín has become a global reference for violence reduction. The case of Comuna 13 illustrates the power of reclaiming gray spaces, where collective action and social investment converge to create safer and more resilient neighborhoods.[54]

Use of participatory visual methods seeks to seize the gray spaces between official and unofficial planning, implying a shift in knowledge production by making visible communities uses and conceptions of identity and space but also enable planners to make decisions informed by real, daily, grounded accounts from inhabitants' perspectives. Implementing participatory visual planning methods might bring us closer to an urban planning through and for care, equity, and justice, arriving at more granular, sensible, and grounded solutions.

This chapter wants to highlight how planning has become a crucial instrument in changing territorial identities, calling attention to the need for "more deliberative forms of governance and participatory planning processes."[55] The chapter has aimed to show how the exclusion of communities from planning processes perpetuates systemic and epistemic violence, reinforcing cycles of territorial stigmatization based on community identities. By adopting more inclusive, bottom-up planning practices that recognize and celebrate identity, communities can appropriate or reclaim their spaces. This fosters place identity, ownership, and empowerment, which may help mitigate structural and identity-based mass violence.

We push for recognition of the multilayered composition of identity, especially in cities, and of how identity can be weaponized. Identity is religion, ethnicity, class, gender, and much more. The diversity of users and people living in the city is, in the end, what cities are made from and for. In other words, we have argued that planning reflects active social engineering based on identity, an identity that is multidimensional and complex, such as in the context of informal settlements and beyond.

Notes

1. Hauge, "Identity and Place: A Critical Comparison of Three Identity Theories." *Architectural Science Review* 50, no. 1 (2007): 44–51.
2. Lombard, "Constructing Ordinary Places: Place-Making in Urban Informal Settlements in Mexico." *Progress in Planning* 94 (November 2014): 1–53, 15.
3. Hull et al., "Place Identity: Symbols of Self in the Urban Fabric." *Landscape and Urban Planning* 28, nos. 2–3 (April 1994): 109–120.
4. Ujang, and Zakariya. "The Notion of Place, Place Meaning and Identity in Urban Regeneration." *Procedia-Social and Behavioral Sciences* 170 (2015): 709–717.
5. Lefebvre, *The Production of Space*. Oxford, UK and Cambridge, USA, Wiley-Blackwell, (1991).
6. Massey, For Space (1st edition). London, SAGE Publications Ltd. (2005); Lombard, Constructing Ordinary Places: Place-Making in Urban Informal Settlements in Mexico, 2014.
7. Hull et al., "Place Identity: Symbols of Self in the Urban Fabric." *Landscape and Urban Planning* 28, nos. 2–3 (April 1994): 109–120.
8. Hauge, Identity and Place: A Critical Comparison of Three Identity Theories (March 2004): 7.
9. Ibid.

10. Yiftachel, "Critical Theory and 'Gray Space': Mobilization of the Colonized." *City* 13, 2–3 (2009): 246–263.
11. Simard, M., and G. Mercier. "Planning, Participation and Identity in Quebec City: Community Building through Urban Revitalization." *Canadian Journal of Urban Research* 10, no. 1 (Summer 2001): 23–46.
12. Garcia-Cervantes, "Violence and Insecurity in Urban Space: An Analytical Approach Based on the Ecological Framework for Violence." *Revista Geográfica de América Central* 66 (January–June 2021): 25–58.
13. Tchoukaleyska, "Public Space and Memories of Migration: Erasing Diversity through Urban Redevelopment in France." *Social and Cultural Geography* 17, no. 8 (2016): 1101–1119, 1103.
14. (He et al., 2017).
15. Pain and Francis, "Reflections on participatory research". *Area*, 35(1) (March 2003): 46–54, 46.
16. Yiftachel, "Critical Theory and 'Gray Space': Mobilization of the Colonized." (2009.)
17. Knox, "Peace Building in Northern Ireland: A Role for Civil Society." *Social Policy and Society* 10, no. 1 (2011): 13–28.
18. Tchoukaleyska, "Public Space and Memories of Migration: Erasing Diversity through Urban Redevelopment in France" (2016).
19. Weigand, "Kabul: Bridging the Gap between the State and the People." In *Cities at War: Global Insecurity and Urban Resistance*, (2020).
20. Kaker, S. A. "Responding to, or Perpetuating, Urban Insecurity? Enclave-Making in Karachi." In *Cities at war: Global insecurity and Urban Resistance*, (2020).
21. Abello Colak, Lombard, and Guarneros-Meza. "Framing Urban Threats: A Socio-Spatial Analysis of Urban Securitisation in Latin America and the Caribbean." *Urban Studies* 60, no. 2 (April 2013): 10.

22. Jovchelovitch, and Priego-Hernández. *Underground Sociabilities: Identity, Culture and Resistance in Rio De Janeiro's Favelas*. Brasilia, UNESCO, 2013.
23. Sen, "Violence in Identity." In *Values and Violence: Intangible Aspects of Terrorism*, Edited by Karawan, I. A., McCormack, W., & Reynolds, S. E. 3-13. Dordrecht: Springer Netherlands, 2008.
24. Garcia-Cervantes, "The Everyday Effects of Urban Planning: Exploring Perceptions of Violence, Insecurity and Urban Space in Two Mexican Cities." PhD thesis, University of Manchester, (2018).
25. Yiftachel, "Planning and Social Control: Exploring the Dark Side." Journal of Planning Literature 12, no. 4 (1998): 395–406.
26. Purbrick, Aulich, and Dawson. *Contested Spaces: Sites, Representations and Histories of Conflict*. Basingstoke, Palgrave Macmillan, 2007: 4.
27. Bourdieu, 1993: 164.
28. Yiftachel, "Critical Theory and 'Gray Space': Mobilization of the Colonized." (2009): 397.
29. Ibid.
30. Ibid.
31. Ibid.
32. Moncada, "Urban Violence, Political Economy, and Territorial Control: Insights from Medellín." *Latin American Research Review* 51, (September 2016): 225–248.
33. Gormley-Heenan and Byrne, "The Problem with Northern Ireland's Peace Walls." *Political Insight* 3, no. 3 (December 2012): 4–7, 4.
34. McCord, McCord, McCluskey, Davis, McIhatton, and Haran. "Belfast's Iron (ic) Curtain: 'Peace Walls' and Their Impact on House Prices in the Belfast Housing Market." *Journal of European Real Estate Research* 6, no. 3 (November 2013): 333–358.
35. Watson, V. "Shifting Approaches to Planning Theory: Global North and South." *Urban Planning* 1, no. 4 (December 2016): 32–41.
36. Miraftab, "Insurgent Planning: Situating Radical Planning in the Global South." *Planning Theory* 8, no. 1 (February 2009): 32–50.

37. Garcia-Cervantes, "Using Participatory Visual Methods in the Study of Violence Perceptions and Urban Space in Mexico." *International Journal of Conflict and Violence* 13 (November 2019). 1–15, 13.
38. Ibid.
39. Kaza, "Tyranny of the Median and Costly Consent: A Reflection on the Justification for Participatory Urban Planning Processes." *Planning Theory* 5, no. 3 (2006): 255–270.
40. Arnstein, "A Ladder Of Citizen Participation". *Journal of the American Institute of Planners*, 35(4), (November 1969).
41. Miraftab, "Insurgent Planning: Situating Radical Planning in the Global South." (February 2009).
42. Dolan "Radical Responses: Architects and Architecture in Urban Development as a Response to Violence in Medellín, Colombia." *Space and Culture* 23, no. 2 (April 2018: 106–128): 121.
43. Sotomayor, "Dealing with Dangerous Spaces: The Construction of Urban Policy in Medellín." *Latin American Perspectives* 44, no. 2 (March 2017): 71–90.
44. Drummond et al. "Medellin: A City Reborn?" *Focus on Geography* 55, no. 4 (December 2012): 146–154.
45. Ibid.
46. Drummond et al. "Medellin: A City Reborn?"; Samper, *Urban Resilience in Situations of Chronic Violence Case Study of Medellin.*
47. Pain, and Francis, Reflections on participatory research. *Area*, 35(1) (March 2003): 46–54.
48. Ibid., 46.
49. San Pedro Garza García is one of the wealthiest municipalities in Mexico and Latin America, known for its high standard of living, exclusive residential areas, luxury shopping centers, and strong economic activity. Its proximity to Campana Altamira highlights stark socio-economic contrasts between these neighboring areas. For Campana Altamira, being close to San Pedro Garza García is a privilege because it provides potential access to economic opportunities, services, and infrastructure typically unavailable in less affluent areas.

50. Author interview with Blanca, 40-year resident of Campana Altamira, August 2021.
51. Colectivo Tomate, 2016. Available here: https://colectivotomate.org/proyectos/monterrey-colosal/.
52. Lombard, "Constructing Ordinary Places: Place-Making in Urban Informal Settlements in Mexico", 2014: 10, and Roy "Slumdog Cities: Rethinking Subaltern Urbanism". *International Journal of Urban and Regional Research*, 35(2): 223–238 (February 2011).
53. Lombard, Constructing Ordinary Places: Place-Making in Urban Informal Settlements in Mexico, 2014.
54. Sotomayor, "Dealing with Dangerous Spaces: The Construction of Urban Policy in Medellín."
55. Gaffikin, and Morrissey. *Planning in Divided Cities: Collaborative Shaping of Contested Space.* (2011): 4.

References

Abello Colak, A., M. Lombard, and V. Guarneros-Meza. "Framing Urban Threats: A Socio-Spatial Analysis of Urban Securitisation in Latin America and the Caribbean." *Urban Studies* 60, no. 2 (April 2013).

Arnstein, S. R.. "A Ladder Of Citizen Participation." *Journal of the American Institute of Planners*, 35(4), (November 1969) 216–224. https://doi.org/10.1080/01944366908977225.

Dolan, M. "Radical Responses: Architects and Architecture in Urban Development as a Response to Violence in Medellín, Colombia." *Space and Culture* 23, no. 2 (April 2018: 106–128).

Drummond, H., J. Dizgun, and D. J. Keeling. "Medellin: A City Reborn?" *Focus on Geography* 55, no. 4 (December 2012): 146–154.

Gaffikin, F., and M. Morrissey. *Planning in Divided Cities: Collaborative Shaping of Contested Space.* Hoboken, NJ, Blackwell Publishing Ltd, (2011).

Garcia-Cervantes, N. "The Everyday Effects of Urban Planning: Exploring Perceptions of Violence, Insecurity and Urban Space in Two Mexican Cities." PhD thesis, University of Manchester. (2018).

Garcia-Cervantes, N. "Using Participatory Visual Methods in the Study of Violence Perceptions and Urban Space in Mexico." *International Journal of Conflict and Violence* 13 (November 2019). 1–15.

Garcia-Cervantes, N. "Violence and Insecurity in Urban Space: An Analytical Approach Based on the Ecological Framework for Violence." *Revista Geográfica de América Central* 66 (January–June 2021): 25–58.

Gormley-Heenan, C., J. and Byrne, J. "The Problem with Northern Ireland's Peace Walls." *Political Insight* 3, no. 3 (December 2012): 4–7. https://doi.org/10.1111/j.2041-9066.2012.00115.x.

Hauge, Å. L. "Identity and Place: A Critical Comparison of Three Identity Theories. *Architectural Science Review* 50, no. 1 (March 2007): 44–51.

He, L., A. Páez, and D. Liu. "Built Environment and Violent Crime: An Environmental Audit Approach Using Google Street View." *Computers, Environment and Urban Systems* 66, (November 2017): 83–95.

Hughes, J., A. Campbell, M. Hewstone, and E. Cairns. "Segregation in Northern Ireland." *Policy Studies* 28 (January 2007): 28:1, 33–53. https://doi.org/10.1080/01442870601121429.

Hull IV, R. B., M. Lam, and G. Vigo. "Place Identity: Symbols of Self in the Urban Fabric." *Landscape and Urban Planning* 28, nos. 2–3 (April 1994): 109–120.

Jovchelovitch, S., and J. Priego-Hernández. *Underground Sociabilities: Identity, Culture and Resistance in Rio De Janeiro's Favelas*. Brasilia, UNESCO, 2013.

Kaker, S. A. "Responding to, or Perpetuating, Urban Insecurity? Enclave-Making in Karachi." In *Cities at war: Global insecurity and Urban Resistance*, edited by Sassen, S. and Kaldor, M., 133-159. New York, Columbia University Press, 2020.

Kaza, N. "Tyranny of the Median and Costly Consent: A Reflection on the Justification for Participatory Urban Planning Processes." *Planning Theory* 5, no. 3 (November 2006): 255–270.

Knox, C. "Peace Building in Northern Ireland: A Role for Civil Society." *Social Policy and Society* 10, no. 1 (December 2011): 13–28.

Lefebvre, H. *The Production of Space*. Oxford, UK and Cambridge, USA, Wiley-Blackwell, 1991.

Lombard, M. "Constructing Ordinary Places: Place-Making in Urban Informal Settlements in Mexico." *Progress in Planning* 94 (November 2014): 1–53.

Massey, D. B. (2005). For Space (1st edition). London, SAGE Publications Ltd.

McCord, J., M. J. McCord, W. McCluskey, P. Davis, D. McIhatton, and M. Haran. "Belfast's Iron (ic) Curtain: 'Peace Walls' and Their Impact on

House Prices in the Belfast Housing Market." *Journal of European Real Estate Research* 6, no. 3 (November 2013): 333–358.

Miraftab, F. "Insurgent Planning: Situating Radical Planning in the Global South." *Planning Theory* 8, no. 1 (February 2009): 32–50.

Moncada, E. "Urban Violence, Political Economy, and Territorial Control: Insights from Medellín." *Latin American Research Review* 51, no. 4 (September 2016): 225–248.

Pain, R., & Francis, P. Reflections on participatory research. *Area*, 35(1) (March 2003), 46–54. https://doi.org/10.1111/1475-4762.00109.

Purbrick, L., J. Aulich, and G. Dawson. *Contested Spaces: Sites, Representations and Histories of Conflict*. Basingstoke, Palgrave Macmillan, 2007.

Roy, A. Slumdog Cities: Rethinking Subaltern Urbanism. *International Journal of Urban and Regional Research*, 35(2), (February 2011), 223–238.

Samper, J. *Urban Resilience in Situations of Chronic Violence Case Study of Medellin*, Colombia. Massachusetts Institute of Technology MIT, 2012.

Sen, A. "Violence in Identity." In *Values and Violence: Intangible Aspects of Terrorism*, Edited by Karawan, I. A., McCormack, W., & Reynolds, S. E. 3–13. Dordrecht: Springer Netherlands, 2008.

Simard, M., and G. Mercier. "Planning, Participation and Identity in Quebec City: Community Building through Urban Revitalization." *Canadian Journal of Urban Research* 10, no. 1 (Summer 2001): 23–46.

Sotomayor, L. "Dealing with Dangerous Spaces: The Construction of Urban Policy in Medellín." *Latin American Perspectives* 44, no. 2 (March 2017): 71–90.

Tchoukaleyska, R. "Public Space and Memories of Migration: Erasing Diversity through Urban Redevelopment in France." *Social and Cultural Geography* 17, no. 8 (January 2016): 1101–1119.

Ujang, N., and K. Zakariya. "The Notion of Place, Place Meaning and Identity in Urban Regeneration." *Procedia-Social and Behavioral Sciences* 170 (January 2015): 709–717.

Watson, V. "Shifting Approaches to Planning Theory: Global North and South." *Urban Planning* 1, no. 4 (December 2016): 32–41.

Weigand, F. "Kabul: Bridging the Gap between the State and the People." In *Cities at War: Global Insecurity and Urban Resistance*. Edited by Sassen, S. and Kaldor, M. 53–77. New York, Columbia University Press, 2020.

Yiftachel, O. "Critical Theory and 'Gray Space': Mobilization of the Colonized." *City* 13, nos. 2–3 (2009): 246–263.

Yiftachel, O. "Planning and Social Control: Exploring the Dark Side." *Journal of Planning Literature* 12, no. 4 (1998): 395–406.

Natalia Garcia Cervantes is a research professor at Tecnologico de Monterrey and holds a PhD from the University of Manchester. Her ethnographic work draws on adapting ecological frameworks to explore perceptions of violence and insecurity in Mexico in order to identify risk factors at differing social levels.

Open Access This chapter is licensed under the terms of the Creative Commons Attribution-NonCommercial-NoDerivatives 4.0 International License (http://creativecommons.org/licenses/by-nc-nd/4.0/), which permits any noncommercial use, sharing, distribution and reproduction in any medium or format, as long as you give appropriate credit to the original author(s) and the source, provide a link to the Creative Commons license and indicate if you modified the licensed material. You do not have permission under this license to share adapted material derived from this chapter or parts of it.

The images or other third party material in this chapter are included in the chapter's Creative Commons license, unless indicated otherwise in a credit line to the material. If material is not included in the chapter's Creative Commons license and your intended use is not permitted by statutory regulation or exceeds the permitted use, you will need to obtain permission directly from the copyright holder.

Harnessing Art and Crowdsourcing to Prevent Gender-Based Violence

Elsamarie D'Silva

Anjali

Fourteen-year-old Anjali lives in the Satara district of India. She loves math and science. She is curious about the world around her. She enjoys learning and exchanging ideas with her teachers and friends, but she hates the bus ride to school. Every morning her father drops her at the bus stop where a minivan picks up her and a few other girls. Anjali and her peers are crammed into the tiny interior of the bus and are often groped and touched by the male passengers. They feel totally uncomfortable and for the next hour stare at the floor because they cannot bear to face the constant male gaze.

The unwanted and harmful attention Anjali faces during her daily bus rides to school have caused great anxiety and has been affecting her ability to concentrate in school. After six months of this abuse, Anjali felt

E. D'Silva (✉)
Red Dot Foundation, Mumbai, India
e-mail: elsa@reddotfoundation.org

so unwell and anxious that she could not get out of bed. She dropped out of school.

Sexual and gender-based violence is a global pandemic impacting one in three women on an average of at least once in their lifetime.[1] Yet it is normalized and accepted as part of a daily routine forcing women and girls to stay silent. The downsides include that it affects mental and physical health, it limits one's opportunities, and it often restricts people's movement and mobility. Over 90% of the 55,000 people who have reported on Safecity, a crowd map for the anonymous reporting of sexual and gender-based violence, have shared they have not made a police complaint nor will they make an official complaint as they are afraid to engage with the formal system.[2] They are afraid to bring shame and dishonor to their families, or many times it is the families who refuse to let them make a complaint, especially if the girl is yet to be married. This is unfortunate because it makes the violence invisible and then there is not complete data to inform policies, decision-making, or the implementation of resources.

Shortly after Anjali dropped out of school, she attended a program that Red Dot Foundation[3] held in her district. She learned during one of the workshops about the various forms of sexual violence: nonverbal forms such as staring, ogling, leering; verbal forms such as commenting, catcalling, and sexual invitations; physical forms such as stalking, touching, groping, sexual assault, and rape; and digital forms such as morphing, revenge porn, cyberbullying, and more. She also learned that under Indian law, all of these were crimes that carried strict punishments. After the workshop, Anjali volunteered to join a program called "Safety Champions," where youth are trained to be peer educators and first responders to sexual and gender-based violence in their communities.

Anjali observed during these trainings that many other girls and women had similar experiences to hers on the minibus and she realized she was not alone. Anjali was curious how to take action and was happy to learn she could document her experience and have others document their experiences on the Safecity app. She could then use the data to make a representation to her family members and other parents for safe transportation to school. In this case, Anjali, and several of her peers, demanded—and received—a dedicated minibus that would only transport girls. With this change, one month later, Anjali was back in school. Anjali is now planning to complete grade 10 and continue onto college.

Jyoti

Anjali's is just one of many success stories from Safecity, a project that is part of my Indian-based nonprofit, the Red Dot Foundation (RDF). I launched Safecity over 11 years ago as an immediate response to a gang rape and killing of a young woman on a bus in Delhi. Jyoti Singh and her male friend had gone to watch a movie, *The Life of Pi*. After the movie, at 8 PM, they decided to board a bus to return home. The people on the bus were all part of a gang who wanted to teach Jyoti a lesson for being out late at night with a male who was not her relative. They beat her male friend and tied him up. Then they gang raped Jyoti several times, inserting metal rods into her body and removing her innards and finally leaving her on the streets to die.

The incident was so traumatic that it triggered conversations across India about personal experiences of sexual and gender-based violence. My friends started sharing how they were assaulted by their uncles and cousins or neighbors. I remembered an incident when I was 13 years old. I was traveling by train with my mum and siblings. It had previously been a ladies compartment, but unknown to us, it had become general, and men were allowed to travel in it. This switch happened just before we could disembark at our destination whilst we were still on the train. An empty compartment suddenly became overcrowded and stifling. As we prepared to disembark, I suddenly felt someone lifting my skirt and touching my private parts. I wanted to scream but could not as I felt my voice would have been drowned in the noise of the crowd. I wanted to push the hands away but my arms were pinned to my side because there were so many people. All I could think of was that I needed to get out of that compartment. I never told anyone about it because I felt terrible and violated. However, I hated traveling by local train in Mumbai, my home city, and would find every excuse not to take it, instead preferring to travel by car despite the traffic congestion. This was neither sustainable nor cheap in the long run. It was only much later that I made the correlation with my experience and my reluctance to take the train.

Public transport is a critical component of mobility within a city. High-quality and safe public transport should be a basic right. Without it many women and girls would not have access to opportunities such as education, careers, or even social life. Often women spend more money on transport options that are perceived to be safer, for example rideshares, or compromise on the quality of their education by choosing an institution closer to home.[4]

Safecity plays an important role in making the invisible visible. Further, it brings the community together to understand the issue and decide solutions that make sense for them. After all, sexual and gender-based violence is not a woman's fault but a societal issue. It is sociocultural constructs that often value a woman's honor and puts impossible standards for her to live her life. She is often blamed for anything that goes wrong. How often have we heard that a woman deserved the violence she suffered because she had no business being out late at night, or that she was wearing too short or too tight clothing, or that she asked for it in some other way? Never do we question why the perpetrator believes it is his right to violate someone.

"I Am Meera"

Most survivors of sexual and gender-based violence are afraid to challenge societal norms and instead accept it as part of their daily routine. Many survivors are ignorant about what constitutes sexual and gender-based violence and are not aware of their legal rights. Storytelling allows for solidarity, resonance, and a feeling of community. I remember one of my earliest workshops on child sexual abuse prevention with nine-year-old girls. We showed them an excellent movie, *Komal*, made by Childline India, on child sexual abuse.[5] It very simply explains what the private parts of the body are, who can touch them, under what circumstances, and the difference between good and bad touching. The video has been made in several languages and is a great teaching tool. After the workshop, a young girl came up to me and said she now felt confident to tell an uncle that she did not want to sit on his lap and she knew what to do, that she was not wrong. Exposure to such films and videos at an early age can equip children with the knowledge and give them the confidence to stand up for themselves.

Poetry and art can create a space for survivors to share stories and break the silence. A couple of years ago, my organization wanted to engage youths to understand harmful gender norms that promote violence and to feel comfortable breaking the silence to challenge these norms. Most young people are afraid to speak up, especially to an adult. They are also afraid they will be blamed for any incident and their freedom will be curtailed. Through a "Design Challenge Workshop" we shared actual stories of young people facing stigma, discrimination, and bullying while going to school, at school, and in their communities. These were common experiences that the youths could relate to. We then asked them to draw the persona of the person experiencing the harassment—give her a name (Meera), age, and sociocultural identity, including her aspirations and goals, fears, and other emotions. They were asked to think about the society around her, her friends, parents, teachers, etc., and provide a background to their relationship with her. This was done so they could relate to her and her experience. The youths were then divided into three groups and asked to quickly respond to questions in a word or sentence. The questions posed were: What was Meera feeling? What frustrations did she face? What hope did she have for the future? Each line or word contributed by the youths were then arranged into a beautiful poem, which highlights that even in tragic circumstances, one can create something beautiful.

The poem generated captured the feelings and emotions of the youths, especially young women who were at the receiving end of harassment, including in public spaces and transport. It also captured their frustrations of being stared at, being objectified, constantly compromising and being afraid to travel alone by public transport. Many of the youths who attended the workshop later shared how they had similar or exact experiences as the ones shared as case studies. They felt they now had a voice and agency because they were not alone. They also felt that there was hope because one or a few incidents did not define you or your life. The teachers who attended the workshop also felt they now had a tool to engage with their students. Prior to the workshop, talking about sexual and gender-based violence was not easy—they felt awkward and in some cases triggered their own memories of being victims of abuse (Fig. 1).

Talking Walls

My organization uses art and various artistic interventions as a process for healing, for survivors to become aware of their latent trauma, find solidarity with others, build their confidence to break the silence, and develop strategies to take action to prevent or respond to the violence.

As a society, it is important to step up a collective understanding of sexual and gender-based violence, and Safecity can be a great tool to use. It has the largest collection of personal experiences in the world—from 96 countries—to help us understand the context in which the violence takes place. Most of this data has been collected in partnership with grassroots organizations that have been trained to use the app and apply the insights from the data in their local programming. The pervasiveness of these incidents is sobering, but it is important to understand the local nuances (sociocultural factors, physical space, etc.) that contribute to the violence.

The map can be zoomed in to understand the incidents occurring at the neighborhood level—the specific kinds of violence, the exact locations, time of day and day of week trends that pinpoint what might be additional factors that make the space the comfort zone of the perpetrator. Most of what is reported on Safecity would be considered too trivial to report—staring, ogling, commenting, catcalling, touching, groping—because it is so normalized and accepted as part of our daily routine. But anonymous reporting provides the safe space to share the incidents and "feel seen and heard," as one survivor recently shared with me (Fig. 2).

The next step would be to decide what steps need to be taken to make such places safe spaces for women and girls and in fact everyone. In the recent past, we have seen increasing numbers of men and members of the

I am Meera

Why must I compromise?
Stop staring, stop objectifying me
Akash why, why do you stand by
I don't feel safe travelling alone
Why me?

You there, you stand and see me,
I am a daughter, you have a daughter.
I have feelings... I'm upset & helpless
I am being confined for who I am
why me!

NO MORE.
Hope. I need a sign.
I want change, I need change
Nothing is going to stop me
I want to study. I love my college

I wish I could fight
I will speak up
I am ambitious, I will speak up
I will do something!

I will stand against it in any case
The change is me.
My study can be my voice,
my instrument for change
I won't give up, I will rise

Change begins with me
I won't care what others are saying
I am my mother's daughter, I will speak up
Speak up all those around
I will stop all this and pave my own way

We are free, free, free – as we sleep,
as we run, as we sit, free as can be.
On my street, in my house,
in the park–free, free, free as can be...
I am society, Society is me
Change begins with me.

I smile but I want to be happy.
Nothing to stop me... nothing to hold me back...
With every dark night, there is a bright next day with new hopes
that the society will change and give me hope to be secure.
The Sun can shine tomorrow, but not brighter than me,
for I have burnt for my kind more than anyone can see.

Free to sing, free to dance,
free to own my life in the way I like,
free to create, free, free, free
along with voice, we need a way to convey,
I wasn't born to hush my voice.
Free to write terrible poetry
Because I can.
Oh what a safe space!

Fig. 1 The poem "I Am Meera" was generated at a workshop in November 2021 organized by Red Dot Foundation in partnership with professors Verena Thomas and Jackie Kauli from the Queensland University of Technology, Australia (*Source* Red Dot Foundation)

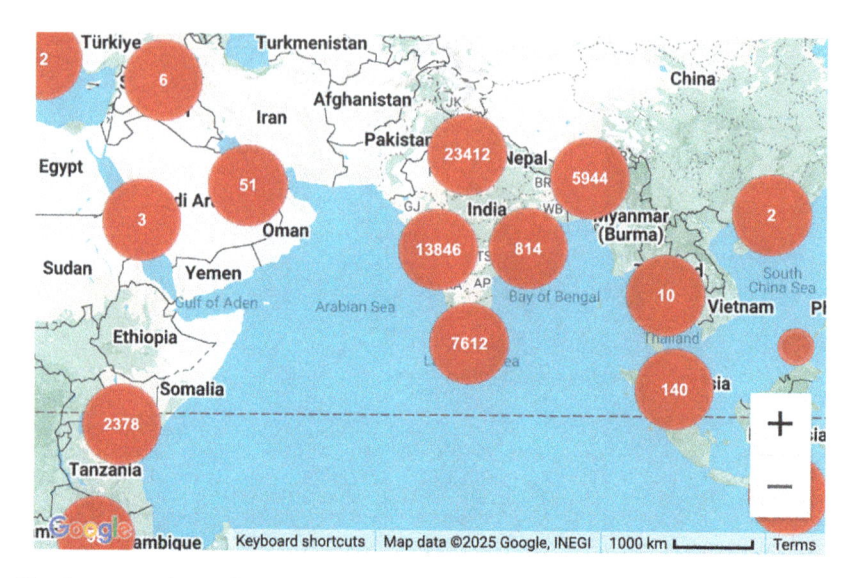

Fig. 2 Screenshot of the Safecity map. The red dots indicate the number of reports per location. Map data: ©2025 Google, INEGI, Safecity https://webapp.safecity.in

LGBTQIA community reporting violence. Most of our users confirm that they have never reported to the police and do not wish to do so, either for lack of trust or the belief that no action would be taken. The data insights compel us to deliberate on such questions as whether the space needs better lighting, or improved walkways, or more patrols. It builds better ally ship and provides ideas on possible ways to intervene and help the survivor.

For example, the Safecity data helped identify a hot spot in an urban slum in Delhi. It was on a main road near a tea stall. Men would loiter there while drinking their tea and intimidate women and girls with their constant staring. When asked what they wanted to change about their neighborhood, the young girls said they would like the staring to stop. So we organized an art workshop for them, and they painted the wall with staring eyes and subtle messaging that loosely translates in English to "Look with your hearts and not with your eyes."

One of the girls, Priyanka, shared that she was intimidated by the constant staring. She felt unsafe, and many of the men would pass comments, quote sexist lines from Bollywood films, and sing ditties with double meanings. She wanted to tell her parents but was afraid they would tell her to stop going to school. In her community, education for girls was not considered important and often not encouraged. Her parents were already pressuring her to get married even though she was only 14. If she shared her concerns, Priyanka worried her parents might stop her from venturing, using the excuse of concern for her safety but really because they were concerned to keep her honor intact for marriage. Priyanka was one of the main leads in designing the wall mural and she felt liberated to be able to express her feelings on the wall without having to challenge someone directly (Fig. 3).

Shortly after the wall mural was painted, the tea stall owner became an ally. He would usher the men along and stop them from making the comments. Other people in the community also became more aware that staring and commenting was making the young girls feel uncomfortable. The staring eyes painted on the wall were useful to spotlight the bad behavior. The staring, loitering, and commenting stopped. The girls, including Priyanka, could now walk comfortably, with no stress, to school, college, or work without fear of being intimidated by the men.

The intervention of using art on walls is now called "talking walls" where the feelings of women are expressed through the paintings in a

Fig. 3 This wall mural in Lalkuan, India, translates in English to "Look with your hearts and not with your eyes." It was created during an art workshop where survivors shared their feelings and co-created the design along with the artist, painting it with her (*Source* Red Dot Foundation)

public space. It serves to put the community on notice and highlights there is an issue. It has been used successfully in many different places, outside public toilets, in front of girls' colleges, and at hot spots on local streets.

Often pop culture promotes harmful gender norms and stereotypes. In a campaign titled "Bollywood vs Bioscopes," RDF partnered with Ogilvy and Mather, a renowned advertising agency, to challenge Bollywood to refrain from promoting sexism and misogyny in the name of love. The campaign used colorful handmade bioscopes to engage people in several small towns of India to critically think about the movies they were consuming.[6] Dialogues and clips from three Bollywood films featuring popular male heroes were artistically illustrated. Young men and women were interviewed after watching the first part, which entailed the actual scenes from the movies. Men felt that stalking, passing comments, and ogling were all expressions of love and interest. They were motivated by their film heroes to actually do the same in real life. Several women too felt there was "good stalking" and it was acceptable for a man to express his love in that form. However, when they were asked to see the rest of the film, where the laws were explained and a different ending was depicted, many of them realized that they should be more careful when consuming content, that they should be aware of the laws, and that the woman must consent before any action is taken. These were new perspectives for them, and they had never realized that this behavior could adversely affect women (Fig. 4).

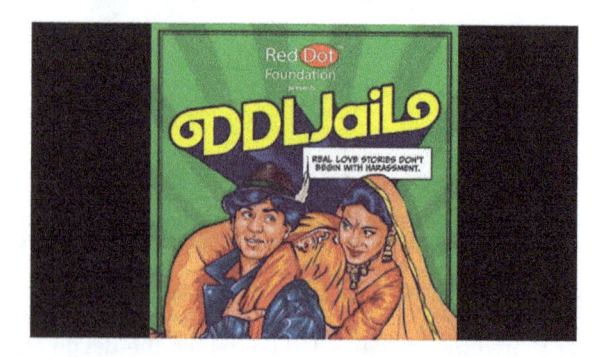

Fig. 4 A poster calling out sexism in Bollywood (*Source* Red Dot Foundation)

This is not surprising as the latest National Family Health Survey reveals that over 75% of women across three states in India believe it is acceptable for their husbands to beat them up.[7]

Changing cultures of violence is partly about policies, but it is also about giving people a voice. By making it easy for people to share their stories and report, and thus transparently showcasing data, it is possible to hold institutions accountable while also incorporating institutions into solution setting. RDF has several examples where on presenting the data, police have changed beat patrol timings and increased patrolling, and municipal authorities have fixed street lighting and made safe, public toilets available. Institutions too can proactively use the data to enhance their decision-making processes and effectively deploy resources. For example, knowing the hot spots enables the police who are scanning closed-circuit TV footage to look for incidents and make public announcements calling out the inappropriate behavior.

It is important to engage men and boys to be allies in preventing violence. One of the hot spots identified on the Safecity platform was in Delhi near a public toilet. A group of young men had placed a couch outside the public toilet complex and intimidated the women and girls who used the space. The toilet complex itself was badly maintained, with no proper lighting and broken doors and windows, making the women and girls feel vulnerable. The young men would crack jokes, take pictures, and film these women and girls while they used the facility.

After attending Safecity workshops, the women and girls shared how they disliked using the facility but did not have a choice as there were no toilets in their homes. They would restrict their food and drink to minimize the visits to the toilet and feel afraid to confront the young men. If they shared their fears with their parents, they would be blamed. After strategizing what action could be taken, they invited the young men for a dialogue. The young men came and heard the women's and girls' stories and, more importantly, their fears. One of the young men, Manoj, was so moved he decided to join the campaign and become a peer educator.[8] He did not realize his actions were causing so much distress among the women. There are many men like Manoj who, after being engaged and trained, have become advocates for safety. This is important because without the active engagement of men and boys, it will not be possible to stop sexual and gender-based violence (Fig. 5).

Polycom Development for Girls, a Safecity partner in Kenya, has also actively engaged young men to stop being perpetrators. One of the hot spots identified was in the informal settlement of Kibera where, on their way to school, girls were bullied, harassed, and touched by young men. It was distressing but also left the girls with little choice. If they changed their route to school, they ran the risk of being kidnapped or trafficked, or if their parents found them in a different part of the settlement, they would be grounded. When Jane Anyango, the executive director of Polycom understood the problem, she engaged the local religious leader, whose institution was quite close to this spot. Anyango showed the data to the priest, who was horrified and immediately started counseling the young men and incorporating messages in his sermon denouncing this

Fig. 5 Safecity engages young men to be agents of change to end gender-based violence. This young man, Manoj, is holding a placard saying "badlav" which means "change." Photo by the author

behavior. It had an immediate impact on the young men. Finding influencers in the community who are well respected by young men can be a game changer.

Brazil: Carnival

Safecity works with partners around the world to bring greater awareness and solutions to the epidemic of gender-based violence. During Carnival in Brazil, for instance, the Safecity team engaged local businesses such as restaurants and pubs in Belo Horizonte and trained them in bystander intervention strategies. They distributed thousands of posters and pamphlets encouraging people to speak up when they see or experience sexual harassment. They also publicized help information for both reporting incidents as well as mental health support. After Carnival, a survey was carried out amongst young women on their perceptions of safety. Many of them felt it was one of the safest carnivals they had experienced. This was because they felt people around them were informed and aware about sexual and gender-based violence with help resources were easily available (Fig. 6).

Blank Noise

Blank Noise and Why Loiter, two feminist initiatives that began in India, use an interesting method to get women and girls to occupy a public space and reclaim their agency. Their campaign is called "Meet to Sleep," and it encourages women to take a mat and lie down in a park. To build women's comfort and risk-taking ability to be alone in a public space such as a garden, the campaign calls for women to go alone and not in a group. It is interesting to see how men react to women in such situations. Often the security guard of the park will ask the woman to leave as he believes she is going to create trouble. Other men might stare, make moves on the woman, or pass comments. For the woman it can be intimidating. One does not often see women by themselves reading a book, lying on the grass, or just being by herself. One of my friends

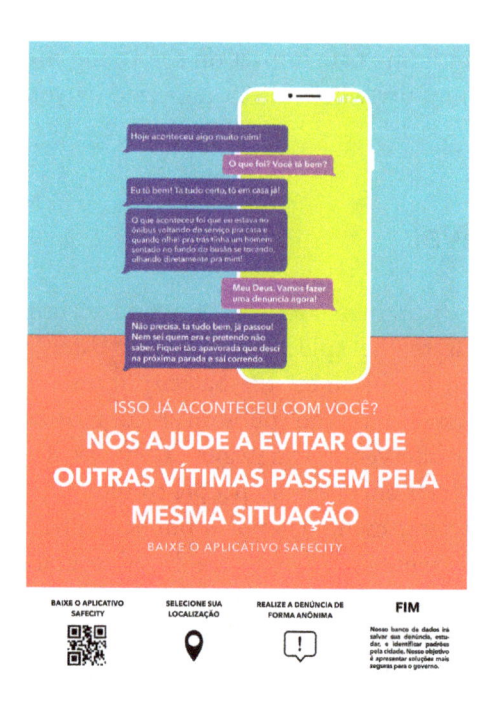

Fig. 6 A poster promoting the Safecity app used in Brazil during Carnival (*Source* Red Dot Foundation)

participated in this activity and found it initially frightening to be lying on the grass even if it was in broad daylight. But after explaining to the security guard that she had every right to be in that space as the men, he had no choice but to let her be. She braved on and withstood the comments and stares. The very act of occupying the space and holding her ground was liberating. We need more people to accept women in public spaces at all times of day and night, by themselves or in a group or with whomever they want to be. It is not an invitation to perpetrate any form of violence against them. Men have to give up space and share power and learn to coexist in peace (Fig. 7).

Fig. 7 Satya heroically participating in the "Meet to Sleep" action (*Source* Blank Noise Meet to Sleep)

Conclusion

From visualizing incidents on a map to storytelling, talking walls, street theater, poetry, movies, and more, there are many success stories in getting women and girls to break their silence, building solidarity and engaging local communities to take action. These artistic interventions help bring voice to the issues while also aiding in the healing process. The disaggregated data at the neighborhood level helps identify possible solutions and unlikely stakeholders who might be engaged as allies to end sexual and gender-based violence. United Nations Secretary-General Antonio Guterres, at the opening of the 78th session of the UN General Assembly, referred to sexual and gender-based violence as an "age old scourge." In order to end it, we will need to think outside the box, which is just what Safecity/RDF is doing with partners around the world.

> We are free, free, free—as we sleep,
> as we run, as we sit, free as can be.

On my street, in my house,
in the park—free, free, free, free as can be…
I am society, Society is me
Change begins with me
I smile but I want to be happy.
Nothing to stop me…nothing to hold me back….
With every dark night, there is a bright next day with new hopes
that the society will change and give me hope to be secure
The Sun can shine tomorrow, but not brighter than me
for I have burnt for my kind more than anyone can see.
Free to sing, free to dance,
free to own my life in the way I like,
free to create, free, free, free
along with voice, we need a way to convey.
I wasn't born to hush my voice.
Free to write terrible poetry
Because I can.
Oh what a safe space!

(from the poem "I Am Meera")

Notes

1. UN Women. 2019. "What We Do: Ending Violence against Women." UN Women. UN Women. 2019. https://www.unwomen.org/en/what-we-do/ending-violence-against-women.
2. Red Dot Foundation, "Safecity," webapp.safecity.in, December 1, 2020, https://webapp.safecity.in/.
3. Red Dot Foundation, "Red Dot Foundation," reddotfoundation.in, November 3, 2014, https://reddotfoundation.in/.
4. Girija Borker, *Safety First: Perceived Risk of Street Harassment and Educational Choices of Women*, Policy Research Working Paper 9731, World Bank, Washington, DC, July 2021, http://hdl.handle.net/10986/36004.
5. Childline India, *Komal*, video, https://youtu.be/VkY0xqtw6W8?si=OD06WG1YII8qvjeP.
6. A bioscope is an early generic name for a movie camera and especially a traveling movie show in rural India.

7. Government of India, Ministry of Health and Family Welfare, National Family Health Survey (NFHS-5), 2019–21, March 2022, https://dhsprogram.com/pubs/pdf/FR375/FR375.pdf.
8. "Manoj" is not his real name.

ElsaMarie D'Silva is the founder of Red Dot Foundation (India) and President of Red Dot Foundation Global (USA). She created the platform Safecity, which crowdsources personal experiences of sexual violence and abuse. Her work has been recognized by the UN secretary-general, UN Alliance of Civilizations, German Federal Foreign Office, and others.

Open Access This chapter is licensed under the terms of the Creative Commons Attribution-NonCommercial-NoDerivatives 4.0 International License (http://creativecommons.org/licenses/by-nc-nd/4.0/), which permits any noncommercial use, sharing, distribution and reproduction in any medium or format, as long as you give appropriate credit to the original author(s) and the source, provide a link to the Creative Commons license and indicate if you modified the licensed material. You do not have permission under this license to share adapted material derived from this chapter or parts of it.

The images or other third party material in this chapter are included in the chapter's Creative Commons license, unless indicated otherwise in a credit line to the material. If material is not included in the chapter's Creative Commons license and your intended use is not permitted by statutory regulation or exceeds the permitted use, you will need to obtain permission directly from the copyright holder.

Urban Violence: Common Elements of Good and Promising City-Led Prevention and Protection Practices

Flávia Carbonari

Identity-based mass violence is not a widely known or agreed-on concept used by policymakers or practitioners in the urban violence or atrocity prevention fields, but rather a framework under construction. When reviewing prevention practices oriented around urban violence with those around atrocity prevention, one finds common drivers that have to do with systemic violence targeted at specific identity groups. While the manifestation of such systemic violence may seem different whether looking through an urban violence or atrocity prevention lens, it is nonetheless true that violence in urban spaces, and consequently responses to such violence, tends to be focused on specific populations and identities, and often on places where they congregate.

This chapter examines effective and promising urban violence prevention and protection practices. It argues that strategies to address identity and systemic violence and urban violence can be similar if they tackle shared root causes related to exclusion and structural inequality. The

F. Carbonari (✉)
The World Bank and Peace in Our Cities, Rosario, Argentina
e-mail: flaviacarbonari@gmail.com

selection of cases mentioned is primarily based on consultations with select experts and a review of the existing literature. They are focused on the United States because of the high rates of lethal violence in the country compared to other high-income countries; and the Latin American region, considered the world's epicenter of urban violence. They try to represent different contexts and realities and include strategies to reduce violence in the near term as well as those that aim to prevent violence and build peace in the longer term. Although a growing number of evaluations demonstrate the effects of specific policies and programs on different forms of violence, these are still limited, and more-robust evidence is needed about some of the experiences mentioned.[1] However, they already tell interesting stories and reinforce common elements. A final word of caution: even among the most-studied and replicated practices, sustainability of peace remains a challenge.

Incorporating a Public Health Approach and Expanding the Role of Cities

Violence, in all of its forms, is a complex and multifaceted phenomenon that requires multisectoral and integrated responses. While this understanding may seem common today, its translation into policy and programming has evolved throughout time. Limited criminal justice punitive approaches, which were the default response in the 1980s and 1990s in Latin America and the United States (and have seen a comeback today), have been criticized for some of their consequences. These include high rates of mass incarceration; the exacerbation of social and economic disparities through the disproportional targeting of minority and vulnerable groups; and the reduced focus on rehabilitation, which also contributes to persistent high rates of recidivism. The effectiveness of these approaches has also been extensively debated, with some studies suggesting that the severity of punishment does not necessarily correlate with reduced crime rates.[2] In light of these limitations, there is a growing consensus on the need to address violence risk factors and root causes, often linked to processes of social exclusion that affect most heavily certain groups and territories.

In Latin America, the redemocratization processes of the 1980s and 1990s and the failures of hardline approaches tried in some countries in the early 2000s[3] contributed to the emergence of the concept of citizen security. The term represented the expansion of a focus of public security policies on safeguarding state institutions to include activities targeted at preserving the safety and rights of citizens,[4] moving toward a broader concept that involved a wider range of actors and looked at drivers and solutions from a public health perspective. With this shift, crime and violence started to be understood as a complex phenomenon resulting from the intersection of various factors in which social policies in education, health, social assistance, culture, and urban development also had a role to play.[5]

In the United States—which leads the most-developed countries in gun-related homicide rates[6] and mass shootings[7] (with substantial variation by state, gender, and major racial/ethnic groups)—the use of public health approaches to prevent violence also emerged in the 1980s. During that decade, the risk of homicides reached epidemic proportions, especially among youth and minority groups. These high rates of violence forced a reckoning and an exploration for solutions. Taking inspiration from the treatment of infectious diseases, violence prevention advocates began to consider ways to apply public health thinking to violence.[8] Parallel to that, child maltreatment and intimate partner violence began to be recognized as social problems, reinforcing the need to move beyond criminal justice responses to solve violence-related problems.

Globally, the World Health Organization (WHO) has continuously contributed to mainstreaming the public health approach. Its work in violence prevention can be traced back to the 1990s, when it adopted a resolution that recognized violence as a major public health issue and called for the development of a comprehensive violence prevention strategy.[9] In 2002, the organization launched the first World Report on Violence and Health,[10] emphasizing the need to address the underlying drivers or risk factors that contribute to violence through a multisectoral approach.[11]

Looking through a public health lens implies understanding violence as a type of disease that spreads primarily through close contact and whose prevention could use health methods to stop outbreaks and reduce the risks of contagion. This framework has shaped some of the best-known prevention programs, as will be further discussed.

The incorporation of the public health perspective into urban-violence-prevention approaches meant understanding that exposure to violence is linked to risks at multiple levels: individual, interpersonal/relationship, community, institutional, and societal. This complex interplay of risk factors associated with different forms of violence is often depicted in WHO's public health socioecological model. This framework conceptualizes violence as the outcome of a variety of interrelated factors at these different levels, such as an individual's age, education, income, and history of abuse; a person's closest social circle of peers, partners, and family members; a community physical and social environment; and social and cultural norms that may accept violence as a possible way of resolving conflict.[12] The combination of risk and protective factors is unique to each individual. This helps explain why some people and communities survive and even thrive in high-risk environments while others do not. Within this framework, it is important to note that there is no mechanical relationship between these factors and outcomes: risk factors do not cause violence, and protective factors do not prevent it. Rather, they influence the way individuals and communities respond to violence. Programs based on this model can be divided into three main categories: primary prevention, focused on the broad population; secondary prevention, targeted at individuals at a higher risk of perpetrating violence; and tertiary prevention, directed at those who have already engaged in violence.

In the mass atrocity prevention field, Randle DeFalco argues that reframing atrocities as "public health catastrophes, rather than spectacles of violence," would help to improve the understanding of this type of violence as "complex social processes of large-scale intentional harm causation" and lead to policy responses that, instead of focusing on individual behaviors, include a combination of short-term interventions to stop violence and longer-term efforts focused on structural changes that address social factors contributing to it.[13] The public health perspective applied to this field is connected to what experts in mass atrocities commonly refers to as "upstream prevention," which also aims to address the root causes and risk factors that contribute to mass violence, including inequality, discrimination, and historical grievances and social injustices. Upstream prevention recognizes the complex intersection of social, political, economic, and cultural factors, in which identity may play a key role in the onset of violence, and proposes measures for early intervention. These include broad strategies to promote human rights and the rule of law, strengthening social cohesion and participatory processes, addressing structural poverty and inequalities, and others that resonate with multisectoral integrated violence prevention plans.

The incorporation of the public health approach into prevention and protection practices therefore confirms that solutions to violence in the urban space must go beyond criminal justice approaches in order to address the root causes of violence. This is especially the case with identity based violence, given its systematic and structural drivers. There is also a growing evidence base suggesting that a combined public health and criminal justice approach, which includes social prevention policies targeted at the root causes of violence as well as deterrence policies, is most effective in reducing violence at the city level.[14]

The shift in conceptualization and consequent demands to revise responses to violence was increasingly accompanied by an urbanization trend that placed municipal governments at the heart of responses. Local authorities usually possess an acute understanding of their city context, communities, and constituencies. In theory, they would therefore be in a great position to target resources more effectively to the geographic areas and populations where they are most needed,[15] if provided with the adequate resources and having the political will (both being significant caveats).

From an atrocity prevention perspective, cities can also play a key role in the implementation and support of the Responsibility to Protect. This principle was endorsed by world leaders at the United Nations World Summit in 2005 as a representation of the global commitment to prevent and respond to "genocide, war crimes, ethnic cleansing, and crimes against humanity," and of states' responsibility to protect their populations.[16] City-led protection efforts can help address structural violence, providing capacity building to strengthen local institutions and civil society organizations working on conflict prevention, peacebuilding, and by promoting initiatives to foster dialogue and strengthen social cohesion.

Common Elements in Successful City-Led Urban Violence Prevention and Protection Efforts

Balanced and Focused

When cities are placed at the heart of combined public health and criminal justice policy responses to violence, a few trends emerge around effective local-led responses. First, integrated strategies that are needed include targeted interventions toward higher-risk groups, individuals, neighborhoods, and behaviors.[17] This principle responds to the evidence-based knowledge that violence in the urban space is a concentrated phenomenon, occurring in specific microenvironments, in many cases down to the street level. It is also usually committed by a small number of people and linked to certain high-risk behaviors, such as carrying a gun, belonging to a criminal organization, or substance and alcohol abuse.[18] Consequently, targeting resources toward these geographic hot spots increases the effective potential of prevention efforts. This knowledge has led to the mainstreaming of three key approaches to violence prevention programming: place based, people based, and behavior based.

Place-based approaches focus on the influence that the built and social environments can have on criminal behavior. Crime Prevention Through Environmental Design (CPTED) is one operational tool of this approach. It proposes interventions to improve and adapt the urban environment to reduce the opportunity for crime. Hot-spot policing is another strategy, used by law enforcement to deploy more resources to areas with higher rates of crime. Problem-oriented policing, which uses data collection to shape law enforcement to community conditions, and community-oriented policing, which helps to strengthen the relationship between communities and the police, are other types of place-based programs that have shown promising results.[19]

People-based approaches with the strongest evidence on violence prevention outcomes include cognitive behavioral therapy[20]; early childhood interventions, such as positive-parenting training; school insertion; employment programs; and focused deterrence (also commonly known as Ceasefire or Group Violence Reduction Strategy, or GVRS), which consists of targeting specialized police forces, social services, and community stakeholders toward the needs of a small group of violent offenders.[21]

Finally, behavior-based approaches include restriction to access to firearms as well as to alcohol consumption, for example through the increase of prices or limitation of hours when it is sold, improving safety of bars and clubs, and enhancing services for substance abusers. It also includes restorative justice interventions that promote dialogue between offenders and victims and their families to promote healing and reduce recidivism.

Most of the promising practices of urban violence prevention and protection implemented in the United States and Latin America over the past decade have taken into account some of the above-mentioned approaches. Palmira, located in southwestern Colombia, is one example. In 2020, the local government launched a strategy to reduce homicide rates by providing opportunities to the city's youth and diverting them from gangs and illicit economies (see Box 1).

Box 1 Palmira's Efforts to Interrupt the Cycle of Violence and Build Resilience Located in southwestern Colombia, Palmira has ranked for years among the 50 most violent cities in the world, according to the Mexican nongovernmental organization Seguridad y Paz. In 2011, the city's homicide rate was 98.1 per 100,000, almost three times the national average at the time. The majority of homicide victims were youths, and territorial control by criminal organizations and gangs, as well as an overall lack of opportunities for youth and interpersonal conflicts at the community level, were identified as some of the main causes of the high levels of violence.

In that context, in 2020 the local government launched the Peace and Opportunities Strategy (PAZOS, *Paz y Oportunidades*), aimed at reducing homicide rates among those 14–29 by providing targeted youth with social and economic opportunities to divert them from gangs and illicit economies. The integrated strategy, with a strong social component and targeted at the most violent neighborhoods in the city, is divided into five mains pillars of intervention: interruption, which tries to dissuade violent behavior through the mediation of some sort of violence interrupters; intervention, by providing psychosocial support, social-emotional learning, training, and economic support, aimed at providing legal income-generating activities; prevention, which offers social and cultural opportunities for youth in their free time, conflict resolution, and interventions to reduce the use of psychoactive substances; safe environments, focused on improvements in the urban spaces affected by violence, opening adequate areas for community congregation; and access to justice, which includes activities of restorative justice. PAZOS's implementation involves a large network of partners, from different levels of government (i.e., national, state, and city) and sectors (e.g., education, health, justice) to the private sector, international cooperation, and community-based organizations.[22]

A recent evaluation of one of PAZOS's flagship programs, *Forjar Oportunidades*, funded by the Open Society Foundations, found sufficient statistical evidence to attribute four avoided deaths with the implementation of the intervention between 2021 and 2022. The evaluation also showed positive results in the lives of the almost 300 youths involved in the program. One year after joining the program, 85% of the participants reported a reduction in the use of psychoactive substances; 86% wrote their Curriculum Vitae and 67% responded to job opportunities, demonstrating increased involvement with the labor market; and 50% reported agreeing to settle differences through dialogue rather than violence. In 2022, Palmira's PAZOS strategy won the United Cities and Local Governments (UCLG) Peace Prize 2022, an award that celebrates local governments that implement successful peace initiatives in their communities.[23]

Examples of Place-, People-, and Behavior-Based Interventions

Street Outreach and Violence Interruption

Balanced and focused approaches include violence reduction programs that use basic concepts of epidemic control methods, such as community violence interruption, outreach to those at highest risk, community mobilization, and social norms and behavior change. The Cure Violence model, first implemented in Chicago in 2000 and adapted to several other cities, is a pioneer in that regard. Based on the concept of violence transmission previously described, its main objective is to stop the spread of violence through targeted interventions focused on the smaller portion of places and people that concentrate lethal violence. The program trains community members to deescalate potentially violent conflicts and connect high-risk individuals with broader services to deter violent behavior and promote a shift in norms and behaviors. Outreach workers are selected from the target communities, based on their credibility with and access to individuals at highest risk of being involved in violent episodes.

In New York City and Chicago, Cure Violence has been credited with a decrease in shootings of 63% and 48% respectively. In Trinidad and Tobago, a 45% reduction in lethal violence was reported.[24] However, different analyses have suggested that the overall evidence base about this model is promising but mixed[25] and not as consistent across sites.[26] Critics of the model point to high numbers of staff turnover among those who have strong and credible relationships with target communities. The links of the program with law enforcement can also be a challenge because of the historical problems of trust between agents and target communities.

Group Violence Reduction Strategies

The GVRS or Ceasefire model (also known as focused deterrence) follows some similar principles of violence interruption but relies on a stronger engagement with law enforcement. Its ultimate goal is to promote behavior change among high-risk individuals through the implementation of combined actions led by the police, community mobilization, and the provision of social services. Different evaluations have found this type of program to have the largest direct impact on reduction of crime and violence.[27] However, some critics of the model point to its elevated focus—even if well targeted—on the traditional criminal justice system, that is, policing and incarceration.[28]

In Oakland, a city that has gained significant attention for having cut its annual shootings and homicides nearly in half between 2012 and 2019,[29] Ceasefire—a key component of the city's overall violence prevention strategy—has been identified as largely responsible for the overall crime reduction (see Box 2).[30]

> **Box 2 Oakland's Ceasefire Strategy** Oakland's approach to violence reduction has gained significant attention in recent years. According to an evaluation by Anthony Braga et al., its main strategy—Oakland Ceasefire—was largely responsible for the overall violence reduction in the city.[31] This strategy is based on a partnership between community members, social service providers, and law enforcement officials, and divided into five main components: analysis of violence incidents and trends; in-person communications with high-risk individuals to warn about the risks of ongoing violence and offer assistance; provision of social services to high-risk individuals through the Oakland Unite network of community-based organizations; focused law enforcement actions by the Oakland Police Department's Ceasefire Section and training in the principles of procedural justice and other strategies to improve police-community relationships; and an integrated management and coordination structure that provides for regular communications between partners. In 2017, the city also created, for the first time, a Department of Violence Prevention. One of the main objectives of this office is to improve responses to victims and families, building a strong support network of people with credibility and trust to access communities. A broad report on lessons learned from this case highlighted the importance of community engagement and partnerships established for its achievements.[32] Despite this success, there have been criticisms from

communities with histories of mistrust with the police, who at times perceived the strategy as based too much on its policing element.

Gang Violence Prevention

The discussions above also apply to the prevention of youth involvement in gangs. Youth gang or group involvement is often grounded in a search for collective identity—a shared sense of belonging with a broader community or group, especially when protective factors to be provided by the state, community, or families are not in place. Although poverty, social exclusion, and lack of educational and job opportunities for youth have been commonly associated with high levels of gang violence,[33] a significant body of research has demonstrated how gang affiliation and gang violence are also connected to deeper issues that are directly linked to identity.[34] In the absence of other role models, these groups represent discipline, leadership, comradery, and social connection in gang members' lives.[35]

Effective prevention of gang violence relies on the collaboration of a wide range of stakeholders, especially communities themselves, and should combine primary, secondary, and tertiary prevention efforts and include tutoring, mentoring, life skills training, case management, and parental and school involvement.[36] Los Angeles and El Salvador provide interesting lessons in that regard. While gang violence remains a great challenge in both places, Los Angeles has seen positive results in the implementation of a comprehensive program to tackle these issues, whereas El Salvador has been linked to dangerous hardline approaches that violate basic due process guarantees and human rights and could be seen as identity based violence in itself, given its indiscriminate targeting of male youth (see Box 3).

Box 3 Los Angeles and El Salvador Responses to Gang Violence In El Salvador, hardline/*mano dura*[37] policies have been the default government response to gang violence since the 2000s. This policy approach has led incarceration rates to skyrocket, pressuring even further already-low-capacity institutions, allowing prisons to become headquarters for the organization of gangs, and increasing reporting of several human rights abuses. More recently, the administration of President Nayib Bukele took that approach to another level. In 2022, he placed the country in a state of exception and implemented over 15 legal reforms that made sentences for gang-related crimes harsher. As a result, more than 75,000 people have been arrested since, according to the government, and El Salvador now has the highest incarceration rate in the world.[38] Although homicides have declined, in a trend that had started prior to Bukele's administration, critics have reported massive human rights violations and unjustified arrests of thousands of people.[39]

The capacity of such measures in sustaining the decline in violent crime is also uncertain. El Salvador's history with *mano dura* policies has made clear that homicide rates eventually reescalate. These quick fixes not only do not address the root causes of the problem, but, on the contrary, may exacerbate them further in the longer run, as seen in the past.[40]

In stark contrast, in 2007, Los Angeles established the Office of Gang Reduction and Youth Development (GRYD). GRYD follows a comprehensive strategy and whole-family approach that includes community engagement, with activities targeting the entire community to build resilience against risk factors linked to gang affiliation and violence; prevention services for youth development and support to their families; intervention services targeted at youth already involved in gang activity, with family case management services and the provision of alternatives for youth; and interruption and peacebuilding activities. A multiyear evaluation published in 2015 found that GRYD implementation coincided with a decline in gang violence at the city and community levels and pointed to positive findings at the individual and family levels. However, the study identified mixed evidence when looking at the performance of GRYD Zones with comparison areas.[41]

Acknowledging Structural Inequalities and Discrimination

Violence prevention and protection practices targeted at specific places and people often overlap with the predominance of higher social vulnerabilities of specific groups and an overall absence of the state.[42] The socioeconomic marginalization that tends to define these areas and populations are often the manifestation of structural inequalities and historical discrimination. Therefore, targeted policy responses should also acknowledge the role that institutions have played on the legacies of targeted discrimination and include measures that respond to this, such as capacity building of the police in the area of human rights.

The most recent violence prevention plan developed by Baltimore offers a good example of efforts to prevent violence while acknowledging the city's institutions' legacy of targeted discrimination. Baltimore's multiyear Comprehensive Violence Prevention Plan[43] has a strong focus on promoting healing and reconciliation and rebuilding trust between citizens and law enforcement (see Box 4).

Box 4 Baltimore Efforts to Prevent Violence by Promoting Equity and Healing and Building Trust Gun violence, police brutality, and social inequality have for decades defined the lives of many Baltimore residents. Recognizing these challenges and the different lived experiences of specific groups, such as Black youth, immigrants, and the LGBTQ+ community, in 2021, the mayor launched the city's first holistic public safety strategy, the Comprehensive Violence Prevention Plan.[44] Although community members still criticize the government for the overall lack of safety, it represents a shift from an overreliance on policing, prosecution, and arrests, traditionally targeted at young Black males, and has a strong focus on promoting healing and reconciliation and rebuilding trust between citizens and authorities. The plan is anchored on three key pillars: (1) a public health approach that identifies the causes or risk factors associated with violence in order to establish the proposed solutions and take them to scale, and that focuses on gun violence prevention, victim services, youth justice, community healing, and trauma-informed practice and reentry; (2) community engagement, stakeholder coordination, and collaboration focused on improving relationships with the police, building key partnerships, improving interagency coordination (local, state, and federal), and investing in neighborhood engagement and capacity building; and (3) evaluation and accountability that emphasize community perception of safety and police accountability.

Baltimore's plan proposes a multisectoral approach that acknowledges that equitable access to basic services and community development are tied to feelings of safety and violence dynamics, and that different sectors, institutions, agencies and organizations, beyond the police, have a role to play in preventing violence. As part of its focus on building community trust and reconciliation, the plan also includes actions by the police department to acknowledge and repair harm done to Black communities through the promotion of permanent spaces for dialogue with communities, and other city agencies to recognize and transform their role in the perpetuation of structural and institutional racism.

The plan also emphasizes a trauma-responsive, healing-centered, and equity-based approach, recognizing the impacts of untreated trauma and retraumatization that communities experiencing high incidents of violence suffer, and includes interventions to build community capacity for self-healing and the expansion of services for survivors of gun violence and different forms of gender based violence, such as interpersonal violence, sexual assault, and human trafficking.

The development of this new strategy was accompanied by the creation or strengthening of dedicated offices that aim to address the needs and healing of specific groups. It is also aligned with a recent national effort—the US Comprehensive Strategy to Prevent and Respond to Gun Crime and Ensure Public Safety, also launched in 2021—which placed significant investments in evidence-based community violence interventions.

At the programmatic level, Safe Streets is one example of community violence interventions targeted at disadvantaged and Black communities in Baltimore that has been running for a long time and will continue to be part of the city's public safety strategy.[45] Inspired by the Cure Violence interruption model, the program is implemented in neighborhoods that have high levels of gun violence and have suffered from structural racism and lack of investments. It operates through the intermediation of frontline workers who are able to engage with people at highest risk of committing violence and mediate disputes, promote nonviolent norms for settling disputes, and connect program participants to services. Safe Streets was fully operational in 11 Baltimore neighborhoods between 2007 and 2021; in six of those sites for less than three years. In the most recent impact evaluation of the program, Daniel Webster, Carla Tilchin, and Mitchell Doucette found an average reduction of 32% in homicides in the five longest-running sites in the first four years of implementation but no significant change in homicides in the six newer program sites.[46] The SideStep Youth Diversion Program is another community violence intervention included in the plan and codeveloped with communities in select neighborhoods of the city following the death of Freddie Gray in 2015 in police custody. The design of the program was part of truth-and-reconciliation conversations. Instead of immediately referring youth to the criminal justice system after they commit a mistake, the program provides community-based support.

Principles of Good Practice

Data Driven

All the elements and interventions described above require a significant number of investments in data collection and analysis. In order to implement balanced, focused, and integrated interventions, local governments need good data to establish which areas, people, and behaviors need to be targeted, and they need solid monitoring systems to hold different sectors and stakeholders accountable. From a programming perspective, in Latin America this has translated into the implementation of local observatories of public security (or similar mechanisms) responsible for collecting and analyzing detailed crime-related data to understand trends and patterns and design strategic responses.[47] These agencies have contributed to the development of local diagnostics to inform local prevention policies and plans. In the United States, such plans are often based on problem-analyses exercises, which consist of systematic processes of data collection and analysis used by law enforcement and criminal justice professionals to understand, assess, and address specific crime-related issues within a city or community, as done in the case of Baltimore and Oakland. In all city cases mentioned in this chapter, platforms (or similar tools) were created to disseminate crime and violence data and promote accountability.

Data-driven plans and strategies also mean investing in evidence-based programs, which have been tested and evaluated before. This is the case of Pelotas in southern Brazil, which designed a multisectoral violence prevention program comprising a series of evidence-based interventions (see Box 5).

Box 5 Pelotas Data-Driven Public Health and Criminal Justice Approach to Violence Reduction The city of Pelotas, Brazil, saw an unprecedented spike in violence and crime starting in the early 2000s, with homicide rates jumping from 6.6 per 100,000 residents in 2000 to 31.5 in 2017. As a response, in 2017, the city government launched the Pact Pelotas for Peace, a multisectoral strategy to promote peace and reduce crime and violence designed in partnership with two civil society organizations. The strategy included over 30 different programs, mostly evidence based, around five main areas of intervention: police and justice, administrative oversight,[48] technology,[49] social prevention,[50] and urbanism.[51]

The programs comprised a series of evidence-based primary, secondary, and tertiary prevention interventions, from a positive parenting program to youth violence prevention interventions focused on youth at risk to develop an individual life plan, with psychosocial support and life skills; social reinsertion for those who have been in the criminal justice system; restorative justice; school interventions; and focused deterrence. When combined, all the interventions' activities span the life cycle of an individual and cover the different dimensions of the social ecological model of public health: individual, family and peers, community, and societal levels. It also included training and capacity building support for local security guards, including on human rights.

> This complex multisector strategy also involved the creation of different structures of government to improve coordination among different actors and sectors, such as the Municipal Security Secretary; the Integrated Management Committee; an integrated committee focused specifically on prevention; and a public security observatory. Findings from an impact evaluation[52] showed that the pact has led to an overall 9% reduction in homicide and 7% reduction in robbery in the city. Although the authors of the evaluation caution that some results may have been influenced by other factors, they suggest that the pact is a good example of how city-level interventions that combine public health and criminal justice approaches can be effective in tackling violence.

Participatory, Legitimate, and Community Oriented

Another promising practice is the establishment of permanent spaces and mechanisms for constant dialogue between governments, civil society, and communities, which allow for the institutionalization of citizen engagement throughout the violence-prevention-and-mitigation policy process. The maintenance of these spaces can be challenging, as they need to overcome histories of mistrust between communities and authorities, especially the police. For this reason, participatory processes, from Diagnostics or Problem Analyses of the local security context to the design, prioritization, monitoring, and implementation of interventions and policies, are crucial to ensure local ownership, adaptation to local contexts, representation of community needs, and sustainability over time. Furthermore, citizen involvement and the transparent dissemination of information play vital roles in establishing the legitimacy of governmental initiatives executed on a local scale.[53]

Another component among policy responses that has been increasingly highlighted in the literature is its community-driven factor. While some of the discussed practices may rely more or less on community members and networks, and others still ensure a heavy link with traditional criminal justice system elements, all of them acknowledge the importance of implementing evidence-informed strategies through community-centered initiatives. Ultimately, community violence interventions are based on a relationship of trust and engagement of individual and community assets to provide a series of services and help disrupt cycles of violence.

Medellín, Colombia, offers a great example of participatory approaches to violence prevention and protection, with citizens playing a key role in the identification of local needs and decision-making priorities, through the development of territorial-based Integrated Security and Coexistence Municipal Plans. This was key to help rebuild trust and legitimacy between communities and authorities and ensure sustained periods of peace.[54] Although challenges remain, the city has continued to innovate in this area throughout the years (see Box 6).

> **Box 6 Medellin Holistic and Participatory Approach to Violence Reduction** Medellin, Colombia's second-largest city, was known in the early 1990s as the most violent city in the world, with homicide rates nearing 400 per 100,000 people as a war against Pablo Escobar's cartel unfolded. With his death in 1993 and the decay of his criminal organization, a significant reduction in violent crime followed. Homicides started to pick up again with the urbanization of the country's long-standing conflict and insurgent and counterinsurgent groups controlling entire territories of the city.
>
> In 2002, with homicide rates at 179 homicides for every 100,000 inhabitants,[55] a major integrated effort between different levels of government was launched, and the city was able to make a real turn. Over the following decade, a combination of measures led to a period of sustained crime decline and stability. These included national and locally led security policies to retake control of some areas, the demobilization of paramilitaries, control by drug lord and paramilitary leader Don Berna over criminal groups' violent behavior, and massive investments in integrated urban and social interventions.[56]
>
> For the next fifteen years, the city's integrated, holistic, and participatory approach to security—focused on social investment, urban development, citizen engagement, and improvement of local government capacities in security[57]—became a model duplicated by many other local governments in the region. The city's strategy represented a recognition

of the local government potential to address some of the structural causes of violence, linked to poverty, inequality, lack of opportunities, and exclusion. Its investments in education, health, housing, and social inclusion, and targeted at vulnerable territories and youth at risk, was seen as contributing to improving communities' well-being and social behavior, and to promoting trust and community integration.[58] The participatory approach in the identification of local needs and decision-making priorities was also key to help rebuild trust and legitimacy.[59] Research tried to measure the specific impacts of interventions on the public transit system and local infrastructure on violence reduction, with one (limited) study pointing to a 66% greater homicide reduction in neighborhoods that had benefited from them, compared to others that hadn't, over four years.[60]

Parallel initiatives to improve police training and promote community policing efforts, among other actions with law enforcement and justice, were also promoted. Similarly, many researchers emphasize the need to acknowledge the importance of criminal organizations' control over violence in the overall reduction of lethal crime in the city.[61]

The Medellin case and its continuous innovation in social and urban investments and other civilian alternatives to policing still provide important lessons for other cities. In 2018, the city government launched the Coexistence Operation (*Operación Convivencia*). Similar to city efforts in the United States to increase broad-based local civilian capacity for prevention and first response to violence, the program initially created a task force to prioritize Medellin's main service agencies (including dispute resolutions officers and basic services, such as street lights) in 40 communities. Each of these neighborhoods then received a full-time representative from the city government, responsible for helping to strengthen community government organizations, identifying and articulating public service needs, and connecting disputants to professional mediators or family-services officials from the government in the case of serious issues. The overall objective was to expand a broad range of regular municipal services and community organization. The program lasted 20 months, and an evaluation of it found, surprisingly, no overall impact on reported governance, legitimacy of the state, or crime. However, the authors did find significant differences in results in neighborhoods where the state began weak (i.e., was more absent) versus those where the state had a much stronger presence (e.g., in terms of service provision) from the start, and where the program delivered, state legitimacy increased, and crime and emergency calls declined.[62]

In 2022, Medellín had its lowest number of murders in decades—fewer than 15 per 100,000.

In the United States, the recognition of the importance of engaging communities in the responses to violence has led to significant investment in community violence interventions. Ideally, such investments include connecting a city's violence prevention infrastructure with offices that often work in silos—such as public health, urban planning, and development—together with community-based organizations, to implement multisectoral strategies that address violence dynamics.[63]

Community-driven efforts have been particularly crucial when it comes to protection responses to identity based violence perpetrated against specific groups. In New York, for example, the creation of the Office for the Prevention of Hate Crimes helped the city strengthen its coordination with community-based organizations and improve prevention and response services to identity based violence (see Box 7).

Box 7 New York City Interagency and Community-Oriented Approach to Hate Crime Prevention and Response In 2019, in response to an escalation of identity based violence, New York City government created the Office for the Prevention of Hate Crimes (OPHC).[64] Tasked with preventing and responding to hate crimes, the OPHC coordinates multisectoral efforts that act on the issues that fuel identity based violence (such as prejudice, bigotry, and hate) and supports community-driven strategies and practices that promote healing of victims and their communities. Its prevention work is focused on public education and community outreach and safety models. When crime occurs, the office and its partners enhance response actions beyond the typical law enforcement methods, building on community initiatives to bring communities together through joint activities and dialogue. The office also works with law enforcement to provide training and improve

> its responses in order to address the concerns of vulnerable communities and improve the reporting of hate crimes.
> Through an Interagency Committee on Hate Crimes, the OPHC coordinates a citywide response that includes civil society organizations who provide mental health services to victims and families. In 2021, the OPHC launched the Partners Against the Hate initiative with six anchor organizations, investing $2.4 million in funding on hate crime prevention and response. These organizations were able to subcontract others, building an unprecedented capacity to address hate crime in the city. These flexible funding mechanisms enabled organizations not traditionally funded by government agencies or lacking the required institutional structure to secure contracts, directly allowing the office to expand its reach and fostering more-diverse coalitions.
> One of the OPHC key areas of focus is to enhance data collection and dissemination about hate crimes. The office has its own dashboard to monitor hate crimes in the city.[65] When gaps in data provided by law enforcement are identified, for example, partner organizations can conduct needs assessments with communities. Now in its third year of operation, the OPHC is applying for funds to evaluate some elements of its program. The results of the evaluation may provide important lessons for the city and other cities in the country in their fight against hate crime.

Multsectoral, Multiactor, Coordinated, and Institutionalized

Balanced, targeted, and legitimate practices are also inherently multisectoral and need to be led by a multitude of actors and partners in an integrated and coordinated manner.[66] Designing integrated local plans or strategies such as the ones implemented in Baltimore, Medellín, Oakland, and Pelotas is key to ensuring that different and interrelated forms of city violence are addressed, context-specific problems are prioritized, and different sectors and actors will work together toward the same overall goals. This also implies ensuring the political prioritization and institutionalization of the violence prevention and protection agenda, for example through the creation of different bureaucracies such as municipal offices of violence prevention and coordination mechanisms to ensure that the whole of government works effectively.

The presence of intrainstitutional coordination mechanisms can also contribute to the continuity of policies and programs across various administrations, provided they receive adequate funding and staffing, operate within a robust bureaucratic framework, and are supported by reliable information systems. In Baltimore, for example, the development of the recent public security strategy was accompanied by the creation or strengthening of dedicated bureaucracies that aim to address the needs and healing of specific groups, such as the new Mayor's Office of LGBTQ Affairs, the Mayor's Office of Immigrant Affairs, the Mayor's Office of African American Male Engagement (all funded by the city government), and community-based organizations. In Oakland, in 2017, the city created its first Department of Violence Prevention.[67]

Finally, it should be mentioned that national legislation and policy guidelines, as well as global frameworks (such as R2P and the Sustainable Development Goals[68]), can also serve as important incentives for local governments to implement effective prevention and protection practices. In Colombia, for example, a national policy requires that local governments design the Integrated Security and Coexistence Municipal Plans. In the United States, the Comprehensive Strategy to Prevent and Respond to Gun Crime and Ensure Public Safety, launched in 2021, placed significant investments in evidence-based community violence interventions. National mechanisms can also play a role in strengthening community and local actors' actions, stimulating the expansion of local knowledge about the law, implementing community-based early warning systems, and securing human rights documentation.

Conclusions

This chapter highlights the fact that city-level prevention and protection efforts have the potential to address structural and acute violence. By directing resources toward marginalized places and groups affected by social and economic exclusion, these efforts aim to mitigate the impact of structural inequalities and historical discrimination. Moreover, these initiatives recognize the identities and potential of these marginalized groups as active contributors to solutions.

The intentional design and targeting of such policies and programs, guided by an equity and justice lens, are evident in the increased incorporation of public health approaches within public security policies, with a combination of social interventions and improvements in criminal justice responses, along with enhanced capacities of authorities and communities to prevent violence and improve responses. The integration of a public health approach is particularly crucial for addressing the root causes of various forms of violence, especially identity-based violence with its systemic and structural drivers.

These targeted policy responses also acknowledge the role of institutions in perpetuating targeted discrimination and include measures such as strengthening the police's human rights' knowledge. Additionally, they also emphasize the involvement of communities as key partners in driving these processes.

While this chapter recognizes the challenge of sustaining the results of such interventions, even with a combination of short- and long-term measures, it emphasizes that there is sufficient evidence available from which valuable lessons can be learned.

Acknowledgements The author thanks the following experts for their invaluable contributions: Alberto Koptike, Annie Bird, Bojan Cruz, Daniel Friedman, Daniel Hooton, Guillermo Cespedes, Hassan Naveed, Jairo Garcia, Jeremy Biddle, Paul Devulder, Pilar de La Torre, Santiago Tobon, and Sara Batmanglich.

Notes

1. A recent review of impact evaluations of city-level (or equivalent) violence and/or crime reduction strategies identified 13 quantitative studies among 1,721 articles on the topic, five of which were conducted in the United States and two in Brazil. Nonetheless, the authors of the review conclude that violence prevention

programs led by city governments are effective tools to address violence, but they emphasize the urgent need for more evaluations. Michelle Degli Esposti et al., "Effects of the Pelotas (Brazil) Peace Pact on Violence and Crime: A Synthetic Control Analysis," *Lancet Regional Health—Americas* 19 (2023): 2. Another significant gap in evaluation efforts related to violence prevention is linked to programs to specifically address violence perpetrated by state actors in urban areas, which range from excessive use of force to extrajudicial killings and disappearances. F. Carbonari et al., "A Review of the Evidence and a Global Strategy for Violence Prevention," New York University/CIC Working Paper, 2020.
2. Chioda, Laura. *Stop the Violence in Latin America: A Look at Prevention from Cradle to Adulthood*. Washington, DC, World Bank, 2017.
3. Basombrío, C., and L. Dammert. *Seguridad y populismo punitivo en América Latina: lecciones corroboradas, constataciones nove dosas y temas emergentes*. Wilson Center, Latin American Program, 2013.
4. Muggah, Robert. "The Rise of Citizen Security in Latin America and the Caribbean." In *Alternative Pathways to Sustainable Development: Lessons from Latin America*, 291–322. International Development Policy series no. 9. Geneva, Boston: Graduate Institute Publications, Brill-Nijhoff, 2017.
5. Ibid.
6. In 2021, the United States ranked first in gun-related homicides among high-income countries with more than 10 million people, with a rate of 4.52 per 100,000 population. This was 19 times greater than the rate registered in France, 77 times greater than in Germany, and 33 times than in Australia. Leach-Kemon, Katherine, Sirull, Rebecca and Glenn, Scott. "On Gun Violence, the United States Is an Outlier." Institute for Health Metrics and Evaluation, October 31, 2023.
7. A 2023 study found that between 1998 and 2019, the United States accounted for 73% of 139 mass shootings that occurred in developed countries, registering 101 attacks and 816 deaths over that period. The study considered a mass shooting an incident involving at least four victims and "a gun violence incident

carried out in one or more public or populated locations within 24 hours, involving at least some victims chosen at random and/or for their symbolic value." Silva, Jason R. "Global Mass Shootings: Comparing the United States against Developed and Developing Countries." *International Journal of Comparative and Applied Criminal Justice* 47, no. 4 (March 2023): 317–340. https://doi.org/10.1080/01924036.2022.2052126.
8. Dahlberg L. L., and J. A. Mercy. "History of Violence as a Public Health Issue." *AMA Virtual Mentor* 11, no. 2 (February 2009): 167–172. http://virtualmentor.ama-assn.org/2009/02/mhst1-0902.html.
9. In 1997, the World Health Assembly adopted resolution 49.25, which established the prevention of violence as a public health priority. World Health Assembly. Prevention of Violence: A Public Health Priority. WHA 49.25, 49th session, May 25, 1996. https://www.emro.who.int/violence-injuries-disabilities/resolutions/resolutions.html.
10. World Health Organization. World Report on Violence and Health. Geneva: World Health Organization, October 3, 2002. https://www.who.int/publications/i/item/9241545615.
11. Today, the WHO has a Prevention of Violence Unit focused on preventing interpersonal violence in all its forms, especially violence against children. The unit provides strategic leadership and capacity building for governments; develops evidence, norms, and standards; and promotes global advocacy around the topic. For more information, see World Health Organization. "World Health Organization Violence Prevention Unit: Approach, Objectives and Activities, 2022–2026." World Health Organization, 2022. https://www.who.int/teams/social-determinants-of-health/violence-prevention.
12. Dahlberg L.L., and E. G. Krug. "Violence: A Global Public Health Problem." In *World Report on Violence and Health*, edited by E. G. Krug, L. L. Dahlberg, J. A. Mercy, A. B. Zwi, and R. Lozano, 1-21. Geneva, Switzerland: World Health Organization, 2002.

13. DeFalco, Randle. "(Re)Conceptualizing Atrocity Crimes as Public Health Catastrophes." In *Public Health, Mental Health, and Mass Atrocity Prevention*, edited by Jocelyn Getgen Kestenbaum, Caitlin O. Mahoney, Amy E. Meade, and Arlan F. Fuller, 17–31. London: Routledge, 2021, 25. https://ssrn.com/abstract=3908637.
14. Esposti et al. "Effects of the Pelotas (Brazil) Peace Pact on Violence and Crime: A Synthetic Control Analysis." *Lancet Regional Health—Americas* 19 (2023); Krug E. G., J. A. Mercy, L. L. Dahlberg, and A. B. Zwi. "The World Report on Violence and Health." *Lancet* 360 (2002): 1083–1088; World Bank. *Pathways for Peace: Inclusive Approaches to Preventing Violent Conflict*. Washington, DC: World Bank, 2018. https://doi.org/10.1596/978-1-4648-1162-3; K. Hughes et al., Hughes, K., M. A. Bellis, K. A. Hardcastle, Butchart, A.,Dahlberg, L., Mercy, J. A., Mikton, C. "Global Development and Diffusion of Outcome Evaluation Research for Interpersonal and Self-Directed Violence Prevention from 2007 to 2013: A Systematic Review." *Aggression and Violent Behavior* 19, no. 6 (November–December 2014): 655–662; Cerdá M., Tracy M., Keyes K.M. "Reducing Urban Violence: A Contrast of Public Health and Criminal Justice Approaches". Epidemiology. 2018 Jan; 29(1): 142–150. https://doi.org/10.1097/EDE.0000000000000756. PMID: 28926374; PMCID: PMC5718925.
15. Beato, C., and A. M. Silveira. "Effectiveness and Evaluation of Crime Prevention Programs in Minas Gerais." *Stability: International Journal of Security and Development* 3, no. 1 (May 16, 2014): 20. DOI: http://doi.org/10.5334/sta.dr.
16. Sitther, Theo, and Rachel Locke. "Preventing Identity-Based Mass Violence in Cities." Discussion paper, Stanley Center for Peace and Security/Impact Peace, December 2020.
17. Peace in Our Cities, Guiding Principles and Inspiring Actions: Operationalizing the Resolution to Reduce Urban Violence, October 2022.
18. Carbonari et al., "Review of the Evidence."
19. Ibid.
20. M. P. Bhatt et al. "Predicting and Preventing Gun Violence: An Experimental Evaluation of Readi Chicago." *The Quarterly Journal*

of Economics, Volume 139, Issue 1, February 2024, Pages 1–56, https://doi.org/10.1093/qje/qjad031.
21. Carbonari et al., "Review of the Evidence."
22. Alcaldía de Palmira. "Estrategia de Prevencion Social de la Violencia PAZOS." Palmira City Government Website, 2020, https://palmira.gov.co/wp-content/uploads/2022/09/Infografia-PAZOS-L.pdf.
23. Open Society Foundations. "Q&A: How One Colombian City Is Tackling Violent Crime." Voices. Open Society Foundations, December 15, 2022. https://www.opensocietyfoundations.org/voices/q-and-a-how-one-colombian-city-is-tackling-violent-crime; Alcaldía de Palmira. "Indicators for the Monitoring, Follow-Up, and Result of the Strategy Aimed at the Reduction of Violence in Palmira, Colombia." October 4, 2022. https://palmira.gov.co/wp-content/uploads/2023/03/Indicators-for-the-monitoring-of-violence.pdf.
24. Sheyla A. Delgado et al. *The Effects of Cure Violence in the South Bronx and East New York, Brooklyn*. John Jay College, 2017. https://johnjayrec.nyc/2017/10/02/cvinsobronxeastny/; Henry, D. B., S. Knoblauch, and R. Sigurvinsdottir. *The Effect of Intensive Ceasefire Intervention on Crime in Four Chicago Police Beats: Quantitative Assessment*. Robert R. McCormick Foundation, 2014; Maguire, E., M. Oakley, and N. Corsaro. *Evaluating Cure Violence in Trinidad and Tobago*. Inter-American Development Bank, 2018.
25. Butts, J. A., C. G. Roman, L. Bostwick, and J. R. Porter. "Cure Violence: A Public Health Model to Reduce Gun Violence." *Annual Review of Public Health* 36 (March 2015): 39–53.
26. Ibid.; Skogan, W. G., S. M. Hartnett, N. Bump, and J. Dubois. *Evaluation of CeaseFire-Chicago*. Northwestern University, 2009; Webster, D. W., J. M. Whitehill, J. S. Vernick, and E. M. Parker. *Evaluation of Baltimore's Safe Streets Program: Effects on Attitudes, Participants' Experiences, and Gun Violence*. Baltimore, MD: Johns Hopkins Center for the Prevention of Youth Violence, 2012.
27. Abt, Thomas, and Christopher Winship. *What Works in Reducing Community Violence: A Meta-Review and Field Study for the*

Northern Triangle. United States Agency for International Development, February 2016; Braga, Anthony, Weisburd, David and Turchan, Brandon. "Focused Deterrence Strategies and Crime Control: An Updated Systematic Review and Meta-Analysis of the Empirical Evidence." Criminology and Public Policy 17, no. 1 (February 2018): 205–250. https://onlinelibrary.wiley.com/doi/epdf/10.1111/1745-9133.12353.
28. Berman, Greg. "No Program Is a Panacea: The Fate of Focused Deterrence." *Vital City*, March 2, 2022. Accessed August 15, 2023. https://www.vitalcitynyc.org/articles/no-program-is-a-panacea-the-fate-of-focused-deterrence.
29. Since the Covid-19 pandemic, Oakland has seen a spike in different types of crime.
30. Braga, Anthony et al. *Oakland Ceasefire Impact Evaluation: Key Findings*. Northeastern University and Rutgers University, August 10, 2018. https://www.kron4.com/wp-content/uploads/sites/11/2018/08/Oakland20Ceasefire20Impact20Evaluation20Key20Findings_1534990511552_52781602_ver1.0.pdf.
31. Ibid.
32. Giffords Law Center to Prevent Gun Violence. *A Case Study in Hope: Lessons from Oakland's Remarkable Reduction in Gun Violence*, April 23, 2019.
33. Ward, Thomas W. *Gangsters without Borders: An Ethnography of a Salvadoran Street Gang*. Oxford: Oxford University Press, 2013.
34. Family stress, peer pressure, and youth struggle for self-identity are among the complex factors that James Diego Vigil identifies as drivers of the emergence and persistence of gangs in Los Angeles. The author, a former youth worker, teacher, and parent, reveals, through interviews with actual gang members, how in the absence of other roles models, these groups represented parents, school, and law enforcement in gang members' lives. Vigil. *Barrio Gangs: Street Life and Identity in Southern California*. University of Texas Press, 1988.
35. In Central America, studies have also shown that gangs play an important social role in defining identity and social interaction. Thomas Ward's ethnography in El Salvador of the international

criminal organization Mara Salvatrucha, most commonly known as MS-13, demonstrates how survival—partially represented by a general sense of marginalization and disenfranchisement, status, and a deeply ingrained sense of identification, which he defines as a heart connection—helps to explain why youths join these gangs. Although his research focuses mostly on "hard core" MS-13 members, understanding this minority among the larger group helps to shed light on the gang affiliation process in El Salvador, as they represent the most active and dedicated ones while serving as role models for the others. Ward, *Gangsters without Borders*. Similar patterns can be seen in a survey conducted by Jose Miguel Cruz et al. with more than 1,100 active and retired Salvadoran gang members. The survey shows that kids join gangs to find the resources not provided by their families and communities, such as friendship, protection, resources, and self-confidence, and that is how the groups become the center of their lives. Therefore, gangs are not always or necessarily about generating revenue as much as they are about creating a collective identity that is constructed and reinforced by shared, often criminal experiences, especially acts of violence and expressions of social control. Cruz et al. *The New Face of Street Gangs: The Gang Phenomenon in El Salvador*. Florida International University, 2017.
36. Cahill, Meagan, Miriam Becker-Cohen, Jesse Jannetta, Ellen Paddock, Emily Tiry, Maria Serackos, and Samantha Lowry. *Evaluation of the Los Angeles Gang Reduction and Youth Development Program: Final Y1 Report*. Urban Institute, 2015.
37. *Mano dura*, which means "firm hand" in Spanish, refers to a set of policies and approaches that are characterized by a strong, often militarized, and punitive response to crime and violence.
38. Tiziano, Breda. "Why El Salvador's Anti-Crime Measures Cannot (and Should Not) Be Exported." Istituto Affari Internazionali (Rome), March 29, 2023. https://www.iai.it/en/pubblicazioni/why-el-salvadors-anti-crime-measures-cannot-and-should-not-be-exported; Ventas, Leire. "Coming Face to Face with Inmates in El Salvador's Mega-Jail." BBC, February 14, 2024. https://www.bbc.com/news/world-latin-america-68244963.

39. Tiziano, "Why El Salvador's Anti-Crime Measures."
40. While *mano dura* approaches may bring quick wins in reducing certain types of crimes, these tend to be short-lived and come at a very high cost. Among the many tradeoffs of the approach are human rights abuses, with the spread of harsh law-enforcement tactics, arbitrary detentions, extrajudicial killings, and violations of due process, to mention a few; criminalization of vulnerable groups, given the disproportional targeting of marginalized communities; and overcrowded prisons, which not only strain public resources and can decrease any potential for rehabilitation of these facilities but may also contribute to expanding criminal organization within these facilities. In addition, the overall lack of proper legal safeguards can erode public trust and undermine the rule of law in the medium and longer terms. Finally, by only focusing on punitive measures, these approaches ignore the roots causes of crime and violence, contributing to their unsustainability overtime. Carbonari et al., "Review of the Evidence"; "The Guardian View on El Salvador'S Crime Crackdown: A Short-Term, High Cost Fix." Editorial, *The Guardian* (London), July 2, 2023. https://www.theguardian.com/commentisfree/2023/jul/02/the-guardian-view-on-el-salvadors-crackdown-a-short-term-high-cost-fix.
41. Cahill et al., *Evaluation of the Los Angeles Gang Reduction and Youth Development Program: Final Y1 Report*.
42. Markowitz, Ariana. *Big Events on a Small Scale: Exploring Identity-Based Mass Violence in Cities*. Stanley Center for Peace and Security/Impact Peace, December 2020.
43. Scott, Brandon M. *Baltimore City Comprehensive Violence Prevention Plan*, July 1, 2021. https://mayor.baltimorecity.gov/sites/default/files/MayorScott-ComprehensiveViolencePreventionPlan-1.pdf.
44. Ibid.
45. Baltimore City Government. Mayor's Office of Neighborhood Safety and Engagement webpage. https://monse.baltimorecity.gov/safe-streets-new.

46. Daniel Webster, Carla Tilchin, and Mitchell Doucette. *Estimating the Effects of Safe Streets Baltimore on Gun Violence 2007–2022.* Johns Hopkins, 2022. https://publichealth.jhu.edu/sites/default/files/2023-10/estimating-the-effects-of-safe-streets-baltimore-on-gun-violence-july-2023.pdf. The authors also found an association of the program with a 23% reduction in nonfatal shootings across the full implementation period in all 11 sites and estimated an average of $7.2–$19.2 in economic benefits for every $1 invested in Safe Streets. According to evaluators, given the racial disparities in gun violence and incarceration rates in the country, programs of this type also help promote healthy equity and social justice.
47. Examples of such data are type, location, date, and time of occurrence of a crime, and characteristics of victims and offenders such as age, gender, race, and socioeconomic status.
48. Includes activities focused on preventing disturbance of the peace and preventing illegal commercialization of goods. See more at https://www.pelotas.rs.gov.br/pacto/25.
49. Includes the use of technological solutions to support violence prevention strategies, such as street cameras and vehicle tracking, all monitored in an integrated center of operations. See more at https://www.pelotas.rs.gov.br/pacto/22.
50. Includes primary, secondary, and tertiary prevention activities, such as social and economic program targeted at youth. See more at https://www.pelotas.rs.gov.br/pacto/19?estrategia=1.
51. Includes urban renewal interventions, such as the revitalization of parks. See more at https://www.pelotas.rs.gov.br/pacto/24.
52. Esposti et al., "Effects of the Pelotas (Brazil) Peace Pact."
53. Beato and Silveira, "Effectiveness and Evaluation."
54. Carbonari et al., "Review of the Evidence"; Peace in Our Cities. "Peace in Our Cities Symposium: Innovations in Urban-Violence Reduction." Preconference Food-for-Thought Note, 2023.
55. Salazar, B. P. "Social Urbanism as a Crime Prevention Strategy: The Case of Medellín, Colombia." In *Practical Approaches to Urban Crime Prevention*, edited by M. Shaw and V. Carli. Proceedings of the Workshop held at the 12th UN Congress on Crime,

Prevention and Criminal Justice, Salvador, Brazil, April 12–19, 2011, 92–101. Montreal: International Centre for the Prevention of Crime, United Nations Office on Drugs and Crime.
56. Carbonari F., A. Willman, and R. Sergio de Lima. "Learning from Latin America: Policy Trends of Crime Decline in 10 Cities Across the Region." 2017. Background report for *Know Violence in Childhood Initiative* flagship report. http://www.knowviolence inchildhood.org/images/pdf/Background-Paper_Carbonari-F.A.%20Willman%20and%20R.%20Sergio-de-Lima-2017_KV.pdf.
57. Peace in Our Cities, "Peace in Our Cities Symposium."
58. Salazar, "Social Urbanism."
59. Carbonari et al., "Learning from Latin America"; Peace in Our Cities, "Peace in Our Cities Symposium."
60. Cerda, M., J. Morenoff, B. Hansen, K. Hicks, J. Tessari, L. F. Duque, A. Restrepo, and A. V. Diez-Roux. "Reducing Violence by Transforming Neighborhoods: A Natural Experiment in Medellín, Colombia." *American Journal of Epidemiology* 175, no. 10 (April 2012): 1045–1053.
61. For example, one study on criminal governance discusses how state and gang rule can be strategically complementary at times, showing how in Medellin some of these organizations choose to maintain order to decrease citizens' demands for law enforcement and their eventual collaboration with police officers, helping to protect the organizations' illicit activities. Today, the city is estimated to have approximately 400 of these organizations, called combos, who control drug trade in their neighborhoods and participate or regulate informal and sometimes also formal legal local markets. Blattman, Christopher, Gustavo Duncan, Benjamin Lessing, and Santiago Tobon. "Gang Rule: Understanding and Countering Criminal Governance." National Bureau of Economic Research (NBER) Working Paper 29692.
62. The authors conclude that "the divergent results suggest the importance of existing state capacity, plus the dangers of over-promising and under-delivering. This may be especially important in Latin America, where cities like Medellín compete with gangs

for local problem-solving and legitimacy." Blattman et al., "Gang Rule," 1.
63. Buggs, Shani. *Community-Based Violence Interruption and Public Safety*. Arnold Ventures, 2022. https://craftmediabucket.s3.ama zonaws.com/uploads/AVCJIReport_Community-BasedViolenc eInterruptionPublicSafety_Buggs_v2.pdf.
64. In 2019, hate crime incidents reported in New York State increased 17.7%, in a reverse trend after two years of decline. The number of incidents of this type registered by law enforcement agencies (619) was the highest in a single year since 2012, in part due to a spike in the number of anti-Jewish incidents. New York State Division of Criminal Justice Services. *Hate Crime in New York State 2019 Annual Report*. Criminal Justice Research Report, 2020. https://www.criminaljustice.ny.gov/crimnet/ojsa/ hate-crime-in-nys-2019-annual-report.pdf. The same trend was seen in other places in the country the year before. According to the Center for the Study of Hate & Extremism at California State University San Bernardino monitoring reports, hate crimes rose 9 percent in major cities in the United States in 2018, for a fifth consecutive year, to decade highs. In that study, race-based or anti-African American hate crimes were the top bias categories in most cities, followed closely by anti-gay and anti-Jewish hate crimes. Center for the Study of Hate & Extremism. *Report to the Nation: 2019 Factbook on Hate & Extremism in the U.S. & Internationally*, 2019. California State University San Bernardino. https://www. csusb.edu/sites/default/files/CSHE%202019%20Report%20to% 20the%20Nation%20FINAL%207.29.19%2011%20PM_0.pdf.
65. The OPHC has its own dashboard to monitor hate crimes in the city: NYPD Hate Crimes Dshboard, https://app.powerbigov. us/view?r=eyJrIjoiYjg1NWI3YjgtYzkzOS00NzcOLTkwMDAtNT gzM2I2M2JmYWE1Iiwidcl6IjJiOWY1N2ViLTc4ZDEtNDZ mYi1iZTgzLWEyYWZkZDdjNjA0MyJ9.
66. For a more detailed discussion on legitimacy, see Peace in Our Cities, *Guiding Principles and Inspiring Actions*.
67. Giffords Law Center to Prevent Gun Violence, "Case Study in Hope."

68. United Nations Sustainable Development Goal 16 aims to achieve "peaceful, just and inclusive societies which are free from fear and violence." United Nations, *Transforming Our World: The 2030 Agenda for Sustainable Development* (New York: United Nations, 2015).

References

Abt, Thomas, and Christopher Winship. *What Works in Reducing Community Violence: A Meta-Review and Field Study for the Northern Triangle*. United States Agency for International Development, February 2016.

Alcaldía de Palmira. "Estrategia de Prevencion Social de la Violencia PAZOS." Palmira City Government Website, 2020, https://palmira.gov.co/wp-content/uploads/2022/09/Infografia-PAZOS-L.pdf.

Alcaldía de Palmira. "Indicators for the Monitoring, Follow-Up, and Result of the Strategy Aimed at the Reduction of Violence in Palmira, Colombia." Palmira City Government October 4, 2022. https://palmira.gov.co/wp-content/uploads/2023/03/Indicators-for-the-monitoring-of-violence.pdf.

Baltimore City Government. Mayor's Office of Neighborhood Safety and Engagement. Baltimore City Government Website. https://monse.baltimorecity.gov/safe-streets-new.

Basombrío, C., and L. Dammert. Seguridad y populismo punitivo en América Latina: lecciones corroboradas, constataciones nove dosas y temas emergentes. Wilson Center, Latin American Program, 2013.

Beato, C., and A. M. Silveira. "Effectiveness and Evaluation of Crime Prevention Programs in Minas Gerais." *Stability: International Journal of Security and Development* 3, no. 1 (May 16, 2014): 20. https://doi.org/10.5334/sta.dr.

Berman, Greg. "No Program Is a Panacea: The Fate of Focused Deterrence." *Vital City*, March 2, 2022. Accessed August 15, 2023. https://www.vitalcitynyc.org/articles/no-program-is-a-panacea-the-fate-of-focused-deterrence.

Bhatt, M. P., S. B. Heller, M. Kapustin, M. Bertrand, and C. Blattman. "Predicting and Preventing Gun Violence: An Experimental Evaluation of

Readi Chicago." The Quarterly Journal of Economics, Volume 139, Issue 1, February 2024, Pages 1–56, https://doi.org/10.1093/qje/qjad031.

Blattman, Christopher, Gustavo Duncan, Benjamin Lessing, and Santiago Tobon. "Gang Rule: Understanding and Countering Criminal Governance." National Bureau of Economic Research (NBER) Working Paper 29692.

Braga, Anthony, Weisburd, David and Turchan, Brandon. "Focused Deterrence Strategies and Crime Control: An Updated Systematic Review and Meta-Analysis of the Empirical Evidence." *Criminology and Public Policy* 17, no. 1 (February 2018): 205–250. https://doi.org/10.1111/1745-9133.12353.

Braga, Anthony, Zimmerman, Gregory, Brunson, Rod K., and Papachristos, Andrew V. *Oakland Ceasefire Impact Evaluation: Key Findings.* Northeastern University and Rutgers University, August 10, 2018. https://www.kron4.com/wp-content/uploads/sites/11/2018/08/Oakland20Ceasefire20Impact2 0Evaluation20Key20Findings_1534990511552_52781602_ver1.0.pdf.

Buggs, Shani. Community-Based Violence Interruption and Public Safety. Arnold Ventures, 2022. https://craftmediabucket.s3.amazonaws.com/upl oads/AVCJIReport_Community-BasedViolenceInterruptionPublicSafety_B uggs_v2.pdf.

Butts, J. A., C. G. Roman, L. Bostwick, and J. R. Porter. "Cure Violence: A Public Health Model to Reduce Gun Violence." *Annual Review of Public Health* 36 (March 2015): 39–53.

Cahill, Meagan, Miriam Becker-Cohen, Jesse Jannetta, Ellen Paddock, Emily Tiry, Maria Serackos, and Samantha Lowry. *Evaluation of the Los Angeles Gang Reduction and Youth Development Program: Final Y1 Report.* Urban Institute, 2015. https://www.urban.org/sites/default/files/public ation/77956/2000622-Evaluation-of-the-Los-Angeles-Gang-Reduction-and-Youth-Development-Program-Year-4-Evaluation-Report.pdf.

Carbonari F., A. Willman, and R. Sergio de Lima. "Learning from Latin America: Policy Trends of Crime Decline in 10 Cities Across the Region." 2017. Background report for *Know Violence in Childhood Initiative* flagship report. http://www.knowviolenceinchildhood.org/images/pdf/Background-Paper_Carbonari-F.A.%20Willman%20and%20R.%20Sergio-de-Lima-2017_KV.pdf.

Carbonari, F., A. Willman, F. Manolio, S. Reinach, and D. Marques. Forum Brasileiro de Seguranca Publica and Pathfinders for Peaceful, Just and Inclusive Societies, "A Review of the Evidence and a Global Strategy for Violence Prevention" (March 2020).

Center for the Study of Hate & Extremism. *Report to the Nation: 2019 Factbook on Hate & Extremism in the U.S. & Internationally*, 2019. California

State University San Bernardino. https://www.csusb.edu/sites/default/files/CSHE%202019%20Report%20to%20the%20Nation%20FINAL%207.29.19%2011%20PM_0.pdf.

Cerda, M., J. Morenoff, B. Hansen, K. Hicks, J. Tessari, L. F. Duque, A. Restrepo, and A. V. Diez-Roux. "Reducing Violence by Transforming Neighborhoods: A Natural Experiment in Medellín, Colombia." *American Journal of Epidemiology* 175, no. 10 (April 2012): 1045–1053.

Cerdá, M., Tracy, M., Keyes, K.M. "Reducing Urban Violence: A Contrast of Public Health and Criminal Justice Approaches". Epidemiology. 2018 Jan; 29(1):142–150. https://doi.org/10.1097/EDE.0000000000000756. PMID: 28926374; PMCID: PMC5718925.

Chioda, Laura. Stop the Violence in Latin America: A Look at Prevention from Cradle to Adulthood. Washington, DC, World Bank, 2017.

Cruz, Miguel, Rosen, Jonathan D., Amaya, Luis Henrique, and Vorobyeva, Yulia. *The New Face of Street Gangs: The Gang Phenomenon in El Salvador*. Florida International University, 2017.

Dahlberg L.L., and E. G. Krug. "Violence: A Global Public Health Problem." In *World Report on Violence and Health*, edited by E. G. Krug, L. L. Dahlberg, J. A. Mercy, A. B. Zwi, and R. Lozano, 1–21. Geneva, Switzerland: World Health Organization, 2002.

Dahlberg L. L., and J. A. Mercy. "History of Violence as a Public Health Issue." *AMA Virtual Mentor* 11, no. 2 (February 2009): 167–172. http://virtualmentor.ama-assn.org/2009/02/mhst1-0902.html.

DeFalco, Randle. "(Re)Conceptualizing Atrocity Crimes as Public Health Catastrophes." In *Public Health, Mental Health, and Mass Atrocity Prevention*, edited by Jocelyn Getgen Kestenbaum, Caitlin O. Mahoney, Amy E. Meade, and Arlan F. Fuller, 17–31. London: Routledge, 2021. https://ssrn.com/abstract=3908637.

Delgado, Sheyla A., Laila Alsabahi, Kevin Wolff, Nicole Alexander, Patricia Cobar, and Jeffrey A. Butts. *The Effects of Cure Violence in the South Bronx and East New York, Brooklyn*. John Jay College, 2017. https://johnjayrec.nyc/2017/10/02/cvinsobronxeastny/.

Esposti, Michelle Degli, Carolina V. N. Coll, Eduardo Viegas da Silva, Doriam Borges, Emiliano Rojido, Alisson Gomes dos Santos, Ignacio Cano, and Joseph Murray. "Effects of the Pelotas (Brazil) Peace Pact on Violence and Crime: A Synthetic Control Analysis." *Lancet Regional Health—Americas* 19 (2023).

Giffords Law Center to Prevent Gun Violence. A Case Study in Hope: Lessons from Oakland's Remarkable Reduction in Gun Violence, April 23, 2019.

"The Guardian View on El Salvador'S Crime Crackdown: A Short-Term, High Cost Fix." Editorial, Guardian (London), July 2, 2023. https://www.theguardian.com/commentisfree/2023/jul/02/the-guardian-view-on-el-salvadors-crackdown-a-short-term-high-cost-fix.

Henry, D. B., S. Knoblauch, and R. Sigurvinsdottir. The Effect of Intensive Ceasefire Intervention on Crime in Four Chicago Police Beats: Quantitative Assessment. Robert R. McCormick Foundation, 2014.

Hughes, K., M. A. Bellis, K. A. Hardcastle, Butchart, A., Dahlberg, L., Mercy, J. A., Mikton, C. "Global Development and Diffusion of Outcome Evaluation Research for Interpersonal and Self-Directed Violence Prevention from 2007 to 2013: A Systematic Review." *Aggression and Violent Behavior* 19, no. 6 (November–December 2014): 655–662.

Krug E. G., J. A. Mercy, L. L. Dahlberg, and A. B. Zwi. "The World Report on Violence and Health." *Lancet* 360 (2002): 1083–1088.

Leach-Kemon, Katherine, Sirull, Rebecca and Glenn, Scott. "On Gun Violence, the United States Is an Outlier." Institute for Health Metrics and Evaluation, October 31, 2023. https://www.healthdata.org/news-events/insights-blog/acting-data/gun-violence-united-states-outlier.

Maguire, E., M. Oakley, and N. Corsaro. *Evaluating Cure Violence in Trinidad and Tobago*. Inter-American Development Bank, 2018.

Markowitz, Ariana. *Big Events on a Small Scale: Exploring Identity-Based Mass Violence in Cities*. Stanley Center for Peace and Security/Impact Peace, December 2020.

Muggah, Robert. "The Rise of Citizen Security in Latin America and the Caribbean." In *Alternative Pathways to Sustainable Development: Lessons from Latin America*, 291–322. International Development Policy series no. 9. Geneva, Boston: Graduate Institute Publications, Brill-Nijhoff, 2017.

New York State Division of Criminal Justice Services. *Hate Crime in New York State 2019 Annual Report*. Criminal Justice Research Report, 2020. https://www.criminaljustice.ny.gov/crimnet/ojsa/hate-crime-in-nys-2019-annual-report.pdf.

Open Society Foundations. "Q&A: How One Colombian City Is Tackling Violent Crime." Voices. Open Society Foundations, December 15, 2022. https://www.opensocietyfoundations.org/voices/q-and-a-how-one-colombian-city-is-tackling-violent-crime.

Peace in Our Cities. Guiding Principles and Inspiring Actions: Operationalizing the Resolution to Reduce Urban Violence, October 2022.

Peace in Our Cities. "Peace in Our Cities Symposium: Innovations in Urban-Violence Reduction." Preconference Food-for-Thought Note, 2023.

Salazar, B. P. "Social Urbanism as a Crime Prevention Strategy: The Case of Medellín, Colombia." In *Practical Approaches to Urban Crime Prevention*, edited by M. Shaw and V. Carli. Proceedings of the Workshop held at the 12th UN Congress on Crime, Prevention and Criminal Justice, Salvador, Brazil, April 12–19, 2011, 92–101. Montreal: International Centre for the Prevention of Crime, United Nations Office on Drugs and Crime.

Scott, Brandon M. *Baltimore City Comprehensive Violence Prevention Plan*, July 1, 2021. https://mayor.baltimorecity.gov/sites/default/files/MayorScott-ComprehensiveViolencePreventionPlan-1.pdf.

Silva, Jason R. "Global Mass Shootings: Comparing the United States against Developed and Developing Countries." *International Journal of Comparative and Applied Criminal Justice* 47, no. 4 (March 2023): 317–340. https://doi.org/10.1080/01924036.2022.2052126.

Sitther, Theo, and Rachel Locke. "Preventing Identity-Based Mass Violence in Cities." Discussion paper, Stanley Center for Peace and Security/Impact Peace, December 2020.

Skogan, W. G., S. M. Hartnett, N. Bump, and J. Dubois. *Evaluation of CeaseFire-Chicago*. Northwestern University, 2009.

Tiziano, Breda. "Why El Salvador's Anti-Crime Measures Cannot (and Should Not) Be Exported." Istituto Affari Internazionali (Rome), March 29, 2023. https://www.iai.it/en/pubblicazioni/why-el-salvadors-anti-crime-measures-cannot-and-should-not-be-exported.

United Nations. Transforming Our World: The 2030 Agenda for Sustainable Development. New York: United Nations, 2015.

Ventas, Leire. "Coming Face to Face with Inmates in El Salvador's Mega-Jail." BBC, February 14, 2024. https://www.bbc.com/news/world-latin-america-68244963.

Vigil, James Diego. *Barrio Gangs: Street Life and Identity in Southern California*. University of Texas Press, 1988. https://doi.org/10.7560/776135.

Ward, Thomas W. *Gangsters without Borders: An Ethnography of a Salvadoran Street Gang*. Oxford: Oxford University Press, 2013.

Daniel Webster, Carla Tilchin, and Mitchell Doucette. *Estimating the Effects of Safe Streets Baltimore on Gun Violence 2007–2022*. Johns Hopkins, 2022. https://publichealth.jhu.edu/sites/default/files/2023-10/estimating-the-effects-of-safe-streets-baltimore-on-gun-violence-july-2023.pdf.

Webster, D. W., J. M. Whitehill, J. S. Vernick, and E. M. Parker. *Evaluation of Baltimore's Safe Streets Program: Effects on Attitudes, Participants' Experiences, and Gun Violence*. Baltimore, MD: Johns Hopkins Center for the Prevention of Youth Violence, 2012.

World Bank. Pathways for Peace: Inclusive Approaches to Preventing Violent Conflict. Washington, DC: World Bank, 2018. https://doi.org/10.1596/978-1-4648-1162-3.

World Health Assembly. Prevention of Violence: A Public Health Priority. WHA 49.25, 49th session, May 25, 1996. https://www.emro.who.int/violence-injuries-disabilities/resolutions/resolutions.html.

World Health Organization. World Report on Violence and Health. Geneva: World Health Organization, October 3, 2002. https://www.who.int/publications/i/item/9241545615.

World Health Organization. "World Health Organization Violence Prevention Unit: Approach, Objectives and Activities, 2022–2026." Geneva: World Health Organization, September 2, 2022. https://www.who.int/teams/social-determinants-of-health/violence-prevention.

Flávia Carbonari is a senior social development, violence prevention, and gender specialist. She has been consulting for the World Bank and other multilaterals for over 15 years, working on investment, research, and technical assistance projects focused on social inclusion, citizen security, conflict, gender, and gender based violence. Carbonari has worked in more than 20 countries in Latin America, Africa, and East Asia. She has consulted for several NGOs, research institutes and think tanks, in Brazil, Argentina, and the United States, leading research on violence prevention, violence against women, and social issues. Carbonari worked as a journalist covering international politics and economics. She has been a non-resident fellow at the Chicago Council on Global Affairs since 2018, and since 2020 has been acting as a Technical Advisor to the Halving Global Violence Task Force at the Pathfinders for Peaceful, Just, and Inclusive Societies. Carbonari holds a MA in Latin American studies from Georgetown University, and graduated from Pontifícea Universidade Católica of São Paulo with a BA in International Relations and a BA in Journalism.

Open Access This chapter is licensed under the terms of the Creative Commons Attribution-NonCommercial-NoDerivatives 4.0 International License (http://creativecommons.org/licenses/by-nc-nd/4.0/), which permits any noncommercial use, sharing, distribution and reproduction in any medium or format, as long as you give appropriate credit to the original author(s) and the source, provide a link to the Creative Commons license and indicate if you modified the licensed material. You do not have permission under this license to share adapted material derived from this chapter or parts of it.

The images or other third party material in this chapter are included in the chapter's Creative Commons license, unless indicated otherwise in a credit line to the material. If material is not included in the chapter's Creative Commons license and your intended use is not permitted by statutory regulation or exceeds the permitted use, you will need to obtain permission directly from the copyright holder.

To Get Revenge or Not, That Is the Question

José Luis Pardo Veiras and Felipe Luna Espinosa

The following is an oral history of Plateros, a neighborhood in Mexico's capital city. Here, in the midst of the militarization the country has endured over the past few decades, some police officers asked questions before shooting, because they understood that a few people are responsible for most of the killing and that a murder can be just one murder or the first of many. In the last few years, the number of homicides has gone down by sixty percent, according to official statistics. This is the story of the police officers and the people from Plateros who decided not to pull the trigger (Fig. 1).

J. L. P. Veiras (✉)
Dromomanos, Mexico City, Mexico
e-mail: joseluis@dromomanos.com

F. L. Espinosa
Dromomanos, Mexico City, Mexico

Fig. 1 Lomas de Plateros's proximity to major roads makes it a key passageway between different areas of Mexico City, adding to its strategic significance. In the background, the financial district and upscale neighborhood of Santa Fe. Photo by Felipe Espinosa

Act 1

Plateros: The Neighborhood Where the Days Are Nights and the Nights Days

The setting for this story is Plateros, a neighborhood on the east side of Mexico City with a deceptive name. The only thing that shines here is the sun reflected from the skyscrapers of Santa Fe, one of the financial centers of the city, which rise up at the edge of the landscape like modern cathedrals. In Plateros there are alleyways, twisted staircases, and impossible slopes. There are houses painted pale yellow and maroon; others are sky blue, a coat of paint courtesy of city hall, an illusion of order in a place dominated by conflict. On the sidewalks a few luxury cars are parked. Some of the small altars dedicated to the Virgin of Guadalupe and those who have died, the majority murdered, mark places where drugs are sold, where invisible boundaries begin. In the mornings the neighborhood is calm, silent, almost empty. The only thing to see is the rare open store and a gang member on lookout, watching for outsiders. Those who live in Plateros often say, "The days are nights and the nights, days."

One day in October 2022, Rafael and Carlos, 21 and 19 years old respectively, brothers who were not raised together, are at their family home. They live there along with close to twenty-five people, among them uncles, aunts, cousins, and siblings. Rafael is in his room. Carlos is on the rooftop with his younger brothers and sisters. On the opposite corner of the alley is the spot where drugs are sold. This is how the two brothers reconstruct the murders of their mother and grandmother.

RAFAEL: You could say it was a stupid situation. It wasn't our fault, we didn't start it. One of the young guys that sells drugs left that day looking for trouble in one of the other places where they also sold drugs. They got into a fight. The guys from the other place told him that if they saw him in the neighborhood, they were going to shoot him. For him it went in one ear and out the other, but they came for him. The guy started to run, and the first thing that occurred to him was to come into our house. We always kept the door shut, but that day it was open. Five minutes before I was outside playing with my mom. She used to call me "hairy little thing" because I have hairy feet. I don't know what they were thinking, but they started to shoot. First I started to hear screams. When I got downstairs and was turning the corner I saw the first shots coming in. One of my cousins had a bullet hole here in her butt cheek. I saw how they shot my mom; I saw how they shot my grandma.

CARLOS: I heard the explosions on the corner and then when I heard them downstairs in my house I came down and said, "What's going on?" When I saw the whole thing play out I was in shock. And when I saw my mom, she started yelling to me, saying her daughters, her daughters, and my sisters were outside in the street, but thank god a neighbor got them inside her house. My mom was on the ground bleeding. She had been hit by three bullets, one in her heart. What I remember is that I went and kneeled down next to her; I held her and I told her, "No, hold

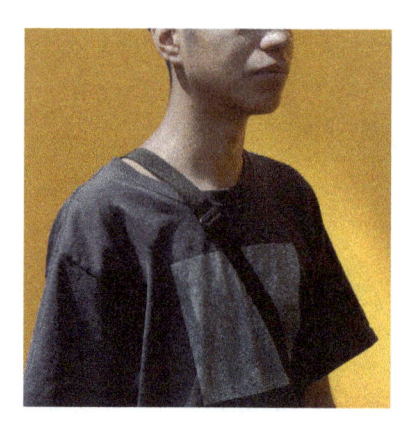

Fig. 2 Carlos (19). Photo by Felipe Espinosa

on Mom, you are a warrior, I don't want my sisters to live the same life as me, hold on Mom, hold on," but my mom didn't hold on.

RAFAEL: I talked to the guys in the neighborhood, all of this is known in the neighborhood, and they told me who did it. In that instant I got pissed. I said, "Damn, I know who they are, what time they are here, we have to go get them." I wanted to kill those people. I wanted to kill them, and I also wanted to kill the guy from my street too because it was his fault that they went and killed my mom and my grandma. I wanted revenge (Figs. 2 and 3).

Act 2

A Strange Police Story (I)

One reason Plateros is the setting of this oral history is because violence has been a fundamental part of its past. A few years ago, the Mexico City police divided this neighborhood of some 300,000 inhabitants into two zones, Plateros I and Plateros II, in an attempt to control it. But that would have made it just another violent place in Mexico. Between 2006—when the military started fighting the so-called war on drugs under the orders of then-president Felipe Calderón—and 2020, now under the presidency of

Fig. 3 Some of the small altars dedicated to the Virgen de Guadalupe mark boundaries or places where drugs are sold. Photo by Felipe Espinosa

Andrés Manuel López Obrador, the number of homicides rose 341 percent. In this period, saying "the most violent year in modern history" has become almost commonplace. The response to the violence has been militarization. The army's budget over the past few years has grown by 163 percent, and the marines' by 300 percent. Close to 200 civilian government roles have been given to the military.

Above all, Plateros is the scene for this story because four years ago, Alto al Fuego (the Ceasefire program) was created. In contrast to the common security strategy, some police officers came to the neighborhood and asked questions before shooting, because they understood that a few people do most of the killing and that a murder can be just one murder or the first of many. In Plateros, the killing continues. It continues to be one of the major points of concentration of violence in Mexico City, and according to police data, dozens of criminal groups are still operating there. Over time, however, there has been a reduction in the number of murders. In 2019, 58 homicides were committed; in 2024, 24. A 59 percent drop.

Pablo Vázquez, former coordinator of the pilot program Alto al Fuego and current security secretary, speaks from his office at the Department of Public Security in Mexico City's police headquarters.

PABLO: Now people talk to us when before they were afraid of us. That is one of the objectives. The structural cause of the violence is a lack of well-being; we don't do this, but what Alto al Fuego does is gradually work its way in the social dynamics that generate violence and tend to repeat cyclically. The majority of the violence in any area or community is caused by one organized group working collectively, but it's a tremendous minority. Less than one percent tends to commit 50 or 60 percent of the homicides or the injuries by firearms. For over a year and a half, we analyzed some 200 homicides. The information was shared to find out who were those who were supposedly responsible, who was fighting with whom. What we do is get close to the social circle of those who commit violence, which doesn't necessarily have to be the perpetrators of violence themselves, sometimes it's their family members. We tell them about the consequences of committing a homicide. Ninety-nine percent of people don't understand the penal code, they don't know it exists, they've never read it, and they don't really know the consequences of committing murder, at least the legal consequences. We also inform them

Fig. 4 Rafael (21). Photo by Felipe Espinosa

that in life there are other ways of behaving other than through violence, and we offer them alternatives (Fig. 4).

Act 3

Whether or Not to Pull the Trigger (I)

Rafael is seated on a park bench in Mexico City. It's noon on a sunny October day. It's a happy day for him: he just graduated from high school. It's also a strange day. At 21 years old, good memories are scarce and the number of bad ones continues to grow. That's why, as he remembers, he averts his eyes under a light blue Golden State Warriors hat with the shyness of an adolescent. His voice breaks with a sob that one can't be sure is born of sadness, rage, or impotence.

RAFAEL: They took my mom and my grandma away from me, they took away my family. And the guy that they were after lives on my street. I see him every day. I was full of pain, full of hatred.... I have had a gun in my hand, I've had it loaded, and I have had that person in front of me, just like that tree is right now.

Rafael makes his hand into a pistol and points at the closest tree.

Carlos sits down on the same bench as Rafael. They are brothers, but they didn't grow up together. Rafael was raised by an aunt, Carlos by his mother. Between the ages 9 and 12 Carlos lived at a group home run by nuns, until he ran away. Today, he's 19. He speaks with the cadence and slang of his neighborhood. His eyes have an unmistakably mischievous glow.

CARLOS: In my neighborhood, there are a lot of guys who steal and a lot of police chases and people going after each other. My neighborhood is a red zone, it's heavy. If you come in and somebody recognizes you, you leave, because if you don't, you'll end up robbed or dead. Your life is always at risk in the neighborhood. There is fun, but there's also violence along with the fun.

Carlos almost always has a big smile. He says with pride that he got it from his mother. But sometimes he looks like a sad clown who laughs while he's crying inside.

CARLOS: My life was not the life of a normal kid. At the group home they beat me. If you misbehaved, beatings; if you stole, beatings; if you talked back, beatings; and if you didn't do anything, beatings. One day I misbehaved and they punished me with a week without food. I don't like to talk about it, but since they had dogs, the only thing I could do was eat dog food. My mom didn't come to see me. Neither did my dad. My dad left when I was three or four years old; he lived in the neighborhood with his other family. My dad was very violent and a womanizer. He died three years ago. He sold drugs, and they arrested him; he ended up in prison, and there he got a stomach infection. He wrote me a letter from prison in which he told me things he'd never told me before, that he was going to change. I never had a father's love, he wasn't the type that saw me and hugged me. When I went to see him he rejected me. But I always had hope. When he died, my dream of having a father came crumbling down.

The laughter fades away.

My mom taught me to respect women. And another thing that I'll always remember is that she told me she was my best friend. I was a rebellious kid; I raised my voice to my mom, insulted her, I said things I never should have said, I ran away. I started smoking weed and doing drugs. I couldn't continue with that life, and I started to help her. And she told me, "Now I am going to start trusting you," and I told her, "Finally I'm going to have [my] mother's love." And she died.
Only the sad clown remains (Figs. 5 and 6).

A Strange Police Story (II)

Aarón Perez, the head of the policing element of Alto al Fuego, is in a lounge on the ninth floor of the Department of Public Security. A group of agents sit in front of their computers, where they have all the data from the program, but Aarón likes to keep a rudimentary paper map on the wall with 129 cutouts of mug shots, one for each case. They remind him of those first months when Plateros was just another violent place he'd heard about during his 16-year career as a police officer in Mexico City. At that time, Francisco Vázquez, alias Pancho Bolas, a man who led a gang of more than 40 people, became his main target. Aarón is a quiet man with a stony gaze; he speaks with a prodigious memory about the cases he's worked on and of the spider web of names and nicknames of the delinquents and gangs in Plateros. Names like Bryan Fuentes Sanchez, who sources said committed more than 22 homicides. One day, he killed his girlfriend; another girl, a minor, survived. One of the fathers of the victims spoke with the police and obtained an arrest warrant, but before the police arrived, Bryan's partner, El Gabacho (the American), killed him. There's a video where a truck can be seen running him over. There's also El Manitas (Tiny Hands), who was born without his left hand, with a stump and just one small finger. He was at war with another group and they arrested him for double homicide. He killed El Perros (the Dogs), who bullied him as a child.

There was also Lenin Cachola (Pig Face), whom he arrested in Monterrey; then there was El Fresa (the Strawberry); La Momia (the Mummy); El Pañal (the Diaper); and El Espagueti (Spaghetti).

Fig. 5 Located on a perilous gorge, Lomas de Plateros is well known for its complex alleyways, twisted staircases, and impossible slopes, making police persecution and monitoring a constant challenge. Photo by Felipe Espinosa

Fig. 6 Elements from Alto al Fuego conduct routine inspections and visits to individuals participating in the program. The neighborhood continues to be one of the major points of concentration of violence in Mexico City. Photo by Felipe Espinosa

AARÓN: All we knew was that someone named Pancho was the one in charge, but even they confused him with a different Pancho. It's an all-too-common name. An ex-police captain got me to the right place, he told me that he operated between Andador 2 Street and Central Street, where the Virgin of Guadalupe altar is located. But I knew not to say who'd given me the information. In the neighborhood they called him "Don Pancho Bolas." But after going back many times and [getting a tip from] a source, I got into their close circle. They arrested him in Mexico City. We did a great job. For a long time I imagined how it would be, I'd been after him for a long time. The chief always told me that he was like my Moby Dick. I saw him washed up. His knees ached. He walked with crutches. He treated me with respect, like a boss. He was in solitary confinement (Fig. 7). He wanted Dirse [his partner who is at another prison] to visit, and medical attention. I asked him to talk with his people in Barrio Norte (the North Side). When I left I asked myself: "Who was his guard? Would someone follow me afterward?".

Fig. 7 Aarón Pérez, a 16-year veteran, is head of the policing element of Alto al Fuego, based in the Department of Public Security. Photo by Felipe Espinosa

Whether or Not to Pull the Trigger (II)

DANIEL: I don't remember anything until I woke up in the hospital. I couldn't feel anything from my legs to my belly button. To this day I don't have any feeling there. The doctors said I wouldn't walk again. In my way of thinking, I wanted to grab a phone to start investigating because in the neighborhood everyone knows everything. I thought, "I'm going to kill them, I'm going to throw a bomb at their families."
The ground floor of the house where Daniel lives serves as a small workshop for his aunt, his mother, and other women. In the upstairs living room there are some cardboard boxes with golden crosses and religious messages and a mural with photos of Daniel's past ten months. The first shows him in the hospital bed, looking almost cadaver-like.
I was in really, really, really bad shape, I was close to dying. I remember I was having a beer when I saw two guys, one got close and I saw him pull out a gun. He shot me from six meters [twenty feet] away and says, "Now you're fucked." So I started shooting at him too. I thought I had enough to beat them, no? Enough so they wouldn't get me, but "what if?" doesn't exist. My mistake was knowing I didn't have any more bullets and pulling the trigger anyway. It was a revolver, a 0.38, and the hammer clicked. And the other guy starts yelling, "Kill him, kill him." I remember the first shot came at my face, but it hit my hands and I threw the gun and started screaming. I felt a strong burning sensation.
Daniel shows how he isn't able to bend one of the fingers on his right hand.
The bullets started to hit my stomach. The two of them started to shoot from a meter and a half [five feet] away, and the only thing I could do was cover myself and turn around. When I did, they got me in the back, close to my lung. When I started running, I think, I don't know, I don't remember how many meters it was...they had already hit my spine. My feet no longer responded; I passed out.
Daniel has the face of a boxer, with small eyes, a broad nose, and a square jaw. He's a hard guy. Even sitting in a wheelchair, his presence is imposing. He reflects on the violence like a presence that has been with him all his life.
I used to do really bad things. Really bad. I started committing a lot of crimes, a lot. I started to do a lot of shootings. I don't know if anyone died, but I did it. I did six and a half years in prison, I went in five or

six times, for robbery, for shoot-outs. There I finished elementary and middle school. I grew up here in this house with my aunts and uncles, I didn't have a dad. One of my uncles was a cop and he taught me to do things on the straight and narrow, but I liked easy money, to feel the adrenaline. I don't remember my first fight well, but I do remember that it was with a kid from my school. They just recently killed him. I started boxing when I was eight, but when my uncle died I felt that there wasn't anyone to come down on me anymore. When I was 16 I bought my first pistol, it was cheap. I bought it and started doing crimes with it. So I could pull off bigger robberies, no? Like stores, I don't know, I even thought about robbing an armored truck, which never happened. [Committing crimes] I made 80,000 pesos [$4,700] a month, whereas working with my cousin as a construction worker, carrying things, I made 2,500 pesos [$150] per week. I did really bad things. I can't get out of my head a guy that I stabbed in the neck with a knife. I can't stop thinking about it because he told me not to take anything from him, not to do anything to him, that what he had was for his kids. When my daughter was born I calmed down, but since I was into drugs I ended up going back to everything. So I feel that what happened to me was because one of those guys couldn't let it go and said, "That's enough from this guy." Everything happens for a reason. The first months after it happened I used to say to the homies, "Come get me and I'll shoot them from the back seat of the car." But after six months I started to change. I found God, I have my daughter, the psychologist taught me how to breathe. Selma [the prison social worker for the government's social program] helped me a lot, I completed the Independent Life program, they taught me how to get around in a wheelchair. I am beginning to understand that revenge is a story that never ends. I see it like a circle that never ends until all of our families are dead.

Daniel goes out onto the small terrace where his family has put up two metal bars so he can do his exercises. He stands up from the wheelchair with help, and with effort starts to walk with his hands on the bar using his two prosthetic legs (Fig. 8).

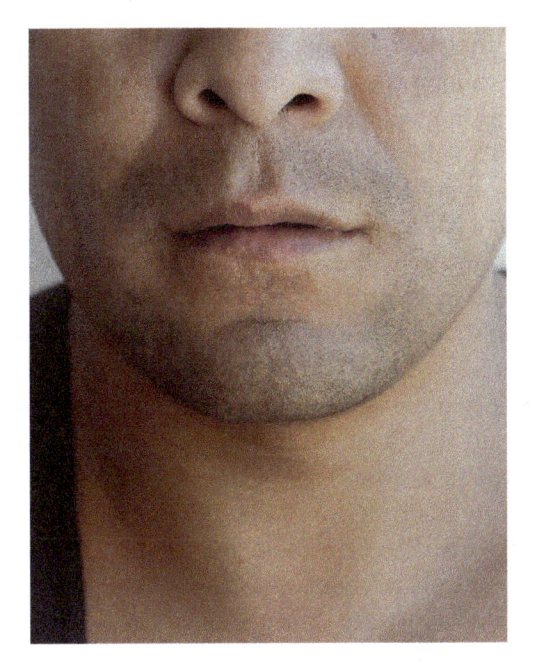

Fig. 8   Daniel. Photo by Felipe Espinosa

A Strange Police Story (III)

At the entrance of Barrio Norte there is a warning painted on an orange construction barrier: NO UBERS. A few meters away is a police kiosk, a tiny jungle gym, a basketball court, and an altar in memory of one of the men from the neighborhood who was killed. At this point "El Corral" begins, one of the nuclei of drug sales in Plateros. It's a small labyrinth of sky-blue houses crammed together. The alleyways are so narrow that at some points one person can barely fit through. It's morning. The silence is almost sepulchral. Among the agents walking and greeting the few people who are out are Karla Moctezuma and Percival Cruz, two patrol officers from Alto al Fuego. They are both in their 20s and grew up in complicated neighborhoods. Karla has a square jaw and sharp face, her tone of voice is hard, and she has a tough posture. Percival, on the other hand, has softer features and a round, childlike face.

KARLA: In the military they teach you rules, but they are their rules, and even though there are opportunities it's very sexist. Here the treatment is more humane, more understanding. You learn other rules. Sometimes, at first, you might come across really aggressive people in the neighborhood and it's not easy for them to calm down, but when they see you are calm, they soften and a lot of times even open the doors of their homes to you. After all those visits and [they see] everything you've told them was the truth, that it's not just making promises and talking, I would even say that they even begin to feel affection for you, that's the word I would use.

PERCIVAL: My mom had brothers and cousins who were police officers, and they killed two of them. I was a rebellious kid and I liked fashion. I worked in a store. I picked up my love for law enforcement when I did my military service. I saw those clean uniforms and those airplanes and I wanted to be a pilot. But in the end I started working as a back-up police officer, doing rounds with the police. What I always enjoyed was the analysis, the information. Now I know who is whose family member, why they are fighting. Alto al Fuego has become more than a strategy. I think it's become a way of building trust, a sense of empathy with people. Finally I see it like this: we are cops, but before becoming a cop, I was a kid, a youth, a teenager, and I was a regular citizen. We belong to this society.

Their colleagues affectionately call Karla and Percival Los Percis (The Percis) because they usually go out on patrol together. They both agree on which story hit them the hardest during their time working in the neighborhood.

KARLA: It was a year ago. She was a woman with two kids, one seven and the other had just turned three. She'd been going out with a guy for three or four months, and he asked if he could take the little one to a kids' party with his family, that there would be cake. He only invited the three-year-old. At nine o'clock at night, he came by with his brother for the baby. From that moment on, he and the mother only communicated through WhatsApp. They'd agreed that he would bring him back that night, but in the end he didn't bring him back. He told his mom that he was taking care of him, that he was asleep, and that he would bring him home in the morning. In the morning the guy called her saying, "Come get Santi, come get Santi, I gave him breakfast and he's choking on a cookie." He also called the police and an ambulance for help. When they arrived the little one had already died. There were bite marks all over his body, they'd ripped out his hair, broken his jaw, they completely broke it, they destroyed it. It was nine in the morning and he'd been dead since four.

PERCIVAL: According to the autopsy, the cause of death was trauma. I was part of the research team, and we investigated the subject. He had four different Facebook profiles. In his social network accounts he had friends from Iraq, Iran, from Turkey, Israel, and other countries in the Middle East. They were groups that recorded or took videos of violent scenarios.

KARLA: We visited his brother. We saw him a little while ago. He didn't know how his little brother died, it was simply explained to him that his brother wasn't going to be there anymore and that he had gone to heaven. We visited him as it got close to the Day of the Dead because he told us that he and his brother used to dress up in costumes together. At Christmas too. We went once a week and later every fifteen days. And when we visited, he said, "Why haven't you come anymore? I thought my police friends weren't going to come anymore." He ran to us and hugged us (Figs. 9 and 10).

Whether or Not to Pull the Trigger (III)

MARÍA: With Bruno everything was beatings and more beatings. I used to say, "And if I go? And I leave him?" Oh no, then I'd have to go back home, with my mom, everyone crowded together. It's better if I stay with him. I had my car, my house. Even if he kept abusing me, in the end that was just how my life was. If he wasn't insulting me, I would say he didn't love me anymore. It was a toxic love. The love I knew. We lived with my brother-in-law's family; we were two families there. His children grew up with mine, there was an age gap of a few months between them. Everything was going OK until Gabriel turned 14. He started to hang out with the kids from our street and started stealing. Then he took José along with him. There started to be conflict between my nephew

Fig. 9 Percival. Photo by Felipe Espinosa

and Esteban, because of jealousy. Esteban was a troublemaker. I'm not going to say my son was a really good kid. He got into trouble, he had a motorcycle and another one for racing. So the other one, well, he wanted to be like him; he even compared himself to him. And I don't know where he got them, but he also had motorcycles. Then, well, Esteban killed him.

María lives by herself in a tiny, 25-square meter [270 square foot] room, where the bed, the kitchen, the table, and the bathroom are just a few steps away from one another. At 50, María, with her short hair, big eyes, and fast and powerful way of speaking, spends her days between this diminutive space and the pharmacy where she works nights cleaning. María's husband, Bruno, and two of her three sons, Esteban and José, are in prison. The three of them ended up there because of what happened on a night in 2017 at the family

Fig. 10   Karla. Photo by Felipe Espinosa

home. On visiting days, María works from 9 PM to 8 AM, and then goes to the prison and gets home at 5 in the afternoon.

MARÍA: My husband used to drive a government water delivery tanker. That day we went shopping at Suburbia with the vouchers they gave him. And we got home and we were eating dinner, I remember it well, and my son and my nephew started arguing about the parking spot. My son shot him in the stomach. My nephew died instantly. Esteban left immediately. They caught him two years later in Durango and brought him back. We had to leave our house. They arrested my husband two months later. His brother had reported him; he said he was at the window shouting, "Kill him, kill him," and they locked him up as an accomplice. At that moment I was alone and I started looking for a job. I don't know at what moment Jesús got the crazy idea, but two years after what happened with Esteban, he went and picked a fight with the brother of the one who had died. They went and shot my nephew. Fortunately the bullets barely touched him. Two hours later they came for Jesús and locked him up for attempted homicide. Esteban was with his dad in the East Prison, but after he went in things got really bad with drugs;

they moved him up to the North, which is maximum security. He got 35 years. Bruno can get out whenever. But he has a business inside prison to take care of himself on his own. He sells shirts, shorts, socks, boxers, pants. Toothpaste, he sells everything. I take him the merchandise. I make 1,500 pesos [$88] for rent. I go see one, then the other…Jesús is in the South. He got 15 years.

On the shelf that also serves as a wardrobe are some paper flowers that one of her sons gave María from prison for Mother's Day. Hanging on the wall is a dreamcatcher woven by another one of her sons. María looks at them with a tender and pained expression (Fig. 11).

Fig. 11 María (50). Since 2017, her husband and two of her three sons are in prison, convicted of murder. Photo by Felipe Espinosa

Whether or Not to Pull the Trigger (IV)

Rafael is in the park. He stops pointing at the tree with his hand.
RAFAEL: I had the opportunity to kill him, but I didn't get up the courage. The cops told me that they understood that I was mad, understood my desire for revenge, but that I wasn't going to want to go from being a victim to a victimizer. I'm not that kind of person. I'm not going to hold myself back, I'm not going to ruin my life. Since I was little I was drawn to becoming an astronaut, then a firefighter, now I'm interested in becoming a soldier, in feeling what it's like to be a person like that. What I want is to get out of my neighborhood.

Daniel continues with his workout and puts on some videos of a Colombian man in a similar situation who was able to walk again.
DANIEL: Now when people from the neighborhood ask, I tell them what I'll do when I can stand again, no? But I don't really want to do it. I still can't feel my feet, I can only feel muscle cramps.

Aarón, in the ninth-floor lounge of the Department of Public Security, talks about something personal without losing his stony expression.
AARÓN: I know that revenge doesn't get you anywhere. In 2019, they killed my cousin in Iztapalapa, you can imagine the state she was in when they found her. And my friends said to me, "We found out who it was, we're going to kill them." I told them no, that maybe that would make them feel better in the moment but it would bring with it a lot of consequences. What I did, even though I wasn't involved in the investigation, was provide a lot of information. Finally they caught them. The only thing getting revenge would have gotten us is another loss. Who was going to bring my cousin back to us?

María has gone up to the rooftop of her building. From there, the sun's reflection shines on the skyscrapers of Santa Fe and the Chapultepec forest, one of the largest urban forests in Latin America.
MARÍA: Ivan also needs help, and he's getting it from the Sanar [Healing] Program [a government mentorship program that accompanies victims of violence]. He always used to get vertigo, and now he works as a professional welder, hanging from the twenty-fifth, thirtieth floor, out of necessity. He went back to the house where he was raised. Now I'm not in a relationship with him. I suppose he blames me because

I have a partner, I'm with Enrique, and, well, they twist things and Diego thinks I abandoned our family. I even feel guilty sometimes. Because with Esteban, he brought women to the house and I ran them out. But I have worked a lot with a psychologist, with Sosa (a mentor), with Sintia (a program coordinator).... The psychologist always tells me: "What do you owe them? Nothing." But I'm not going to abandon them. In the prison I see a lot of moms, some are in worse shape than me. Now there are people that look at me and say that I look good, and before I was in bad shape, along with my blood sugar levels. So I think, "I shouldn't be doing badly." I fell madly in love with my husband, with Enrique I'm getting to know a different kind of love. When he sees me he says I'm the most beautiful woman in the world, he takes care of me. When he can he takes me to the prisons on his motorcycle.

Carlos puts on a song in the background that reminds him of his mother.

CARLOS: My mom's dream was that I join the military. I don't like the idea, I want to be a DJ, but I'm doing it for her. My dream was for her to see me succeed, but those dreams no longer exist. I still can't accept that my mom isn't here, and it feels terrible because I always go by places where I was with her. It's the same place, but without her. "What would you be doing with your mom?" I have changed my life. It's really something being bad. Now I stay in shape, play soccer, fronton.... Yeah, well, I've got a lot of life ahead of me. But I'm between a rock and a hard place. What do I do? Should I leave? Should I leave my family? Should I stay away from my brothers and sisters? Should I live a different life, like I want to? Or do I live this life? Or run away? I don't know (Fig. 12).

Note: The testimonies have been edited and shortened in order to synthesize and clarify the reading of this report, while always respecting the meaning of the individuals' words. The police officers were interviewed at different times over a period of one month. The conversations are excerpts from their individual testimonies. The names of the inhabitants of Plateros were changed to protect their identities.

Fig. 12 Since Alto al Fuego was initiated, the number of homicides in Lomas de Plateros has gone down by 60 percent. Photo by Felipe Espinosa

José Luis Pardo is co-founder and editorial director of Dromómanos, a journalism production company. His work has appeared in the *New York Times*, *El País*, and other publications. He is coauthor of *Narco América: From the Andes to Manhattan, 55,000 Kilometers on the Trail of Cocaine* (Barcelona: Tusquets, 2015), and of *The 12 Poorest Mexicans* (Madrid: Planeta, 2016). His awards include Spain's 2014 Ortega y Gasset Prize and 2013 National Journalism Prize.

Felipe Luna Espinosa is an independent photographer, reporter, and editor based in Mexico. His work has been featured in Bloomberg, *El País*, the *Los Angeles Times*, and the *New York Times*. He has worked with nongovernmental organizations, designers, videographers, and visual artists. He is an active member of Diversify Photo and Frontline Freelance Mexico.

Open Access This chapter is licensed under the terms of the Creative Commons Attribution-NonCommercial-NoDerivatives 4.0 International License (http://creativecommons.org/licenses/by-nc-nd/4.0/), which permits any noncommercial use, sharing, distribution and reproduction in any medium or format, as long as you give appropriate credit to the original author(s) and the source, provide a link to the Creative Commons license and indicate if you modified the licensed material. You do not have permission under this license to share adapted material derived from this chapter or parts of it.

The images or other third party material in this chapter are included in the chapter's Creative Commons license, unless indicated otherwise in a credit line to the material. If material is not included in the chapter's Creative Commons license and your intended use is not permitted by statutory regulation or exceeds the permitted use, you will need to obtain permission directly from the copyright holder.

Hafiz

Shukria Dellawar

On September 11, 2001, I felt crippled with fear and pain as I saw the horrifying images of people jumping out of the Twin Towers hit by the terrorists. The images I saw as I sat glued to my desktop praying for all those innocent souls continue to haunt me to this day. I was traumatized as an American, and a few weeks later, my trauma deepened as an Afghan. Unfortunately, very few Americans are truly aware of the dire consequences of the flip side of 9/11—the inferno imposed on the Afghan people, even though there was not a single Afghan among the 9/11 hijackers.

Reports of the overwhelming air assaults and frequent images of horrendous rocket attacks and bombings that were televised on news channels have left an indelible mark on my mind and a constant fear in my heart. The world turned a blind eye to the atrocities committed by both sides. A great number of civilians were killed in the crossfire, and

S. Dellawar (✉)
Lotus Anchor LLC, Centreville, VA, USA
e-mail: sdellawar@lotusanchor.com

mass graves continue to haunt hundreds of thousands of Afghan families who lost their loved ones without a trace.

My family was one of them.

A week before Thanksgiving of 2001, I received a call from my youngest brother, Hafiz, who had traveled from America to Afghanistan to spend time with my father. Our immediate family was scattered between countries (Afghanistan, Pakistan, and America) as our family became refugees during the Soviet invasion of Afghanistan. Hafiz could not get out; the borders had been shut down in an effort to prevent terrorists from escaping Afghanistan. Unfortunately, many civilians—including my brother—got trapped and could not leave the country.

All hell had broken loose for countless innocent civilians after Operation Enduring Freedom was launched by the US and Coalition forces to remove the Taliban from power. My family and I were very concerned for Hafiz's safety because he was in northern Afghanistan, where the US-Coalition-backed Northern Alliance fiercely clashed with the Taliban. Many civilians were caught in the crossfire and paid with their lives.

The last time I heard my brother's voice was when I happened to answer his phone call. He was calling from Afghanistan to say he was alive and well. I could hear shells exploding in the background. I begged him to be careful and not venture out to dangerous areas. I remember his response distinctly: "Where should I go? They are bombing everywhere."

It did not occur to me that it could be the last time I heard his voice. One of my biggest regrets in life is that I did not pass the receiver to my mother; I thought if she heard explosions in the background, her fear for her son's safety would get worse. Yet in trying to protect her I ended up depriving her of hearing her youngest son's voice one last time. That guilt has haunted me for years.

My trauma is so deep that as I write this, I cannot help but cry. I had asked Hafiz to call back Thanksgiving weekend. That call never came. Agonizing days, weeks, months, and years passed without any information about his fate. Was he killed by a stray bullet or a bomb? Or was he caught in the crossfire of rival factions? Did a rocket hit him? Or was it a mistaken identity? Is he still alive and trapped somewhere? We never found out. He simply disappeared in the catastrophe. Two decades later, he is still missing. My family has had no closure because we could not even hold a funeral for our beloved Hafiz. This tragedy changed the direction of my life and turned me into a full-time peace advocate.

Searching for Meaning

My brother's disappearance in northern Afghanistan, where mass graves were dug and signs of vicious atrocities revealed, left me emotionally paralyzed. Before this tragedy, life was good in general, and I was mostly a carefree spirit. I had surmounted most of the usual immigrant family challenges. But losing my brother instilled endless fear for his safety in my heart and guilt for not having done something differently to avoid the tragic outcome. Although it was not something anyone could have predicted or stopped, guilt became a dominant part of my grieving process. I never felt at peace not knowing what happened to my brother.

Overnight, my young life turned into an abyss of pain and suffering. I helplessly watched my siblings suffer in silence, my mother crying endlessly for her youngest child, my father praying for his safe return—all of which left me at the same time restless and emotionally frozen. I was no longer the happy, fun-loving, carefree spirit who always found joy in small things. The sudden, ugly turn forced a drastic change in my life, and in my overall personality. I lost interest in socializing. The social butterfly that I was turned into a news junkie. I would read anything I could get my hands on to better inform myself in the hope that somehow, I could find Hafiz or find out what happened to him. Those initial years I just wanted to find my brother and end my own and my family's pain. Those years were deeply painful. I became introverted and turned to my family for the love and support I had always taken for granted. Losing Hafiz taught me lessons I wish I hadn't had to learn in such a difficult way. Perhaps the greatest lesson was to never take any of my family members for granted. It is during such tragedies that families either break or come closer together. Hafiz's loss took a toll on each member of my family—he was a brother, a son, an uncle, a friend, and just a fun-loving and gentle soul. He was loved by all, and our hearts still long for him every day.

Despite the support from family and close friends, I went into depression. The only things that kept me occupied the first few weeks and months were work and taking care of my mother. But that feeling of helplessness kept building inside me. I realized I needed to do something different. My work at a patent and trademark law firm doing legal filings started to feel empty. I needed to channel my pain into something more meaningful—something that would serve the purpose of peace.

The lessons I had learned from my parents' lived experience of the Cold War were now like my own. Wars were ugly, often unnecessary, and caused the death of mostly innocent people; invariably atrocities take place, and crimes against humanity are not prevented; the powerful control the narrative, and the corporate media broadcast it to the people. Our family tragedy helped me mature overnight. I was sick of the charade. I was tired of reading reports about the war that did not match reports from the ground in several provinces in Afghanistan, including the capital Kabul. I was tired of stereotypical and mostly Islamophobic nonsense repeated in Western media. I resolved to do something about it by better educating myself and working for peace.

For all the Afghan Americans (as well as the Afghan diaspora across the globe) who experienced the loss of their loved ones, the tragedy of 9/11 was personal on multiple fronts. We felt the pain of millions of innocent Afghans caught in a war they did not cause. We felt the discrimination against Muslims after 9/11. But we also felt the pain, sorrow, and fear of our fellow Americans watching the coverage of the 9/11 attacks rebroadcast on our TV screens. I felt the sorrow and pain of the families who lost loved ones on 9/11, the sorrow of the families of countless soldiers who died needlessly in the war, and the endless, painful stereotyping that came my way as an Afghan-American and a Muslim.

At times it was difficult to honor my two identities as an American and an Afghan equally. The endless war in Afghanistan, mounting civilian casualties year after year, the constant wondering if my brother was still alive languishing in a dungeon somewhere, and the fabricated reports of progress by multiple generals disheartened me. But they also made me more determined to become an advocate for peace and reconciliation. With all these realities weighing on my mind, I had to struggle to get up every day and go to work, function normally, and pretend to feel fine.

No words could explain the complexity and layers of suffering of those first few years. The onset of the war in 2001 felt like my right arm was fighting my left arm, and my body and mind were paying the price.

To fulfill my new goal, I joined George Mason University's Conflict Analysis and Resolution program, known today as the Carter School for Peace and Conflict Resolution, and received my bachelor's and master's degrees. My concentration was on international conflicts, and I was determined to start working for peacebuilding as soon as possible. I was young and naïve. I didn't realize what the future would bring.

Power, Propaganda, and No Peace

I learned after multiple fact-finding trips to Kabul that most of the officials in power were not interested in peace—neither the US government leadership nor the many corrupt officials and warlords in the Afghan government. Only the Afghan people and countless foreign service members and their families wanted an end to the war and to achieve peace, all of them similarly helpless in influencing the outcomes driven by the elite and powerful in Kabul and Washington, DC (along with capitals of Coalition countries). Most Afghans wanted the rulers of Kabul to engage in peace talks with the Taliban, and they wanted a normal life to return. They were tired of worrying about their children not returning from school, their sons and husbands getting killed, their family members maimed or killed by aerial bombs and suicide bombers, and the bombings of weddings and funerals due to poor intelligence. Afghans wanted what everyone in the world wants: peace, shelter, livelihoods, their human rights, and human dignity.

Several US politicians, major defense contractors, and their media allies seemed to have an interest in prolonging the war by populist psychological means. The phrase "they hate our freedom" was repeated ad infinitum to stoke fear in the American public, blurring lines between extremists and an entire innocent population. The result was the longest war in American history, two decades of death and destruction with heavy loss of blood and treasure on both sides. It is estimated that approximately 70,000 Afghan civilians were killed during the two-decade war. But this is an inaccurate number. When the attacks were unfolding, the numbers were always contested by local Afghans and foreign militaries. Countless Afghans lost their lives and an unknown number suffered major injuries, including the loss of limbs. Those numbers also don't account for the ongoing mental and psychological damage and the invisible scars of war that will continue for generations.

Post-9/11 anti-Afghan propaganda from US politicians and media misled many Americans. Though my parents immigrated when I was 10, I quickly had to educate myself on Afghanistan's history to answer misinformed questions as overnight I was seen as only "Afghan." Colleagues and friends asked questions like why did Afghans attack the United States (they didn't, it was Osama bin Laden and al-Qaeda), why did Afghans give terrorists a safe haven (they didn't, terrorism is a global phenomenon), and why do Afghans hate our lifestyle (they don't, they want their freedom and human dignity like everyone else). The Afghan population had no connection to 9/11; Bin Laden, once a US ally, financed Afghan resistance against the Soviets. Yet voters and taxpayers failed to hold the government accountable for misleading narratives, leading to a war based on false premises. Journalists would visit Afghanistan briefly, claim expertise, and produce sensationalized stories. Despite no Afghan involvement in 9/11, the war continued, ending in defeat and abandoning Afghanistan back to the Taliban.

Thirty-eight million Afghans were on the receiving end of the world's most sophisticated military, along with its coalition, which utilized conventional war tactics such as carpet bombing, cluster bombs, missiles, heavy armory, etc. These weapons are highly likely to cause indiscriminate harm to civilians. In 2017, the United States dropped one of the largest nonnuclear weapons ever used by its military in Afghanistan, called the "mother of all bombs." Any counterintelligence expert would tell you that such sophisticated weaponry is not needed to fight terrorist and insurgent groups who use guerrilla warfare tactics and often remain invisible as they are blended with the public. Would it not have made sense to use more-targeted intelligence to go after individual terrorists and radical groups than drop heavy bombs and assess later if the target was killed?

Finding My Own Expression

I was one of the first six graduates of George Mason University's bachelor's program for conflict analysis and resolution. My focus was on international conflicts, and I wrote endless papers on Afghanistan and South Asia. There were heated debates with classmates that often exacerbated the pain I was living through. I learned to speak up during class discussions on war and peace to challenge the stereotypes and explain the complexities. I left the law firm the first year of my master's program and started working to help build increased understanding between Afghan and American policymakers in an effort to sow the seeds for peace. I worked on women's rights, peacebuilding, atrocity prevention, policy, and lobbying. I kept running into a pattern where I was hired for my expertise to tell those who hired me what they often did not want to hear.

There is so much suppressed trauma, anger, and frustration in me that has made it excruciatingly painful for me to relive this experience through writing about it. I have pondered the question of loyalty for a long time. Am I more loyal to Afghanistan or to America? How could I know when I was accused by both sides of favoring the other constantly? In reality, I understand both sides and empathize with them, but it took me nearly two decades to reconcile myself to the fact that I own my own narrative despite how the two sides view me.

I worked with several organizations over the past 15 years, during which I experienced three burnouts. Academia does not prepare you for this type of thing. Burnouts are real, and one does not see them coming. I was too passionate about working for peace, and I always went above and beyond my job description, so it was bound to catch up with me. My first burnout happened in 2011 after bearing witness to ground realities in Kabul during fact-finding trips. It was eye opening for me to learn to what extent the American people were being lied to by the leadership who continued to push for war without focusing on political negotiations that would end the conflict and pave the way for troop withdrawal.

This was two years before my father passed away. I visited him in 2012 in Mazar-e-Sharif, just wanting to see him and spend time with him. We had endless conversations. My father was *the* pillar of strength for me, and unlike the horror stories one may have heard about strict Afghan men, he was the kindest and most compassionate soul in my life. I was very close to him since I was a little girl—he was more of a friend than a father. We endlessly discussed politics every time we were together. But on this trip, our conversation was more about spiritual topics. My father was spiritually evolved, he had lived through so much, but he never lost love and compassion for humanity in his heart. Perhaps that was his biggest gift to all his children, something we all embody in our own unique way. As for my spiritual journey, my father was my first spiritual teacher. His teachings about the importance of forgiveness, love, unity, and remembrance of God still ground me through trials to this day.

During my last visit with my father in 2012, he gifted me poetry books of Rumi, Hafiz, and Saadi, the great Persian metaphysical poets, before I returned to the United States. It was surreal when he told me they would be my friends from now on as I departed for the airport. One year later, he died. The pain of his loss broke me in ways I didn't think I would survive. There went my mountain of strength, and I was broken in spirit and brutally burnt out for the second time. Something had to give. A few weeks after his loss, a creative channel opened, and I started writing poetry. My father knew it before I did. I never trained to be a creative writer, yet somehow the very first poem was a deep source of comfort:

> When a sea of sorrow is leaving your eyes
> Drop by drop
> Know that you are being cleansed
> Of the worries of the world
> When an ocean of light
> Is moving in your direction
> Know that you are being given
> A new life
> When the earth and the sky fail to sooth you
> Know that God is about to save you.

And I was saved. Day by day, I felt that my pen became my contact with the supernatural world as I would get creative poetry downloads that soothed my soul. This journey also led me deeper in the practice of meditation and love for nature. That's how I came out of burnout and eventually returned to work, as peace in Afghanistan remained an unfinished dream. Somehow these practices helped me through another decade of working toward peace. I continued with fact-finding trips to Kabul and briefed the US Congress on the Afghanistan conflict multiple times.

In 2015, I experienced another burnout after two years of work on Afghan women and women's rights globally. I started to notice a pattern of war, a pattern of human rights violations, and a pattern of exploitation of locals who didn't understand regional and global politics. This burnout took a full year of lounging by the beach and writing to recover. I moved to Florida for a year and explored my creative side, giving it wings. This was also the year my mother's health began to fail, and I knew I had to return to Virginia. I wanted to be around my siblings, as I knew from my mother's diagnosis that she didn't have much time. I flew to Pakistan to visit her for what I knew would be the last time. She passed away shortly after. She died without her last wish granted, which was to see her baby boy Hafiz alive and well. It took a lot of inner spiritual work for me to find solace in the heart knowing she is now watching from Heaven, and all is well, as her suffering in this world ended and her soul has journeyed on.

I fully occupied myself again with work. Finally, in 2021, the US and Coalition forces exited from Afghanistan unceremoniously. I was working on atrocity prevention at the time. I took two months' leave without pay to regain my sanity and composure from my third burnout. For 20 years I had written policy papers, provided sound advice to many organizations, policymakers, the US administration, and Congress. However, my voice was not heard, and my warnings were ignored. I felt let down, but my phone kept ringing with requests for help with evacuating human rights defenders. The US government completely miscalculated the endgame. And again the price was paid by ordinary Afghans, not the corrupt Afghan leaders who filled their pockets and ran. After an exhausting five weeks, I went to Turkey for the last three weeks of my leave. I had done what I could to fulfill all the requests for assistance. It was my turn to have some peace and deal with my own emotions. I traveled to Turkey, as I had always wanted to visit Rumi's shrine.

After a few days in Konya, my heart found some solace. This is a poem I wrote to express what could not be expressed as a professional:

> Afghanistan—It will more than break you
> It will throw you in a dark treacherous storm
> You will feel like scattered debris
> With fierce winds throwing you in every which way
> Believer or not
> It will make you scream
> "Oh my God"
> Over and over again
> It will force you to take endless deep sighs
> Gasping for air
> You will find yourself at its dominion
> Until the storm settles
> And a new dawn breaks
> Leaving you to look around
> With weary eyes
> and see for yourself
> That the world has never really been fair
> That you didn't want to be part of this storm
> That you were pulled in
> Against your own will
> But here you are
> Scattered like broken glass
> What now?
> What else?
> Can your soul find its way around?
> Can you transcend body and mind?
> Now that both have failed you
> Can you rise above the dark clouds?
> Can you cling to a sliver of light?
> Can you endure the continued nightmares?
> Can you dream a better dream?
> Can you hold on?
> Just a little longer
> Until a new vision is realized?
> Oh yes
> A little more endurance is needed

Until the sun of mercy rises
Will it make you a believer?
Or will it take away all your faith in mankind?
Tell me
Oh soul
How will you come out of this storm?
For sure not the way you entered
But upon departure
Will you pay a special tribute?
A standing ovation?
Perhaps a humbling salute
Or some words of gratitude
For the lessons you have been taught.
Or will you go about life
living like a wounded soldier
You decide…how will you come out?
A martyr, a believer, an atheist, or a saint?

My third burnout was hard. I didn't bounce back so easily. I left my full-time job and became a consultant. I lost faith in knocking on congressional and administration doors trying to move policymakers toward decisions that would bring about peace and prevent atrocities. After some months of reflection in 2023, I realized that my true strength lies in integrating my creative side with professional work. While I will continue to take up projects that impact peacebuilding positively around the world, I am now equally nourishing the more creative side of me.

For me, poetry is like therapy. It is healing. The pen and the blank paper offer me a safe space to articulate my experience, my emotions, and the complexity of what I have learned and understood. Here, I can own my narrative. It helps me untangle the light and darkness we experience; it offers my soul a place to remain true and intact. It transcends the mental space, and drops me in the heart, and helps me heal my own wounds while allowing me to voice the collective pain that transcends linguistic, cultural, and political barriers. It helps me connect with our shared humanity.

The Work Continues

As an Afghan American working on issues of peace and security from Washington, I often had to suppress emotions that would either be triggered or would surface when dealing with professional work. Kabul, the city I was born in, is not the only city that left its mark on my heart and psyche. My journey to become a peacebuilder and work in Washington as an advocate/lobbyist for peace was not short of its own challenges. I often felt I didn't belong, yet I did, but then again, I didn't. Over and over in my profession, I witnessed and experienced many forms of violence. From outright racist comments like "Afghans just don't want peace" to deep structural issues that live in plain sight.

This most recent phase of my professional career feels too raw. Sometimes I feel like I wasted the last two decades of my life educating myself, working on peacebuilding, and trying to move policymakers toward rational decisions. All three previous US presidents—and one current—did considerable damage to Afghan society in the name of freeing them from the Taliban and helping them with nation-building, building democracy, and human rights/women's rights (while actively putting many warlords and corrupt politicians in power).

This brings me to an important point. Peacebuilding is not just outer work. Washington and Kabul are cities where power is brokered and decisions are made, often without the input of those whose lives will be impacted by those decisions. There is little to no accountability for policy mistakes. This can feel hopeless. But it's not. It requires that we do our inner work to stay resilient and effective. For me, the practice of daily meditation is key to navigating the inner work of healing, forgiveness, and letting go while continuing with outer work.

An Open Wound, a Colossal Failure

What was the point of the 20-plus years of war to save Afghans from the Taliban and the massive cost in blood and treasure, both American and Afghan—to hand the country right back to them anyway? As someone who spent two decades of her life calling for talks with the Taliban to end the war and negotiate peace, I cannot help but call out the four US presidents. It has been a colossal failure of leadership not to end the war in a way that withheld Afghan societal progress and honored the loss of American lives. I was personally exhausted taking part in congressional and administration briefings on Afghanistan highlighting repeatedly the need for engagement with the Taliban as the only way to end the conflict. This does not mean I agreed with the Taliban's politics, but I understood that without negotiations, the US coalition would eventually lose the war. As it did.

It was clear after several fact-finding trips that the mostly puppet governments the United States helped set up in Afghanistan, consisting of known corrupt figures and warlords with Afghan blood on their hands, were not going to share power if the United States refused to hold that space. Unfortunately, by the time the United States started engaging in talks, it was too late. Those talks came because the United States was failing militarily—not because the leadership was pursuing peace through a political settlement. That is the simple truth.

The Afghan people, not the Taliban leadership, continue to suffer. As for human rights, they were not even considered when the United States was negotiating the exit agreement with the Taliban since no Afghans were included except for Taliban representatives. The process went from the United States resisting any negotiations to a complete sellout, without even a decent agreement for an organized withdrawal of all foreign forces. Adding insult to injury, no representatives of the Afghan government nor any other organization, group, or any women at all were included in the final negotiations.

As a result, the people of Afghanistan continue to suffer under additional humanitarian, economic, and human rights challenges. The Biden administration froze 7 billion Afghanistan Central Bank funds in August 2021. These assets belong to the Afghan people, not the Taliban or any other government. The continued economic hardship caused by a sudden foreign troop withdrawal and frozen Central Bank funds resulted in famine and severe economic hardship for ordinary Afghan citizens the last few years.

This is why the Afghan people's sentiment has turned against the American government. Two wars: one resulting from the Cold War and the other from 9/11. Both times the Afghan people were used and abandoned—the first time to take down the Soviet Union through a proxy, and the second time to show the world a fierce and capable military force out to punish the perpetrators of the 9/11 crimes.

The next poem captures the suffering of the Afghan people through decades of war, and also the suffering of humanity everywhere war crimes and atrocities continue to unfold today:

> When you unleash your bombs
> On our people and our lands
> Do you see us burn to ashes
> Lit on fire
> How deep does it satisfy you?
> Our blood splashed on ruins
> Broken bones, bleeding limbs
> Missing arms and legs
> Spread across dust and concrete
> Little children under rubble
> Babies, women and men slaughtered
> Do you get a cheap thrill?
> When you rain down your bombs
> Do you wait around to see who got killed
> Does your army rejoice?
> Forget our bodies
> That's just flesh and blood
> No value to you
> But tell me, do you see our spirits
> Of course not. You are blinded
> By hate and revenge
> Because you have disturbed and destroyed
> Our people and our land
> And slaughtered us for decades
> As the world watches in deafening silence
> Blurring lines between truth and lies
> Still our spirit rises from our dead bodies
> Witnessing something more horrific
> Your bombs and your guns and your soldiers
> Continue taking innocent lives
> But you can't see the real calamity

You, yourself, with your own hands
Have KILLED YOUR OWN HUMANITY.

Shukria Dellawar is founder and President of Lotus Anchor, a consulting firm specializing in conflict prevention and peacebuilding. She holds a BA and an MS in conflict analysis and resolution from George Mason University's Carter School for Peace. She has testified before Congress and was instrumental in the passage of the Elie Wiesel Genocide and Atrocities Prevention Act and the Global Fragility Act.

Open Access This chapter is licensed under the terms of the Creative Commons Attribution-NonCommercial-NoDerivatives 4.0 International License (http://creativecommons.org/licenses/by-nc-nd/4.0/), which permits any noncommercial use, sharing, distribution and reproduction in any medium or format, as long as you give appropriate credit to the original author(s) and the source, provide a link to the Creative Commons license and indicate if you modified the licensed material. You do not have permission under this license to share adapted material derived from this chapter or parts of it.

The images or other third party material in this chapter are included in the chapter's Creative Commons license, unless indicated otherwise in a credit line to the material. If material is not included in the chapter's Creative Commons license and your intended use is not permitted by statutory regulation or exceeds the permitted use, you will need to obtain permission directly from the copyright holder.

Policy Recommendations and Ways Forward

Rachel Locke and Jocelyn Getgen Kestenbaum

The authors of this volume have taken us to diverse urban centers across the globe—Mexico City, London, Aleppo, Baltimore, Rio, Mumbai, and more—to build a better understanding of identity-based mass violence (IBMV), its causes and consequences, and unique strategies for prevention in cities. While representing varied disciplines and geographies, the authors use myriad tools and frameworks to unearth and expose the harms to—and the humanity of—individuals and collectives rendered invisible, those excluded from the realms of safety and security afforded to others. These incredible experts include storytellers, artists, journalists, academics, practitioners, and policymakers who have labored together in community to tackle the pressing challenges of addressing, mitigating,

R. Locke (✉)
Peace in Our Cities, San Diego, CA, USA
e-mail: rachel@peaceinourcities.org

J. G. Kestenbaum
Cardozo Law Institute in Holocaust and Human Rights, Cardozo School of Law, New York, NY, USA
e-mail: jocelyn.getgen@yu.edu

and preventing structural and acute violence against individuals and groups based on their multiple and intersecting identities.

What this volume emphatically reminds us is that violence exerted repeatedly and at scale requires a combination of intentional disempowerment, dehumanization, brutalization, exploitation, and isolation. The collective works herein expose these forms of marginalization and othering. Once exposed, particularly in our oversaturated information environment, the works put forward a call to action: to continue advocating for the kind of transformative change our contributors and those on the losing side of IBMV demand and deserve.

This volume draws intentionally from both the atrocity-prevention and urban-violence prevention fields, a framing that helps to ensure the narrative throughout weaves across the hyperlocal to the national and global levels. The tools and approaches of much of our multilateral systems have been oriented around the cessation of conflict in the world. While valuable, this has resulted in systems that are not well set up to address or prevent structural violence. They are, rather, much more oriented around the presence of or escalation toward large-scale, acute violence. In part because of this, their designs all too often replicate the very structural violence this volume unearths. When politicians, policymakers, and practitioners focus too narrowly on mitigating acts of spectacular violence without also upending and transforming the systems, structures, institutions, and processes that enable and sustain such violence, we see cycles of harm repeat and endure.

While this volume respects the value and urgency of response systems, the concrete policy recommendations outlined in this chapter seek to direct a much greater balance of resources toward the transformation of the structures, institutions, and systems that enable violence. This commitment to address the structural conditions forces new thinking and requires operating in new, specific, targeted, and sometimes imaginative ways.

Every contributor has highlighted, either subtly or directly, alternatives to the present reality: recommendations that represent shifts in practice, alterations to norms, and overwhelming changes to social structure. These calls to action are directed primarily to reform-minded individuals who have power and influence to transform our urban spaces and prevent

IBMV. Here, we aim to consolidate many of these calls to action in the form of concrete recommendations, highlighting the value of outcomes themselves and the processes through which change comes about.

Guiding Principles

Developing the concrete recommendations below relied on particular methods of deep listening, reflexivity, and centering affected individual and community voices, the same principles required for future action. This volume upends traditional hierarchies of knowledge production by explicitly weaving together the voices of those typically left out of more-conventional academic spaces together with voices of those who are more institutionally oriented. In so doing, this volume unlocks an opportunity to rethink and reorient policy approaches that center the knowledge, expertise, and solutions of those most immediately grappling with acute and structural conditions of violence through a deeply collaborative process.

The authors and editors gathered in community through a series of workshops to understand diverse perspectives, contexts of acute and structural violence, and the causes and consequences of such violence. From these gatherings and the resulting chapters, we have compiled some of the most salient themes and recommendations for future positive peace in urban spaces across the globe. These discussions and deep reflections make clear that local communities—the affected populations themselves—are best positioned to articulate the change they want to see. But it is crucial to recognize these voices are often being kept intentionally silenced; maintaining a sheen of invisibility to the harm inflicted on certain communities serves traditional power structures, reinforces harmful social norms, and allows for abuses to continue unabated. To realize transformative change, existing power differentials—and who is best served by them—must be acknowledged and addressed.

The mosaic of power competition demands that process-oriented recommendations be prioritized as equal to—if not more than—outcome-oriented recommendations. A sole focus on outcomes otherwise risks replicating whose voice matters, and whose does not.

1. Recommendations must be process oriented as well as outcome oriented.

Process recommendations address how to determine goals and strategies. They must include participatory, inclusive, and intersectional methods (i.e., who is and who is not at the table, and being intentionally reflexive, feminist, and decolonial), while outcome recommendations must be evidence based, data driven, and locally tailored (i.e., must be careful to not transplant and replicate solutions without context, and must take into consideration the specifics of the historical and present contexts).

Focusing on process is crucial. Individuals and collectives who experience acute and structural discrimination and violence based on identity often have been the objects of legal and policy solutions, largely without consultation or consideration on equal footing with other stakeholders. Transformative change requires that legal and policy decision making engage in consensus-building methods in which individuals collaborate on developing solutions together.

Stakeholders can implement participatory methods that involve bringing historically excluded individuals and groups to the table to engage their knowledge and expertise on local challenges and solutions. Participatory methods in policymaking address problems, such as lack of trust among the public for their governance institutions and perceptions of weak legitimacy. Additionally, participatory processes must intentionally seek out individuals in urban spaces with multiple and intersecting identities to ensure that all voices of those who experience structural and acute violence are centered.[1] Particularly at a moment of global retrenchment when it comes to inclusivity, sufficient protective mechanisms must be in place for meaningful participation.

Solutions must be based on evidence and grounded in knowledge that tackles challenges identified through inclusive, consensus decision-making processes. As Gary Milante reminds us in Chapter 4, "Often, we draw on data (typically statistics) that have been collected by trusted actors and are objective and replicable. But statistics alone do not constitute evidence; equally rigorous is the collection of qualitative evidence....

Further, 'official statistics' or the 'establishment' versions of facts may be insufficient to construct a historical record, contested as it may be."

2. Recommendations must be rights based, trauma informed, and survivor centered, and must be considered at the individual, collective, and societal levels.

A rights-based approach to developing and implementing laws, policies, and programs toward IBMV prevention means incorporating a conceptual framework that protects and promotes human rights and focuses on state obligations and accountability to all individuals and collectives within its borders.[2] Thriving, peaceful cities are those that establish systems, structures, norms, institutions, and public policy that guarantee human rights equally to all without discrimination while respecting inherent differences across and diversity of its population.

Trauma-informed approaches incorporate methods to better address and accommodate trauma in affected communities, including across generations. Methods can include providing resources for resilience skills when working within and against legal, policy, and other structures that perpetuate identity-based discrimination and mass violence. Trauma-informed approaches may also consider altering timelines to build in the space for dialogue, building trust, and confronting deeply held pain. As Kate Ferguson reminds us, timelines are often cited by power holders as the reason for lack of flexibility, inclusion, or adaptation, which can reinforce status-quo systems.

A survivor-centered approach is a methodology that places the rights, wishes, needs, safety, dignity, and well-being of victims-survivors at the center of all violence-prevention and response measures.[3] A survivor-centered approach will depend on specific survivors' needs and will be context specific. The process of consultation and iterative, participatory policymaking with survivor communities will ensure that policymakers prioritize their needs for safety and dignity. All states and local municipalities should endeavor to fully incorporate existing international standards and protocols that emphasize survivor-centered approaches.

Once participatory and inclusive processes incorporate these frameworks for consultation and process, solutions must be developed to address and prevent individual harms, collective harms, and wider, social harms. The consideration of the myriad ways in which identity-based discrimination and mass violence cause harm will identify particular downstream consequences of such harm. In turn, identifying harms in all of these ways may lead to tailored solutions that promote healing and trust building at the individual, community, and larger societal levels.

3. Recommendations must prioritize building trust, and (re)building and repairing relationships and community. Toward that end, recommendations must respect and integrate varied forms of expression and knowledge in pluralistic urban settings.

People who experience identity-based discrimination and mass violence in urban settings must understand and navigate dominant cultures for survival and resistance.[4] Too often, however, individuals in positions of power and privilege in government or other policymaking circles do not experience or occupy nondominant worlds, or a "double consciousness,"[5] because they are not harmed by, and many times benefit from, the very structures and systems that perpetuate IBMV. Such understanding comes from learning about the continuum of urban violence and the accompanying human rights violations perpetrated against affected communities that have been largely left unredressed.

Thus, as policymakers or government actors tasked with developing and implementing legal, policy, and other solutions to prevent and adequately address IBMV in urban settings, it is not enough to work with affected communities or advocate for their rights. Stakeholders also must understand their own roles in—and continued benefits from—structures and institutions that perpetuate discrimination and violence against certain identity groups in cities. These structures and institutions must be remade away from the hierarchical domination and subjugation of certain identity groups over others, to a place of valuing collective ways of being, centering new forms of knowledge and expertise.[6]

4. Recommendations must be made to a multitude of actors operating across diverse sectors, including multilateral institutions, government representatives and policymakers, educational administrators

and academics, business entities, and norm-setting institutional actors (e.g., journalism/media, museums, historical associations).

Diverse stakeholders implement policies and programs that can either perpetuate identity-based discrimination and mass violence or build and promote lasting peace in urban settings. Mapping such stakeholders and their roles and responsibilities to prevent and adequately respond to IBMV in cities is the first step toward developing sector-specific tools and solutions. Once identified, these stakeholders must understand the pathways of structural and acute violence—and these pathways' influence within the urban ecosystem—toward developing methods and action items to respond in preventative and transformative ways.

Journalists, for example, must be supported and protected to investigate the root causes and consequences of structural and acute violence against marginalized, minoritized communities. Additionally, affected communities and their allies must train media to use language that confronts stereotypes and calls out dehumanizing and other discourses that perpetuate IBMV. Museums must rethink narratives about historical and present moments of social unrest and must center affected communities' perspectives in such narrative (re)tellings.

5. Recommendations should lean into deep understanding and community building across related fields of study, including, but not limited to: transitional justice, international criminal law, reparations, restorative justice, conflict prevention, peacebuilding, urban violence prevention, human rights, the responsibility to protect, the security sector, community organizing, history, and memory studies.

One of the many benefits of bringing such diverse authors and editors across multiple geographies and disciplines was the start of mutual, respectful, and cross-disciplinary language understanding. That is to say, professional areas of study are siloed, but through cross-pollination and deep listening there is an extraordinary amount of insight, knowledge, and collective action that can be achieved. The combination of identity-based discrimination and mass violence is a complex social, economic, political, legal, environmental, and structural problem that requires a multidisciplinary, field-building approach. By using the common language of IBMV, this volume weaves together individuals from across different communities of practice in order to inspire and transform communities through togetherness and solidarity.

6. Recommendations must orient around transformative change, requiring a focus on both acute and structural forms of violence to address immediate harms and root causes of violence.

Preventing IBMV is an achievable goal. In order to build institutions and structures that actively prevent violence, however, we must recognize risks and warning signs, as well as understand and commit to viable options for prevention at every level across the continuum. Upstream, or primary prevention, is assessing and responding to structural risk factors that enable discrimination or violence against minority groups. Midstream, or secondary, prevention efforts include immediate, real-time response or relief efforts—including the prevention of further escalation—as moments of crises unfold in forms of acute violence against individual members of minority groups. Downstream, or tertiary, prevention is an acknowledgment and accounting in the wake of violence toward fostering resiliency, reestablishing trust, and rebuilding communities. Each of these moments along the violence continuum are important entry points where prevention of (additional) harm is possible. Each of these areas needs sustained effort and investment if prevention and/or mitigation is to be successful.

Most importantly, policies, programs, plans, and practices must address immediate harms at the same time as they tackle the underlying drivers and root causes of identity-based discrimination and mass violence in urban spaces. Undertaking immediate response actions will make policymakers and other stakeholders good at putting out fires. Without combating root causes, however, the fires will continue to spread unabated and wreak persistent and unrelenting havoc on our cities, disproportionately impacting affected communities at risk of violence.

Taking these guiding principles as a frame, the remainder of this chapter discusses how these transformative ideas apply across practical areas that include funding, training, capacity building, research methodologies, and localization. Our recommendations will not focus on blueprints; rather, these ways forward aim to shift away from prescriptive policy solutions toward new ways of thinking about policy that are more appreciative of the themes of identity, power, and space as a transformative, preventative agenda.

Throughout this collection, the editors and authors have attempted to demonstrate a broader perspective on what we should be thinking about when we think about atrocities. All too often conversations in the atrocity prevention space focus on definitions, both legal and moral. These are important dialogues, and this volume does not attempt to deny the value of legal distinctions and norms. However, while definitional analysis is taking place, time and energy that could be valuably invested in supporting the tapestry of social, economic, and political relationships that can build up preventative capacity are being left behind.

At the same time, the atrocity prevention field has largely ignored the vital role of cities in prevention, especially in upstream, or structural, prevention. The IBMV frame, with its focus on the acute and the structural, as well as the practical, provides an anecdote to the spin cycle of policy deliberations by focusing on the concrete. The focus on cities opens a toolkit of who can—and indeed should—do this work and how it can be done.

Practical Areas for Action

1. Reframing Narratives

Critical to disrupting and preventing identity-based discrimination and mass violence is framing or reframing narratives. While history is often believed to be the collection of facts, a majority or elite view of the historical record sanitizes the past from the people and collective experiences that shape our varying understandings of history. While historical events may take place at certain times and locations, they are recounted differently across groups in ways that are crucial to shaping an understanding of not just the past but also the present. Atrocities, or mass violence, do not take place in a vacuum; they rest on a foundation of socially constructed perspectives and on relative power positions. Only through understanding these varied perspectives and being open to a reframing of how we view ourselves in our collective society can we get to the solutions that respect the humanity and value of all individuals and collectives.

At its essence, much of what we are talking about in this volume is the brutalization, exploitation, and exclusion of certain groups of people by other groups of people. This brutalization, exploitation, and exclusion is both intentional (i.e., individuals explicitly casting others as less than human) and unintentional (i.e., individuals benefiting from systems that dehumanize without acknowledging or calling out the harm inflicted on specific identity groups). The city provides us with a space to observe and then shift these exploitative practices, calling on accountability for those responsible for upholding systems of structural and acute violence but also calling in partners to help transform and fully realize peaceful, vibrant urban centers.

As Ariana Markowitz discusses so eloquently in Chapter 8, forms of structural or slow violence become so ubiquitous as to be nearly invisible while simultaneously leaving scars and fissures that are deeply felt. Preventing mass atrocities starts with preventing structural violence. Whether defined as upstream prevention, social-cohesion promotion, or human rights protection, the term matters far less than a deep appreciation of how dehumanization works, and how absolutely fundamental the appreciation of and respect for all human life and dignity is.

2. Shifting Policy Orientations

Reinforcing the second Guiding Principle above, policy orientations must shift from being needs based to rights based. For far too long, "development" has overtaken "rights." In place after place, entire neighborhoods, communities, and sometimes even cities are razed or people evicted from their homes in the name of "growth and development." If we start by acknowledging that development is something done *to* people rather than *for* people, and institutions are not always rights oriented, funders—including philanthropies—should invest more in those actors and collectives, such as the Housing and Land Rights Network or Slum Dwellers International, that provide a lens of accountability and work to reinforce human rights and human standards of habitation. As Ammar Azzouz reminds us in Chapter 2, "reconstruction" must not take the place of investment in equity and prevention, nor should reconstruction be understood purely in building and infrastructure terms. People are social; their histories, artifacts, stories, and places of common meaning are essential to living contented and dignified lives. Reconstruction must center attention on collective meaning and humanity.

As many of our authors point out, the slow destruction that is both violence in its own right and also precedent to more spectacular forms of acute violence can be seen if we care to look. As al-Hakam Shaar writes in Chapter 11, "public services, security, and permits can be viewed as intentional forms of punishment, exclusion, or suppression in response to challenges to existing power structures." The very way in which groups of individuals are forced to navigate the everyday aspects of living demonstrates for whom society works and against whom systems work. When combined with the "invisibility" of harm, it is crucial work to document how groups of individuals experience life in the city based on their identity and resulting from these systemic inequalities.

Cities bring this into focus given their density of habitation as well as their diversity. Cities join together political and personal identities with the physical space. When this joining together results in practice that is exclusionary, the propensity for violence is often reinforced. The fluidity of boundaries within and around cities can, for many, define their very being, where they walk, with whom they talk, how they work, shop, marry, or fight. Recognizing the intersection of identity with space is crucial in our framing of rights, individual liberty, and mass-violence prevention.

One concrete pathway to ensure the recognition and protective mechanisms above and below are priorities is to create specific Offices of Violence Prevention within cities. There is a growing movement of such offices around the world, with some very intentionally focused not only on reducing the presentation of physical violence but also addressing the deep scars and manifestations of generational violence and trauma. While much of the writing here is aspirational, it is also factual to say cities are taking up the mantle and—in many cases—doing this very hard work.

3. Focusing on Urban Conflict

After meaningful and hard-won declines in global conflict, the last several years have seen an upsurge, with more conflicts playing out today than at any time in the post-World War II era. Not only are more conflicts playing out around the world, but wars increasingly and deliberately target civilians and are increasingly multi-actor, involving a range of state, quasi-state, and nonstate actors. The increasing complexity of violent conflict makes it both difficult and imperative to endeavor to disambiguate how strategies of IBMV are precedents to violent conflict, core to the very strategy of war making, or pursued in the devastating wake of conflict (which may also precede future conflict). While this volume explicitly places focus on IBMV whether or not the violence occurs in conflict, it simultaneously recognizes that diagnosing the relationship to organized conflict remains of paramount importance, particularly at a time of increased global war making.

The rules of war remain unchanged: civilians must not be targeted disproportionate to any military advantage gained. But rules do not equal facts, and civilians are increasingly both "collateral damage" and intentional targets of war-making parties. As the majority of humanity continues its move to cities, war and the violence it brings will accompany such movement, increasingly resulting in urban landscapes as theaters of conflict.

Several of our authors point out ways conflict creates new identity groups. We have seen this in Syria, as Shaar discussed, as well as a range of other locales around the world. Identities are never static. Entire communities can arise from the emergence of shifting identity formation, including in the onslaught or aftermath of war. But it is also crucial not to romanticize the formation of identity, even when formed in reaction to conflict or violence. Newly formed communities that bring people together in the face of conflict can also reinforce some of the same harmful patterns that gave rise to their creation. The need for community is human, but the formation of community is value neutral. Some aspects of some communities may be exceptionally prosocial and peaceful, while others can be destructive and predatory. Peace negotiations, mediation, and other efforts toward conflict and violence cessation should pay great attention to how identity is shaped, recast, and forges itself in community while simultaneously attending the practical and tangible aspects of laying down of arms.

The United Nations (UN) is forged around ending conflict and upholding human rights. The international community must continue to invest in the accountability authority of the UN system to bring perpetrators of atrocity crimes to justice and engage in transitional justice processes, albeit in a way that is decolonial and survivor centered.

For some, accountability looks like fines, restitution, jail time, formal apologies, statements, etc. UN special rapporteurs can also offer expert investigations and statements that help foster accountability, and the Security Council can suspend its use of the veto power in the case of atrocity-crimes perpetration. Further, advocates must not abandon their strategies to bring survivors' claims to international courts to hold states responsible for human rights violations and individuals to account for international crimes, but must include additional, restorative, and other community-based approaches to their advocacy toolbox to center victims' and survivors' needs for healing and transformative, structural changes.

Finally, it is worth being clear eyed that even institutions run the risk of capture by powerful interests. This should not mean we abandon institutions altogether; rather we must either invest in their legitimacy, integrity, and operational focus, or we must create new institutions that respond to the needs of excluded and subaltern peoples.

4. Institutional Localization

As Ammar Azzouz discusses in his chapter, communities can be labeled as undesired, unwanted, illegal, or terrorists based on identity. Violence takes different forms against them as their communities are seen as disposable "sacrifice zones."[7] A localization agenda should go beyond just ensuring national actors have seats at tables and local organizations are funded. It should also understand the mosaic of power and disempowerment at the hyperlocal level to ensure efforts to localize do not end up reinforcing the very abuse and discrimination that is creating and reinforcing disposable communities.

International institutions are hugely valuable and have a great role to play. But they must never take the place of or be valued more than the people, institutions, and social structures on the ground they purport to serve and protect. Over the past several years, there has been significant investment in a localization agenda, with significant policy emphasis placed on ensuring greater voice, leadership, and power of local actors in decision making, knowledge generation, and program implementation. There have been tangible, positive benefits to this agenda in terms of financing and voice, but the localization agenda should extend further.

As Kerry Whigham states so precisely in Chapter 13, "One aspect of both acute and structural violence that is often overlooked...is the actual structures it produces, that is, the built environment that surrounds us." Placing importance on "geographies of domination" is key to understanding and preventing the replication of power dominance by some over others in ways that reproduce and reinforce violence.[8]

And, as Flávia Carbonari explores in Chapter 21, balanced, integrated, and fair strategies are key, but this looks different from one microneighborhood to the next. Understanding what an integrated strategy means and having the local sensitivity to put it into practice will have huge dividends from prevention and peacebuilding perspectives. These ideas extend into urban planning, which is all too often carried out in the interest of the majority or the elite, with great harm done to certain communities. From pedagogy to practice, the field of urban planning must be reframed around *all* the people who inhabit the urban environment, taking into consideration who benefits, who is harmed, and who has the most to gain or lose from urban planning investments. In Chapter 7, Michal Braier and Efrat Cohen Bar provide clear examples of when urban planning works to discriminate, while Friederike Bubenzer (Chapter 15) and Kerry Whigham (Chapter 13) offer examples of a different kind of urban planning.

5. Investing in Dialogue

This volume walks an important line of articulating the imperative of practice that is based on data and evidence while reckoning with the fact that traditionally, data and evidence are included or excluded depending on whether voices, knowledge, or lived experience is valued. What is or is not collected also often serves certain interests, for example, *not* keeping data on child recruitment into armed groups as a signal of conflict cessation, even when such practices continue. If we believe knowledge is power, we must also acknowledge power can be used for both harm and benefit. This volume argues in substance and in style for an equality of voices and perspectives. That knowledge is not prioritized or undermined according to one's identity, position, or academic credentials.

In practice, this means convening dialogues on mass violence, atrocity prevention, and urban violence prevention should value knowledge and intent over these markers. Contributors to this volume spoke passionately about being invited to meetings to provide testimony of their trauma—harm done to them and their communities—while simultaneously being excluded as experts in dialogues on how such harms should be understood and addressed. Those with lived experience of harm must not be seen simply as fetishized voices to speak only of their experiences but rather as knowledge holders whose perspective, interpretation, and ideas are valued and centered in policy solutions.

6. Rethinking Funding Priorities

Discussing policy, legislation, and plans without talking about resources risks creating ideas without action. What is crucial to acknowledge here is that there are more challenges in need of action than there are resources that have been prioritized to address them. What this volume suggests is that rather than recognizing a problem and then programming against it, it is essential to place social cohesion and protection of marginalized individuals and groups at the center of all priorities. This is less a call for specific programming funds and more a call for an ethos that demands equity and rights for all, regardless of identity or economic status.

This also becomes a call to invest equitably. As Braier and Cohen Bar's chapter demonstrated so pointedly, Jews and Palestinians have wildly different opportunities that stem in part from very different levels of investment in basic infrastructure and community services. Similarly, higher-quality services and facilities are found in Jewish-Israeli areas, and public transportation, health, welfare, and community services are segregated.

Most project-based funding includes little support for built-in, overhead costs as well as process-oriented costs, including the time it takes to build relationships and engage with broad constituencies of people. Organizations reliant on grant funding for their work continuously raise this as a primary obstacle to institutional security and programmatic consistency. Because so many funders retain these time-limited, project-based models, organizations carrying out crucial work are often forced to rely on the same local experts over and over again, as developing new connections and taking the time to learn from diverse voices takes time—time that is often unfunded. Meaningful integration of more voices, including those directly impacted and those who have done harm—who are also often victims themselves—is crucial to finding off-ramps to cycles of harm. This might mean expanding allowable costs, timeframes, or the types of eligible participants in project-based work.

7. Investing in Community

As this book aims to represent and as so many of our authors show in their chapters, art is a means through which to connect to people on both intellectual and emotional levels (Whigham). It can elevate the voice of those otherwise ignored and attach meaning to place in a way that words are insufficient to do. Policymakers can enable the environment of urban spaces through, *inter alia*, human rights protections to free speech and peaceful assembly, and police training and reform to implement a rights-based approach to embrace art and demonstration as part of civic life in urban spaces. As many of our contributors discuss, art is also a way of healing trauma and ensuring the space for expressing emotion to heal harmed communities. Because art has the power to heal and to translate meaning, as well as to help people find joy and identity (which authoritarians would often seek to control or repress), it is often viewed as a threat to dictators or those seeking to maintain a grip on power. Investing in protection of artists, through organizations such as the Artistic Freedom Initiative, is crucial to keeping art flourishing.

Around the world there is a rise in authoritarian regimes and an associated crackdown on civil societies, civil liberties, freedom of movement, and freedom of expression. These repressive measures are being coordinated primarily by national governments. City leaders have, in many instances, formed barriers of resistance to these efforts, striving to uphold individual and collective rights. The ability to reinforce such rights, however, is highly dependent on the political system within the respective country and how decentralized it may be. Regardless of system and context, there is an urgent need to invest in organizations that work to protect human rights defenders, journalists, academics, political prisoners, and all those who are being persecuted for their beliefs, their opposition to political elites, or their identities.

People need community and places to gather to find meaning, to find joy, and to find solace, particularly in contexts of harm, discrimination, and exclusion. Having safe public spaces that are humanity reinforcing rather than concrete blocks provides the physical shell for the emotional, mental, and spiritual needs of people to flourish. Protecting public spaces means also preserving cultural heritage and must be done in a way that is participatory and inclusive of trained and untrained urban planners (see Chapter 9 and the Guiding Principles above).

The emergence of public health approaches to understanding violence helps to treat many forms of violence as a disease that has contagion trajectories, points of origin, and pathways for remediation and prevention. A public health approach also sees both individual and social forms of responsibility for harms, rather than hoping to kill, punish, arrest, or detain our way out of violence. Investing in improved diagnosis of violence can help to prevent its cyclical nature, with significant benefit to address both structural and acute forms of violence. Randle DeFalco argues that reframing atrocities as "public health catastrophes, rather than spectacles of violence," would help to improve understanding of violence pathways and lead to policy responses that focus on structural changes to address root causes.[9] Flávia Carbonari emphasizes that upstream, rights-based prevention policies, such as multisectoral, integrated, violence-prevention plans, are integral to address root causes of violence and reduce the incidence of urban violence. Our critical caution is to also look at state-sponsored violence and to protect individuals, collectives, and communities designated by the state as "sacrifice zones" from IBMV and erasure.

As important as the funding discussion above is, the reality is that around the world budgets are contracting and spending on violence prevention, peace, and justice is being slashed. Budgets or funding, however, are not always determinative. Often, people in positions of power insist on expanding the table to include those directly impacted who have less institutional power. As Wiebe and Turner discuss in Chapter 9, investing in individuals can be transformative and can—in turn—help to inform the transformation of entire systems and communities. People need agency to change their lives and investing in that agency can change thousands of lives. Journalists (Chapter 22), ethnographic researchers (Chapter 5), artists (Chapter 3), and others are telling these crucial stories. Decision-makers—and those who elect them—must take time to listen, to see the humanity in people who may not look like, sound like, or believe like they do.

8. Training and Capacity Building

As Bobbi Sherrod reminds us in Chapter 16, coping strategies, including the very human imperative to seek safety in an environment in which one's safety is threatened or undervalued, can be misunderstood or misdiagnosed to place blame on the individual or individuals under risk of harm, rather than to actually see the forces causing harm. Having the right training, the right sensitivities to understand this phenomenon is key. ElsaMarie D'Silva reminds us of this as well in Chapter 20, making clear that young women are not avoiding school out of a dislike of education but rather as a protective mechanism in the face of real danger. Those whose responsibility it is to analyze social patterns—whether in legal, transportation, education, healthcare or other systems—must be trained or have the training capacity to understand these protective mechanisms, which are context and identity specific.

Furthermore, education systems, whether primary, secondary, or tertiary, have roles to play both in educating themselves on how identities impact the safety experience of students in their care and in how they teach and communicate empathy and humanity. For example, universities can advance research and data-collection processes that acknowledge the voices of those who have traditionally been left out, intentionally including such voices in academic pursuits. Schools can do better in hiring staff representative of their student body while also looking beyond immediate behavioral issues to understand what deeper, root causes may be at play.

Beyond training, urban networks can hold space through which professionals across disciplines can be brought together to discuss how their individual efforts—as educators, as transport engineers, as librarians, as city managers, and others—can inform and support one another to build safe, resilient communities. Creating space for cross-disciplinary collaboration is crucial, as it will reinforce training and capacity building in helping to understand and realize the priorities and rights of different communities. Further, researchers and city governments can collect data to hold unique departments or agencies accountable to living up to the standards set through collaborative processes. Far too often, training is not accompanied by accountability and does not, therefore, get put into practice.

Beyond all the recommendations mentioned above, it is also crucial to acknowledge the pain inherent in all of what is being discussed. A clear through line between structural and acute violence is trauma. Understanding the pathology of trauma, its pathways and, crucially, opportunities for addressing trauma, are essential to creating real, lasting safety. Our authors are our guides in how we share, the spaces we encumber, and the work we do for ourselves. Rose Mbone counsels, "The trauma process has been able to support all of these groups in their understanding of ways of communicating, including that it's possible to criticize but still maintain dignity. We can work together, and we still maintain respect for each other." Friederike Bubenzer reminds us that addressing trauma doesn't simply mean providing counseling or space for talking, but also considering the literal construction of places for healing and well-being. And, as Shukria Dellawar reinforces the so crucial point, this work "requires that we do our inner work to stay resilient and effective."

The Guiding Principles and Practical Areas for Action sections above are not one-size-fits-all solutions. Nor are they directed at a singular institution or small set of institutions. The work described here is big and complicated, and it requires resources to co-create and implement solutions that are bold and transformative for lasting, positive peace. We invite readers not to take these recommendations as pro forma but rather to use them to inspire new ideas, new collaborations, and new energies that can shift our cities toward urban centers that are more peaceful, interdependent, and inclusive of all human beings and their collective diversity.

Notes

1. G. Rowe and L. Frewer, "Public Participation Methods: A Framework for Evaluation," *Science, Technology & Human Values* 25, no. 1 (2000): 3–29.
2. Prisca Benelli, *Human Rights in Humanitarian Action and Development Cooperation and the Implications of Rights-Based Approaches in the Field*, ReliefWeb, https://reliefweb.int/report/world/human-rig hts-humanitarian-action-and-development-cooperation-and-imp lications-rights, July 15, 2023; Andrea Cornwall and Celestine Nyamu-Musembi, "Putting the 'Rights-Based Approach' to Development into Perspective," *Third World Quarterly* 25, no. 8 (2004): 1415-1437.
3. United Nations Inter-Agency Standing Committee, *IASC Definition & Principles of a Victim/Survivor Centered Approach*, https://perma.cc/AV3D-P2CW, IASC 3, June 6, 2023.

4. See Haunani-Kay Trask, "Feminism and Indigenous Hawaiian Nationalism", Vol. 21 SIGNS 906-916 (1996).
5. Double consciousness refers to "a 'sensation,' a consciousness of one's self, but which falls short of a unified, 'true' self-consciousness." "Double Consciousness," *Stanford Encyclopedia of Philosophy*, Feb. 16, 2023, https://plato.stanford.edu/entries/double-consciousness/. The term was coined by W. E. B. Du Bois to describe a feeling of "twoness" caused by the oppression and "disvaluation" of African Americans in a white-dominated society. Ibid.
6. See Jocelyn Getgen Kestenbaum and Caroline LaPorte, "Unsettling Human Rights Pedagogy and Practice in Settler Colonial Contexts," American University Journal of Gender, Social Policy & the Law, Vol. 31, Issue 3 2023): 441-83.; D. Purdue, "Whose Knowledge Counts? 'Experts,' 'Counter-Experts,' and the 'Lay' Public," *Ecologist* 25, no. 5 (1995): 170-72.
7. Sacrifice Zones is a term of art used in violent dispossession of groups of people, especially in urban extractivism. It is also used in the environmental justice movement to define areas where residents, typically from disenfranchised or marginalized communities, face higher levels of environmental harm than in neighboring areas. See, Bullard RD. "Sacrifice Zones: The Front Lines of Toxic Chemical Exposure in the United States." Environmental Health Perspective. 2011 Jun;119(6):A266.
8. Steve Pile, "Introduction: Opposition, political identities, and spaces of resistance," in *Geographies of resistance*, ed. Steve Pile and Michael Keith (London: Routledge, 1997), 1–32.
9. Randle DeFalco, "(Re)Conceptualizing Atrocity Crimes as Public Health Catastrophes," in *Public Health, Mental Health and Mass Atrocity Prevention*, ed. Getgen Kestenbaum, Mahoney, Meade, Fuller. (Routledge: 2021).

Jocelyn Getgen Kestenbaum is professor of law at the Benjamin N. Cardozo School of Law, where she directs the Benjamin B. Ferencz Human Rights and Atrocity Prevention Clinic and the Cardozo Law Institute in Holocaust and Human Rights. She holds a JD from Cornell Law School and an MPH from the Johns Hopkins Bloomberg School of Public Health.

Open Access This chapter is licensed under the terms of the Creative Commons Attribution-NonCommercial-NoDerivatives 4.0 International License (http://creativecommons.org/licenses/by-nc-nd/4.0/), which permits any noncommercial use, sharing, distribution and reproduction in any medium or format, as long as you give appropriate credit to the original author(s) and the source, provide a link to the Creative Commons license and indicate if you modified the licensed material. You do not have permission under this license to share adapted material derived from this chapter or parts of it.

The images or other third party material in this chapter are included in the chapter's Creative Commons license, unless indicated otherwise in a credit line to the material. If material is not included in the chapter's Creative Commons license and your intended use is not permitted by statutory regulation or exceeds the permitted use, you will need to obtain permission directly from the copyright holder.

Identity-Based Mass Violence and Cities: Concluding Thoughts

Rachel Locke, Kelsey Paul Shantz, Andrei Serbin Pont, and Jai-Ayla Sutherland

This volume is a compendium of perspectives that, first and foremost, shed light on pervasive violence that is often visible yet ignored—made to appear invisible, unseen, or acceptable. Weaving from the personal and heartfelt to the more removed and analytical, this volume asserts that our collective knowledge on the fundamental structures of identity-based mass violence and how it can be addressed is made stronger when informed by more-complete perspectives and expressions of evidence. Put another way, evidence of the occurrence of identity-based mass violence and how to prevent it is best reflected by combining

R. Locke (✉)
Peace in Our Cities, San Diego, CA, USA
e-mail: rachel@peaceinourcities.org

K. Paul Shantz · J.-A. Sutherland
Stanley Center for Peace and Security, Muscatine, IA, USA

A. Serbin Pont
Economicas y Sociales, Coordinadora Regional Investigaciones Económicas y Sociales, Buenos Aires, Argentina

quantifiable, tested data and case studies with the essential knowledge from within communities, held by those who understand first-hand the experience of violence and who have been part of healing.

While each contribution offers unique perspectives, expertise, and analytical frames, the whole—the entirety of this volume—is truly greater than the sum of its parts. This field-building, innovative, and disruptive compilation reflects hours of honest and vulnerable reflection, convening, sharing, listening, critique, and creativity—through laughter and tears—to expose the gaps in the legal and policy architecture of violence prevention and response, as well as to generate and center locally driven solutions toward transformative change. At its core, this effort has been to prevent and address the societal underpinnings that lead to violent death, and to realize the equality and dignity of all human beings in urban spaces. The current realities of ongoing structural, institutional, and acute violence along identity lines in cities across the globe demand urgent action. Until and unless these structures are reformed, certain urban communities will continue to be the sacrifice zones for the benefit of the elite and privileged few.

As thinkers and doers—whether through art, activism, poetry, narration, policy development, academic research, or otherwise—the contributors to this volume force a reckoning with violence in all its manifestations and what that means for how to harness the capacities that exist to create environments that are more peaceful, more just, and more safe. Throughout the process of developing this volume, it's been important to acknowledge that the word "violence" itself can be divisive. For some, the word brings to mind a specific or acute incident or event that is easy to see, to identify, even to count. For others, the word evokes a much broader set of violations or harms, including those that are not easily observed but still result in death, disease, disability, discrimination, disenfranchisement, and lasting, generational trauma. This volume asserts affirmatively that we must care about preventing all forms of violence, without prioritizing "spectacular incidents" of violence over the slower-burn manifestations. This is not simply because human rights demand that we value both. It's also because the slower-burn manifestations of harm are precisely what set the stage for the larger, more spectacular, and—at times—genocidal levels of violence.

The world today is increasingly dangerous, with conflicts, violence, and weapons flows all on the rise at the same time multilateral systems are buckling and national governments are falling prey to the appeal of authoritarianism. The legal tools, policies, and frames on which we currently lean most heavily to check power and address the root causes of violence have proven limited in preventing and responding adequately to identity-based mass violence in urban spaces. Indeed, all too often, whether as intended or not, structures and institutions are operating to perpetuate discrimination, exclusion, and violence against marginalized urban populations. Although difficult and perilous to navigate, times of crisis can surface opportunities for innovation and transformative change.

We as co-editors recognize that this volume does not capture the entirety of identity-based mass violence in cities; in fact, the magnitude of the everyday unseen or ignored levels of violence warrants a reckoning of empathy, study, community building, and policy solutions. Our hope is that this volume and the tremendous chapters from our contributing authors provide a sound basis for further study, practice, and action. We invite further study, including on other forms of identity we may not have included here. We invite you, our reader, to consider where you are best positioned to facilitate healing and change, including where you see systems of violence or where identity is weaponized, and where you have the ability to create change. We are unlikely to have always gotten it right; any errors are our own. But we created this volume not to be "right"—we created it so that those whose lives may be at risk due to identity-based violence that is large scale or structural may never face that preventable outcome. This volume was created to honor all lives; shining a light to make the invisible visible so all people can live in peace.

While complex in practice, what this volume asserts is simple in mission. It argues for a centering of rights and dignity for all. Every day, cities navigate a range of competing interests, ideas, religions, norms, and values. And every day, cities—including the people within them—do this peacefully and in such ways that are invigorating, caretaking, and beautiful. But this requires intentionality. It is not that every city in the world needs to undertake a cookie-cutter set of reforms; they should not. Rather, it is that urban inhabitants need to see themselves in one another, and urban leaders need to see the value of interdependence and connectedness. At a time when leaders around the world are manipulating differences to nefarious, violent ends, seeing humanity in others is an act of resistance, an act of peacebuilding, and, for many, an act of courage.

The world faces a severe empathy gap. For far too long we have seen our earth, our home, even our fellow humans in purely utilitarian or instrumentalized ways. It is well past time to truly look at one another. To see one another's humanity and to understand the actions that we can all take to uphold that humanity, to live the lives we are all worthy of living. This volume calls on each of us to truly see one another and to lean into the hope that through working together we can make this world a place of promise and prosperity for all.

Open Access This chapter is licensed under the terms of the Creative Commons Attribution-NonCommercial-NoDerivatives 4.0 International License (http://creativecommons.org/licenses/by-nc-nd/4.0/), which permits any noncommercial use, sharing, distribution and reproduction in any medium or format, as long as you give appropriate credit to the original author(s) and the source, provide a link to the Creative Commons license and indicate if you modified the licensed material. You do not have permission under this license to share adapted material derived from this chapter or parts of it.

The images or other third party material in this chapter are included in the chapter's Creative Commons license, unless indicated otherwise in a credit line to the material. If material is not included in the chapter's Creative Commons license and your intended use is not permitted by statutory regulation or exceeds the permitted use, you will need to obtain permission directly from the copyright holder.

Index

A
abuse 166, 322
accessibility 304, 305, 311, 313, 314
action 532–534
activism 32
acute violence 3–5, 7, 204, 205, 209, 218, 219, 221, 222, 322, 510, 512, 515, 516, 518, 519, 527, 532
advertising 30–33
Afghanistan war 496
Alawites 204, 205, 209–215, 220
Alto al Fuego (Ceasefire program) 474, 477, 480, 483, 484, 491
analysis 531
Arab Spring 203, 215
Argentina 256–260, 268
armed conflict 178, 184, 185, 194
armed violence 177–180, 182–184, 187, 190, 192, 194, 195

art 257, 259, 260, 262–264, 266–268, 532
Assad 204, 205, 208–216, 218–221
assault 51–53
atrocity prevention 2, 3, 5, 499, 501, 531

B
Ba'ath Party 204–206, 210–212, 214
Baltimore 52, 322
Bassa 341–347, 349–353, 364
Bhuba, Gyang 341, 347
Black girls 321, 323, 324, 329, 333, 335–337
Black women 323, 324
Bosnia 41, 258, 264–266
boxing 163, 165, 175
Brazil 31, 38, 50, 56

Bristol (UK) 161–164, 167–169, 172, 173, 175
Brown people 325
Bukele, Nayib 238
bullying 321, 324, 329, 332, 333

C
caravans 66, 68–70, 72, 73
chronic violence 3
cities 4–9
civil war 205
class 167, 172
coach 163, 173–175
collective kitchens 68, 69, 76
Colombia 52, 257, 261–264, 268
commerce 33
community 81–83, 85, 87, 88, 90, 94, 96–101, 509, 511, 514, 515, 520, 521, 524, 525, 532, 533
community-based training 371
community engagement 341, 351, 360, 363
community ownership 359
community-police relations 377
community violence 437, 442, 446, 448, 450, 474
concentrated violence 474, 479
conflict 1, 43, 49–51, 54, 56, 57
consumption 34
copresence 35
creative expression 493
crimes against humanity 43–46, 54
crimes of aggression 43–45
cultural heritage 17, 21
culture 33, 36
cycles of harm 204

cycles of violence 371, 205, 208, 218, 379

D
deterritorialization 36
dialogue 341, 344, 346, 351, 353–355, 360, 362, 363
dictatorship 248
dignity 299, 301, 303, 308, 315
disappeared 52
discrimination 163
displacements 204, 221, 222
division 172
domicide 13, 15, 18, 22, 52
drugs 162–166, 471, 473, 476, 477, 482, 483, 487

E
early warning 54
economic fractures 161
education 323, 326
"Eighties Events" (student) protests 212, 213, 215, 216
El Salvador 235, 238, 241, 248, 249
emotional violence 326
empathy 484, 533, 534
employment 163
enclaving of cities 207
ethics of care 299, 301–303, 305, 306, 308, 311, 313, 315
ethnic violence 4
ethnonational segregation 110
executions 213
extortion 51
extrajudicial killing 369, 370, 372, 375
eyewitness account 51

F

farmer-herder conflicts 341, 342
Flint (MI) 55
focus group 48, 52
forced displacement 203
forced disappearance 219

G

gangs 161, 163, 165, 171, 238, 241–248, 471, 477
gang violence 439, 440
Gaza 42
gender 412–416, 420, 422, 423, 425
gender-based violence 412–414, 416, 422, 423, 425
Genocide 41, 43–46, 53, 54, 58
gentrification 164
gun violence 476, 481

H

hate crimes 45, 46, 51–53, 58
healing 257, 265, 267, 268, 341, 347–351, 353–355, 361, 503, 504
health 9, 130–132, 135, 139
heat 130–134
historical roots of conflict 341
home demolition 116, 117
homicides 469, 474, 477, 487, 491
hope 371, 374, 379, 476
humanitarian crisis 342, 343

I

identity-based mass violence (IBMV) 1–9, 382–387, 389–392, 400–402, 531, 533

identity conflict 493
India 52
Indigenous wisdom 341, 350, 355
inequality 162, 163, 167
informal-formal duality 215
informal settlements 216, 222, 369, 371, 372, 377, 378
institutions 33, 34
intent 42, 44–46, 49, 53, 54
intercommunal clashes 341–343
internally displaced person(s) 221
International Criminal Court 43
ISIS 217, 218
Israel 43

J

judicial 53
justice 256, 257, 260–262, 265, 267, 268, 369, 371, 376, 379

K

Kenya 54
knife crime 164

L

lambe-lambe 32, 35
LGBTQ+ 73
light 129, 133, 135–138
lived experience 531
local peacebuilders 341, 342, 346, 347, 351, 352, 354–361

M

Madaki, Danlami 341, 347
marginalization 127

markets 33, 34
martial law 214
mass violence 1–7, 9
measurement 41, 42, 47, 48, 57, 58
memory 256, 263, 265, 266
mental health 163, 169, 377, 379, 469
Mexico 469, 470, 472, 474, 475, 477, 479, 480
migrants 66, 67, 69, 75
militarization 469, 474
militias 179, 182, 185, 189, 190
mortality 49–51
mural 163, 164

N

negative peace 54
neighborhoods 469–472, 474, 476, 479–481, 483, 484, 489
New York City 51
Nigeria 341, 342, 361–364
nonstate violence 45, 50

O

one-sided violence 43, 45, 50
oppression 1, 6
organized crime 186
(organized) criminal groups 474

P

palimpsest 37
Palmira 50
participatory planning 389, 391, 401
participatory processes 52
peacebuilding 2, 3, 379, 497, 499, 503, 504, 534

Pelotas 56
perpetrators 4, 5
Phoenix 55
physical violence 326
Plateau State 341, 342, 344, 347, 361–365
police 469, 472, 474, 476–478, 483–485, 490
police violence 45, 51, 58
policy 2, 8, 9, 532, 533
political action 33
political science 9
political violence 43, 45, 54
politics 3, 7, 9, 33
posters 31–33, 37
poverty 371
power 2, 3, 5–9, 33, 203–205, 208–215, 218–220
practice 533
preparedness 102
prevention 81–83, 85, 86, 88, 91, 92, 94, 97, 98, 100, 102, 509, 510, 513, 515–519, 522, 523, 525, 526
private sector 54
profit 34
property crime 51
public art 32
public health approach 430, 431, 433, 441, 451
public space(s) 256–258, 260–264, 266–268, 298, 300, 305–308, 313
public transport 298, 304, 307, 314

R

race 161, 167, 324, 326, 335
racial violence 4

Index

racism 167, 172
reconciliation 341, 343, 344, 346, 348–351, 353, 354, 356, 361, 363
reeducation 34
regime 235, 238, 241, 247, 248
reintegration 373
relationships of violence 78
religious tensions 341, 342
resilience 302, 310, 311, 342, 348, 351, 353, 354, 361, 364, 370–377, 379
restorative 301–303, 307
restorative circle 321, 322, 328, 329, 331, 332, 335
restorative conversations 321, 327, 328, 331, 333–335
restorative justice 322–328, 331, 335–337
retributive violence 469
revenge killings 472
revolution 203, 213–216, 221, 223
rights 532, 533
risk 52–56
risk factors 87–89, 92, 98, 99
Riyom 341–347, 349–353, 363
robbery 482

S

Safecity 412–414, 416, 418, 421–425
safer cities 414
schools 163, 166, 167, 171, 321–331, 333–337
self-care 376
sexism 484
sexual and gender-based violence 4
sexual violence 51, 412

shootings 51
slow violence 13
social 31–34, 36, 474, 482, 485
social dimension 66
social dynamics of violence 474
social exclusion 220
social fabric 341, 342
social housing 129, 137–139
socioeconomic cleaving 206, 216
sociology 9
solidarity 66, 77
sources 42, 44, 47, 48, 50, 51, 53, 56, 57
South Africa 55
stabbing 164, 167
state government 43
state violence 45, 51
statistics 41, 42, 46–53, 56
stigmatization 165
storytelling 531
street art 34
structural change 82
structural violence 4, 46, 47, 52, 54, 55, 58, 128, 129, 140, 204, 208, 209, 211, 213, 218–222, 297, 298, 322, 333, 336, 337, 376, 474, 510, 511, 518, 522, 532
suicide 163, 169
Sunnis 205, 210–212, 215, 217, 220
survey 42, 51
survivors 51, 52
Sustainable Development Goal 16 49
sustainable peacebuilding 342, 355
Syria 51, 203–205, 210–213, 215–219, 222
systemic violence 43, 46, 50, 55

Index

T
territorialization 36
terrorism 45, 56
Tijuana 52
Tilly, Charles 182, 183, 187, 188, 191, 195
trauma 223, 323, 370–377, 379, 485, 493, 494, 499
trauma awareness 374
trauma healing 371, 374, 376, 377, 379
trauma-informed 372
trauma transformative 302
trust 48, 484
trust-building 358
Twelver Shia 210

U
United States 51–53
upstream prevention 432
urban art 32, 34, 37
urban cleaving 207
urban design 299, 301, 303, 314
urban planning 95, 96, 109, 115, 116, 118, 204, 381, 388, 394, 396, 400, 401
urban studies 9
urban violence 2, 3, 8, 178, 179, 181, 183–185, 188, 189, 194, 195, 429, 435
urban-violence prevention 305
urban violence reduction 531
urbicide 208, 222

V
victims 4, 5
violence 161–165, 175
violence against migrants 4
violence prevention 392
visibility 128, 129
visual art 33, 35, 36

W
war crimes 43, 44, 54
war on drugs 472
war-torn cities 13
well-being 298–306, 308, 312–314, 474
white people 324
white teachers 324

Y
youth/young person 34, 161, 163, 165, 166, 173–175, 322, 324, 330–332, 369, 371–373, 377, 378, 484